TRANS-PACIFIC
Japanese American Studies

TRANS-PACIFIC
Japanese American Studies
Conversations on Race and Racializations

edited by Yasuko Takezawa and Gary Y. Okihiro

University of Hawai'i Press
Honolulu

© 2016 University of Hawaiʻi Press
All rights reserved
Printed in the United States of America

21 20 19 18 17 16   6 5 4 3 2 1

Library of Congress Cataloging-in-Publication Data

Names: Takezawa, Yasuko I., editor. | Okihiro, Gary Y., editor.
Title: Trans-Pacific Japanese American studies : conversations on race and racializations / edited by Yasuko Takezawa and Gary Y. Okihiro.
Description: Honolulu : University of Hawaiʻi Press, [2016] | Includes index.
Identifiers: LCCN 2015051047 | ISBN 9780824847586 cloth : alk. paper
Subjects: LCSH: Japanese Americans—Study and teaching.
Classification: LCC E184.J3 T73 2016 | DDC 973/.04956—dc23 LC record available at http://lccn.loc.gov/2015051047

University of Hawaiʻi Press books are printed on acid-free paper and meet the guidelines for permanence and durability of the Council on Library Resources.

Contents

Note to the Reader ix
Acknowledgments xi

        Introduction 1
        Yasuko TAKEZAWA and Gary Y. OKIHIRO

PART I   Orientation 11
       1 Shifting Grounds in Japanese American Studies: Reconsidering "Race" and "Class" in a Trans-Pacific Geopolitical-Historical Context 13
          Yasuko TAKEZAWA

PART II   Racializations 37
       2 The Unbearable Whiteness of Being: The Contemporary Racialization of Japanese/Asian Americans 39
          Michael OMI

       3 Negotiating Categories and Transgressing (Mixed-) Race Identities: The Art and Narratives of Roger Shimomura, Laura Kina, and Shizu Saldamando 60
          Yasuko TAKEZAWA

PART III Communities 83
       4 Trans-Pacific Localism and the Creation of a Fishing Colony: Pre–World War II Taiji Immigrants on Terminal Island, California 85
          Yuko KONNO

       5 Vernacular Representations of Race and the Making of a Japanese Ethnoracial Community in Los Angeles 107
          Fuminori MINAMIKAWA

6 Negotiating the Boundaries of Race, Caste, and Mibun: Meiji-era Diplomatic and Immigrant Responses to North American Categories of Exclusion 133
Andrea GEIGER

PART IV Intersections 159

7 Americanization and Beika: Gender and Racialization of the Issei Community in California before World War II 161
Yuko MATSUMOTO

8 Sansei Women and the Gendering of Yellow Power in Southern California, 1960s–1970s 183
Valerie J. MATSUMOTO

PART V Borderlands 211

9 Nakayoshi Group: Postwar Okinawan Women's Articulation of Identity in America 213
Wesley UEUNTEN

10 What Brings Korean Immigrants to Japantown?: Commodifying Racial Differences in the Age of Globalization 238
Sachiko KAWAKAMI

PART VI Reorientations 255

11 The Making of a Japanese American Race, and Why Are There No "Immigrants" in Postwar Nikkei History and Community?: The Problems of Generation, Region, and Citizenship in Japanese America 257
Eiichiro AZUMA

12 Reorienting Asian American Studies in Asia and the Pacific 288
Rika NAKAMURA

PART VII Pedagogies 313

13 Teaching Asian American Studies in Japan: Challenges and Possibilities 315
Masumi IZUMI

14　Japanese American Progressives: A Case Study in Identity Formation　342
Mari MATSUDA

PART VIII　Dialoguing Subject Positions　367

Notes from Shinagawa, July 28–29, 2012　369
Gary Y. OKIHIRO

Thoughts on Positionality　372
Noriko K. ISHII

Asian American History across the Pacific　378
Lon KURASHIGE

Japanese Americans in Academia and Political Discourse in Japan　385
Okiyoshi TAKEDA

Location, Positionality, and Community: Studying and Teaching Japanese America in the United States and Japan　389
Yoko TSUKUDA

Positions In-Between: Hapa, Buddhist, and Japanese American Studies　393
Duncan Ryûken WILLIAMS

Toward More Equal Dialogue　396
Yasuko TAKEZAWA

Contributors　401
Index　407

Note to the Reader

Throughout this book, Japanese names, including those of Japan-based contributors and scholars, figures in Japan, and immigrants in the United States, are written as given names first and family names last. Although this does not conform to Japanese practice, we follow this to avoid confusion for English-language readers.

Acknowledgments

This book is a product of several years of trans-Pacific conversations between North America–based and Japan-based scholars specializing in Japanese American studies. We benefited a great deal from our colleagues, friends, and audiences in attendance at a series of conferences and meetings held in Tokyo, Kyoto, and Los Angeles. At those meetings, Karen Ishizuka, Duncan Ryûken Williams, Charles Lawrence, and Miya Shichinose-Suga provided commentaries, while Brian Masaru Hayashi, Lon Kurashige, Ayako Takamori, Clement Lai, and Lane Ryo Hirabayashi provided valuable comments that helped to improve the essays in this anthology.

Our special gratitude goes to Lane Ryo Hirabayashi, who co-organized with Yasuko Takezawa the conference held in October 2012 at the University of California, Los Angeles. Also thanks to Brandon Shindo and Eri Kameyama at UCLA for their logistical support. We appreciate the aid and hospitality received from the UCLA Asian American Studies Center, Department of Asian American Studies, and Terasaki Center for Japanese Studies, along with the Japanese American National Museum in Los Angeles.

The administrative support from the Tokyo Office and the Institute for Research in Humanities of Kyoto University contributed to the success of the conferences held in Tokyo and Kyoto.

The publication of this anthology as well as the conferences would not have been possible without the generous funding from the Grant-in-Aid for Scientific Research (S), "A Japan-based Global Study of Racial Representations" (No. 22222003, Principal Investigator: Yasuko Takezawa), based at the Institute for Research in Humanities of Kyoto University. The project has been supported by all its staff members, and for this anthology, special thanks go to researchers Go Oyagi, Chiori Goto, and Noriko Watanabe and the secretariat, Yoshimi Murata, for their continued diligent work and support.

All of the Japan-based scholars owe a debt of gratitude to Gary Y. Okihiro, Dylan Luers Toda, Jenn Lee, and Crystal Uchino for editing their essays with an eye toward the English language. Masako Ikeda of the University of Hawai'i Press greeted our manuscript with enthusiasm and provided welcome support for this anthology. Our deep appreciation also extends to the two anonymous reviewers of the manuscript who provided insightful comments and encouraging words.

We hope that the publication of this anthology will contribute to vitalizing the wider realm of conversations in Japanese American studies and other related fields across nations and oceans.

Yasuko Takezawa and Gary Y. Okihiro

**TRANS-PACIFIC
Japanese American Studies**

Introduction

Yasuko Takezawa and Gary Y. Okihiro

Trans-Pacific Japanese American Studies began as a conversation regarding the state of Japan-U.S. trans-Pacific academic discussions on the racializations of Japanese Americans. As a result of that conversation, four conferences on the subject were held, twice in Tokyo, once in Kyoto, and once in Los Angeles over the course of several years, leading to the publication of this volume.

In designating this a "trans-Pacific" engagement, we recognize the hegemonic nature of discourses across the Pacific without considerations from Oceania. Moreover, we acknowledge differences among Japanese American studies in Hawai'i and the U.S. continent, as well as differences among Japanese American studies in the United States and the Japanese imperial orbits of Okinawa, Guam, and other Pacific Islands. The subject positions of some of our contributors to this anthology emerge from that consciousness within Oceania.

In Japan and the United States, there is an abundance of academic literature on, as well as public interest in Japanese Americans. In Japan, the subject is one of the most popular research areas in fields such as American and migration studies. Moreover, the last several years have witnessed a proliferation of publications, art exhibits, television programs, and conferences on the topic directed at the general public.[1] In the United States, not only are Japanese Americans the focus of a vast body of scholarship, particularly in Asian American and ethnic studies, but the forced removal and confinement of Japanese Americans during World War II is now also recognized—at least in education and by the U.S. federal government—as a lesson on how racism can operate during a national crisis with lasting consequences for the affected group and society as a whole.

This book's subject, Japanese Americans, is a part of "A Japan-based Global Study of Racial Representations," a five-year interdisciplinary research project (led by Takezawa) funded by the Japan Society for the Promotion of Science. While we focus on race and racializations, we also consider their intersections with gender, class, nation, and other socially significant categories.

The contrasting social positions of Japanese in the United States and Japan serve as a useful starting point from which to explore the subject of their respective racializations. Whereas Japanese in the United States have been part of a historically marginalized minority group, in Japan, they have been an overwhelming majority. The issue of "multicultural coexistence" began to receive attention only after the 1995 Great Hanshin-Awaji Earthquake, an event that led to the increased visibility of ethnic and migrant minorities. Some scholars have also questioned the essentialized category "Japanese."

Although the study of Japanese Americans has reached a stage of maturity, contributors to this collection recognize important historical and contemporary areas of neglect in the historiography and literature. Prominent reasons for the neglect lie in the history and nature of Japanese American studies in Japan and the United States, as well as in differences in the subject positions of scholars engaged in the field.

In this age of accelerated globalization, we witness an increasing number of dialogues within and across the Pacific. The field of Asian American studies is unexceptional in this regard. Topics emerging from such engagements include the question of Asian American studies in Asia, the U.S. centrism of the field and its decentering, the impacts of U.S. imperialism, and the subject positions and subjectivities, in time and space, of scholars (e.g., Wang 2012; Chuh 2003; Ueki 2000; Okihiro 2001).

In this volume, with few exceptions, we do not engage in a critique of Japanese American studies. Beyond exploring absences in the field, we are keenly interested in how a scholar's subject position generates contrasting choices, approaches, and interpretations, even on similar topics. To that end, we encouraged our authors to engage one another as is reflected in several chapters of this book.

The issue of positionality was the focal point of our 2012 summer conference held at Kyoto University's Tokyo Office in Shinagawa. After several brief presentations by U.S.- and Japan-based scholars, Gary Okihiro posed an intriguing series of questions to the participants: What are the personal investments of scholars in the field of Japanese American studies regarding race, gender, and nationality? What are the problems inherent in a field of study framed as "Japanese American" studies? How can we engage in more equal exchanges across nation-states, especially when the field defines itself as "Japanese American"? Okihiro, having asked those questions within the context of Japan, was mainly interested in hearing Japanese scholars' views in order to identify differences and commonalities between them and U.S.-based scholars with regard to epistemology, training, language, and personal investment. The final section of this volume as well as part of Chapter One by Takezawa, is the product of that occasion, containing contributions from both presenters and the audience.

We note, however, that the positionalities of the contributors to this volume are multilayered and cannot be reduced to a "Japan-U.S." binary and framework. Factors such as discipline, age, generation, gender, ethnicity, location, upbringing, and social context generate significant differences in epistemologies, sensitivities, and research topics and frameworks.

The U.S.-based contributors' relationship to Japan is by no means monolithic. Some have only visited Japan briefly, and others have spent more than a year at Japanese universities or made multiple trips to Japan. Some even bear the title of immigrant scholar. Similarly, the Japan-based contributors are not representative of Japanese scholars as a whole, and they differ in their relationships to America. More than half of them have received advanced degrees from U.S. and Canadian institutions, and all of them continue to engage in international dialogues. It is probably safe to say that the trans-Pacific academic experiences of U.S.- and Japan-based scholars alike—regardless of their scope—have led them to question their positionalities. Still, our engagements triggered and inspired, consciously or unconsciously, their reflections on their subject positions and stakes in the field of Japanese American studies.

Although we recognize the diversity of scholars on both sides of the Pacific, we believe that the dialogues found in this volume can help readers further understand how the nation-state has shaped the academic tradition of Japanese American studies in both countries. That is, scholars carry agency in their intellectual productions, but they are also constrained by the nation-state, their respective histories, archives, traditions, and languages.

Organization

We begin with Yasuko Takezawa's commentary on Japanese American studies in Japan. Her discussion in the first half of the chapter provides an orientation to our conversations across the Pacific. In this helpful synopsis, Takezawa traces the literature of Japanese American studies in Japan. This accounting is particularly valuable for scholars of Japanese American studies in the United States. The second half of the chapter raises some questions regarding how salient concepts such as "race" and "class" are interpreted and consumed differently between Japanese American studies in the United States and those in Japan according to their respective socio-geo-political contexts. For historiographies of Japanese American studies in the United States, see Eiichiro Azuma's account in his chapter in this anthology and Gary Y. Okihiro's *The Columbia Guide to Asian American History*.

In the second section, Michael Omi and Yasuko Takezawa reflect on "racializations." Michael Omi contends that accompanying the changing demography of the United States is the greater visibility accorded Asian and Japanese Americans within the U.S. racial formation. That contemporary condition illustrates the complexity of how race is created, lived, and changed, he writes. Intermarriage and mixed race; the articulations of race with class and of biology with culture; the nation, citizenship, and the perpetual foreigner designation; ethnic and religious diversity within the single category "Asian"; and the model minority stereotype and "whitening" of Asian Americans exemplify some of the complexities involved in untangling the contingent racial formation. Relative and relational, the racial formation, Omi concludes, still upholds white supremacy.

Social categories and movements based on race, ethnicity, gender, or sexuality entail a risk of essentializing the categories as well as supplying an indispensable means for resistance. They constitute, following Antonio Gramsci and Gayatri Spivak, strategic essentialisms. At the same time, we witness a growing assertiveness by border crossers, particularly among multiracials whose identities are fluid, flexible, and multiple. With those issues in mind, Yasuko Takezawa, drawing on her ethnography on the works and narratives of three artists, Roger Shimomura, Laura Kina, and Shizu Saldamando, poses the question of the context regarding how collective categories such as "Japanese American," "Asian American," and "hapa" can be mobilized.

In the book's third section, "Communities," Yuko Konno, Fuminori Minamikawa, and Andrea Geiger discuss factors such as localism, language, and race and caste that reveal agency in subjectivities and community formations. Using her multisite archival study, Yuko Konno presents a historiography of migration from Taiji, Wakayama to Terminal Island in California, demonstrating how and to what degree a "trans-Pacific localism"—not nation-state—framework is useful for understanding those migrants as active agents who, while utilizing personal networks and resources in their homeland, contributed to the development of a new community. Although this case is somewhat exceptional in the geographical concentration of the Japanese group studied therein, Konno details the community's internal structure while providing rich, concrete data. Interestingly, it was an invitation by Taiji administrators who had been waiting for someone to shed light on the emigration history of their village as part of its globalization project sparked Konno's study.

Fuminori Minamikawa explores the vernacular representations of Japanese migrants in California-based Japanese-language newspapers by focusing on two Japanese terms, *minzoku* (nation/race/ethnicity) and *jinshu* (race). To survive the anti-Japanese campaign of the time, Japanese migrants strengthened their solidarity and unity by creating a discursive "patchwork" from their rearticulations of the two concepts. Minamikawa argues that through such practices Japanese migrants were able to resist racism in the United States as well as adapt to the racialized ideology of international politics faced by their home country.

Andrea Geiger examines how her subjects, Japanese migrants during the Meiji era, negotiated the material conditions of American racism and Japan's social formation. The process reveals how the *mibunsei,* or status system, including such associations as outcaste status, shaped and mediated Japanese American responses to the limitations and opportunities available in Canada and the United States. Drawing on her larger, prize-winning study *Subverting Exclusion: Transpacific Encounters with Race, Caste, and Borders, 1885–1928* (2011), Geiger notes that Meiji officials mirrored anti-Asian rhetoric in seeking to elevate their "civilized" selves in comparison with their "barbaric" Chinese others and cautions that Japanese historical agency was fired and tempered by American racism and Japanese history and culture. Geiger's chapter follows the footnoting practiced in the discipline of history to remind readers that writing styles and conventions mark disciplinary choices and epistemologies or ways of knowing.

In "Intersections," Yuko Matsumoto with Valerie J. Matsumoto articulate the social formation of race, gender, and nation in the lives of Japanese American women. Yuko Matsumoto shows the multiplicity and fluidity of the boundaries of U.S. citizenship for Japanese migrants by examining Issei leaders' interpretation and promotion of *beika* (Americanization) as well as the discourse of white agitators in the anti-Japanese movements of the period. What the anti-Asianists depicted as the alleged mistreatment of Japanese women (such as being "forced" to work long hours in the fields as well as do housework) became a justification for the anti-Japanese movement and, in turn, informed the racialization and gendering of Japanese Americans.

The pages of *Gidra,* an Asian American student monthly from the University of California, Los Angeles, published from 1969 to 1974, reveal *sansei* (third generation) women's challenges to gendered racializations within the U.S. and Japanese American communities during the 1960s and 1970s, writes Valerie J. Matsumoto. Holding third world women revolutionaries as their role models, *sansei* women articulated subjectivities in relation to black and brown power, white racism, sexism, stereotypes arising from the U.S. war in Southeast Asia, and the relations among the United States, Japan, and the third world. They, Matsumoto writes, insisted on self-determination under the banner of yellow power and forged solidarities to create a new subjectivity while serving the people.

The section "Borderlands" examines some of the contours of the "Japanese American" subject. As with all subjectivities, Japanese America was and is a work in progress. Its definitions have been struggled over by Japanese and non-Japanese alike. Imperial Japan, like the imperial United States, absorbed peoples deemed to be "foreign" and thus inferior, such as the Ainu, Uchinanchu (Okinawans), and Zainichi (Koreans in Japan). Wesley Ueunten and Sachiko Kawakami examine those borders in their studies of Okinawan women and Korean immigrants.

Okinawan subjectivity, Wesley Ueunten points out, involves the intellect as well as the affect. The Nakayoshi Group of the San Francisco Bay Area, a collective of Uchinanchu immigrant women who laugh, eat, and sing songs they "own," Ueunten claims, illustrates how song can embody subjectivity and reproductive labor. Central to their experiences as Okinawan women is violence, beginning with the World War II Battle of Okinawa and the continuing U.S. occupation and militarization of Okinawa. Although unstated, the Nakayoshi Group exists in cultural resistance to the erasures of U.S. military violence, Japan's colonial rule, and white supremacy and patriarchy in the United States. Ueunten argues for a more inclusive Japanese American history and community that accounts for the voices of all of its diverse members.

In spite of the abundance of writings on San Francisco's Japantown, we know little about Korean merchants and residents in that neighborhood. This is partly due to the research framework of Japanese and Korean American studies, which is based on the nation-state and ethnicity. Sachiko Kawakami, drawing from her fieldwork and experiences living in the United States, South Korea, and Japan, depicts the worldviews, survival strategies, and everyday practices of Korean immigrants and their descendants, whose presence is both visible and invisible in Japantown. Her study shows that, although living between Japanese and Korean American communities, Korean immigrants and their children in Japantown have created their own space where they can express their ambiguous, flexible, and expansive (Asian) subjectivities.

In the next section, titled "Reorientations," Eiichiro Azuma and Rika Nakamura add to the discussion of the making of "Japanese America." Eiichiro Azuma reflects on his subject position as a *shin issei* (newly arrived immigrant) and the category's exclusion from the normative narratives and formations of Japanese America. As he points out, the silence betrays the writer's assumptions and purposes in defining a "Japanese American race" and subjectivity. Expanding on that insight, Azuma calls attention to the intricate, mutually reinforcing relations between the writing of history and community formation broadly and their specificities of place, time, and social location. The West Coast and California especially dominate in those representations, which then marginalize Hawai'i and places "east of California." Intellectuals ignore workers and the class distinctions among Japanese migrants, and anti-racists rush to defend Japanese America by subscribing to the U.S. frontier hypothesis and the superpatriotic "model minority" stereotype. In the process, they distance themselves from American Indians, who "vanish" in the engagement with the expanding frontier, and African Americans and Latina/Latinos, whom they chastise with the Japanese American "model minority." Accordingly, Azuma concludes, although it domesticates the formerly alien Japanese "race" by adopting the hegemonic anthem of the U.S. nation-state, the normative narrative of Japanese America alienates others of its erstwhile members deemed "queer"—*kibei, shin issei*, workers, war brides, and multiracials.

By examining the writings of four U.S.-based Asian American studies scholars, Rika Nakamura explores the meanings and possibilities of Asian American studies when it is relocated to Asia. She brings our attention to the importance of the perspective that arises from the "majority-minority twist," which enables us to practice empathy and critique, or identification and disidentification, in situations like those Japanese nationals—members of an ethnoracial majority in their home country—find themselves in when doing research on ethnoracial minorities in Western imperial nations. At the same time, she presents an often overlooked critique of the phenomenon of some U.S.-based Asian American scholars—domestic minorities in their home country—engaging in an imperial mission of uplift when they participate in a "one-way teaching" process and demonstrate little eagerness to engage in mutual learning. She posits that the intellectual encounter between Asia and Asian America opens it to interrogation of its complicities with U.S. imperialism in its representations of Asia while constituting a significant moment for U.S.- and Asia-based scholars to engage in the histories of atrocities in Asia.

In "Pedagogies," Masumi Izumi and Mari Matsuda ponder the possibilities of learning from the past and from the contexts in which our teaching arises. Masumi Izumi reflects on her position of being continually challenged by her students, some of whom have internalized the myth that Japan is a homogeneous society or express frustration about the increasing number of new immigrants in Japan. Izumi describes her struggles and experiments as those of a Japan-based teacher/scholar teaching Asian and Japanese American studies. Although many have criticized the "Japanese diaspora" approach to Japanese American studies because it can easily be used for nationalist and racist purposes, Izumi argues that such a perspective can connect students with a wider context by which to grasp the Japanese American experience that is neither restricted to the United States nor detached from experiences in Asia.

Mari Matsuda begins with her father's sage observation that the Okinawan subject position depends on place and time. Subjectivities shift, he declared, and they operate variably within particular historical and geographic contexts. Japanese American progressives, often reviled as *aka* (reds), Matsuda informs, shaped history with their political identifications and commitments. Moreover, they organized social movements across national boundaries to end injustices and advance a more democratic world. In that light, the current apparent paralysis among youth is puzzling. Still, the exemplars of the past, those generations of resistance, inspire, Matsuda insists, and despite their unfinished cause of social change, they ignite anew the fires of freedom.

In the book's final section, "Dialoguing Subject Positions," Gary Y. Okihiro offers his observations drawn from the 2012 Shinagawa conference as a preface to the essays by Noriko K. Ishii, Lon Kurashige, Okiyoshi (Oki) Takeda, Yoko Tsukuda, Duncan Ryûken Williams, and Yasuko Takezawa, reflecting on their subjectivities as scholars of Japanese American studies across the Pacific. All wrote their essays after having participated in the discussions at the 2012 Shinagawa conference. In them, the scholars underscore the need to articulate how our subject positions, whether as teachers or students, influence our writings, readings, and political commitments. They also affirm the critical necessity for open, honest, and anti-imperial engagements across national borders of histories, literatures, and traditions.

This appeal, to complicate Japanese American studies and subjectivities, is in fact a theme common to all the contributions to this engagement across the Pacific. Japanese America and its scholarly representations, they declare, are much too deep, rich, and varied to contain in a singular narrative or subject position.

Notes

1 Some recent examples include U.S.-based arts-related events that toured Japan (the exhibition *Art of Gaman: Arts and Crafts from Japanese American Internment Camps, 1942–1946*, which was originally shown to much acclaim at the Smithsonian American Art Museum from May 2010 to January 2012, and Nikki Nojima Louis's play *Breaking the Silence*, first performed at the University of Washington in 1985), the annual conference on Japanese American experiences run by the Japanese American Leadership Delegation under the leadership of Irene Hirano (founding chief executive officer of the Japanese American National Museum and now the president of the U.S.-Japan Council) and sponsored by the Japanese Ministry of Foreign Affairs, and the five-episode November 2010 TV drama *99 Years of Love: Japanese Americans,* which was produced by the Japanese television company TBS for its sixtieth anniversary. The latter achieved high ratings for a show of its type—15.3 percent on average and 19.1 percent on the last night.

References

Chuh, Kandice. 2003. *Imagine Otherwise: On Asian Americanist Critique.* Durham, NC: Duke University Press.
Geiger, Andrea. 2011. *Subverting Exclusion: Transpacific Encounters with Race, Caste, and Borders, 1885–1928.* New Haven, CT: Yale University Press.

Okihiro, Gary Y. 2001. *The Columbia Guide to Asian American History.* New York: Columbia University Press.
Ueki, Teruyo. 2000. "Past, Present, and Future of Asian American Studies." *Asian American Literature Association Journal* 6: 53–64.
Wang, Chih-ming. 2012. "Editorial Introduction: Between Nations and across the Ocean." *Inter-Asia Cultural Studies* 13(2): 1–11.

PART I

ORIENTATION

CHAPTER 1

Shifting Grounds in Japanese American Studies
Reconsidering "Race" and "Class" in a Trans-Pacific Geopolitical-Historical Context

Yasuko Takezawa

In this chapter, inspired by our series of transnational conversations, I will provide some historical and social contexts for the emergence, growth, and consumption of Japanese American studies in Japan and shed light on some translation and interpreting issues involving the meanings of "race" and "class." The first section of this chapter provides a sketch of the historical development of Japanese American studies in Japan, and the second discusses some of the transnational conversations we engaged in at the Shinagawa conference, particularly those regarding the field's subject matter, institutional production of knowledge, and gender imbalance. In the third section of the chapter, I discuss issues surrounding the act of translation with a focus on the Japanese terms translated into English as "race" and "class." This chapter may be read as a supplement to the Introduction.

Historical Development of Japanese American Studies in Japan

Japanese American studies in Japan can be described as having roots in three different but mutually related streams: local history, emigration studies supported and promoted by emigration agencies, and studies of U.S.-Japan relations and American studies. Scholarship originating within the field of local history has contributed significantly to the development of Japanese American studies, particularly in regions known for extensive overseas emigration, such as Okinawa, Hiroshima, Yamaguchi, and Wakayama. In these regions, there is an abundance of archival documents that in addition to qualitative data and narratives contain detailed statistics relating to population, emigrants, remittances, and so on. The field of local history has used such information on the prefectural—and occasionally village or town—level to produce scholarship on Japanese people who went to America.[1]

Emigration agencies affiliated with the Japanese government such as the Japan Emigration Service have produced a large number of academic bulletins and reports about overseas Japanese migrants and their children because emigration was part of the national policy from the Meiji period through the post–World War II years.[2] One interesting point is that the postscript to the final 1996 volume of the Japan Emigration Service's academic bulletin refers to the foundation of the *Annual Review of Migration Studies* (the journal of the Japanese Association for Migration Studies) in the previous year, mentioning the desire of the Japan Emigration Service to have the tradition and the leadership of Japanese migration studies be inherited by journal (Yamawaki 2013, 173).

Finally, the fields of U.S.-Japanese relations and Japanese American studies became a locus of scholarship on Japanese Americans as early as the first half of the 1960s with the publications of several scholars who returned from the United States.[3] A popular focus for them was the anti-Japanese laws and other acts related to Japanese exclusion on the West Coast. From the late 1960s through the 1970s, the publication of books, articles, and related reports on "Japanese immigrants overseas," including Japanese Americans, dramatically increased. There were a number of contributing reasons behind that growth, in particular, the centennial of Japanese immigration to North America, the emergence of American studies as a field of "area studies," and the translation into Japanese of a number of important books covering Japanese American internment, such as Carey McWilliams' *Prejudice: Japanese-Americans, Symbol of Racial Intolerance* (1944, translated in 1970), Michi Weglyn's *Years of Infamy: The Untold Story of America's Concentration Camps* (1976, translated in 1978), Dillon Myer's *Uprooted Americans: The Japanese Americans and the War Relocation Authority during World War II* (1971, translated in 1978), and John Okada's *No-No-Boy* (1957, translated in 1979).

Another factor contributing to the rapid growth of Japanese American studies during this period might have been the popularity of Nihonjin-ron (theories on the uniqueness of the Japanese race and its culture), which culminated in the 1970s and early 1980s when Japan's increasing global presence was becoming visible as reflected in the then popular phrase "Japan As

Number One." Moreover, the shift from a fixed to a floating exchange rate between the U.S. dollar and the Japanese yen in 1973 (the value of the former was 360 yen until 1971, then decreased to 308 yen until 1973) also spurred Japan's globalization.

This long tradition of scholarship in the field of Japanese American studies may not be surprising, considering that Japanese immigrants remained "aliens ineligible for citizenship" until as recently as 1952. Until then, Issei (first-generation immigrants) were denied their right to claim their status as Americans and U.S. citizens.

Having been shaped by these factors, Japanese American studies in Japan has for decades—and still does to some extent—seen Japanese Americans as "overseas Japanese," or an extension of the "Japanese" people. This slowly began to change in the 1970s, when a small number of scholars who earned master's and/or doctoral degrees from American universities assumed teaching positions in English-language literature and English or American culture at Japanese institutions of higher education. However, it was not until one or two decades later that studies started to appear in Japan that took into account the wider parameters of the American social context, such as religion, ethnicity, community, the media, and economic relations.

From Transnational Conversations between U.S.-based Scholars and Japan-based Scholars

Having outlined the historical development of Japanese American studies in Japan, I will next draw from the conversations on Japanese American studies we engaged in at the Shinagawa conference, to show how such different evolutions in the two countries have shaped in part the differences in subject matter, institutional production of knowledge, and gender imbalance in contemporary Japanese American studies across the Pacific.

Subject Matter

For many of the pioneers of Asian American studies in the United States, including Gary Okihiro and the late Yuji Ichioka, their initial motivation to engage in Japanese and Asian American studies was to resist the "invisibilization" of Japanese and Asian Americans in both the American academic world and society at large. The history of migrants from various parts of Asia and the experiences of their descendants in the United States remained, in Ichioka's words, a "buried past," with even issues such as the massacres of early Chinese migrants in the latter half of the nineteenth century and the forced removal and incarceration of Japanese Americans hardly touched upon in school textbooks. Likewise, Japanese and Asian American art and culture were largely excluded from mainstream media. As a result, as Okihiro stated during our 2012 Shinagawa conference, Japanese/Asian American studies "was a pursuit of social justice, a reclaiming of our past defined by us."

During our discussions, Eiichiro Azuma described how Yuji Ichioka was critical of some Japanese scholars who studied Japanese Americans only for academic reasons detached from U.S. political realities. Many Asian Americans inside and outside academia have shared that stance. Irrespective of the individual variations among scholars, such as their lived experiences in the United States and choice of research topics, Asian Americans have at times been and may remain suspicious of scholars who grew up in Japan, questioning their sensitivity to issues surrounding racism, sexism, and other forms of social oppression. Problematic comments regarding other minority groups such as African Americans and Latinas/os by Japanese politicians and other related incidents, particularly menacing in the 1980s, only hardened the stereotype of the Japanese as people insensitive to minority issues.

One unfortunate consequence of this stereotype is that it can intimidate Japanese students and scholars or turn them away from the field. Noriko Ishii (see Part VIII), as she has written in her essay in this volume, decided to change her research topic away from Japanese American studies as a result of such an experience. In a similar vein, in my essay, I recall a story of being told by a moderator at the Association for Asian American Studies meeting in 1989 that only Asian Americans, not Asians from Asia, have credentials to apply for positions in the field because the latter "may sympathize but cannot empathize with the Asian American experience as they did not grow up in that community" (see Part VIII).

For many of the field's founders, Japanese and Asian American studies provided a means for self-determination by reclaiming ignored histories and cultures. They gave agency to people who were not only denied the freedom promised in America but also strived to have their voices heard in larger society. The field of Asian American studies was thereby closely tied to political issues and demands within American society over concerns of racism, oppression, inequality, and social injustice. Asian American scholars were keenly aware of the racism that homogenized Asians in Asia and Americans of Asian ancestry in the United States. U.S. Orientalism underwrites that essentialism, and the events of the 1970s and 1980s only added to that brand of U.S. Orientalism: the redress and reparations movement, the intense U.S.-Japanese "trade war," the murder of Vincent Chin in 1982, and racist remarks by Japanese politicians. The social contexts pertaining to American society at those times conditioned scholars to restrict their analyses to a nation-state framework. Last, a nationalism operating under a banner of self-determination discouraged non-Asian Americans from engaging in Asian American studies. The anecdotes offered by Ishii and Takezawa in this collection should be understood against this wider social context.

In Japan, some of the participants in the conference argued that research topics in the field tend to be broader in contrast to subject focuses in the United States due to the institutional history of ethnic studies. Furthermore, aside from a handful of scholars with multilingual skills, U.S.-based scholars have generally shown little interest in Japanese-language materials, whereas Japanese and Japan-based scholars by necessity read materials in both English and Japanese.

That being said, Japan-based scholars may suffer subject matter constraints for reasons different from those of U.S.-based scholars, particularly with regard to a relative weakness in English. At the Shinagawa conference, several participants voiced concern that some Japanese historians limit and spend much of their energy "discovering" new Japanese-language archives and documents without articulating their scholarly significance. At the same time, diaries, documents, and other valuable materials written in Japanese are being lost, and the number of Japanese-language-competent scholars in the United States is declining. Without studies by Japanese and other scholars who are highly proficient in Japanese, important elements of Japanese American history will never be brought to light. Japanese students studying at American universities are often pressured by their academic advisers to conduct research that specifically exploits their Japanese-language skills. This phenomenon is not limited to Japanese American studies but extends to the humanities and social sciences in general, contributing to a restricting and compartmentalizing of Japanese students in the United States (see Takezawa's short essay in Part VIII).

The scope of research topics among American-based scholars in the fields of Japanese American studies and Asian American studies has expanded considerably since the late 1990s as a result of the increasing influence of the post-1965 generation on scholarship in the field, the increase of multiracial/multiethnic people, and the post-redress era. Topics such as diaspora and transnational/transracial adoption demonstrate a shift from the nation-state framework. Moreover, as can be seen in this volume, affected by postmodern and postcolonial conceptions, we can observe that academic influence is not unidirectional. For example, elsewhere in this volume, Lon Kurashige explains how, inspired by his longtime friend and Japanese university professor Brian Masaru Hayashi, as well as his firsthand experience of living and teaching in Japan, he expanded the scope of his scholarship.

As the number of Japanese scholars with American degrees has gradually increased, many of these scholars after returning to Japan have begun to question their position as members of the social "majority." Some have reflected on how observations and theories developed in the field of Asian American studies can be used to address social injustice, inequality, and the conditions of migrants and minority groups in Japan. Others have returned those insights back to America in a reciprocal liaison. As a result, influence has flowed between the United States and Japan and back again in multiple directions and at concurrent times.

Institutional Production of Knowledge

Despite a large body of literature that examines the roles of institutions such as museums, universities, and other research entities on the production of knowledge, there is a dearth of scholarship on the institutional production of knowledge within Japanese and Asian America. Through its exhibits and educational programs, the Japanese American National Museum in Los Angeles has played an important role in imparting the concentration camp experience as well as developing the concept of the Japanese "diaspora." In Japan, the Yokohama Japanese Overseas Migration Museum, run by the Japan International Cooperation Agency (JICA), and the Kobe Center for Overseas Migration and Cultural Interaction, affiliated with the city of Kobe, have produced comparable programs on Japanese Americans. The Japan International Cooperation Agency, as a partial successor to the Japan Emigration Service, continues to be affiliated with the Japanese government. Both museums narrate the overseas Japanese experience through topics such as the history of emigration journeys, the hardships and struggles of the Issei, wartime experiences, postwar achievements, and the diversification of contemporary communities.

Besides museums, the media exerts a tremendous influence on the general public's understanding and image of Japanese American experiences. Several Japanese scholars have criticized the approach typically found in Japanese television dramas and documentary programs, which depict Japanese overseas immigrants and their offspring as a direct extension of the "Japanese" people. Although recently an increasing number of television programs and book titles refer to Japanese immigrants in the United States as "Americans,"[4] others express the concern that the normative narrative can be easily linked to nationalism and racism.

Such interpretations are also popular in the United States, despite decades of criticism over the Japanese and Asian American "success story." In mass media, art, and public talks, the story of Japanese Americans rarely ventures beyond incarceration, achievements in the postwar period, and contemporary racism. It is unclear whether "breaking the silence" around the World War II incarceration remains a pressing issue in Japanese America as Nisei (second generation) and Sansei (third generation) grow older and pass away, or whether Japanese Americans have found another way to forge their identity as a people and community.

At the Shinagawa conference, some U.S.-based scholars pointed out that although there is not much difference in theory in the social sciences such as sociology and anthropology in Japan and the United States, there is a significant difference in approach in the field of history. According to those historians, U.S.-based scholars tend to pay greater attention to theory than their Japanese counterparts, for whom it has been argued that historical studies on Japanese and Asian American studies tend to be weak in their theoretical orientations. That criticism is often levied by some Japan-based scholars as well, who note that in Japan the antitheoretical tendency leans toward empirical studies and philology.

Gender Imbalance

Although no hard statistics are available, male Japanese American studies scholars seem to be outnumbered by female scholars, with perhaps a few exceptions for certain areas such as emigration, religious institutions, and media studies. In contrast, in the United States, it appears that the representation seems to be more gender balanced. Although this gender disparity can be seen in immigration and minority studies in Japan in general, it appears to be even greater in Japanese American studies. This can be partially explained in that oftentimes those in the Japanese and Asian American studies field are obligated to teach English as part of their responsibilities, an area in which, again, there is an overwhelming female presence. Another factor may relate to educational institutions themselves; for example, some women's colleges in particular have grown strong Japanese American studies programs.

Reconsidering "Race" and "Class"

Scholars in the field who use both Japanese- and English-language sources continually face translation issues surrounding concepts such as race, class, multiracialism, and nation. These difficulties are sometimes caused by the absence of equivalent terms in Japanese, and at other times by changes in the meaning of words over the years. The act of translation is also one of definition. All of these difficulties can lead to not only confusion but also misinterpretation. It is beyond my abilities to engage in positivist research on this topic in the style of the field of history, so I have limited myself to raising questions through my analysis. Although there is excellent trans-Pacific historiographical scholarship in the field of Japanese American studies (e.g., Ichioka 1988; Hayashi 2004; Azuma 2005), more work is needed to explore the historical and geopolitical background behind the emergence of concepts critical to understanding Japanese America. To do such research, it is necessary to trace back to the late Edo (1603–1868) and the early Meiji periods (1868–1912), a time predating the rise of the Japanese nationalism and imperialism that these works focus on. Here, it is not my intention to create a comprehensive history. Rather, by offering some snapshots from my current research, I hope to pose questions regarding interpretations associated with translation in previous studies.

"Race"

The decision in *Takao Ozawa v. United States,* 260 U.S. 178 (1922), marks a critical moment in Japanese American history. In delivering the opinion of the U.S. Supreme Court—that the Naturalization Act of 1790 grants naturalization rights only to immigrants who are "free white persons" (which the judge defined as "Caucasian") and that Ozawa was "clearly of a race which is not Caucasian"—Justice George Sutherland thereby denied Japanese immigrants naturalization rights for the next three decades. Below, I will provide the context for the belief that led Ozawa and the Japanese community in the United States to fight a losing game all the way to the Supreme Court.

Elsewhere, through an analysis of geography books and textbooks published in the early Meiji period, I have argued that the process of translating "race" contributed to the transformation of Japan's position in relation to its geopolitical "others" in the context of struggles associated with "Leaving Asia, Entering Europe (*datsu-a nyū-ō*)," the slogan the new Meiji government promoted to join civilized European nations by distinguishing itself from the rest of Asia (Takezawa 2015).[5] Here, I show that the issue of whiteness in the Ozawa case needs to be understood in light of the geopolitical and historical situation surrounding Japan during the late Edo and Meiji periods.

Before Japan was exposed to the European construct of race in the late Edo period, a time of national isolation, the classification of humans based on skin color and head shape was non-existent, and the skin color of Europeans was depicted no lighter than that of Japanese women and upper-status Japanese men (see Wagatsuma 1967; Screech 1995). Furthermore, as John Russell has pointed out, prior to the introduction of Euro-American prejudice toward black people in the early modern period, negative images of them were nowhere to be found (Russell 2007).

Following the 1868 Meiji Restoration, when the country made a drastic change in foreign policy from centuries-old seclusion to an open door, the new government swiftly embarked on a project to establish an elementary school system throughout the country to "eliminate uneducated households" (Nakagawa 1978, 11). In classrooms, teachers spent the most amount of time on foreign geography, and the textbooks on the topic they employed focused primarily on race, followed by language and religion. In the 1870s and 1880s, popular textbooks featured translations of American and European publications, such as those by the Americans Sarah S. Cornell and S. Augustus Mitchell and the Rev. J. Goldsmith (a pseudonym of the British author Sir Richard Phillips).

Some of these textbooks spent a considerable number of pages discussing "stages of civilization." For example, the top two best-selling textbooks of the time—*Sekai kunizukushi* (All the Countries of the World, Meiji 2 [1869]), which was compiled by the influential intellectual Yukichi Fukuzawa, and Masao Uchida's *Yochishiryaku* (Condensed geography, Meiji 3 [1871])—both cover the topic.[6] *Sekai kunizukushi* divides the people of the world into four categories: (1) "chaos" (*konton*), which is composed of the "most inferior people," such as the "natives" (*dojin*) of Australia and inner Africa, (2) "barbarian" (*ban'ya*), which comprises groups "one stage above savage people," (3) "as of yet uncivilized (*mikai*) or half-civilized (*hankai*)," and (4) "civilized" (*bunmeikaika*), for which the United States, England,

France, Germany, and the Netherlands are presented as examples (Fukuzawa 2002 [1869], 14–17). In this way, through translation, textbooks uncritically embraced the European and American racial hierarchy that asserted a vast gulf between illiterate African and Australian "savage natives" and fully civilized European and American Caucasians and inserted the intermediary stages of "not-yet civilized" and "half-civilized" into this empty space.

Such developmental schemes were not uncommon in American geography textbooks. For example, Harper & Brothers' *Harper's School Geography: With Maps and Illustrations*—one of the most popular sources for early Japanese geography books—presents five stages: savages, barbarians, half-civilized nations, civilized nations, and enlightened nations, with detailed definitions and descriptions (Harper & Brothers 1886, 18).

From the late Edo period to the first half of the Meiji period, Japanese intellectuals were keenly aware of not only domestic upheaval but also the increased international tensions that surrounded it. European countries and the United States were in intense competition throughout the world to expand their territories and power. In this context, Japan's neighbor China found itself further and further under the sway of England after the Opium War (1839–1842) and the Arrow War (1856–1860), eventually resulting in its cession of Hong Kong. Falling to a similar fate was Japan's worst nightmare.

In fact, as early as 1839, Kazan Watanabe, a leading "Dutch learning" (*Rangaku*) specialist, expressed deep anxiety about Europe's expanded colonialism and the possibility of its invading eastern Asia, stating, "All the five continents on the earth with the exception of Asia belong to Europe. Furthermore, within Asia, only the three countries of China, Persia, and our country have avoided the 'defilement of Westerners'" (Watanabe 1971 [1839], 49). As Shōsuke Satō notes, "This awareness was the reason that Kazan developed a deep sense of crisis as he engaged in Dutch learning research" (Satō 1971, 631). Kazan's alarm was heightened as he observed from the vantage point of his new knowledge about foreign countries the shadow of a Europe encroaching upon Japan. Thirty years later, the aforementioned intellectual Yukichi Fukuzawa revealed a similar concern in his *Sekai kunizukushi*. After providing an overview of Britain's defeat of China, the subsequent indemnity payments, and its takeover of Hong Kong, Fukuzawa states that China came to "in the end receive the contempt of other countries because there were truly no people who held patriotic thoughts" (Fukuzawa 2002 [1869], 78). Fukuzawa states, "It is my sole hope that this book *Sekai kunizukushi* makes mainly children and women understand the formation of the world, opens the door to this knowledge, and thereby establishes the basis of welfare and happiness under heaven" (Fukuzawa 2002 [1869], 64). Fukuzawa thought that whether Japan would fall to the same fate as China or enter Europe as a civilized nation depended on common people's acquisition of knowledge. Furthermore, he believed that the country could become civilized, strong, wealthy, and happy by mimicking civilized lifestyles and temperaments. Therefore, the book provides a considerable amount of detail on the subject at the expense of topography and climate. It was in this historical context as well as the four-way geopolitics involving Europe, the United States, Japan, and China that production and circulation of the knowledge on race and "stages of civilization" took place in the early Meiji period.

Textbooks from the early Meiji period generally do not explicitly state Japan's civilizational level, but as time passed, they began to take on a patriotic hue. After the magazine *Nihonjin* (*Japanese People*) and the newspaper *Nihon* (*Japan*) were launched in 1888, one can find the compound *minzoku* (race/nation) in them. Here it can be seen that this term was closely connected to the word *Nihonjin* (Japanese), at least in its inception (Yun 1994, 38–41). In this context, *minzoku* can mean "race," for example, *Nihon minzoku* (the Japanese race).

In the next decade, some textbooks began to group the Mongolian race and Japanese people with the Caucasian race. This is markedly different from—one could also say a distortion of—European raciology theories.

> Within the five races, the two races of Europe and Asia are advanced in their knowledge and are civilized or half-civilized. (Hata 1891, 20)

> People of the Caucasian and Mongolian races, who live in the moderate northern climates, are the most civilizationally progressed, and are powerful. . . . (Yamada 1893, 8)

Thus, a new understanding emerged that asserted the existence of, on the one hand, the "Caucasian race" and "Mongolian race" ("Asian race") and, on the other, "the other three races." This rejected the dualistic "white races versus colored races" framework that was taken for granted in Europe and America.

Furthermore, just as some racial theories emerged around the turn of the twentieth century in America and Europe that posited a hierarchy within Europe (e.g., Ripley 1899; Deniker 1900), some texts asserted that Japan and China were superior to the other races found in Asia. Some textbooks would subsequently drop China from this pair and state that only the Yamato (mainland Japanese) stock was at a level equal to the European race:

> The Japanese, although belonging to the Mongolian race according to racial divisions [*jinshu no kubetsu-jō*], are superior to other Mongolians, tending to prize *chū* [loyalty], *kō* [filial piety], and *shingi* [faith]. (Yamada, 1893, 8)

> Among the yellow race, we Japanese as well as the Chinese are . . . the most advanced, [and people of the white race comprise] the nations with outstanding intelligence and the most power in the world. (Kinkōdō shosekikaisha henshūjo 1894, 37)

> By learning about the various countries of the world, we know how our empire excels more than other countries of the world. By learning about the natural features [of our empire], we know in what way its nature and natural features are beautiful, and in what way its climate is moderate. (Yazu 1896, 2–3)

> As for the Asian race, its power has generally declined, with the exception of our Yamato Minzoku. . . . As for the African race . . . there are many who have still not escaped from an ignorant and savage state. (Chiriki-kenkyūkai 1913, 78–79)

However, not all textbooks published during the late nineteenth century emphasized the superiority of the Japanese, and some intellectuals also started to show doubts about white supremacism during this time.[7] Amid such questioning and a European- and American-influenced racial discourse that saw the Japanese as being low on the worldwide racial hierarchy, Japan began to undulate between Westernization and de-Westernization.

Now let us return to my initial assertion concerning the *Takao Ozawa v. United States* case. I believe we can see in it a discrepancy in the Meiji-educated Issei leaders' understandings of race and civilization (including the "whiteness" of skin) and those of the white-centered court system. For Ozawa and the Japanese community who received the education of Meiji Japan, "race" was inseparably connected to the Japanese (including those overseas) civilizational stage, rather than the Eurocentric paradigm of "whites" and "colored." They saw the highest stage ("civilized") as being attainable through cultivation and modernization. In fact, after more than a decade of research on this case and its relationship to the 1906 naturalization law, the Japanese Association of the Pacific Coast concluded that the latter was intended to "judge a person in accordance to one's manner, character, and educational level" (Japanese Association of the Pacific Coast 1918). Moreover, Ozawa's attorneys claimed that his skin was even whiter than some of "white" Americans. In other words, their understanding of "whiteness" defined by this law was the physical tone of the skin as well as, but more importantly, a designation one could obtain by becoming civilized and modern.

Japan's humiliating experience in the Ozawa case was a repeat of another incident when its Racial Equality Proposal, an attempt to counter legal racism against Japanese immigrants on the West Coast of the United States, was rejected by the United States and its allies at the Paris Peace Conference of 1919. These two critical incidents involving Japanese immigrants in the United States made Japan and Issei leaders finally recognize that the dream of joining, along with Europe and America, the highest rank of "civilization" was unattainable, no matter how "civilized" individuals became.

"Class"

Let us now turn our attention to the translation of *katō shakai* as "lower class." This Japanese term appeared in a famous confidential memorandum exchanged in 1891 between the consul of San Francisco, Sutemi Chinda, and the Japanese foreign minister, Shuzō Aoki. The following passage appears in a document entitled "Record concerning exclusions of Japanese citizens, Diplomat Record" that was part of a lengthy cable from Chinda to Aoki dated April 25, 1891 (Chinda 1891):

> With people from *katō shakai* swarming together one after another as they have been recently, it has brought disgrace on the entire Japanese people and a bad influence is exerted. . . .

To my knowledge, Donald Teruo Hata's 1970 dissertation, published as *"Undesirables": Early Immigrants and the Anti-Japanese Movement in San Francisco 1892–1893*, is one of the first instances of English-language scholarship that discussed Chinda's memorandum extensively and used the English translation of "lower class" (Hata 1970):

> In recent years . . . it is the poor and needy, prostitutes and outlandishly dressed fellows who had landed in ever increasing numbers at this important port . . . and the increasing arrivals of *lower class Japanese* will provide a pretext for . . . pseudo politicians . . . to exclude the Japanese from this country." (Hata 1970, 122–123, emphasis added)

Hata used "unpublished translations of documents from the Foreign Ministry archive," part of the Japanese American Research Project (JARP) of the University of California at Los Angeles. It is uncertain whether Hata relied on a translation done by JARP staff or employed "lower class" from the English language newspaper clippings that will be discussed shortly.

In their *East to America* (1980), Robert A. Wilson and Bill Hosokawa also cite the same Chinda memorandum:

> An unrestricted mass migration of *lower class Japanese* . . . will, without doubt, arouse and aggravate suspicion among the working class in this country. (Wilson and Hosokawa 1980, 114, emphasis added)

Since then, this translation of *katō shakai* as "lower class" has been reproduced and become established in Japanese American history scholarship. The phrase generally appears as part of this quotation or in an indirect reference to it (e.g., Ichioka 1977; Sawada 1991; Geiger 2011).

This translation might have been chosen because of the phrase's use in "American newspapers' seditious coverage" of the increasing number of Japanese prostitutes and other "undesirables." Included in the aforementioned document from Chinda to Aoki are multiple newspaper clippings glued to notepaper with the letterhead of the San Francisco Consulate of Japan. Although the newspapers from which they came is unclear, it is highly possible that Chinda himself sent or instructed someone to send them to Aoki. For example, a newspaper article in *Vancouver Daily News-Advertiser*, dated July 19, 1893, states, "the lower class Japanese are by no means . . . desirable settlers . . ." Another clipping of a newspaper article dated April 24, 1891, also mentions "a very low class" in the following statement:

The Commissioner states that the Japanese on both the [ships] Remus and Pemptos are of a *very low class and densely ignorant* [emphasis added].⁸

Let us first consider what the word "class" originally meant in this context. Although the *Oxford English Dictionary* includes several definitions of the word, "class" in this sense is defined as "a social division based on social or economic status." According to Raymond Williams's famous work *Keywords* and other sociology encyclopedias and dictionaries, "class" began to take on its contemporary meaning when the Industrial Revolution occurred, from the middle of the eighteenth to the middle of the nineteenth centuries:

> Development of class in its modern social sense, with relatively fixed names for particular classes (lower class, middle class, upper class, working class and so on), belongs essentially to the period between 1770 and 1840, which is also the period of the Industrial Revolution and its decisive reorganization of society. (Williams 1983 [1976], 61)

In other words, after the Industrial Revolution, "class" no longer meant an innate social status determined by birth (as was the case in premodern England); rather, like today, it primarily referred to an economic stratum. It is thus a concept inseparable from capitalism. Whereas capitalism had grown considerably in the United States by the end of the nineteenth century, Japan at the time was not necessarily in a similar situation. Japanese historians have generally agreed that capitalism took root in the country during the period between the Sino-Japanese War (1894–1895) and the Russo-Japanese War (1904–1905), but such development was limited to industrialized cities like Tokyo and Osaka. Only in this context did the economic disparities and poverty arising from the working class's low wages begin to emerge as a social problem in the form of a "metropolitan *kasō shakai* [下層社会 low strata society]" (e.g., Yokoyama 1985 [1899]; Nishinarita 2006). Gennosuke Yokoyama's classic work *Nihon no kasō shakai* (Japan's *kasō shakai*) discussed "Tokyo's poor," laborers, craftsmen, and tenant farmers as *kasō*, not *katō*.

As can be seen here, in Japanese there is also the term *kasō shakai*. Like *katō shakai*「下等社会」, it starts with the character *ka* ("low") and ends with the compound *shakai* ("society" or "community"); its second character is *sō* 層, not *tō* 等. In contemporary dictionaries, *sō* is defined as "strata," and *tō* is defined as "grade," "quality," or "class." It appears that this has led previous U.S.-based scholars to translate *katō shakai* as "lower class."

However, these words should be translated in light of their contemporary context and usage during the Meiji period. *A Dictionary of Chinese Character Compounds in Use Today from the End of the Edo and Early Meiji Period* defines "*kasō*" as "the bottom part of something layered" and "a stratum with a low social position." "*Katō*," in contrast, is defined as "low-quality, or appearing to be so" or "having a low level within the same group of humans," and "*katōjin*" [*jin* means person) as someone with bad character or vulgar attitude (Satō 2007, 108, 117).

Akihiko Ishidō presents more usage examples in his research, including one ranking individuals depending on their newspaper reading habits (*Eiri Shimbun,* Dec. 7, 1875, called readers of high-brow newspapers "cultured *jōtō* [upper grade]," readers of popular newspapers "half-civilized *chūtō* [middle grade]," and those who don't read the newspaper "uncivilized *katō* [low grade]"; Ishidō 2012, 64) and on their devotion to others ("people who serve the country" are *jōtō*, "people who serve people" *chūtō*, and "people who spend their days . . . within their capabilities" *katō*). He also points out that *katō* implies scorn, which is important to keep in mind understanding the word's difference from *kasō* (Ishidō 2012, 65).

Words parallel to these Japanese words did exist in classical Chinese. As Shūichi Katō notes, "Western-language texts were able to be translated into Japanese because, above all, the Japanese lexicon included an abundance of Chinese words" (Katō 1991, 349). When considering concepts from this time, examining Japanese words of Chinese origin is indispensable.

I searched for usages of these terms in the Database of Chinese Classic Ancient Books (中国基本古籍庫) Academia Sinica Chinese Full-text Database (中央研究院漢籍電子文献) (http://hanji.sinica. edu.tw/), a database that includes approximately ten thousand entries of basic classic Chinese-language texts produced up until the former half of the twentieth century.[9] The major Chinese dictionary *Hanyu dacidian* defines *xiadeng* (the same characters for *katō* in Japanese) as follows: (1) the person with the lowest position (within a certain social status); (2) low grade, low position; (3) low grade and vulgar; not refined and elegant.

Although there are many *katō* usage examples in the aforementioned database, they all refer to statuses only within a specific category and indicate scorn regarding "bad character" and the like. There are no examples from the nineteenth century or earlier of the compound being used to refer to a group within society as a whole. Since Liang Qichao, who studied in Japan, spread in China the contemporary usage (Meiji-period usage) of *jinshu* (race) and *minzoku* (nation/race) in the beginning of the twentieth century, we cannot rule out the possibility that these concepts crossed Japan's borders and spread in China as well.

Xiaceng (the same characters for *kasō* in Japanese), on the other hand, is defined as follows in the *Hanyu dacidian:* (1) the bottom stratum or substratum; (2) low-strata; or *xiadeng* (*katō*). The number of search results for *xiaceng* (*kasō*) is overwhelmingly lower than that for *xiadeng* (*katō*). Furthermore, documents from before the nineteenth century use the word *xiaceng* (*kasō*) only in a physical sense, in other words, when referring to parts of structures or concrete things. Examples of it referring to part of society's overall class order do not appear until the early twentieth century.

From this database search, we can conclude that, at the very least, at the end of the nineteenth century when Chinda sent his telegram, the meaning of *katō* and *kasō* matched that of *xiadeng* and *xiaceng,* respectively, in Chinese as well as in Japanese observed in the dictionaries and various writings of this era.

In sum, the word *kasō*, based on an ideology of socioeconomic hierarchy, has similar meanings as "lower class" in English, whereas *katō*, used to refer to bad character or vulgar behavior and clothing, meant a low level of civilization, cultivation, and modernity. Although these two words are highly correlated with each other, they should be conceptually distinguished. One possible English translation is "uncultivated segment of society/ uncultivated people" or "people of lesser civility." It may not be identical in meaning and nuance to *katō shakai,* but one closest in terms of referring to level of civilization, cultivation, and implying scorn.

Scholars have also not seriously considered the fact that the extent to which "civilization," "cultivation," and "modernization" shaped people's lives was related to their proximity to cities, particularly larger ones like Tokyo and Osaka. Rural areas in the countryside, from which the majority of immigrants to the United States came—Chinda states (perhaps exaggeratedly) in the aforementioned cable that "eight or nine out of ten [immigrants] are pure farmers"—were far less influenced by these government-sponsored projects.

Moreover, we must also consider the structures of hierarchy operating within the family at this time. The majority of immigrants were second sons or younger who often found themselves in positions of tremendous disadvantage in their hometowns in regard to their earnings as farmers or fishermen, their resources, and their level of privilege. An immigrant who was a second or younger son of a farmer's or fisherman's family in a rural area, who carried only the minimal amount of money, spoke only the local dialect, did not know how to write his own name, would have most likely been considered "uncivilized," "ill mannered," and "vulgar."

It is in this context that Chinda and Aoki repeatedly expressed their concerns about "undesirables," such as "prostitutes," "the poor," "the uneducated," "the illiterate," and "the unsanitary," all of whom they saw as an "embarrassment" and a "disgrace" to the entire Japanese community in the United States, a potential cause of serious immigration policy (Chinda 1952 [1891]). They voiced their concern within the context of a specific Japanese insecurity in America. Their worst nightmare was a repeat of the Chinese Exclusion Act of 1882, a version targeting Japanese immigrants.

Although it is possible to interpret "lower class" as referring to a social status (*mibun*), in this case, *burakumin*, a former outcast group in Japan, based on its classical usage, dictionary definitions cannot be used to make precise historical claims. It remains uncertain to what extent this "*katō shakai*" included *burakumin* (whose *mibun* during the Edo period was located in an entirely different framework from that of rulers and commoners). Japanese scholars specializing in *burakumin* and emigration history unanimously agree that there are almost no historical documents indicating how many *burakumin* were included among those who emigrated overseas. The late Yuji Ichioka repeatedly said to his colleagues that very few people of *burakumin* background had actually been able to leave Japan before 1908 because of strong emigration restrictions by the Japanese government. Regardless, discourses in Japanese American communities surrounding *burakumin* did exist and were often accompanied by prejudice against them. All we can conclude at this point is that no historical evidence exists that indicates whether or not *burakumin* were included among the people whom Chinda and Aoki referred to as *katō shakai,* and even if so, how many.

The expression "lower class" is a catchy phrase—it includes one of American academia's major three concepts ("race," "class," and "gender")— and has attracted attention among U.S.-based scholars in Japanese American studies. However, this attention has been based on the inaccurate assumption that Japan as a whole was a class society like the United States by 1891 and that these labor immigrants had belonged to the lower class. It involves an anachronistic projection of a concept onto nineteenth-century Japan: it ignores the historical reality that capitalism had not developed enough in the country to produce class differences, particularly in rural areas.

Why have Japanese researchers not pointed this out until now? Discussions surrounding translations surely should have already taken place by now. I believe that part of the problem lies in the scarcity of American researchers who can read Japanese as well as Japanese researchers' lack of initiative when it comes to words' translations into English.

The Future of Japanese American Studies

Young scholars in both the United States and Japan have the latitude to reshape their respective research topics and focus as their understanding and interest in the study of Japanese Americans deepens. We have started to witness scholars on the rise who are shifting the field's focus to encompass the wider context of Japanese American experiences—highlighting internal diversity, interethnic relationships, and trans-Pacific exchanges between social activists prior to World War II. The people and the attributes encompassed by the category "Japanese American" also need to be redefined. Hapa studies, along with the rise in interest surrounding multiracial Asian Americans, marks the academic recognition of a new phase in the field. Regardless of their individual geo-socio-political location, scholars' continual self-reflexive questioning regarding their stake in the study of Japanese Americans and their unique potential contributions to the field remains an important aspect of engaging in Japanese American studies.

The growing number of educational and research exchange programs as well as international conferences have contributed to a widening of perspectives and the development of new research topics in both countries. Japanese American studies seems to have finally reached a point at which scholars in the field have started to recognize the importance of engaging in such dialogues, which can only be seen as a positive and necessary development.

Notes

1 Almost all books and book chapters dealing with *kenjin* (people of the same prefecture) who emigrated abroad were published between the early 1960s and the late 1980s (Imin-kenkyūkai, 2007 [1994]), 23.

2 For example, the Japan Emigration Service (*kaigai ijū jigyōdan* 海外移住事業団) published thirty-three volumes of the research bulletin *Kaigai ijū* 『海外移住』 (*Emigration Overseas*) from 1965 to 1997. For a list of titles and authors

of all back numbers, see http://camp.ff.tku.ac.jp/tool-box/mig/iju.html (in Japanese). The journal continued to be one of the major resources for providing research materials as well as one of the major spaces to publish research findings for scholars in the field. For the literature review of studies related to these emigration agencies and corporations, see Imin-kenkyūkai 2007, chapter 3.

3 For example, Teruko Kachi, who later was a professor at Tsuda College, was probably the first Japanese person to earn a PhD degree in the study of Japanese Americans from an American university (the University of Chicago in 1957).

4 For example, as we write this introduction, on August 15, 2013 (the 68th memorial day for the end of WWII in Japan) and the following day, NHK (Japan Broadcasting Cooperation) aired a two-night documentary entitled 「日本兵になったアメリカ人 (*Americans Who Became Japanese Soldiers*), which used personal narratives of Nisei to shed light on some of the forty thousand Japanese Americans who happened to live in Japan at the outbreak of World War II. This part of their history had hardly been touched on before in the Japanese media.

5 Part of the discussion in this section is based on Takezawa (2015).

6 One million copies of *Sekai kunizukushi* were printed. As for *Yochishiryaku*, the Ministry of Education reported that up to 150,000 copies had already been printed by Meiji 7–8 (1874–1875). See Kikuji Nakamura 中村紀久二, *Kyōkasho no shakaishi Meiji ishin kara haisen made* (*Social History of School Textbook: From the Meiji Restoration to the End of World War II*) (Tokyo: Iwanami Shoten, 1992), 5.

7 As previously discussed, it is well known that during this time period there was also a tendency to see Japan as having been invaded by Western capitalism (although some nationals had grown confident in their country due to its economic development), leading certain intellectuals who had been advocates of international cooperation and free trade (such as Fukuzawa) to switch to conservative or ethno-nationalistic positions.

8 The newspaper title is unknown. Japanese consul, San Francisco, to Foreign Ministry, Tokyo, April 25, 1891. 本邦人ノ米國移民並ニ排斥関係一件 ("Record Concerning Exclusions of Japanese Citizens, Diplomat Record" 外交資料館所蔵外務省記録3門8類2項21号[第1巻]). On the same day, April 25, Chinda sent another memorandum to Aoki, following the memorandum dated on April 24, with several clippings, including the piece above. It is uncertain, though, when, where, and by whom the term "lower class" was first used in English, and whether this happened in the U.S. media or not.

9 Naoto Mochizuki and Tatsuma Matsushima of the Institute for Research in Humanities at Kyoto University assisted me in my Chinese-language database search.

References

Azuma, Eiichiro. 2005. *Between Two Empires: Race, History, and Transnationalism in Japanese America*. New York: Oxford University Press.

Chinda, Sutemi 珍田捨巳. 1891. 外交史料館所蔵外務省記録3門8類2項21号 (第1巻) (The Ministry of Foreign Affairs Record Held by the Diplomatic Archives of the Ministry of Foreign Affairs of Japan, 3.8.2.21, v. 1).

———. 1952 [1891]. 機密第六号 (Confidential Dispatch No. 6). Nihon Gaikō Bunsho, vol. 24, 463–476. Tokyo: Nihon Rengō Kyōkai.

Chiriki-kenkyūkai, ed. 地理研究會編. 1913. 新地理 中学校用概説之部 (Geography for Junior High School). Tokyo: Bungakusha.

Deniker, Joseph. 1900. *The Races of Man: An Outline of Anthropology and Ethnography*. London: Walter Scott.

Fukuzawa, Yukichi 福澤諭吉. 1869. 世界国盡 (All the Countries of the World). Tokyo: Keiō Gijuku Zōhan. Fukuzawa Collection: http://project.lib.keio.ac.jp/dg_kul/fukuzawa_title.php?id=34.

———. 2002 [1869]. 世界国尽 (All the Countries of the World). In *Fukuzawa Yukichi Chosakushū 2 kan*, edited by Shinya Nakagawa, 63–142. Tokyo: Keiō Gijuku Daigaku Shuppankai.

Geiger, Andrea A. E. 2011. *Subverting Exclusion: Transpacific Encounters with Race, Caste, and Borders, 1885–1928*. New Haven, CT: Yale University Press.

Harper & Brothers. 1886. *Harper's School Geography with Maps and Illustrations*. New York: Harper & Brothers.

Hata, Donald Teruo, Jr. 1970. "'Undesirables': Early Immigrants and the Anti-Japanese Movement in San Francisco 1892–1893." PhD diss., Department of History, University of Southern California.

Hata, Masajirō 秦政治郎. 1891. 中等教育 万国地誌 (Secondary Education World Geography). Tokyo: Hakubunkan.

Hayashi, Brian Masaru. 2004. *Democratizing the Enemy: The Japanese American Internment*. Princeton, NJ: Princeton University Press.

Ichioka, Yuji. 1977. "Ameyuki-san: Japanese Prostitutes in Nineteenth-Century America." *Amerasia* 4(1): 1–21.

———. 1988. *The Issei: The World of the First Generation Japanese Immigrant, 1885–1924*. New York: Free Press.

Imin-kenkyūkai. 移民研究会 (Migration Study Group), ed. 2007 [1994]. 日本の移民研究ー動向と文献目録 I (Migration Studies in Japan: Its Trends and Annotated Bibliography, Part I). Tokyo: Akashi Shoten.

Ishidō, Akihiko 石堂彰彦. 2012. 近代日本のメディアと階層認識 (The Media and Perceptions of Social Strata in Modern Japan). Tokyo: Yoshikawa Kōbunkan.

Japanese Association of the Pacific Coast. 1918. 帰化問題に就いて普く同胞に檄す (Appeal for Our Countrymen's Support Regarding the Naturalization Issue). Yuji Ichioka Papers: Research Materials: Social Adaptation and Racial Exclusion—Ozawa Takao correspondence file, 1919–1921. Box 67, Folder 8. Young Research Library, University of California, Los Angeles.

Kato, Shūichi 加藤周一. 1991. 明治初期の翻訳：何故・何を・如何に訳したか (Translation in the Early Meiji Period: Why, What, and How They Translated), in Shūichi Kato and Masao Maruyama, eds, *Hon'yaku no shisō*. Tokyo: Iwanami Shoten.

Kinkōdō shosekikaisha henshūjo 金港堂書籍会社編輯所. 1894. 小学万国地誌 (Elementary School World Geography). Tokyo: Kinkōdō Shoseki.

Nakagawa, Kōichi 中川浩一. 1978. 近代地理教育の源流 (Origin of Modern Geographical Education). Tokyo: Kokon Shoin.

Nakamura, Kikuji 中村紀久二. 1992. 教科書の社会史：明治維新から敗戦まで (Social History of School Textbook: From the Meiji Restoration to the End of World War II). Tokyo: Iwanami Shoten.

Nishinarita, Yutaka 西成田豊. 2006. 産業革命期日本における重工業大経営労働者の「都市下層民」的性格について (上) ("The 'Urban Lower Class' Nature of Laborers in Heavy Industry Companies during Japan's Industrial Revolution Period," Part 1). *Ōhara Shakaimondai Kenkyūjo Zasshi* 568: 1–22.

Ripley, William. 1899. *Races of Europe: A Sociological Study*. New York: D. Appleton and Co.

Russell, John G. 2007. "Excluded Presence: Shoguns, Minstrels, Bodyguards, and Japan's Encounters with the Black Other." *ZINBUN* 40: 15–51.

Satō, Shōsuke 佐藤昌介. 1971. 渡邊華山と高野長英 日本思想体系５５ 渡邊崋山 高野長英 佐久間象山 横井小楠 橋本左内 (Kazan Watanabe and Chōei Takano [An Outline of Japanese Thought No. 55]: *Watanabe Kazan, Takano Chōei, Sakuma Shōzan, Yokoi Shōnan, Hashimoto Sanai*), 607–650. Tokyo: Iwanami Shoten.

Satō, Tōru 佐藤亨. 2007. 現代に生きる 幕末・明治初期漢語辞典 (A Dictionary of Chinese Character Compounds in Use Today from the End of the Edo and Early Meiji Period). Tokyo: Meiji Shoin.

Sawada, Mitziko. 1991. "Culprits and Gentlemen: Meiji Japan's Restrictions of Emigrants to the United States, 1891–1909." *Pacific Historical Review* 60(3): 339–359.

Screech, Timon タイモン・スクリーチ. 1995. 大江戸異人往来 (The Coming and Going of Foreigners in Edo). Tokyo: Maruzen.

Takezawa, Yasuko. 2015. "Translating and Transforming 'Race': Early Meiji Period Textbooks." *Japanese Studies* 31(1): 5–21.

Uchida, Masao 内田正. 1871. 輿地誌略 (A Grammar of Geography for the Use of Schools). Tokyo: Daigaku Nankō.

Wagatsuma, Hiroshi. 1967. "The Social Perception of Skin Color in Japan." *Daedalus* 96(2): 407–443.

Watanabe, Kazan 渡辺崋山. 1971 [1839]. 再稿西洋事情書 ("Revised Report on Conditions in Western Countries"). In *Watanabe Kazan, Takano Chōei, Sakuma Shōzan, Yokoi Shōnan, Hashimoto Sanai,* edited by Shōsuke Satō, Michiari Uete and Muneyuki Yamaguchi, 43–55. Tokyo: Iwanami Shoten.

Williams, Raymond. 1983 [1976]. *Keywords: A Vocabulary of Culture and Society.* London: Fontana/ Croom Helm.

Wilson, Robert A., and Bill Hosokawa. 1980. *East to America: A History of the Japanese in the United States.* New York: William Morrow.

Yamada, Yukimoto, ed. 山田行元. 1893. 新地誌 (New Geography). Uehara Saiichirō.

Yamawaki, Chikako 山脇千賀子. 2013. 日系/nikkei のかなたへ (Beyond the Nikkei). In *Idō to iu keiken: Nihon ni okeru "imin" kenkyu no kadai,* edited by Toshio Iyotani, 163–184. Tokyo: Yūshindō.

Yazu, Masanaga 矢津昌永. 1896. 中学万国地誌 (Junior High School World Geography). Tokyo: Maruzen.

Yokoyama, Gennosuke 横山源之助. 1985 [1899]. 日本の下層社会 (The Lower Social Strata of Japan). Tokyo: Iwanami Shoten.

Yun, Kŏn-ch'a 尹健次. 1994. 民族幻想の蹉跌: 日本人の自己像 (The Failure of the *Minzoku* Illusion: Japanese People's Self-Image). Tokyo: Iwanami Shoten.

PART II

RACIALIZATIONS

CHAPTER 2

The Unbearable Whiteness of Being
The Contemporary Racialization of Japanese/Asian Americans

Michael Omi

In August 2006, Mark Burnett, the creator of CBS's *Survivor,* created quite a furor when he revealed that in the forthcoming fall season of the television show, the twenty *Survivor* contestants would be divided into four "tribes"—Asian American, black, Latino, and white. Protests ensued. The United Methodists of California and Nevada staged demonstrations at select CBS affiliates protesting what Bishop Beverly Shamana said was the network's attempt to "wager the basic tenet of humanity—that we are all one race—for the sake of higher ratings" (Nevius 2006). A *Wall Street Journal* editorial accused the show of "playing up identity-politics in a crude and potentially rancorous way" ("Survival Strategy" 2006). When asked by the Associated Press for his reaction to all the flack, Burnett said that his harshest critics "could look pretty stupid if it becomes the most positive thing for removing stereotypes."

Perhaps. But I do not think Rush Limbaugh got that message. Consider Limbaugh's remarks during the August 23, 2006, broadcast of his nationally syndicated radio talk show (*Media Matters for America* 2006). In assessing what might happen on the new season of *Survivor,* Limbaugh feared that the African American "tribe" would do badly if there were a lot of water events, since blacks are poor swimmers. Limbaugh said that his early money was on the Hispanics

> because these people have shown a remarkable ability, ladies and gentlemen, to cross borders, boundaries—they get anywhere they want to

go. They can do it without water for a long time. They don't get apprehended, and they will do things other people won't do. . . .

The white tribe, I have to tell you—I don't have a whole lot of hope in the white tribe. The Asian—the Asian-American tribe probably will outsmart everybody, but will that help them in the ultimate survival contest?

Apparently, yes. In December 2006, in what was billed as "a classic finale that pitted brains against brawn," Yul Kwon, a San Mateo management consultant with degrees from Stanford University and Yale Law School, was voted the "Sole Survivor" and winner of the $1 million prize (Hua 2006).

But let me return to Limbaugh's racial positioning of different groups and their respective attributes. I evoke this example to raise the contentious issue of how Asian Americans are popularly envisioned and represented in the broader context of racial stratification in the United States. How are Asian Americans currently racialized? And how are contemporary representations of Asian Americans related to their racial formation (Omi and Winant 1994) over historical time?

Arguably, there has never been a more appropriate time to consider the issue of Asian American racialization. According to the 2010 census, the Asian population grew faster than any other race group in the United States between 2000 and 2010. The Asian "alone" population (not counting individuals who classified themselves as Asian in combination with other race groups) increased more than four times faster than the total U.S. population, growing by 43 percent from 10.2 million in 2000 to 14.7 million in 2010. Factoring in the Asian "alone or in combination" (with other racial groups), the numbers grew by 46 percent, from 11.9 million in 2000 to 17.3 million in 2010 (U.S. Census Bureau 2012). Historically clustered in particular regions of the country, such as the West Coast, Asians are now found in large numbers in diverse parts of the United States. Regions that saw the fastest growth in their Asian population were primarily located in the South and the Midwest. The Asian population grew by 200 percent or more in counties in Texas, Florida, Georgia, Minnesota, Ohio, Iowa, and Indiana. Asian immigrants are settling or resettling in "new destination" cities and regions, and their increased presence has been the subject of national and local media coverage.

So, given the exponential growth and increased visibility of the Asian American population, how are they thought about and "positioned" in the current framework of racial classification and racial meanings?

This is a tricky question to address because the racial framework itself is being continually transformed and rendered more complex. The "color line" of the twentieth century has become the "color lines" of the twenty-first. The dramatic growth of both Asian and Latino populations has recast the traditional black/white paradigm of U.S. race relations and focused attention on the emergence of the so-called majority-minority society. Such a social order is characterized by a declining (and aging) white population offset by a growing (and relatively young) population of Latinos and Asians whose growth is based in large part on continuing immigration.

Dramatic transformations in the racial and ethnic demography of the United States have spurred interest in deciphering the meaning of such changes on the broader patterns of race and racism. Speculation has centered on what types of racial and ethnic alignments might emerge from these demographic shifts and their consequences with respect to job opportunities, the distribution of public goods, and electoral political mobilization. Outside of the domestic impact, changes in the racial/ethnic composition of the nation as the result of immigration have had, and will continue to have, profound effects on the U.S. approach to global issues ranging from trade agreements to foreign policy.

So what might the future hold? In an article in *Daedulus,* Jennifer Hochschild (2005) speculated on future racial trends and poses several possible scenarios contingent on different racial constructions and practices. Let us consider four of these scenarios regarding racial stratification:

- The first is black exceptionalism. In this scenario a black/nonblack racial divide is the crucial axis of race stratification, with Asians and Latinos being drawn to the white side of the color line and correspondingly distanced from blacks.
- The second is white exceptionalism. Here, a white/nonwhite racial divide would be in effect, and groups of color would presumably share a common subordinate status to whites.
- Third is the South African model, in which the nation becomes sorted into three groups: whites and "honorary whites" (most Asians, some Latinos, and some biracials), coloreds (some Asians, most Latinos,

some biracials, and a few blacks), and blacks and almost-blacks. This is similar to Eduardo Bonilla-Silva's (2006) notion of the "Latin Americanization" of race relations.
- A fourth scenario has distinct racial and ethnic groups blurring into a multiracial mélange. "A crucial divide in this scenario," writes Hochschild, "would be between those who identify as monoracials and seek to protect cultural purity and those who identify as multiracials and celebrate cultural mixing" (Hochschild 2005).

Each scenario envisions a different organizing principle of social stratification—one that defines group boundaries, shapes group consciousness, and establishes the overall structure of power and privilege. What each scenario gives us, therefore, is a glimpse of what the prevailing racial order might look like and how groups would be situated within such a racialized hierarchy.

We can debate the possibility and relative merits of each scenario, yet a key question remains in thinking about and assessing these racial futures: Who has or will have the power to define and structurally impose a given racial order? This question is fundamental to our discussion. Crucial to evaluating these racial futures, I would contend, is *where* Asian Americans will be positioned in the racial hierarchy and *who* will be doing the positioning.

Neither Black nor White

Where to position Asian Americans in the dominant racial order has historically been clouded by the prevailing black/white paradigm of race in the United States. Historian Gary Y. Okihiro (1994) provocatively posed the question "Is Yellow Black or White?" Indeed, depending on the period in question, Asian Americans have historically found themselves assigned to different sides of the color line. In the nineteenth century, as historian Dan Caldwell (1971) documented, there was a pervasive "Negroization" of the image of Chinese Americans found in opinion-page cartoons. In the early 1970s, by contrast, *Newsweek* assessed and proclaimed that Japanese Americans were "outwhiting the whites." Given these historical shifts, Okihiro noted that the very question of locating Asian Americans within a black/white binary is ultimately "a false and mystifying proposition." The black and white dyad, he argued, ignores "the gradations and complexities of the full spectrum between the racial poles" (Okihiro 1994, 62). Legal scholar Angelo N. Ancheta stated that the black/white paradigm "fails to recognize that the basic nature of discrimination can differ among racial and ethnic groups" and lists the unique aspects of racism directed at Asian Americans, which have included "nativism, differences in language and culture, perceptions of Asians as economic competitors, international relations, and past military involvement in Asian countries" (Ancheta 2006, 13). The point here is that the historical experiences of Asians in America have been distinctive in ways that are difficult to subsume into an analytic model of racial subordination and oppression based on black/white relations.

It is also important to note in passing that whereas Asian Americans have historically lacked the power to determine their racial position, they have not been without agency in seeking to position or reposition themselves on the color line. One could argue, as Ian Haney López (2006 [1996]) does in *White by Law: The Legal Construction of Race*, that the early Asian legal challenges to naturalization laws were complicitous with whiteness to the extent that petitioners argued to be recognized as "whites." Takao Ozawa, in the landmark 1922 U.S. Supreme Court case, argued that his skin color made him a "white person" and that the typical resident of Kyoto was "whiter than the average Italian, Spaniard or Portuguese." In a 1923 U.S. Supreme Court case, Bhagat Singh Thind's request for citizenship rested on the prevailing anthropological classification of Asian Indians not as "Mongolians" but as "Caucasians." Given the pervasive system of white supremacy that Asian Americans have historically grappled with, claims for extended rights and privileges were framed in constant reference to whiteness. Asian American aspirations to be defined as white or "near white" have to be seen in historical context.

Modeling a Minority

What Eric Liu recently referred to as "the tired old warhorse of the model minority" (quoted in Egan 2007) is seen as a child of the sixties, but the root of this image and argument goes back to the immediate postwar era and the experience of Japanese American resettlement. From 1943 to 1946, thousands of Japanese Americans left the internment camps to settle in Chicago, and a University of Chicago team studied the adjustment of this group to life in the city from 1947 until the early 1950s. William Caudill and George De Vos were attempting to account for the rapid social mobility and general acceptance of Nisei in Chicago. Why, they asked, have Japanese Americans achieved more in a few years than other groups have in a longer period of time? In "Achievement, Culture and Personality: The Case of Japanese Americans," Caudill and De Vos (1956) explored the importance of ethnic background in accounting for differences in achievement: A major hypothesis used as an orientation to our research was: there seems to be significant compatibility between the value systems found in the Culture of Japan and the value systems found in American middle-class culture.

Employing a battery of tests on both Issei and Nisei subjects, Caudill and DeVos looked at the achievement goals emphasized in the value system of the specific culture from which the subjects were drawn, the processes by which these goals were implemented, and the types of individual personality adjustment to these goals. They concluded that Japanese Americans have "made it" due to an achievement orientation founded on the "Japanese spirit" (Yamato Damashi):

> The Japanese Americans provide us, then, with the case of a group who, despite racial visibility and a culture traditionally thought of as alien, achieved a remarkable adjustment to middle-class American life because certain compatibilities in the value systems of the immigrant and host cultures operated strongly enough to override the obvious difficulties. What is meant is that, because of the compatibility between Japanese and American middle class cultures, individual Nisei probably have a better chance of succeeding than individuals from other ethnic groups where the underlying cultural patterns are less in harmony with those of the American middle class.

Asian American complicity with this line of argument has continued to be a flashpoint for often heated debate. Have Asian American social scientists, for example, been guilty of aspiring toward whiteness? In 2005, sociologist Setsuko Matsunaga Nishi (2005) wrote and circulated a detailed open letter to anthropologist Jacalyn Harden criticizing Harden's book *Double Cross: Japanese Americans in Black and White Chicago* (2003). Nishi admonishes Harden for misrepresenting her work as well as that of other Nisei graduate students at the University of Chicago who were involved in the resettlement studies. Among other things, Nishi takes issue with Harden's statement that the Nisei researchers were "tormented by struggles, intellectual and personal, to prove that Japanese Americans, by virtue of their culture, should not be considered 'colored'" and that they believed that "Japanese Americans had the skills and cultural traditions to work their way across the color line and blacks did not."

Whatever the intentions of the University of Chicago researchers were, it is undeniable that the research was selectively utilized in the mid-1960s to serve an important ideological function in the midst of glaring racial inequalities and troubling black/white hostilities. Against the backdrop of urban unrest and the insistent emphasis of the National Advisory Commission on Civil Disorders (The Kerner Commission) on the institutional dimensions of racism in the United States, influential journalists and scholars began to herald Asian Americans as a "model minority." Although acknowledging earlier forms of discrimination—including exclusionary immigration laws, restrictive political rights, and (in the case of Japanese Americans) mass incarceration, the literature concluded that Asian Americans had overcome racial barriers and were successfully integrating into the mainstream of American life. Sociologist William Petersen (1966, 21) declared, "Even in a country whose patron saint is the Horatio Alger hero, there is no parallel to this success story." Extrapolating from the Asian American experience, the "model minority" literature argued that the "race problem" was not the consequence of institutional racism, but of blacks and other groups of color not possessing the right cultural stuff.

"Whiteness" and Assimilation

Although the cultural compatibility argument has been dominant and pervasive for some time, I would argue that the current context for racially positioning Asian Americans is the increased scholarly attention being paid to the concept of "whiteness." White racial identity, classification, and consciousness is the subject of a growing literature that seeks to understand historical changes in the categorization of who is "white" and the formation of racial boundaries. Noel Ignatiev's (1995) book *How the Irish Became White* traces how a once despised European ethnic group became incorporated as white, and Karen Brodkin (1998) has explored how Jews became white in her book *How Jews Became White Folks and What That Says about Race in America*. Just as previous "outsiders" have been incorporated into our notions of who is white, speculation now centers on whether Asian Americans are following such a trajectory of inclusion under an expanded definition of "whiteness."

In *Two Nations*, a book about black and white racial inequalities, political scientist Andrew Hacker (1992) argues that the racial category of white is an elastic one. The question is not "who is white?," Hacker asserts, but "who can be considered white?" With this in mind, he believes that Asian

Americans are "merging" into the white category and that whites are "ready to absorb" this population.

The question of Asian American whiteness is also related to another development in social theory—a renewed interest in the concept of "assimilation." Once seen as a disreputable model of "Anglo-conformity" that ignored the experiences of people of color, assimilationist theory is making a big comeback among scholars of contemporary immigration and generational change.

Sociologists such as Richard Alba and Victor Nee (2003) have engaged in a rethinking and substantive reformulation of the concept of assimilation that they claim avoids some of its ideological and teleological flaws. This rethinking, among other things, casts the provocative issue of the "declining white majority" in a different light. Alba and Nee point out that processes of assimilation render racial and ethnic demographic projections problematic because they rest on the assumption that these categories are stable enclosures. Responding to forecasters who predict the decline of the white population, they suggest that our collective notion of who the majority group is might undergo a profound redefinition as some Asians and Latinas/os are merged into the white, European population.

Sociologist George Yancey (2003) in *Who Is White?* argues that Latinos and Asian Americans are undergoing a significant level of structural, marital, and *identificational* assimilation. He draws on survey data to illustrate that the social attitudes of Latinos and Asian Americans on a number of issues are closer to those of whites than blacks. Yancey believes that this indicates that these nonblack groups are beginning to identify with majority group status. He states that a black/nonblack divide is emerging as Latinos and Asian Americans become "white" and blacks continue to endure a specific form of what he calls racial "alienation."

Michael Lind (1998) correspondingly argues in his article "The Beige and the Black" that contemporary intermarriage trends point to a new, disturbing division between blacks and nonblacks. In the twenty-first century, he envisions "a white-Asian-Hispanic melting-pot majority—a hard-to-differentiate group of beige Americans—offset by a minority consisting of blacks who have been left out of the melting pot once again." Such a dire racial scenario and landscape presents a number of troubling political questions regarding the formation of group interests and social inequality.

"It's the Economy, Stupid," or Is It?

The question of whether Asian Americans are becoming white is a complex one. Seen as a "racial minority," Asian Americans are nonetheless not generally regarded as a "disadvantaged" or "underrepresented" one. The prevailing belief is that Asian Americans do not directly experience racial discrimination nor incur social disadvantages by race. Drawing on select social and economic indicators, some researchers have argued that Asian Americans have achieved parity with whites with respect to income and levels of education and, correspondingly, have distanced themselves from other groups of color. An often cited statistic is median household income. In 2010, the median household income for Asian American households was $64,308 compared with $54,620 for non-Hispanic whites, $37,759 for Hispanics, and $32,068 for blacks. The 2010 poverty rate for Asian Americans was 12.1 percent compared with 9.9 percent for non-Hispanic whites, 26.6 percent for Hispanics, and 27.4 percent for blacks (U.S. Census Bureau 2011). With respect to education, 50 percent of Asian Americans twenty-five years or older had a bachelor's degree or higher level of education compared with 28 percent of all Americans age twenty-five years or older.

All these socioeconomic indicators have been subject to debate regarding their meaning and significance. For example, it can be argued that the high median household income for Asian Americans can be accounted for by noting the number of working family members in the household and the concentration of Asian Americans in parts of the country where incomes and the cost of living are relatively high. Perhaps more important, it is crucial to point out that the aggregate statistics reported for all Asian Americans mask the internal diversity within the socially constructed group we so glibly refer to as Asian American. Asian Americans exhibit a bimodal pattern; some groups are doing quite well economically, but others remain mired in poverty. For example, per capita income is seven times higher for Japanese Americans than Hmong. Correspondingly, the poverty rate for Hmong is nine times higher than that of Japanese Americans.

Although much can be said about the interpretation of economic indicators and the bimodal pattern exhibited among Asian Americans, I want to turn to the social and cultural indicators evoked in the literature on Asian Americans and on "whiteness" and how they are read and interpreted. I remain conscious of the symbiotic and dialectical relationship between economic and social/cultural variables, but the literature at hand is more preoccupied with shifting perceptions of race and racial difference and their meaning for an expanded notion of who is white.

Intermarriage, Gender, and "Mixed Race" Identity

The most popularly cited indicator that Asian Americans are becoming "white" has been the high rates of Asian American intermarriage with whites. In the classic model of assimilation, advanced by sociologist Milton Gordon (1964), increasing rates of marriage between minority and majority groups are interpreted as an important indicator of a reduction in group prejudice and discrimination and a lessening of strict social boundaries. Writing in 2003, George Yancey said, "With sufficient time and a sufficiently high outmarriage rate, Asian Americans will lose the social perception that they belong to a different race."

Although Yancey's is an optimistic prediction of dissolving racial group distinctiveness, the meaning of interracial marriages for Asian Americans is filled with contradictions and can be interpreted differently. One important variable to consider is the difference in outmarriage rates by gender, which are sharp and apparent for Asian Americans. In 2010, 36.1 percent of Asian American female newlyweds married a non-Asian, compared with only 16.6 percent of Asian American male newlyweds (Wang 2012). This gender gap, with obvious variation, has persisted for at least forty years. Several factors are at work, but it can be argued that the higher outmarriage rate of Asian American females is reflective of a long history of Asian women being popularly regarded as desirable sexual partners and spouses. Ideas and images about Asian women circulate in a variety of settings, from popular films to pornography, and from dating ads to "mail order bride" services (Shimizu 2007). The point is that "racial difference" is being affirmed, not shed as the model of assimilation would hold. Instead of being read as a crucial indicator of assimilation, increasing intermarriage might simply reflect inequalities in racial power and the persistence of stereotypic notions of race, gender, and sexuality.

The literature on assimilation and whiteness also assumes that with increasing rates of intermarriage among Asian Americans, so-called mixed-race children will lose their distinctive Asian ethnic identities and facilitate the absorption of Asian Americans into an expanded notion of whiteness. The increased visibility of mixed-race Japanese Americans, for example, is obvious. An often quoted census report in 1990 revealed that there were

39 percent more Japanese/white births than monoracial Japanese American births. According to data presented in 2002, Japanese Americans had a 52 percent outmarriage rate and the largest proportion of mixed-race members of any ethnic/racial group. Around 31 percent of Japanese Americans were of mixed race.

What is the broader meaning of this demographic growth of the mixed-race population? Some have suggested that it spells the future demise of Japanese American ethnicity and community. This has been a long-standing view. Consider the following statement from an article, "A Major Ethnic Disaster," that appeared in the Japanese American Citizens League's newspaper, *Pacific Citizen,* in 1977:

> What is the greatest threat to our race here in the U.S.? Is it the FBI? White Racism? Is it the media? The intermarriage problem is by far the worse threat to our existence than a hundred million Manzanars, Tule Lakes, or Pearl Harbors. (Inouye 1977)

Strong stuff indeed. But let us unpack the assumptions. Such a view conflates concepts of race, ethnicity, and culture and assumes that widespread racial outmarriage means the erosion of ethnicity and culture. Is this true? Not necessarily.

Sociologist Rebecca Chiyoko King-O'Riain (2006) provided a comparative study of Japanese American beauty pageants that sheds light on the connections between race, culture, and community. She notes that the eligibility rules over who can enter the beauty pageants render visible the racial and ethnic boundaries of the community, pointing out who is and who is not legitimately Japanese American. Most require that contestants be at least half-Japanese—Seattle's racial rule is 25 percent; Honolulu's was 100 percent until 1999 and is now 50 percent.

King-O'Riain found that the question of authenticity and who should represent the Japanese Amrican community is a contentious one. On the one hand, there were what she calls "cultural impostors"—contestants who are "biologically" Japanese but were assimilated and did not ethnically or culturally view themselves as Japanese. On the other hand, there were hapa (mixed race) contestants, whom she describes as "eggs"—women who looked white on the outside, but who spoke fluent Japanese, were versed in various traditional music and dance forms, culturally saw themselves as Japanese. One monoracial candidate in the study said,

I've met women [in the pageant] who are half Japanese who are more Japanese than me, a lot more culturally. I'm fourth generation. I'm probably more American than most of my friends. My family has been here longer. Does that mean I'm not a good representative of the Japanese community? I don't know. (King-O'Riain 2006, 91)

The point I want to make here is that ethnic identity is continually being redefined, and the assumption that the decrease in the population of racially "pure" Japanese Americans means the end of community and culture, and eventual absorption into whiteness, is a profoundly misleading one. Shifting notions of ethnicity, cultural belonging, and community are not simply anchored in racial phenotype, and claims of blending into whiteness based solely on the increase of a mixed Asian/white population are suspect.

Perpetual Foreigners and Racial Threats

One clear impediment to white status for Asian Americans is the popular social perception of Asians as "perpetual foreigners." It is reflective of the process of racializing people in terms of their presumed affiliation with foreign places. According to cultural studies scholar Lisa Lowe (1996), "The Asian is always seen as an immigrant, as the 'foreigner-within'" and "remains the symbolic 'alien.'" Indeed, the very notion of Asian Americans as the perpetual foreigner presents a sharp challenge to the image of "Asians as honorary whites" (Tuan 1998).

The importance of cultural representations of the Asian American as the "forever foreigner" cannot be understated. This nation has not been able to purge itself of a repertoire of ideologies and practices that are evoked or emphasized in particular historical moments and render Asian Americans foreign, subversive, and suspect.

Both the Asian campaign finance controversy of the Clinton-Gore years and the Wen Ho Lee case provide illustrations of this. A national survey on American attitudes toward Chinese Americans conducted in March 2001 found that 23 percent of Americans held "strong negative attitudes" toward Chinese Americans, and 43 percent held "somewhat negative attitudes." Among other things, 32 percent felt that Chinese Americans were more loyal to China than America. Those surveyed were more "uncomfortable" with an Asian American as president of the United States, CEO of a Fortune 500 company, or supervisor at work than they would be with an African American, a woman, or a Jewish American (Committee of 100 2001).

These attitudes illustrate an important dimension about Asian Americans and racism. The experiences of Asian Americans have been inordinately shaped by the prevailing tenor of U.S. political and economic relations with Asia. Exclusion laws, internment, and the extension of naturalization rights have been the direct result of shifts in these relations. Racial representations, therefore, are shaped by global dynamics and the prevailing images of Asians in America continually remain tied and subject to the twists and turns in trade relations, U.S. foreign policy, and overall geopolitical alignments. Deterioration in relations between the United States and any Asian country profoundly affects how Asian Americans are viewed and treated. This connection has dire implications in the current period. Andrew Barlow (2003), in a book on globalization and race, stated that "as globalization leaves national elites with less capacity to redistribute scarce social resources downward to maintain social order, the politics of maintaining social order become increasingly symbolic and repressive" (p. 77). What we have in this climate is an intensification of racism and national chauvinism.

Competitive fears play out on the local level as well. In a study of perceived group competition in Los Angeles, sociologists Larry Bobo and Vincent Hutchings (1996) found, among other things, that whites feel least threatened by blacks and most threatened by Asians. Interestingly, they also found that Asians are perceived by whites as a threat not because they are deemed racially inferior, but because they are seen as unfair competitors who do "too well."

The images of Asian Americans as both a "model minority" and a competitive racial threat reveal important differential aspects of racism in the United States. Racism is popularly understood as hostility directed against those of a different skin color whom we believe to be "inferior" in intellectual capability, temperament, cultural orientation, and so on. This belief is coupled with structural forms of discrimination with respect to jobs and housing, along with political disempowerment. Blacks in the United States are subject to racism understood in these terms. Asian Americans are subject to a different form of racism. They are often the objects of resentment by other groups who believe they do "too well" and unfairly secure material resources and social advantages.

The consequences of such a perception can be ironic. In 2005, the *Wall Street Journal* examined "The New White Flight" (Hwang 2005). The article looked at Monta Vista High School in Cupertino, California, a school with an outstanding academic reputation that was losing white students as Asian student enrollment increased.

In the article, I was struck by the comments of a white woman who was president of the Monta Vista PTA. She had recently dissuaded a family with a young child from moving to Cupertino because there are so few white students left in the public schools: "This may not sound good, but their child may be the only Caucasian kid in the class. . . . White kids are thought of as the dumb kids." A recent Asian American graduate of the high school said, "If you were Asian, you had to confirm you were smart. If you were white, you had to prove it." As a result of this perceived competition, whites are moving out of Cupertino as Asians move in—thus, the "new white flight." The image of Asian American unassailable intellectual prowess, and the fear it inspires among whites in this instance, dramatically contrasts with the "old" white flight motivated by white fears of black criminality and "deteriorating" schools.

This example suggests the intimate connection between representations of Asian Americans as a model minority and as a racial threat. As Gary Okihiro perceptively noted,

> The yellow peril and the model minority are not poles, denoting opposite representations along a single line, but in fact form a circular relationship that moves in either direction . . . Moving in one direction along the circle, the model minority mitigates the alleged danger of the yellow peril, whereas reversing direction, the model minority, if taken too far, can become the yellow peril. (Okihiro 1994, 142)

Fears that Asian Americans can "outwhite the whites" reflect a continuing racialization and "othering" of Asians—one that historically has led to policies and practices of exclusion and containment.

Caught in the Middle

Recent scholarship has challenged the view that Asian Americans can easily be categorized or recognized as "honorary whites" and, in so doing, has emphasized issues of racial hierarchy and racism and their continued salience. In *The Myth of the Model Minority,* sociologists Rosalind Chou and Joe Feagin (2008) have captured how individual Asian Americans encounter racial hostility and discrimination in different social and institutional sites and the distinct ways they strategically respond to such treatment, including both passive accommodation and active resistance. In *The Racial Middle,* sociologist Eileen O'Brien's (2008) Asian American respondents express racial ideologies and assert social identities that reveal a distinctive positionality within the dominant black/white paradigm of race in the United States.

Group position is a relative and relational thing. In many respects, it is important to see that "whiteness" is being selectively extended to some Asian Americans—principally, East Asian Americans—and denied to others. The heterogeneity of the Asian American population elides enormous social and economic differences within this racial category. *Colorism* is an issue as well, with lighter-skinned Asians being popularly viewed as better candidates for assimilation than darker-skinned Asians.

And if Asian Americans are collectively seen as "not quite white," they may also be increasingly viewed, on the other hand, as "not quite colored." This racial positioning makes Asian Americans potentially vulnerable to attacks from both whites *and* other groups of color.

In October 2006, a controversial editorial was printed in the *Daily Bruin,* the student newspaper of the University of California, Los Angeles (UCLA). Regular contributor Jed Levine (2006) urged students to "wake up and smell the bamboo." He argued that black and Latino student protests against prevailing University of California admissions policies were misdirected at "The Man." Levine argued that whites were not to blame, because whites themselves were an underrepresented minority at UCLA. Although they made up 44 percent of California's population, white students constituted only 34 percent of UCLA's student population. By contrast, Levine noted that although Asian Americans made up only 12 percent of the state's population, they accounted for 38 percent of UCLA's students. He concluded,

> By keeping Asian-American student numbers under control and more accurate to their representation in California, we can free up 26 percent of the student body for members of underrepresented groups. The result is a win-win situation: fewer rolling backpacks, more diversity.

Levine's piece was satirical (I think), but in January 2007, the *New York Times* ran an extensive article on the "overrepresentation" of Asians at elite colleges and universities (Egan 2007). Mentioned is a case regarding a student who filed a complaint with the Department of Education's Office of Civil Rights contending he was denied admission to Princeton because he was Asian. Jian Li had a perfect SAT score and near-perfect grades. To back his discrimination claim, he cited a 2005 study by two Princeton scholars that concluded that if elite universities were to disregard race, Asians would fill nearly four of five spots that were then going to blacks or Latinos. Li argued that affirmative action had had a neutral effect on the number of whites admitted, but that it had raised the bar for Asians. In his complaint, Li said that Princeton's admissions policy "seems to be a calculated move by a historically white institution to protect its racial identity while at the same time maintaining a facade of progressivism."

In a more recent commentary piece in the *Chronicle of Higher Education,* Jonathan Zimmerman (2012) said, "Put simply, it's harder to get into college if you're Asian." He cited a study by Princeton sociologist Thomas J. Espenshade, who found that Asian Americans need 140 more points on their SAT scores than white students—other things being equal—-to get into elite colleges.

Li and others may be challenging whiteness in their claims of Asian discrimination, but it is important to consider that such challenges may come at the expense of underrepresented groups of color. As George Lipsitz (1998) noted, "No magical essence unites aggrieved victims of white supremacy in common endeavors." Communities of color, he wrote, are mutually constitutive of one another and need to "be aware of one another and be prepared for unexpected alliances as well as unexpected antagonisms" (p. 184). This has certainly been the case regarding the highly contested issue of affirmative action.

The Racial Bribe

In January 1996, Governor Pete Wilson of California upheld his support for the decision by the University of California (UC) regents to eliminate affirmative action in admissions, hiring, and contracting. It was the "right decision," he argued, one premised on the principles of equal opportunity for all: "Racial preferences are by definition racial discrimination. They were wrong 30 years ago when they discriminated against African-Americans. And they're wrong today, when they discriminate against Asian or Caucasian Americans" (Wilson 1996).

Wilson's strategic assignment of Asian Americans to the white side of the color line was noteworthy. The very questioning of affirmative action by the UC regents was precipitated by a complaint lodged by Jerry and Ellen Cook, a white San Diego couple who began examining statistical information on the five medical schools in the UC system when their son was denied admission to the UC San Diego Medical School. The Cooks claimed that at one of the UC medical schools they examined, Latinos were offered admission at five times the rate of whites and *nineteen times* the rate of Japanese Americans. In evoking these statistics, the implicit argument was that Asian Americans were harmed by affirmative action policies as much if not more than whites (Omi and Takagi 1996).

The deployment of this particular narrative served an important political purpose. By raising the issue of Asian American victimization, opponents of affirmative action could deflect charges that their opposition to affirmative action merely stemmed from an attempt to preserve white privilege. Asian Americans were strategically evoked to demonstrate that another "racial minority" was being hurt and disadvantaged by affirmative action as well. This disrupted the political discourse surrounding this highly charged racial issue as an expression of white/nonwhite difference and conflict, and new battle lines were drawn playing upon popular constructions of Asian Americans as "friends" of whites and "foes" of African Americans.

What are the political implications of establishing Asian American and white alliances in the face of continuing racial stratification and hierarchy? In their book *The Miner's Canary,* law professors Lani Guinier and Gerald Torres (2002) examined what they call "the racial bribe," which they describe as "a strategy that invites specific racial or ethnic groups to advance within the existing black-white racial hierarchy by becoming 'white.'" This strategy to expand the definition of "white" is advanced, they claim, "to defuse the previously marginalized group's oppositional political agenda"; "to offer incentives that discourage the group from affiliating with blacks"; and "to make the social position of 'whiteness' appear more racially or ethnically diverse."

Although Guinier and Torres focused their discussion on Latinos and possible Latino racial "incorporation," it is apparent that the racial bribe has been extended to Asian Americans as well. And even though some Asian Americans in the United States may relish their emerging status as "honorary whites," the broader question remains, Who is doing the labeling, who is conferring the status, and to what ends?

In this regard, it may be analytically useful to think about the contemporary racialization of Asian Americans as a *racial project*. In racial formation theory, a racial project is "simultaneously an interpretation, representation, or explanation of racial dynamics and an effort to reorganize and redistribute resources along particular racial lines" (Omi and Winant 1994, 56). Racial projects connect discursive practices with social structures to give race meaning in everyday and institutional life. The prevailing representations of Asian Americans as white or "near white" can be seen as part of a racial project to reimagine the color line and consolidate a revised racial hierarchy. It is one in which Asian Americans are strategically incorporated into the white racial category and distanced from other groups of color.

White Like Me?

In *The Accidental Asian,* author Eric Liu (1998) proposed a strange new status—"white, by acclamation": "Some are born white, others achieve whiteness, still others have whiteness thrust upon them." Let us think about this observation a bit. How do we understand the issue of Asian Americans' becoming white? Is it a matter of structural assimilation, shifts in social attitudes, increasing intermarriage? Or does it represent a political effort to reconfigure the racial divide? It could be argued that as whites experience a relative decline in numbers and a loss of dominant status, a shift in racial boundaries can strategically serve to prop up racial power. Incorporation, in this sense, might simply be a function of preserving white privilege.

What is fundamentally missing in the broader debate regarding whether Asian Americans are becoming "white" is a substantive challenge to the problematic category of "whiteness" itself. According to legal scholar john powell (2005),

> Even if more and more people are allowed to pass, and notice the connotations of those words "allowed to pass," it does nothing to transform the meaning associated with that boundary in the first place.... The very need to pass indicates the continued salience of racial hierarchy. (p. 41)

Acknowledging the continuing salience of racial stratification and hierarchy puts a different spin on the topic of whether Asian Americans are becoming white. Perhaps the issue to be addressed is not whether the category of "white" is expanding to include Asian Americans, but why, given the current racial climate, there is a move to expand our notion of whiteness. The prevailing representation of Asian Americans and their assumed incorporation as "honorary whites" might, in this sense, simply reflect a move to preserve white supremacy and privilege.

References

Alba, Richard, and Victor Nee. 2003. *Remaking the American Mainstream: Assimilation and Contemporary Immigration.* Cambridge, MA: Harvard University Press.

Ancheta, Angelo N. 2006. *Race, Rights, and the Asian American Experience,* 2nd ed. New Brunswick, NJ: Rutgers University Press.

Barlow, Andrew L. 2003. *Between Fear and Hope: Globalization and Race in the United States.* Lanham, MD: Rowan & Littlefield.

Bobo, Lawrence, and Vincent Hutchings. 1996. "Perceptions of Racial Group Competition: Extending Blumer's Theory of Group Position to a Multiracial Social Context." *American Sociological Review* 61(6) (December): 951–972.

Bonilla-Silva, Eduardo. 2006. "E Pluribus Unum or the Same Old Perfume in a New Bottle?: On the Future of Racial Stratification in the United States." In *Racism Without Racists: Color-Blind Racism and the Persistence of Racial Inequality in the United States,* 2nd ed., chap. 8. Lanham, MD: Rowan & Littlefield.

Brodkin, Karen. 1998. *How Jews Became White Folks and What That Says about Race in America.* New Brunswick, NJ: Rutgers University Press.

Caldwell, Dan. 1971. "The Negroization of the Chinese Stereotype in California." *Southern California Quarterly* 53 (June): 123–131.

Caudill, William, and George De Vos. 1956. "Achievement, Culture and Personality: The Case of Japanese Americans." *American Anthropologist* 58 (1) (December): 102–126.

Chou, Rosalind S., and Joe R. Feagin. 2008. *The Myth of the Model Minority: Asian Americans Facing Racism.* Boulder, CO: Paradigm.

Committee of 100. 2001. "American Attitudes Toward Chinese Americans and Asian Americans." http://www.committee100.org/publications/survey/C100survey.pdf.

Egan, Timothy. 2007. "Little Asia on the Hill." *New York Times,* January 7.

Gordon, Milton M. 1964. *Assimilation in American Life: The Role of Race, Religion, and National Origins.* New York: Oxford University Press.

Guinier, Lani, and Gerald Torres. 2002. *The Miner's Canary: Enlisting Race, Resisting Power, Transforming Democracy.* Cambridge, MA: Harvard University Press.

Hacker, Andrew. 1992. *Two Nations: Black and White, Separate, Hostile, Unequal.* New York: Scribner's.

Harden, Jacalyn D. 2003. *Double Cross: Japanese Americans in Black and White Chicago.* Minneapolis: University of Minnesota Press.

Hochschild, Jennifer L. 2005. "Looking Ahead: Racial Trends in the United States." *Daedalus* 134 (Winter): 70–81.

Hua, Vanessa. 2006. "San Mateo Man Defeats Asian Stereotypes to Win 'Survivor.'" *San Francisco Chronicle,* December 19.

Hwang, Suein. 2005. "The New White Flight." *Wall Street Journal,* November 19.

Ignatiev, Noel. 1995. *How the Irish Became White.* New York: Routledge.

Inouye, Jon. 1977. "A Major Ethnic Disaster." *Pacific Citizen,* March 25, 9.

King-O'Riain, Rebecca Chiyoko. 2006. *Pure Beauty: Judging Race in Japanese American Beauty Pageants.* Minneapolis: University of Minnesota Press.

Levine, Jed. 2006. "A Modest Proposal for an Immodest Proposition." *Daily Bruin,* October 10.

Lind, Michael. 1998. "The Beige and the Black." *New York Times Magazine,* August 18, 38–39.

Lipsitz, George. 1998. *The Possessive Investment in Whiteness: How White People Profit From Identity Politics.* Philadelphia: Temple University Press.

Liu, Eric. 1998. *The Accidental Asian: Notes of a Native Speaker.* New York: Random House.

Lopéz, Ian Haney. 2006 [1996]. *White by Law: The Legal Construction of Race.* New York: New York University Press.

Lowe, Lisa. 1996. *Immigrant Acts: On Asian American Cultural Politics.* Durham, NC: Duke University Press.

Media Matters for America. 2006. "Limbaugh Handicaps Races in New *Survivor* Series." August 23. http://mediamatters.org/research/2006/08/23/Limbaugh-handicapped-races-in-new-survivor-seri/136459.

Nevius, C. W. 2006. "*Survivor* Wades Right into Racial Stereotyping." *San Francisco Chronicle,* September 14.

Nishi, Setsuko Matsunaga. 2005. "An Open Letter to Jacalyn D. Harden." *Amerasia Journal* 13(1) (January): 179–195.

O'Brien, Eileen. 2008. *The Racial Middle: Latinos and Asian Americans Living Beyond the Racial Divide.* New York: New York University Press.

Okihiro, Gary Y. 1994. *Margins and Mainstreams: Asians in American History and Culture.* Seattle: University of Washington Press.

Omi, Michael, and Dana Y. Takagi. 1996. "Situating Asian Americans in the Political Discourse on Affirmative Action." *Representations* (Summer): 155–162.

Omi, Michael, and Howard Winant. 1994. *Racial Formation in the United States: From the 1960s to the 1990s.* New York: Routledge.

Petersen, William. 1966. "Success Story, Japanese-American Style." *New York Times Magazine,* January 9.

powell, john a. 2005. "Dreaming of a Self Beyond Whiteness and Isolation." *Washington University Journal of Law & Policy* 18: 13–45.

Shimizu, Celine Parrenas. 2007. *The Hypersexuality of Race: Performing Asian/American Women on Screen and Scene.* Durham, NC: Duke University Press.
"Survival Strategy." 2006. *Wall Street Journal,* September 1.
Tuan, Mia. 1998. *Forever Foreigners or Honorary Whites?: The Asian Ethnic Experience Today.* New Brunswick, NJ: Rutgers University Press.
U.S. Census Bureau. 2011. "Income, Poverty and Health Insurance Coverage in the United States." September 12. http://www.census.gov/newsroom/releases/archives/income_wealth/cb12-172.html.
U.S. Census Bureau. 2012. *The Asian Population: 2010.* 2010 Census Briefs. Report by Elizabeth M. Hoeffel, Sonya Rastogi, Myoung Ouk Kim, and Hasan Shahid. March.
Wang, Wendy. 2012. *The Rise of Intermarriage: Rates, Characteristics Vary by Race and Gender.* Washington, DC: Pew Social & Demographic Trends. February 16.
Wilson, Pete. 1996. "Why Racial Preferences Must End." Open Forum, *San Francisco Chronicle,* January 18.
Yancey, George. 2003. *Who Is White?: Latinos, Asians, and the New Black/Non-Black Divide.* Boulder, CO: Lynne Rienner.
Zimmerman, Jonathan. 2012. "Asian Americans, the New Jews on Campus." *Chronicle of Higher Education,* April 29.

CHAPTER 3

Negotiating Categories and Transgressing (Mixed-) Race Identities
The Art and Narratives of Roger Shimomura, Laura Kina, and Shizu Saldamando

Yasuko Takezawa

Introduction

In April 2013, the Japanese American National Museum in Los Angeles launched a new exhibition entitled "Visible & Invisible: A Hapa Japanese American History." This exhibit spotlighted multiracial and multiethnic Japanese American families and individuals, covering the past to the present.[1] The museum has also, since its inception in 2008, been host to the Mixed Roots Film and Literary Festival, now Mixed Remixed Festival, which serves as a forum to commemorate the U.S. Supreme Court's 1967 landmark decision in *Loving v. Virginia,* overturning the nation's remaining antimiscegenation laws, and as a hub to share stories and generate new collective memories celebrating multiracialism.

With individual artists such as Velina Hasu Houston, a pioneer who paved the way with a series of theater plays, and Kip Fulbeck, known for his influential exhibition, "Part Asian, 100% Hapa," which later became a book, as well as the above-mentioned community-organized events, the arts are increasingly serving as a convergent crossroad for diverse and divergent multiracial Asian Americans to share their experiences and identities in this emerging community. These events and activities in the arts may demonstrate the shifting boundaries and community needs of "Japanese Americans" and "Asian Americans."

In chapter 2, Michael Omi offered an admirable critique of academic and popular discourse that portrays the high rate of interracial marriage among Asian Americans as steadily marching on a path toward whiteness and the discourse that operates as a contemporary form of racialization of Japanese and Asian Americans. I share a mutual interest in multiracial issues and boundary formation. In this chapter I turn from the macro level to the micro as I interrogate how individuals, in this case artists, negotiate a fraught terrain and exercise, reject, or transgress, through their art, the racial and other social categories applied to them.

When people on the margins employ social categories such as race, gender, or sexuality, they face a dilemma: although categories can be used as a means for improving political or social status, achieving public recognition, and sometimes securing economic resources, they can also perpetuate, essentialize, and homogenize group boundaries and identities (Benford and Snow 2000; Brubaker and Cooper 2000). As encompassing as a category like "multiracial" might seem, it has not been immune to the problematic paradoxical aspects of categories. Multiracial activists, taking cues from the self-oriented liberal individualism of earlier ethnic and minority movements, have used the multiracial category as part of their effort to bring public attention to their unique struggles (DaCosta 2007). Some criticize the use of the terms "mixed race" or "multiracial," but doing away with these categories could easily lead to the subsumption of such individuals under existing racial categories, placing them in a position in which they could be seen as deviant or rendered invisible. Asian Americans also have much at stake in the shaping of the "multiracial" category (Lowe 1996; Võ 2004). The word "hapa" was originally used as part of the phrase "hapa haole," which referred to people who were a "mix" (hapa) of a native Hawaiian and a white person (haole), and subsequently came to be used to refer to any person of part Asian and/or Pacific Islander descent. Some are critical of this category on the grounds that, like existing racial categories, it is accompanied by the danger of reifying a "mixed race" and thereby constructing a new racial entity. Other critics point out that it conceals diversity and hierarchies within hapa. However, there are some who use "mixed race" from a standpoint that is critical of essentialism, instilling it with the meaning of "mix up" (in the sense of "throwing into confusion").

Some interlocutors in the exhaustive debates on post-identity have represented—sometimes in ways intertwined with "color-blind" dogmas—the increase of multiracialism in the United States as "a visual symbol of a new multiracial order" *and* as "a symptom of the direction of the disappearance of race," as a "bridge between two worlds," or as the romanticized "Happy Hapa" (Ropp 1997; Nishime 2014; Creef 2004; Kina and Dariotis 2013).[2]

However, such an optimistic view can itself actually validate real-world racism.[3] It is premised on a multiculturalism-style plurality of cultures and is a fantasy that grew out of debates about the ideal form of the United States as a nation-state. Furthermore, when one considers the roots of Asian mixed-race people, it becomes clear that this view tends to overlook the layered structures and situations of war, postcolonialism, globalization, and so on that are exemplified by the likes of mail-order brides, U.S. military bases, and refugees. If so, is there a path that can avoid the polar extremes of reification and fantasy? Moreover, is it possible for mixed-race individuals to express the plurality and ambiguity of their positions without being sucked into nation-state discourses, or to contribute to the understanding of visions of the world from their positions—and if so, how?

The art world continues to be an important arena for addressing social and political issues. Asian American artists have played significant roles in mobilizing collective categories and identities using the power of art and visual culture, a trend that has its roots in the 1960s and 1970s, when "an Asian American political and social consciousness emerged among many visual artists" (Machida 2008, 25).

The success of artists with Asian (particularly Japanese) roots is pronounced in cultural and artistic activities related to multiracialism. For example, Ken Tanabe is a leading proponent of the "Loving Day," to commemorate the *Loving v. Virginia* decision on or around June 12 as well as to fight against racism, the Japanese American National Museum supports a film and literary festival on the topic, and Laura Kina (discussed below) cofounded the biannual conference Critical Mix Raced Studies and the journal of the same name. Furthermore, Kip Fulbeck, who has part Chinese heritage, can probably be credited for contributing to the spread of the word "hapa" widely throughout the United States. The backdrop for this phenomenon has been mixed individuals with Asian roots who were compelled to raise their voices and seek societal recognition. In part they were motivated by the frequent oppression and rejection of the interracial couples to which they were born, a rejection that came not only from the white majority but also from those within Asian and Japanese American communities. This stands in contrast with mixed-race Africans, Latinas/Latinos, and Native Americans, groups with a long history of inter-racial mixing.[4]

I have previously discussed the works and identities of the young artists who participated in *One Way or Another: Asian American Art Now*, an exhibition that emerged in the context of the art world's "post-race" and "post-identity" response to "identity-based art" (Takezawa 2011). This chapter builds on my previous work on Asian American artists, this time focusing on three artists in more depth. Two of the artists have mixed-race backgrounds, which will also help us to explore the idea that "the mixed race body and mixed race art have the potential to destabilize the bifurcation between an uncritical multicultural identity and post-identity solutions by providing a more liminal, fluid-reading of art, cultures, and racial politics" (Kina and Dariotis 2013, 8).

The aim of this chapter is neither to engage in an art critique nor provide an art history analysis of these artists' works. Drawing from in-depth anthropological interviews,[5] the chapter explores how each, in her or his own way, grapples with issues of social categories, marginalization, and identification, and if it changes, how. It also examines possibilities for transcending the extremes of reification and fantasy, the nation-state framework, and even categories themselves.

I chose to use art as a space from which to consider issues surrounding multiracialism because art has the unique power to appeal to viewers' sensibilities and transcend language. It can also be an effective medium when one thinks about a "Third Space" (Bhabha 1994) that goes beyond existing frameworks involving power imbalances in representation.

The following discussion analyzes the art and narratives of Roger Shimomura, Laura Kina, and Shizu Saldamando. I chose to focus on these artists for a number of reasons. First, they all specialize in portraits. Portraits provide a useful subject for analysis because "face can be taken as the stereotypic 'Oriental' trope," while at the same time, for people on the margins, "face is our primary external, bodily locus of identity.... Our face can speak back to Orientalist hegemonies" (Kondo 1997, 24–25). Second, they have all gained national recognition in one way or another. Shimomura and Saldamando, along with five other Asian American artists, were selected to participate in the special exhibition *Asian American Portraits of Encounter*, which was first held from 2011 to 2012 at the Smithsonian Institution's National Portrait Gallery and later at various locations across the nation.[6] And Laura Kina, in addition to being an artist, is a major proponent of critical mixed race studies as mentioned above and has co-organized conferences for the field.

Although sharing in common a Japanese American heritage and the professional experience of being artists, they have notably different backgrounds relating to age/generation, ethnicity, location, gender, and class and sexuality consciousness, resulting in their different approaches to the expressions, identities, and/or relationships with their subjects, which are thus reflected in their own styles of art.

Roger Shimomura

When I first met Roger Shimomura at his Kansas studio in 2006,[7] my attention was immediately drawn to his eclectic collection of Halloween masks, salt-and-pepper shaker sets, and other ornamental objects, all of which exhibited "Oriental" stereotypes: slanted eyes, buckteeth, pigtailed men, and women clad in kimonos. These items have served as reference points and inspiration throughout his career.[8] It is interesting to note that he chose Kansas for his after-retirement residence because "being reminded that you aren't white every day" continues to contribute to his inspiration for making art.

Shimomura's work on stereotypes has roots in a conversation he had with a Kansas farmer in 1969. The farmer, attempting to find out *what* Shimomura was, interrogated him: "How have you come to speak English so well?" "Where are you from?" When the farmer learned that Shimomura was an art professor at the University of Kansas, he replied, "Oh yeah, you're Japanese? Konnichiwa!" and "You do pictures of them Geeshee girls wearing them Kamonas?"[9]

This exchange led Shimomura to leave behind the pop culture commercial art world and attempt to reverse the farmer's gaze in his art. From there he developed a new approach to portray the illusionary stereotypes of the Japanese in American society, which eventually culminated in his releasing his satirically named *Oriental Masterprint* series (1972–1978) (plate 1). "I decided to do the first painting [of the series] that looked Japanese as a kind of tongue-in-cheek response," Shimomura recalled.[10]

This "tongue-in-cheek" response employed *ukiyo-e* imagery that included masks based on kabuki actors' "highly stylized makeup patterns" to highlight stereotypes associated with "Japanese" and "Oriental" people. Stacey Uradomo contends that his usage of masks in his paintings functions in two ways. First, the kabuki-inspired masks act to illustrate the inability of mainstream Americans to look beyond superficial stereotypes and appearances, signifying "the manner in which Japanese Americans are often denied subjecthood." Second, "the heroic and iconic status of the white character masks" can also serve as representations of "the image that some Japanese Americans strove for in the post-internment era" (Uradomo 2005, 106–107).

Unless the observer is astute, however, it is difficult for her or him to read the social messages buried in Shimomura's works regarding racial prejudice and discrimination; even Shimomura recognizes that his message has not gotten across to most collectors and viewers. Some experts actually project stereotypes onto his works, describing them as employing the "traditional techniques of his ancestors."[11]

An argument he had in 1980 with his then-wife, a Japanese American theater producer, regarding his art style had a considerable influence on his style. Shimomura says:

> She felt that what I was doing by keeping them [his paintings] in the *ukiyo-e* style was . . . perpetuating the stereotype—people who think that when Asian people go home . . . [they] put on a kimono and eat with ohashi [chopsticks] and things like this. That was the first time I really had to face the option of deciding whether the stereotypical depiction was going to be read as such rather than to support a larger cause, in this case disguising the incarceration in the highly attractive and visually appealing ukiyo-e style.[12]

Over the years, Shimomura's style has evolved from being an indirect political satire that focused on stereotypes to a more explicit and documentary-style portrayal of his subjects with a political aim to educate his viewers. Lippard has argued, "Shimomura has forgone the complex, layered mode of his performances and some other paintings series in order to insure that the audience gets the message" (Lippard 2003, 3). In shedding the *ukiyo-e* style, Shimomura said, "I felt that the bigger chance I would be taking at this point would be to take away that layer [of satire that had been present in my art] and to see what's there. And I felt that at that point in my life I was more suited, more able myself to be able to do that and still be comfortable with it."[13] His *An American Diary* series (1997–1998), a series on incarceration based on his grandmother's diary, won the Most Distinguished Body of Work award by the College Art Association in 2002.

American Infamy #2 (plate 2) in the series of *Minidoka on My Mind* (2006–2012) is a bird's-eye view portrayal of Minidoka, one of ten incarceration camps. In this piece, the view expands over the shoulder of an

American soldier who keeps surveillance on the inside of the camp. Japanese Americans and their parents, inside and outside of the barracks, are killing time, confined by barbed wire and deprived of their liberty. Inspired by *Rakuchu Rakugai zu* (Scenes in and around the capital [Kyoto]), a genre of famous screen paintings around the sixteenth century, Shimomura exhibits his knowledge and aesthetics as an artist. The gold clouds depicted in the original Japanese works are replaced by dark clouds, evoking the aftermath of 9/11 when the idea of mass confinement of Arab Americans was widely voiced, reminiscent of Japanese Americans after Pearl Harbor, the Day of Infamy, which this title, *American Infamy,* sarcastically refers to.

Shimomura has also produced a number of paintings that satirically fuse *ukiyo-e* with American comics, a style that has become his trademark. These contrasting art styles come together in unique compositions that employ flat, precise brushwork and bold colors, creating a distinctive world that juxtaposes fine art and comics, humor and anger. The distorted images of "Japanese" floating in his bold and colorful compositions use humor and irony to compel the viewer to think about stereotypes without turning them away (plates 3, 4, and 5).

This change in his style could be interpreted as a manifestation of the changing political atmosphere and demands for more education and awareness surrounding Japanese American incarceration during that time. In addition to being a recipient of the Civil Liberties Public Education Fund in 1997 for his *An American Diary* series, Shimomura has noted a rise in public speaking opportunities at educational and awareness-raising events as well as in opportunities to exhibit his work in art galleries and museums. The rise of multiculturalism in the art world also favorably impacted Shimomura's career. As one of only a handful of Asian American artists recognized by a white-dominated society around the 1980s and early 1990s, Shimomura often received invitations to participate in multicultural art exhibitions, which further enhanced his profile. The commercial value of Shimomura's work has increased significantly over the years. For example, a 5 × 6 feet painting (Minidoka) that sold for $5,000 in 1976 is valued at $30,000 today. Most of his collectors continue to be white Americans.

Shimomura Crossing the Delaware (plate 6) is a play on the famous 1851 painting *Washington Crossing the Delaware.*[14] The original scene depicts one of the heroic battles from the American Revolutionary War in which George Washington crossed an icy river in stormy weather to lead his troops to victory. Washington is replaced with a self-portrait, which is intended to present a challenge to his viewers.[15] Shimomura explained to me:

> Imagine what historical changes might have been different in order to have a Japanese American instead of George Washington leading the troops across the Delaware River. And/Or imagine how history would have changed afterwards if George Washington were a Japanese American.[16]

This piece is embedded with the deep philosophical questions that Shimomura has continued to pose to American society over the past four decades, as Goodyear also points out: who are Americans and what does patriotism mean? (Goodyear 2013)

At one point, I asked Shimomura's opinion about the inclusion of the words "Asian American" in the aforementioned Smithsonian exhibition's title, referring to the conflicting feelings toward the label among some young Asian American artists (Takezawa 2011). He responded,

> I would prefer not [to have the label] . . . but by the same token, if they didn't have that in there, there would be no exhibition. . . . Look at theater, movie, music, and everything else, and ask yourself the same question, have we arrived yet? I think most people would agree it's better, but it's better because we did identify ourselves that way.[17]

Without categories and names, incarceration camps and racial prejudice cannot be articulated. As signifiers of them, Shimomura's works continue to require the categories of Japanese and Asian American.

When we were finishing an interview, he added, "I want to be American. My preference is to just be an American."[18] Although a casual remark, one can read these words as both an interrogation of an Americanism that involves both exclusion and inclusion, something that he has taken as his life's work, as well as, perhaps, a reflection of the driving force lying in the depths of his mind.

Laura Kina

With floating oil portraits inspired by vintage Bollywood movie posters, Laura Kina formed a virtual mixed-race community of friends, siblings, and strangers in her *Hapa Soap Opera* series (2002–2004), which subsequently developed into a real community network of multiracial individuals on its completion (plate 7). Kina produced the series at a time in the early 2000s when she was "desperate to meet people of similar backgrounds."[19]

Born in 1973, Kina is a self-described "hapa, yonsei, Uchinanchu" (mixed-race, fourth-generation, Okinawan) American visual artist and a professor at DePaul University. Her father is a Hawaiian-born Okinawan American, and her mother has Spanish/Basque and "white" roots. Kina grew up under the influence of her *obaachan* (grandmother), who lived with her family in the small Norwegian town of Poulsbo, Washington, where the visibility of her face and body continually called into her consciousness an uneasiness about her differences.

As a student in Chicago in the 1990s, Kina attended Asian American studies classes and became active in Asian American organizations on campus and in the community. Since then, the label "Asian American" has served as an important part of her identity. Kina describes her relationship to the categories "post-ethnic," "post-race," and "post-identity" as follows:

> Back when I started, I had to ask what to call myself. I agree with David Hollinger's *post-ethnic* preference for the ethnoracial "choice over prescription." . . . But all these "post" terms don't define who I am; they just define what I'm supposedly getting over. I have no desire to "get over" race or ethnicity. (Kina 2012, 8)

Shortly thereafter, Kina became interested in the aforementioned *Loving v. Virginia* 1967 U.S. Supreme Court case. This led her to produce the *Loving* series (2006), consisting of ten life-sized portraits of "mixed race" individuals. In this series, she imparts both a sense of unity to her subjects, by giving them identical postures and adopting a monochromatic charcoal black palette, and a sense of diversity, because some of the subjects, including herself, have "white privilege" and others who have no white heritage, like Weinberger (plate 8), do not (Kina 2012, 9).

Although the Asian American and mixed-race components of Kina's subjectivities are presented as the strongest, they are not the only ones. The *Devon Ave. Sampler* series (2009–2011) illustrates her awareness of the multifacetedness and intermingling of place, history, and identities. Devon Avenue in Chicago was home to an Orthodox Jewish community but is now a thriving community of South Asians. In this series, fabrics of different colors and patterns, text, and illustrations contrast and complement each other in a massive collage, somehow harmonious and whole. A sprinkling of Jewish religious attire symbolizes her conversion to Judaism after marrying a Jewish American; the text and illustrations are the signs of the street's cafes and shops, a historical testament to its present. The use of indigo blue and *khadi* fabric in many of the works in the series is meant to be suggestive of Gandhi and India's independence movement. The patchwork canvas has also been fashioned to resemble Japanese indigo-dyed *boro* quilts. Of significance is that whereas the image shown in plate 9 (along with five other works) features hand-painted text, in thirteen of the remaining works in this series, Kina ordered the hand-embroidered text and illustrations used in the signboard samples from women who are members of a fair trade organization in Mumbai, India. The term "sampler" in the title thus refers both to the embroidery samples and to "sampling" in the sense of cultural appropriation.[20]

Kina has also looked to her family history. Intrigued by the realization that most of her immediate family and relatives were reluctant to talk about the past, she began collecting oral histories and photographs in Hawai'i in order to unearth the history of her family and community. The scarce prewar photographs and fragmented oral histories that she was able to excavate provided rough sketches of the past: glimpses through stories of "picture brides" like her great-grandmother, of the harsh working conditions and poverty on the sugarcane plantation, and of painful World War II memories. Out of these, her *Sugar* series (2010–2011) emerged.

On a superficial level, *Kasuri* (plate 10) appears to be based on a photograph of a 1920s sugarcane workers' strike. However, upon deeper reflection, its complex meaning reveals itself: it is a representation of *obake* (ghosts or ancestral spirits) returning to the earth. The *obake* narrative found in this painting was inspired by the natural volcanic gas phenomenon of *hinotama* (fireballs) that appeared to shoot into the night sky from graves that used to be located on the edge of the sugarcane field in her father's Big Island plantation community. With the obscured faces of her ghost-like ancestors, this piece also speaks to the erased history of Japanese Americans who "assimilated" into American society, burying their past experiences of harsh labor as plantation workers. She states,

> I was thinking about the metaphor of ghosts and the erasure of our past because Japanese Americans often assimilated, we lost the language, we moved towards economic advancement and especially after World

War II. . . . History has just disappeared and specifically women's history has very much disappeared. Then in my own family's case, . . . it was poverty and things, and people don't want to talk about that, so it's erased.[21]

Kina's artistic gaze in her series *Blue Hawai'i* (2012–2013) reaches across the Pacific Ocean to the Ryūkyū island of Okinawa. Her visit there in 2012 with her father to reconnect with extended family inspired her to produce this series, which deals with colonized landscapes and people of Okinawa, as expressed in some of her paintings, which "capture the remnants of war and a continued American military presence" (Kina 2015, 2). The title came from the 1961 film of the same title starring Elvis Presley, a comedy that underscores the cultural differences observed from the mainland-centered viewpoint. Kina, instead, shifts the framework to the trans-Pacific Okinawan diaspora. The painting *Soldier Boys* (2013) (plate 11) features relatives who were conscripted child soldiers, some of whom were forced to commit suicide by the Japanese in the 1945 Battle of Okinawa during World War II. The series can be simultaneously interpreted as both an indication of Kina's expansive interest in a way that crosses national boundaries, as well as her ambiguous position as a person with identities that encapsulate continental America, Hawai'i, and Okinawa, which have had, and still have, unequal relationships.

In 2015, Kina's *Sugar/Islands* was a featured work in a two-artist show at the Japanese American National Museum. Margo Machida, an art critic and independent curator, states that Kina's work "serves to foreground Asian migratory journeys and patterns of settlement embedded in globe-spanning histories of exploration, flows of trade, labor and migration, colonial imposition, and the war" (2015, 35). Kina is one of few artists with Japanese heritage who deeply engage the issue of diaspora. Her works distinctly connect the mainland, Hawai'i, Okinawa, and Japan, producing a new space to interrogate the memories of immigration, the war, and the U.S. military presence that continues to marginalize the people in Okinawa in this trans-Pacific space.

In her work, Kina also deals with the family memories of four generations spanning from Issei (her great-grandmother) to her daughter, "who has blue eyes and light brown hair" (*Gosei* [fifth-generation], plate 12). Her primary audience includes communities of mixed-race people, Asian American artists, Indians, Jews, and women's studies scholars and people in a variety of locations, such as the continental United States, Hawai'i, Okinawa, and India.[22]

Kina's works, which always shine light on marginalized individuals in society, depict the view from her own ambiguous, complicated, and marginalized positions. It appears that she simultaneously feels uncomfortable with existing social categories *and* enjoys them. She states, "I find myself again embracing the restless amorphousness of ambiguity. Perhaps this is right where I belong as an artist. After all, it's not an artist's job to definitively answer questions so much as it is to raise them. I'm happy to be 'half yella'" (Kina 2010, 9).

Shizu Saldamando

A young crowd is enjoying a party in a park with glittering gold and silver banners hanging above them. The painting (plate 13) depicts a space in which a "very ordinary" gathering of young people is taking place. A focus on contemporary Los Angeles youth culture is a prominent theme in Saldamando's work. The background of this painting is a folding screen covered with many layers of gold foil and origami paper, providing a contrast to the oil-painted three-dimensional figures in the foreground, who are defined by light and shadow.

Ambiguity is another aspect that seems to characterize Saldamando's work. In this piece, the race and ethnicity of her subjects are not instantly identifiable from their physical appearance. Here, the scene's location—Highland Park, Los Angeles, an area known as the home of a middle-class Latino community—is the only cue.

Born in 1978 to a Chicano father and a Japanese American mother, Saldamando grew up on Mission Street, which she described as a lower-class Chicana/Chicano community in San Francisco. Her maternal grandmother, a Nisei who learned crafts that employed *washi* (Japanese paper) and other Japanese materials, influenced her mother, who taught art classes for children and in turn shaped Saldamando's aesthetics. Although she makes use of Japanese and Latina cultural materials, she draws a sharp line between so-called identity art and her deployment of these materials, which she was familiarized with in her childhood. She blends these ethnic-related materials into her art while transgressing racially/ethnically framed stereotypical expectations in the mainstream art world. Saldamando repeatedly expresses her deep frustration that stereotypes pressure artists of color to engage in identity politics or diaspora art, something that stands in contrast to the freedom given to white artists. She says:

There are other artists who chose to add diversity to their imagery by showing "geishas" to represent Asians, and "folklorico" dancers to represent Mexican Americans. For me this does nothing to increase the understanding that minorities are contemporary people who are alive now and a part of the American landscape.[23]

In her solid resistance to such stereotypical ideas, Saldamando chooses to depict contemporary images of urban people of color who exist, thrive, and create their own subcultures, fashion, and music outside of what mainstream culture dictates as "normal." To do so, she avoids giving prominence to symbols that are taken to be the basis of permanent identity, such as race-related bodily characteristics, employing instead signifiers that are variable and have historical meanings, like fashion and place.

Her rejection of social constructs is also reflected in her protestation that "Asian American" should be dropped from the title of *Asian American Portraits of Encounter*, the aforementioned exhibition at the Smithsonian. Although her objection was dismissed, it illustrates that although her work is often exhibited at shows classified as "Latina/Chicana" or "Asian American" art, she challenges and rejects the categories that are applied to her on an institutional level.

After being invited to present her work at a Day of the Dead exhibition, Saldamando created a wreath (plate 14) commemorating the experience of her maternal Japanese American relatives and community. This was in part prompted by her discovery through historical photographs that people in incarceration camps made funerary flower wreaths with craft paper due to a scarcity of real flowers, as well as the realization that her older Japanese American relatives and their friends were not talking about their experiences (see also Urton 2008; Wong 2007, 72). For Saldamando, this work does not make political assertions or appeal to her Japanese roots, but rather expresses respect for family and relatives who survived incarceration. Moreover, her presentation of a piece inscribed with Japanese American history at a Mexican American exhibition reflects her resistance to divisions based on ethnic categories and is an attempt to make visible and share her family's experience in a way that transcends categories.

In a conversation on her style, Saldamando articulated her artistic vision:

> It was really important for me to show our historical or social historical legacy and beauty, and that you can be revolutionary in your own right

just by living your own true life without necessarily waving a UFW (United Farm Workers) flag. . . . [People can] create their own center and their own sort of space where they try to become not like minorities . . . [but rather] become whole people. . . . [This is] not so blatantly political but very subtly and I think more relatable somehow.[24]

I originally interpreted this as Saldamando's distancing herself from earlier generations of artists of color who engaged in identity politics following the civil rights movement. However, it became clear in our second interview that this statement referred to her activist parents, particularly her *Sansei* mother, a Japanese American community activist who currently teaches cultural studies at a university. Her father, who as a lawyer used to support asylum seekers fleeing civil war in Central America, now works for the protection of indigenous rights. She sees her parents as continually having been incensed by racial discrimination and as eager to see everything in black and white when devoting themselves to the civil rights movement of the 1960s. She came to create the unique imagery in her paintings in partial defiance of her parents (plates 15, 17):

There are good people and bad people, but people don't seem to realize that there is so much in between. Everybody has good and bad in them, and people have the capacity for both, and so by showing people just being normal people and singing Karaoke at a party or getting drunk or whatever, they become just normal, regular, relatable people.[25]

Saldamando's use of gold in both the title and content of her *Stay Gold* series (2008–2009) reflects her desire to glorify her subjects, whom she sees as everyday heroes and heroines. Saldamando furthermore articulates the "conundrum" entailed in her efforts to decenter whiteness without falling into the "reactive" paradigm against "whiteness," where "whiteness" exists at the center and her work is positioned as a reactive project only in relation to it.

Saldamando notes that she can "pass" as Mexican and at the same time emphasizes her self-awareness of her privileges in a number of domains: being college educated, having lighter skin, being heterosexual, among other things. "I have certain privileges that others may not have, . . . maybe this is why I try to depict only people I have personal relationships with and so I can say my work is a personal narrative."[26] She often paints portraits of one to three friends based on snapshots she has taken. In this way, Saldamando makes use of a distinct atmosphere of intimacy from these affinity networks and trust that allows her to capture the unique gazes of her young subjects.

Plate 16, part of the *Looking at Art* series (2005), is composed of large ballpoint pen drawings of individuals of color looking at artwork. This reflects another approach that Saldamando has played with to decenter "whiteness" in the subject/spectator power relationship. White viewers of these pieces find themselves the object of the subjects' gazes, a reversal of the dominant position of white viewers gazing at nonwhite subjects.[27]

According to Saldamando, although her work is seldom bought by the general public, she has been invited to various museums and conferences and has received a range of grants, thereby raising her profile across the United States. More recently, she designed the artwork for a new metro station in the Palms area of Los Angeles and continues to explore tattooing as a medium for her artwork while working at a tattoo shop.

Negotiating Categories and Transgressing Identities

Several characteristics distinguish these artists' grappling with social, racial, and other categories as well as their expression of multilayered identities and the ways in which they negotiate categories while shifting and transgressing their context-dependent identities throughout the course of their lives.

Roger Shimomura has consistently worked to promote public awareness surrounding dynamics of inclusion and exclusion in Americanism. Labels like "Asian American" or "Japanese American" are racial categories that he strategically employs in an essentialist mode in order to problematize the gaze that rests upon such categories, as well as the images associated with them.

Interestingly, in our personal interviews, he articulated his orientation within a number of spheres, including art appreciation, family, and community historical belonging, somewhat distancing himself from other Japanese Americans or Asian Americans. For example, he often laments the lack of serious interest in art and history among Asian Americans, asserting that they think nothing of throwing out works with historical value from before and during World War II. Almost all of his collectors, art dealers, and supporters have been white Americans. Except for his first wife, he says, he has dated only people of non-Asian ancestry; in his paintings, a figure of a white woman with blue eyes and blonde hair, modeled after his current wife, often appears. One might even venture to say that his personal daily practices take place in a predominantly white, mainstream American world. Whether Japanese and Asian Americans have little interest in art and history may depend on the definitions of "art" and "history."

This apparent disconnect is even more pronounced with regard to Japanese people in Japan. Shimomura's employment of such stereotypes gives credence to an interpretation of his work that sees it as emphasizing his Americanness in a way that draws a sharp line between Americans of Japanese ancestry like himself and Japanese nationals. His interest lies in addressing the racism in American society directed toward Americans, but not the type that is directed beyond national boundaries to places like Japan, where he has only felt alienated as a foreigner when he traveled.

Shimomura says that he strongly desires to be just "American"; however, persistent racism continues to impede the realization of this unmarked identity. Cheryan and Monin (2005) have pointed out that Asian Americans inaccurately categorized as non-U.S. citizens are led to display more of their American cultural knowledge and practices in an attempt to reassert their American identity. A similar dynamic may be at work in Shimomura's constant use of the theme of "Americanism," partly due to his frequent experience of being miscategorized as a foreigner.

Shimomura's life and work suggests that adherence to racial categories is not necessarily a faithful reflection of an individual's identity and social relationships. Regardless of how layered a person's identity is, prevailing racial discrimination and prejudice are grim realities that jeopardize daily life or obstruct advancement in society; unfortunately, racism cannot be made visible without racial categories. Thus, Shimomura tries to bring about change in American society, with which he strongly identifies, through his art that employs racial stereotypes and categories.

In contrast, the works of Kina and Saldamando do not adhere to "Americanism" nor employ racial categories. This arises from composite factors such as generation, place of residence, gender, and monoraciality/multiracialism; the overt racially discriminatory and prejudiced abuse and disregard that Shimomura has experienced nearly daily in Kansas are less familiar to them. Although Kina is occasionally asked, "What are you?"—a depersonalizing question that many mixed-race people encounter—she does not have a strong awareness of herself as someone who is discriminated against. Saldamando, however, says that she can pass as Mexican, in a way evading ambiguity and the discrimination that accompanies being multiracial. The reactions of these two "hapa" women to racism also differ because they are considerably shaped by age, region (Kina is based in Chicago, Saldamando in Los Angeles), and ethnic background (Kina is part white and Saldamando is part Mexican). Saldamando paints a golden light on people as "heroes and heroines," people who are not necessarily as socio-economically privileged as she is.

Kina sought people similar to herself after becoming aware of the multiracial movement in the 1990s, thereafter strengthening her sense of belonging to the category "hapa." Although paying attention to diversity and disparities within the category, as well as its essentializing and homogenizing pressure, she still actively uses "hapa" as an important word for expressing her subjectivity. As her work *Devon Ave. Sampler* demonstrates, after marriage she was prompted to consciously express the plasticity of identity to resist essentialist and deterministic views of race and ethnicity. Through her art, her multilayered identities transgress the boundaries of the individual, family, and nation-state, with a flexibility that openly expands in a trans-Pacific space.

In the various spaces Kina is involved in, she is simultaneously an outsider as well as an insider; she experiences both comfort and alienation. For Kina, the category of "mixed race" and its marginalized position enable it to serve as an arena for critical interrogation of issues surrounding social justice and racial equality, rather than a tool to promote the social recognition of multiracials.

Saldamando rejects socially constructed categories as well as identity politics on the grounds that they all lead to essentialized understandings of the world. Instead, she chooses to feature racially and/or sexually ambiguous subjects in her paintings. By portraying the lived experiences of "ordinary people" in her affinity networks, Saldamando is trying to find a path that disentangles and transgresses the socially constructed categories of race, gender, and sexuality. She emphasizes that in using materials such as *washi*, origami, and stickers and adopting techniques from lowrider and *pinta* (prison) art, she is not trying to represent her racial or cultural identity, but is simply incorporating into her artwork elements of the environment that she was raised in. For a viewer in this contemporary culture fraught with social conditioning, it is, however, difficult to interpret such cultural materials as not doing so, a circumstance that Saldamando is also aware of. Her narrative can be seen as a conscious rejection of these circumstances arising out of an awareness that her love for the culture(s) she has inherited might be misinterpreted as an expression of identity politics.

Saldamando approaches the issue of social categories differently. Some of her works feature queer subjects as shown in plate 17, and interestingly, many of my colleagues and friends, including some Japanese American artists and queer specialists, assumed that she herself identified as queer, with which she does not. Such assumptions reveal the insidious conscious or subconscious lenses that we use to see marginalized people. These boxed frames and essentialized boundaries in contemporary American society demonstrate another problem—only members of the minority groups in question are regarded to have the agency to represent themselves, or give their identities humanity. Saldamando challenges such boundaries again, while paying keen attention to her own educated, middle-class, hetero-privilege and to power relations between artist and subject. At the same time, by centering her art on subjects betwixt and between such categories, those who according to Saldamando are everyday heroes and heroines, she invites us to think about the potential unintended consequences of excessive identity politics and how contemporary youth are dealing with the difficult aspects of this double-edged sword inherited from the civil rights generation.

As Michael Omi has pointed out in chapter 2, the racialization of Japanese and Asian Americans continues in spite of projections of assimilation or integration into whiteness. As has been noted by scholars working in the field of social movement theory, racial categories and identity politics in general form the basis of many social movements and collective action. In his art, Shimomura strategically mobilizes racial/ethnic categories—the very ones upon which stereotypes are also built, calling attention to the "category of practice" that is formed through the buildup of everyday social interactions. His art is his contribution to increase the public's awareness surrounding issues pertaining to the dynamics of inclusion and exclusion present in America, where blatant racism and stereotypes still continue to be a social reality. In contrast, Saldamando's work, in highlighting issues surrounding the structures of center/margin and norm/exotic, problematizes fixed categories that exert their power by reproducing dynamics of inclusion and exclusion, even *within* marginalized groups. Kina, in contrast, seems to manipulate categories depending on her aims: at times, she destabilizes or cuts across conventional categories, and at other times she embraces categories, including "hapa" and "Okinawan," for political and cultural purposes.

Although it may change form, insofar as overt racial discrimination and prejudice aimed at Japanese and Asian Americans continues to exist in U.S.

society, methods of expression like that of Shimomura, who uses clear racial categories, remain indispensable mediums to respond. In contrast, we can observe more pronounced subjectivity that manipulates categories in the works and narratives of Kina and Saldamando. Such resentment of the imposition of racial and other social categories by others, as well as of the expectations that accompany them, may be found among many young minorities in the contemporary world. They do not operate based on simple equations of belonging to the racial/ethnic group(s) of one parent or both parents. The ways in which these three artists engage with categories demonstrate convergent and divergent transgressions of social categories, which may suggest how future generations interpret and respond to these categories.

Notes

1 The exhibition was curated by Cindy Nakashima, Lily Anne Yumi Welty, and Duncan Williams.
2 In resistance to such stereotyping, Laura Kina and Wei Ming Dariotis, with the term "Happy Happa," reclaim "racial pride and a multicultural symbol of undivided wholeness" (Kina and Dariotis 2013, 13).
3 Regarding the harassment of interracial couples in the United States rooted in racist negativism, see Schueths (2014).
4 It is said that Japanese American women who married Filipinos were ostracized by the Japanese American community at internment camps during World War II. Furthermore, more than half of the Japanese American children entrusted to the Japanese American Children's Home of Los Angeles in 1940 were mixed children thrown out by their parents (Spickard 1986).
5 After being introduced to them in 2006 by a curator at the Japanese American National Museum and other artists with Asian American backgrounds, I interviewed each of them in person over the course of three to six sessions for one and a half to two hours and subsequently had brief conversations with them at conferences and other events as well as via e-mail. In 2014, I showed them a draft of this paper and had them check its content.
6 For a brief general review of the show, see O'Sullivan (2011).
7 There is an abundance of essays and reviews covering Roger Shimomura's work and life. For a detailed biography, see Lau and Nakane (2011) and Uradomo (2005).
8 His collection of "stereotype" items was exhibited at his 2011 show *Yellow Terror* at the Wing Luke Museum of the Asian Pacific American Experience in Seattle before being donated to the museum permanently.

9 Personal interview on April 13, 2006, at his studio in Lawrence, Kansas. Confirmed on August 13, 2014.
10 Ibid.
11 For example, the entry on Roger Shimomura in *Encyclopaedia of Asian American Artists* frames his use of the *ukiyo-e* style in the following way: "Similar to other Japanese artists and Japanese American artists, Shimomura experimented with traditional techniques of his ancestors" (Hallmark 2007, 192).
12 Personal interview on April 13, 2006, at his studio in Lawrence, Kansas. Confirmed on August 13, 2014.
13 Ibid.
14 The original oil-on-canvas piece *Washington Crossing the Delaware* was painted by the German American artist Emanuel Leutze in 1851.
15 This piece echoes *George Washington Carver Crossing the Delaware: Pages from an American History Textbook* (1975) by Robert Colescott, a black artist who was well known for satirized paintings with stereotypes associated with blacks, although it was only after he finished his piece that Shimomura learned of Colescott's work using the same motif.
16 Personal e-mail communication on May 19, 2013. Confirmed on August 13, 2014.
17 Personal interview on June 22, 2012, at a cafe in Boise, Idaho. Confirmed on August 13, 2014.
18 Personal interview on June 12, 2012, at a cafe in Seattle, WA. Confirmed on August 13, 2014.
19 Personal interview on June 1, 2012, at a hotel in Los Angeles, CA. Confirmed on August 11, 2014.
20 Laura Kina, http://www.laurakina.com/devon.html.
21 Personal interview on June 1, 2012, at a hotel in Los Angeles, CA. Confirmed on August 11, 2014.
22 Her work has been featured by a wide variety of local and national media outlets (*Times of India,* May 7, 2011; *Indian Express,* December 22, 2009; *Turkey Red Journal,* 2013; *New York Times,* July 27, 2003).
23 Personal e-mail communication on August 14, 2014.
24 Personal interview on November 5, 2006, at the Japanese American National Museum, in Los Angeles, CA. Confirmed on September 4, 2014.
25 Personal e-mail communication on August 18, 2014.
26 Personal interview on June 16, 2012, at a hotel in Los Angeles, CA. Confirmed on September 4, 2014.
27 Although Saldamando's works possess distinctive features, behind this series is a history of the gaze, surveillance, and power that has attracted considerable attention in art for the past two decades, out of which a

number of influential works have emerged that challenge the relations between the subject and the spectator. See, for example, Lippard (1990, chap. 5) and Kaplan (2005). I thank Margo Machida for bringing this point to my attention.

References

Benford, Robert D., and David A. Snow. 2000. "Framing Processes and Social Movements: An Overview and Assessment." *Annual Review of Sociology* 26: 611–639.

Bhabha, Homi. 1994. *The Location of Culture*. Oxford: Routledge.

Brubaker, Rogers, and Frederick Cooper. 2000. "Beyond 'Identity.'" *Theory and Society* 29 (1): 1–47.

Chang, Alexandra. 2009. *Envisioning Diaspora: Asian American Visual Arts Collectives: From Godzilla, Godzookie to the Barnstormers*. Beijing: Timezone 8 Editions.

Cheryan, Sapna, and Benoît Monin. 2005. "Where Are You *Really* From?: Asian Americans and Identity Denial." *Journal of Personality and Social Psychology* 89 (5): 717–730.

Creef, Elena Tajima. 2004. *Imagining Japanese America: The Visual Construction of Citizenship, Nation, and the Body*. New York: New York University Press.

DaCosta, Kimberly McClain. 2007. *Making Multiracials: State, Family, and Market in the Redrawing of the Color Line*. Stanford, CA: Stanford University Press.

Dariotis, Wei Ming. 2007. "Hapa: The Word of Power." *Mixed Heritage Center Spotlight*. http://www.mixedheritagecenter.org/index.php?option=com_content&task=view&id=1259&Itemid=34, accessed September 9, 2014.

Fulbeck, Kip. 2006. *Part Asian: 100% Hapa*. San Francisco: Chronicle Books.

Goodyear, Anne Collins. 2013. "Roger Shimomura: An American Artist." *American Art* 27 (1): 70–93.

Hallmark, Kara Kelley. 2007. *Encyclopaedia of Asian American Artists: Artists of the American Mosaic*. Westport, CT: Greenwood Press.

Houston, Velina Hasu, and Teresa K. Williams, eds. 1997. *No Passing Zone: The Artistic and Discursive Voices of Asian-descent Multiracials*. Special issue. *Amerasia Journal* 23 (1).

Indian Express. 2009. "Blue Print." December 22, 6.

Kaplan, Louis. 2005. *American Exposures: Photography and the Community in the Twentieth Century*. Minneapolis: University of Minnesota Press.

Kina, Laura. 2010. "Half Yella: Embracing Ethno-Racial Ambiguity." In *Embracing Ambiguities: Faces of the Future* (exhibition catalog), edited by Jillian Nakornthap and Lynn Stromick (exhibition catalog). Fullerton: California State University, Fullerton, 5–10 and 39–42.

———. 2012. "In Love with Cat and Carm: Queering Asian American Portraiture in Shizu Saldamando's *Stay Gold*." *Asian American Literary Review* 3 (2): 27–30.

———. 2015. "Exhibition Statement." *Laura Kina: Blue Hawai'i. 2*. Exhibition catalogue. http://www.laurakina.com/bluehawaii-catalog.pdf

Kina, Laura, and Wei Ming Dariotis, eds. 2013. *War Baby/Love Child: Mixed Race Asian American Art*. Seattle: University of Washington Press.

King-O'Riain, Rebecca C., Stephen Small, Minelle Mahatani, Miri Song, and Paul Spickard, eds. 2014. *Global Mixed Race*. New York: New York University Press.

Kondo, Dorinne. 1997. *About Face: Performing Race in Fashion and Theater*. New York: Routledge.

Lau, Alan C., and Kazuko Nakane. 2011. "Misrepresentation: or The Bittersweet Cartoon of Life, The Art of Roger Shimomura." *GIA Reader* 22(3). http://www.giarts.org/article/ misrepresentation-or-bittersweet-cartoon-life, accessed July 31, 2013.

Lippard, Lucy R. 1990. *Mixed Blessings: New Art in a Multicultural America*. New York: Pantheon Books.

———. 2003. "Perilous Times." In *Roger Shimomura: Stereotypes and Admonitions*, 1–3. Seattle: Greg Kucera Gallery.

Lowe, Lisa. 1996. *Immigrant Acts*. Durham, NC: Duke University Press.

Machida, Margo. 2008. *Unsettled Visions: Contemporary Asian American Artists and the Social Imaginary*. Durham, NC: Duke University Press.

———. 2015. "Re-imagining Islands: Asia, America, and the Pacific." In *Sugar/Islands: Finding Okinawa in Hawai'i—The Art of Laura Kina and Emily Hanako Momohara*, edited by Krystal Hauseur, 30–35. Los Angeles: Bear River Press.

Murphy-Shigematsu, Stephen. 2012. *When Half Is Whole*. Stanford, CA: Stanford University Press.

New York Times. 2003. "The Asia Within Us: Bicultural Eyes and What They See." July 27.

Niemi, Paul. 2014. *Under Cover Asian: Multiracial Asian Americans in Visual Culture*. Urbana: University of Illinois Press.

Nishime, Leilani. 2014. *Under Cover Asian: Multiracial Asian Americans in Visual Culture*. Urbana: University of Illinois Press.

O'Sullivan, Michael. 2011. "Identity That Goes beyond Stereotypes." *Washington Post*, September 2.

Ropp, Steven Masami. 1997. "Do Multiracial Subjects Really Challenge Race?: Mixed-Race Asians in the United States and the Caribbean." *Amerasia Journal* 23 (1): 1–16.

Schueths, April. 2014. "'It's almost like white supremacy': Interracial mixed-status couples facing racist nativism." *Ethnic and Racial Studies* 37 (13): 2438–2456.

Spickard, Paul R. 1986. "Injustice Compounded: Amerasians and Non-Japanese Americans in World War II Concentration Camps." *Journal of American Ethnic History* 5 (2): 5–22.

———. 1989. *Mixed Blood: Intermarriage and Ethnic Identity in Twentieth-Century America*. Madison: University of Wisconsin Press.

Takezawa, Yasuko. 2011. "New Arts, New Resistance: Asian American Artists in the 'Post-Race' Era." In *Racial Representations in Asia,* edited by Yasuko Takezawa, 93–123. Kyoto: Kyoto University Press and Melbourne: Trans Pacific Press.

Telles, Edward E., and Christina A. Sue. 2009. "Race Mixture: Boundary Crossing in Comparative Perspective." *Annual Review of Sociology* 35: 129–146.

Times of India. 2011. "City-Based Artist's Exhibition to Open in Florida Now." May 7, 2011.

Turkey Red Journal. 2013. "Nature's Gallery: Shelly Jyoti and Laura Kina," 18 (1). http://www.turkeyredjournal.com/gallery.html, accessed July 31, 2013.

Uradomo, Stacey Mitsue. 2005. "Legacies: Family Memory, History, and Identity in the Art of Roger Shimomura, Tomie Arai, and Lynne Yamamoto." PhD diss., University of Southern California.

Urton, Michelle. 2008. "Shizu Saldamando." In *Phantom Sightings: Art after the Chicano Movement* (exhibition catalog). Rita Gonzalez, Howard N. Fox, and Chon A. Noriega. Berkeley: University of California Press.

Võ, Linda Trinh. 2004. *Mobilizing an Asian American Community*. Philadelphia: Temple University Press.

Williams-León, Teresa, and Chynthia L. Nakashima, eds. 2001. *The Sum of Our Parts: Mixed Heritage Asian Americans*. Philadelphia: Temple University Press.

Wong, Martin. 2007. "Loca Motion: Eastside Art." *Giant Robot Magazine* 50: 70–73.

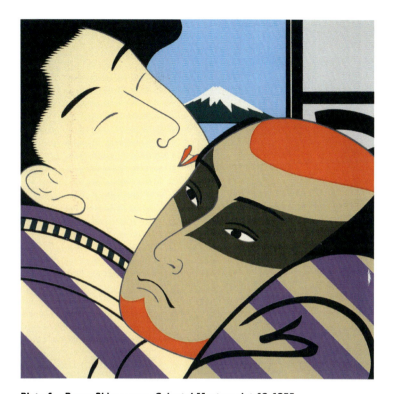

Plate 1   Roger Shimomura, *Oriental Masterprint 10*, 1975
Color screen print on woven paper.
Image 14 15/16 × 15 inches, Sheet 16 7/8 × 16 7/8 inches.
(Metropolitan Museum of Art, New York, NY)

Plate 2   Roger Shimomura, *American Infamy 2*, 2006
Acrylic on canvas, 4 panels, 72 × 30 each panel, 72 × 120 overall inches.
(Boise Art Museum, Boise, Idaho)

Plate 3 Roger Shimomura, *Not Pearl Harbor*, 2003
Acrylic on canvas, 20 × 24 inches.
(Courtesy of the artist)

Plate 4 Roger Shimomura, *American vs. Japs 2*, 2010
Acrylic on canvas, 54 × 54 inches.
(Flomenhaft Gallery, New York, NY)

Plate 5 Roger Shimomura, *American Hello Kitty*, 2010
Acrylic on canvas, 18 × 18 inches.
(Flomenhaft Gallery, New York, NY)

Plate 6 Roger Shimomura, *Shimomura Crossing the Delaware*, 2010
Acrylic on canvas, triptych, 6 × 12 feet.
(Smithsonian National Portrait Gallery, Washington, DC)

Plate 7   Laura Kina, *Hapa Soap Opera #1* (Misty Fujinaga, Sean Stoops, Laura Kina, Sam Kina, Ian Wan), 2002
Oil on canvas, 72 × 48 inches.
(Courtesy of the artist)

Plate 8   Laura Kina, *Shoshanna Weinberger, Loving Series,* 2006
Charcoal on paper, 42.5 × 34 inches.
(Courtesy of the artist)

Plate 9 Laura Kina, *Devon Ave. Sampler*, 2009 Acrylic on hand-sewn patchwork quilt, 53 × 77 inches. (Courtesy of the artist)

Plate 10 Laura Kina, *Kasuri*, 2010 Oil on wood panel, 30 × 45 inches. (Private collection, Chicago, IL)

Plate 11 Laura Kina, *Soldier Boys*, 2013 Oil on canvas, 30 × 45 inches. (Courtesy of the artist)

Plate 12　Laura Kina, *Gosei*, 2012
Oil on canvas,
30 × 45 inches.
(Courtesy of the artist)

Plate 13　Shizu Saldamando, *Highland Park Luau*, 2009
Oil and gold leaf on found screen, 32 × 64 inches.
(Courtesy of the artist)

Plate 14　Shizu Saldamando, *Farewell to Rohwer*, 2006
Washi paper, ribbon, wire and glue, flower stand, graphite on paper.
(Courtesy of the artist)

Plate 15 Shizu Saldamando, *Waiting for the Band in Between Sets,* **2010**
Color pencil on paper, 23 × 36 inches.
(Private collection, Laguna Beach, CA)

Plate 16 Shizu Saldamando, *Arnoldo, Looking at Art 2,* **2005**
Ballpoint pen on canvas, 24 × 48 inches.
(Courtesy of the artist)

Plate 17 Shizu Saldamando, *La Otra Gerry*, 2009
Oil paint, gold leaf, washi paper, collage on wood panel, 60 × 30 inches.
(Courtesy of the artist)

PART III

COMMUNITIES

CHAPTER 4

Trans-Pacific Localism and the Creation of a Fishing Colony
Pre–World War II Taiji Immigrants on Terminal Island, California

Yuko Konno

On February 27, 2011, about 120 people attended the New Year's party and reunion of the Taiji-jinkei Club (Taiji People's Club) in Torrance, California. Six officials from the town of Taiji (Wakayama Prefecture, Japan) also attended the event, hoping to renew ties with Taiji immigrants and their descendants in Southern California. In fact, Taiji, a small town near the southern tip of the Kii peninsula with a population of 3,500 to 4,000, played a central role in making this event happen. Taiji villagers, who began migrating in large numbers to the United States in the late nineteenth century, formed the Taijijin-kai (Taiji Village Association) in 1916 on Terminal Island, Los Angeles. Although there were times when it took a brief hiatus and changed location during World War II, the association remained in existence until it finally disbanded in 2006. However, when the people of Taiji town began digging into its emigration history around 2008, they successfully convinced one of the former club members to create a new organization in Southern California. Attracting people both young and old, the 2011 New Year's party served as an occasion for participants not only to renew their friendships but also to celebrate the association's reestablishment (participant observation, Taiji-jinkei Club New Year's party, February 27, 2011).

This new relationship between home and abroad has materialized as the small town has reached out globally in recent years. Although now at the center of an international controversy surrounding the infamous dolphin drive hunt, long before activists came to town, Taiji had been exposed to foreign influences due to its history of whaling and overseas emigration. To educate the youth, the town's current charismatic mayor crafted plans to make full use of Taiji's cultural heritage. He recruited a Japanese assistant curator working at the New Bedford Whaling Museum in Massachusetts so that Taiji's would become the leading whaling museum in the world. Fluent in English, skilled in communication, and capable of historical research, the new curator helped revive Taiji as a community once again open to foreign cultures. He not only brought his knowledge of whaling history to the museum but also played a big role in the town's various projects to send its youth overseas and renew contacts with emigrants and their descendants abroad. It is in this context that Taiji began collecting historical documents and artifacts related to emigration as well as pressing for the reunion of people from Taiji in Southern California (Akio Usagawa, personal communication, June 28, 2010; Hayato Sakurai, personal communication, February 27, 2011).

I happened to come across this gold mine of emigration history in 2010 as I was looking for a "model" migration community that would serve as a good topic for my dissertation. My goal was to write a history of a migration community from its beginnings to its maturity. More specifically, following the lead of certain Japanese and American scholars who suggested that local immigrant identity was key to connecting emigration and immigration, I was hoping to show the roles the village played in these two processes.[1]

At the time, I had no connections to Wakayama. I was merely looking for "a case," and my preliminary research of old passport records indicated that the prefecture was a potentially interesting place to do research. After several phone calls to various town offices in Wakayama, one official in Kushimoto referred me to Taiji's untapped archive of emigration history. In this way, my encounter with Taiji was coincidental. However, thanks to the town's hospitality and openness, I was able to avail myself of the community's rich trans-Pacific past. My search for a case of localism led me to a town trying to reach out globally.

Focusing on the relationship between Taiji and its prewar immigrant fishing colony on Terminal Island, this chapter highlights the formation of a community shaped by localism that was rooted in Japan and yet crossed over the Pacific. Paying attention to this trans-Pacific localism entails looking at both emigration and immigration contexts in order to understand how personal connections and resources from one village traveled across national borders and created new opportunities and contacts for residents in foreign locales. This movement made it possible for immigrants to actively participate in the affairs of their village of origin. Although the phenomenon and experiences of migration and community formation explored in this chapter are "transnational" in the sense that they relate to two different national contexts, I believe the term "trans-Pacific" more accurately captures the worldview of immigrants from southern Wakayama. To many of them, international migration was the process of settling in a new land by going beyond the boundary of their village and across the ocean. What ultimately shaped the lives of immigrants and those left behind was the connection between particular locales on both sides of the Pacific, which the term "transnational" does not reflect.

Taiji–Terminal Island connections, however, did not offer the "model" case for considering immigrant localism, because the way Taiji immigrants adapted themselves to American contexts was rather peculiar. The population became heavily concentrated in one corner of the island where the majority of people hailed from neighboring villages in Wakayama and worked primarily in fisheries. Thus, they re-created an overseas community in an environment characterized by familiarity and psychological proximity among its members—perhaps more so than in other Japanese communities in America. Because many residents were from the same prefecture, internal diversity within this particular society meant different village or town identities.

As much as Japanese people on Terminal Island looked to their villages of origin, it was difficult for them to simply remain villagers from Wakayama forever. As they lived and worked alongside other racial and ethnic groups, immigrants sought ways to cope with the reality of their being "Japanese" subjects. Their efforts consisted of, above all, maintaining a good relationship with local whites. A dearth of evidence makes it difficult to judge how the Japanese viewed local Mexicans and Filipinos, but they most likely perceived themselves as different from and yet equal partners to whites as long as they were engaged in their chosen profession as fishermen, an area in which they had comparable if not superior skills.

In this chapter, I emphasize two aspects of Taiji immigrants' identity: their connection to Taiji, which was rooted in trans-Pacific localism, and their "Japaneseness," which was shaped by U.S. race relations as well as local occupational settings that favored Japanese fishermen. In the end, these two ways of identifying themselves supplemented each other, enabling immigrants to form a unique fishing community different from other Japanese communities in the prewar United States. Although Taiji immigrants may be outliers in the larger narrative of the Japanese immigrant experience, their stories serve as an important reminder that trans-Pacific human connections as well as occupational and numerical strengths have worked to alleviate most damaging consequences of racialization.

Emigration: Taiji, Wakayama Prefecture, Japan

Pre–World War II emigration from Wakayama prefecture primarily originated from three locations. The first group of emigrants hailed from the northern part of Wakayama. The pioneers of this group were from the northeastern area of the prefecture, around the villages of Ikeda and Tanaka (currently Kinokawa City) in Naga County. Young men wishing to study in the United States led emigration from the area, including a successful businessman who invited fellow villagers to work in California. Immigrants from Naga and those from the neighboring county of Kaisō in the northwest tended to choose the continental United States or Hawai'i as their destination. Those in Kaisō might have obtained information about foreign countries from that businessman, or perhaps through a different channel in Wakayama City, the prefectural capital. The second group consisted of fishing migrants from the central coastal area around the village of Mio (currently Mihama Town), many of whom ended up in Canada. And the third group came from a number of coastal villages in southern Wakayama, and usually went to Australia or the United States. The first emigrants of those groups went overseas in the 1880s and 1890s (Wakayama-ken 1957, 147–221). Emigrants from Taiji, who belonged to the third group, were influenced by stories of successful immigrants and returnees from nearby villages, just like their counterparts in other villages.[2]

Global and national factors dictated the flow of international migration, and village social networks shaped emigrants' actual decisions. Without any guidance from neighbors, friends, relatives, or family members, it would have been difficult for a villager to imagine what opportunities living abroad could offer. The phenomenon of villagers migrating in groups to specific foreign locales can well be explained by the presence of successful returnees, who remodeled their houses, bought Western-style furniture, and showed other signs of affluence.

A geographical analysis of passport records corroborates the significance of local connections. The year 1906 was one of the peak years of emigration from Wakayama villages, brought on by the depression after the Russo-Japanese War (1904–1905). With the exception of Mio, all the villages that sent seventy emigrants or more in that year are located in the southern coastal area. Furthermore, besides Wakayama City, only one village in the northern part of the prefecture sent more than fifty emigrants. In short, there were more villages in southern Wakayama than northern Wakayama that sent a considerable number of emigrants overseas. Emigration from northern Wakayama reached its zenith in 1899, the year before the Alien Contract Labor Law (1885), which banned foreign contract labor in the United States, took effect in Hawai'i as a result of the United States' annexation of the kingdom. After the turn of the century, although emigration fever never disappeared from the area, it did not return to the high levels seen in the late nineteenth century. Due to severe immigration restrictions enforced by the Australian government, by 1906 southern Wakayama emigrants' primary destination had become North America instead of Australia (Documents and Tables, 1906; Kodama 1992, 466–468).

Although Taiji had supplied pearl divers to Australia since the 1890s, the popularity of the country had already declined among emigrants from the village by 1906. In that year, seventy passports were issued to prospective Taiji emigrants by the government of Wakayama, of which only two were for those going to Australia: one's destination was listed as Thursday Island, Australia, and another's was "China," which probably meant the state of Western Australia. The other passports were issued for four people going to the continental United States, one to Canada, fifty-three to Hawai'i, and ten to Mexico. The majority of those who chose Hawai'i or Mexico probably intended to enter the continental United States eventually, a very common practice among labor migrants on the eve of the Gentlemen's Agreement (1907–1908). Thus, the continental United States had become the most popular destination among Taiji migrants by 1906.

The culture of overseas *dekasegi* (work away from home) emigration had become prevalent by the turn of the twentieth century, as records of Taiji Elementary School show (see Table 4.1). Among children who entered school in 1904, 27 percent had family members abroad for work. In 1905 and 1906, the percentage was higher: 35.7 percent and 32.7 percent, respectively. In other words, during those years, approximately three out of every ten new pupils had family members abroad. The United States was the most popular destination, particularly in the latter two years, followed by Australia. Even these partial data demonstrate that overseas

Table 4.1 Overseas Emigration from Families of Students at Taiji Elementary School, 1904–1906

Year of Entrance: 1904. Ten out of thirty-seven children (27 percent) had family members abroad.

Who:	Where:
- Parents: 7	- The United States: 5
- Siblings: 2	- Australia: 4
- Unknown: 1	- Unknown: 1 (#)

Year of Entrance: 1905. Fifteen out of forty-two children (35.7 percent) had family members abroad.

Who:	Where:
- Parents: 8	- The United States: 11
- Siblings: 7	- Australia: 4
- Unknown: 1	
* One family had both a parent and a sibling abroad.	

Year of Entrance: 1906. Eighteen out of fifty-five children (32.7 percent) had family members abroad.

Who:	Where:
- Parents: 10	- The United States: 10
- Siblings: 6	- Australia: 3
- Unknown: 3	- Unspecified foreign country: 3
* One family had both a parent and a person with an unknown relationship abroad.	- Canada: 1
	- Unknown: 1 (#)

Source: Taiji Jinjō Kōtō Shōgakkō, Records of Characters and Behaviors, ca. 1902–1914, Taiji Historical Archives, Wakayama, compiled by the author.
Note: Detailed records on every schoolchild's character, behavior, and family background were kept by teachers at Taiji Elementary School. The data here are taken from entries between 1904 and 1906, because of the consistency of the content as well as special emphasis on family backgrounds as they pertained to overseas emigration.
(#) The "unknown category" might have included people who moved to other areas in Japan.

migration was quite common among villagers (Taiji Jinjō Kōtō Shōgakkō, ca. 1902–1914).

From 1907 onward, after the Gentlemen's Agreement banned new labor migration by Japanese nationals to the continental United States, specifically prohibiting them from entering the country by way of Hawai'i, Canada, or Mexico, the majority of immigrants to America were the wives, children, or parents of bona fide residents, or those who had come before

1908. So-called *yobiyose* (bringing over) migration became popular as those who had entered the United States prior to the Gentlemen's Agreement sent for their spouses and children.

Despite state control of migration on both sides of the Pacific, Japanese immigrants came up with ways to evade laws. For example, because it was legal for the children of bona fide U.S. residents to enter the country, some prospective emigrants became the adopted children of those already there by having their names inserted into the residents' family registers (a practice very similar to the "paper sons" phenomenon among Chinese immigrants).

This led to the so-called Kotsubo Incident in Taiji. Before applying for passports, prospective emigrants needed to have their documentation verified by the local police. In Taiji, knowing what overseas emigration meant to local people, a police officer named Kannosuke[3] Kotsubo ignored the fact that applicants were abusing the family registration system, and between 1912 and 1915 approximately eighty people from Taiji reportedly immigrated to the United States thanks to his leniency. However, at one point a villager who had had trouble having his name entered into a family register reported the "crimes" to the authorities, leading to the imprisonment of Kotsubo and one registrar at the village office. Feeling deeply grateful to Kotsubo, many villagers pleaded for mercy on his behalf, but to no avail. Concerned villagers, together with immigrants in the United States, provided financial assistance to him and his family after he was removed from office. In this way, in order to have access to the wealth that America was thought to offer them, prospective emigrants did not hesitate to challenge laws and nations. They even praised people who helped them with fraudulent means (Ichihara 1959, 50; Taiji Chōshi Kanshū Iinkai 1979, 799–801).

Even after the Gentlemen's Agreement, illegal migration remained prevalent, with Mexico continuing to act as a convenient entry point for Japanese migrants, who relied especially on ties formed through trans-Pacific localism. Many Taiji immigrants who made a living by fishing from East San Pedro (part of Terminal Island) or San Diego would hide their compatriots in their boats when sailing near the coast of Mexico and bring them to the shores of Southern California in secrecy. The spirit underlying those localist ties is expressed succinctly in Taiji's official history, which states, "No matter what sacrifice they had to make, fellow locals sheltered and made special arrangements for immigrants." Social networks based on local ties thus helped sustain the migration flow from Taiji (Taiji Chōshi Kanshū Iinkai 1979, 804–805).

Accordingly, overseas migration from Japan continued despite immigration regulations in North America and Australia thanks to family-based immigration policies and audacious lawbreakers taking advantage of local connections. Although the 1924 Immigration Act nearly halted Japanese immigration to the United States, those who had already entered the country by then were determined to stay. In 1930, there were 335 Taiji immigrants living in the continental United States, 74 in Australia, 66 in Mexico, 19 in Canada, 11 in Singapore, 7 in the Philippines, 2 in Hawai'i, and 2 in Great Britain. In total, 516 people from Taiji lived abroad at the time, accounting for approximately 14 percent of the town's total population of 3,693. The popularity of overseas emigration again can be seen in school records. Of the 58 female students enrolled at Taiji Elementary School during the 1930s, 26 had family members abroad.[4] Of those, 16 had family members in the United States, and 3 had been born in San Pedro. After graduating from high school, 2 of these American-born students returned to San Pedro, 4 others migrated there, and 1 went to Monterey, a fishing community in northern California.[5] Furthermore, 16 of the 58 girls' families had *dekasegi* workers in cities and towns within Japan, and 5 of these families also had members working abroad. One family whose patriarch had passed away had its oldest son working at a trading company in Hyōgo, Japan, the second-oldest son working as a mechanic in an unspecified mine, the third-oldest son working as a pearl diver in Australia, the fourth-oldest son working as a mechanic at a steeling factory in Osaka, and two sisters working somewhere else, most likely as maids in other households. When these school records were taken, of all the families of the 58 girls enrolled at Taiji Elementary School, only 20 had no members working outside of Taiji. Thus, despite a series of immigration regulations having been implemented, overseas emigration had a significant impact on the lives of people left in Taiji in the 1930s (Taijikō Takushokubu, ca. 1931–1933 and Taiji Jinjō Kōto Shōgakkō, ca. 1936–1940; Wakayama-ken 1933, 21–30).

One of the reasons Taiji people continued to emigrate overseas was the money it brought to families and the entire community. In 1931, a total of 206,102.12 yen was remitted or brought by hand to Taiji by 282 immigrants in the United States, Canada, Australia, and Singapore. This means that each person contributed an average of more than 730 yen to the community.

When only the remitted amount of 174,602.12 yen sent by 257 immigrants is taken into account, the average declines to about 680 yen. Still, when compared with the average amount per immigrant of 590 yen that was remitted to Wakayama Prefecture from overseas in the same year, it becomes clear that Taiji immigrants brought greater wealth to the community than the average immigrant from other areas of Wakayama.[6] Indeed, the amount of money sent or brought to Taiji in 1931 is comparable to the value of all the fish caught in 1932 (204,778 yen) by members of Taiji Suisan Kyōdō Kumiai (Taiji Fisheries Cooperative). Money sent or brought by overseas residents would have been enough to support the local economy if fishermen had gone bankrupt (Taijikō Takushokubu, ca. 1931–1933; Miscellaneous Records 1931; and Taiji Chōshi Kanshū Iinkai 1979, 526–527).

Because overseas emigration was so important to the community in social and economic terms, practical instructions regarding emigration were given to the youth. To educate those who would go abroad after graduating from school, a supplementary school attached to Taiji Elementary School created the Ishokumin-ka (Department of Emigration and Colonization) in 1931. The department offered a one-hour course once a week in which students learned the procedures and laws related to going overseas as well as history relating to emigration and colonization. They also received practical training in driving cars and handling fishing boats. Because going to America as a new emigrant had become impossible by this time, those who took the course might have had other regions of the world in mind, such as countries in South America or Asia, including territories colonized by the Japanese Empire. At any rate, the establishment of a department specializing in emigrant education symbolizes the local emigration fever at the time as well as the community's matter-of-fact awareness of its dependency on "overseas development" to support and sustain itself (Wakayama-ken 1957, 203–204).

In pre–World War II Taiji, overseas emigration influenced both the local economy and culture to a considerable degree. As the wealth brought over from abroad changed village society, the "home" functioned as a system to sustain migration flows to specific foreign locales. As is most clearly shown in the case of illegal (undocumented) migration, the "village" worked as more than a simple unit of identification for immigrants. Rather, immigrants used the connections offered by this affiliation to gain access to resources necessary for their survival.

As immigrants created a new home abroad, they not only retained a close relationship with their home village but also faced the reality of race in their new settlement. Once on Terminal Island, Taiji immigrants as well as other Japanese from southern Wakayama helped establish a fluid trans-Pacific community where money, goods, and people were continually on the move. At the same time, they resisted being simply categorized as a racial minority, which was made possible by their large numbers and special skills as fishermen.

Immigration: Terminal Island, Los Angeles, California

Terminal Island is a small island of 4.46 square miles located approximately 25 miles south of downtown Los Angeles. Administratively, the eastern half of the island belongs to the city of Long Beach and the western half to the city of Los Angeles. The latter used to be under the jurisdiction of San Pedro, a city across Main Channel to the west of the island. In 1909, however, Los Angeles was in need of a safe and spacious commercial port, so San Pedro was incorporated into it and the Port of Los Angeles was created in San Pedro Bay. Since then, San Pedro and the western half of Terminal Island have been part of Los Angeles, although a slight distance between the center of the city and the island has led to the formation of an almost independent community with a peculiar culture of its own (Fogelson [1967] 1993, 108–117; Zangs [1991] 1999, 6, 11).

The urban center initially supplied Japanese labor to areas around San Pedro. In 1901, a group of twelve to fifteen Japanese discovered abalone in the San Pedro region. Originally they had worked as fishermen in Japan; however, at the time of their abalone discovery, they were employed by the Southern Pacific Railroad, working as car cleaners and mechanics in Los Angeles. Feeling that the life of a fisherman was more exciting and enjoyable than a car cleaner or mechanic's, those Japanese men started a business, catching, processing, and selling abalone at White Point, about four miles west of San Pedro. At first they sold dried abalone to a Japanese-run trading company in Los Angeles, but in 1903 after a Japanese man built a canning company in San Francisco, they began shipping dried abalone and shrimp there. The business appeared to be going well, but unexpected hostility led to its end. The sight of deep-diving abalone catchers aroused suspicion among some white Americans, with one newspaper reporting that the Japanese were "spying the coast line of Southern California."[7] After the article's publication, some whites threw stones on the sheds in which the Japanese lived.

Finally, in 1905, the state of California ordered that the enterprise be put to an end. Forced to disband their company, the Japanese pioneers moved out of White Point to other nearby communities, such as San Pedro, Terminal Island, and Wilmington.

In 1906, other Japanese people working in and around Los Angeles began to gather in San Pedro to fish for albacore. One of them, a former candy store owner, confessed that he had been waiting for an opportunity to become a fisherman, having been born and trained as a son of a fishing family.

White Americans had not eaten albacore until this point. The invention of canned albacore (branded "Chicken of the Sea") led to a rapid increase in its demand. This fortune attracted fishermen of other ethnic groups, such as Italians, Russians, and Scandinavians, to San Pedro. It was also around this time that Japanese fishermen began living in sheds built on Terminal Island. In this way, the Japanese community on the island had its roots in the Japanese laborers who had originally been based in Los Angeles. It did not take long for those laborers with connections to fellow Japanese people who were interested in fishing and had experience as fishermen to find out about San Pedro and Terminal Island (Kawasaki 1931, 31–43; Ryono 1994, 3; Queenan 1983, 59–62; Takeuchi 1937, 27–29, 58; Wakayama-ken 1957, 381–382).

A Japanese village on Terminal Island emerged quickly. In 1907, there were already around six hundred Japanese fishermen there, of which a quarter (one hundred fifty) were from Taiji. A Japanese fishermen's association was established in the same year, although it disbanded three years later. Three canning companies were also built around this time. Most of the Japanese were concentrated at East San Pedro (Higashi San Pīdoro), which was north of Fish Harbor, an area where more canning companies were built and fishing boats docked. The number of Japanese residents in East San Pedro increased, especially in the early 1920s after a large fire in Port Los Angeles (in Santa Monica, not to be confused with the Port of Los Angeles) destroyed the fishermen's camps in 1918. It also attracted fishermen who did not succeed in Monterey, as well as farmers driven out of business due to the Alien Land Laws. Those Japanese quickly occupied one corner of the island and created a village that thrived on fisheries (Kawasaki 1931, 16, 43–46, 52–53).

East San Pedro was a self-segregated community separate from Terminal, another residential section one mile west of it. The latter had primarily whites, Mexicans, and Filipinos, with some Japanese residents as well. According to the 1930 census, close to 97 percent of the population in East San Pedro were Japanese, whereas Japanese composed only 5.3 percent of those in Terminal and other areas of the western part of the island (see Table 4.2). In fact, Terminal was predominantly occupied by white Americans, with Mexicans being the second-largest group. The Japanese village on Terminal Island as mentioned in immigration literature, then, was essentially East San Pedro. Little is known about the multiethnic/racial community next to it.

Occupationally, East San Pedro residents depended heavily on the fisheries industry while residents of Terminal worked as laborers in lumber mills, canneries, railroads, oil refineries, docks, and shipyards (see Tables 4.3-1 and 4.3-2). In the former community, about 70 percent of the working population engaged in fishing, and fish canneries employed more than 15 percent. In the latter community, lumber mills and fish canneries were the major employers. Since most of the Japanese lived in East San Pedro, naturally the "Japanese village" on Terminal Island is recognized in immigration literature as a fishing community.

The peculiarity of Terminal Island Japanese was not only that they congregated in East San Pedro in large numbers, but also that they largely

Table 4.2 Racial Composition of the Population on Terminal Island (under the Jurisdiction of Los Angeles), 1930

Race	East San Pedro		Terminal and Other		
	N	%	N	%	
Japanese	1,850	96.8	58	5.3	
Mexican	5	0.3	349	31.7	Blank/unclear
White	56	2.9	632	57.4	
Filipino	0	0.0	56	5.1	
Other	0	0.0	7	0.6	
Subtotal	1,911		1,102		19
Total			3,032		

Source: 1930 U.S. census, Los Angeles County, California, population schedule, San Pedro district (hereafter cited as 1930 U.S. Census, Los Angeles County, Cal., pop. sch., San Pedro dis.), Ancestry Library Edition (accessed from the Los Angeles Public Library), compiled by the author.

Note: As no maps exist to show the exact locations of East San Pedro or Terminal, I have categorized people's places of residence based on street names. I counted respondents whose addresses are on the following streets as residents of East San Pedro: Albicore St, Cannery St, Fish Harbor Wharf, Pilchard St, S Seaside Ave, Terminal Way, Tuna St, Ways St, and Wharf St.

Table 4.3-1 Occupational Composition of the Population in East San Pedro, 1930

Occupation	N	%
Fisherman	571	69.1
Cannery worker	128	15.5
Proprietor	27	3.3
Clerk	13	1.6
Other	87	10.5
Total	826	100.0

Table 4.3-2 Occupational Composition of the Population in Terminal and Other, 1930

Occupation	N	%
Lumber mill worker	148	29.0
Cannery worker	144	28.2
Railroad worker	22	4.3
Fisherman	20	3.9
Oil industry worker	18	3.5
Dock worker	15	2.9
Shipyard worker	12	2.4
Other	131	25.7
Total	510	99.9*

Source: 1930 U.S. census, Los Angeles County, Cal., pop. sch., San Pedro dis., compiled by the author.
Note: While they reported their occupations, many respondents were actually jobless at the time the census was taken, possibly as a consequence of the Great Depression.
*The total does not add up to 100 percent due to rounding.

came from a limited number of communities in Japan. Table 4.4 lists the top seven villages/towns that sent emigrants to Terminal Island; all are located in the southern coastal area of Wakayama. Emigrants from Taiji formed the largest group, making up 13.7 percent of the entire Japanese population on pre–World War II Terminal Island. This situation—in which neighbors in the home country became new neighbors in the United States—contributed to an atmosphere where immigrants could feel at home even though they were physically apart from their native villages.

Because many Japanese on Terminal Island came from nearby towns and villages in southern Wakayama, the internal diversity in the Japanese

Table 4.4 Top Seven Villages where Japanese Residents in Terminal Island Originated

County*	Village/town	N (sample)	% (100= 161 residents)
Higashimuro	Taiji	22	13.7
Higashimuro	Shimosato	18	11.2
Nishimuro	Esumi	16	9.9
Nishimuro	Tanami	10	6.2
Higashimuro	Ugui	8	5.0
Higashimuro	Tawara	8	5.0
Nishimuro	Wabuka	6	3.7

*All in Wakayama Prefecture.
Source: Registrants' Cards, 1909–1941, Boxes 164–225, Japanese American Research Project, Charles E. Young Research Library, University of California, Los Angeles, compiled by the author.
Note: To create this table, a random sample of 4,104 cards of family heads was taken from the approximately 50,350 registration cards that Japanese people filed with the consulate in Los Angeles, and 161 cards from this random sample with addresses in Terminal Island were chosen for analysis. The cards are from between 1919 and 1939, but most of them are from the early 1920s. Since some people moved out of Terminal Island and others joined the community later on, not all of the 161 individuals represented by these cards lived on the island at the same time. Furthermore, five of these individuals were Nisei, although they all had registered domiciles in Japan.

community meant differences in places of origin within Wakayama rather than in prefectures of origin. Thus, the *sonjin-kai* (village association) played a greater role on the island than the *kenjin-kai* (prefectural association). Beginning with the one founded by Tawara villagers in 1905, a number of *sonjin-kai* appeared on Terminal Island from the late 1910s to the early 1920s. The aforementioned Taijijin-kai was created between 1914 and 1916, and had about 130 members by 1937.

The members cultivated friendships by holding picnics and parties and expressed their nationalism by welcoming training squadrons from Japan. One of the most important activities of the *sonjin-kai* was to give monetary assistance to the home village. Members of the Taijijin-kai financially supported the relocation of Taiji Elementary School, the purchase of fire pumps, and the establishment of a local shrine. They particularly cared about the education of local children and created and funded an award called the San Pīdoro Taijijin-kai Shō (San Pedro Taiji Village Association Prize) that was given to especially good students at Taiji Elementary School. This award, which included gifts and certificates, was given every year from 1923 to 1940 to one male and one female student in each grade who performed well (see Figure 4.1). The Taijijin-kai's continuous support to Taiji children reflected the immigrants' strong commitment to

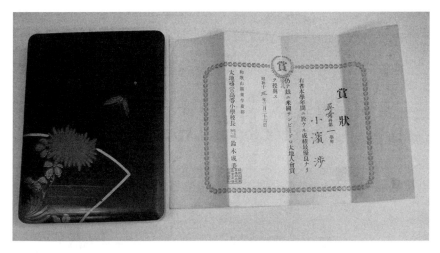

Figure 4.1 An Inkstone Case and a Certificate of Merit Given to Wataru Kohama, Winner of the San Pīdoro Taijijin-kai Shō (San Pedro Taiji Village Association Prize), 1938
(Courtesy of Taiji Historical Archives)

the affairs of their home village (Takeuchi 1937, 169–192; Taiji Jinjō Kōtō Shōgakkō, ca. 1923–1940).

Monetary contribution was not the only way to assert and maintain village identity. Immigrants frequently returned to their home villages in Japan, sometimes staying for more than a couple of months at a time to take care of their parents or manage other familial issues. For example, Chiyomatsu Ryōno of Taiji came to the United States in 1907, worked at a lumber mill in Seattle for ten years, and then became a fisherman in East San Pedro. In 1915, he returned to Japan as a member of a tourist group and came back to the United States with his wife the next year, buying a fishing boat shortly thereafter. He once again went back to Japan in 1924 with his family and left his two children there before returning to the United States. In 1928, he embarked on deep-sea fishing with a new boat. In October 1935, he visited his parents in Japan and did not come back to the United States until March of the next year. Narratives of this kind abound in biographies of immigrants. Such behaviors suggest that Japanese residents in the United States were, to a certain degree, prepared for the day when they could return to Japan permanently. Frequent trips to Japan meant that they had somewhere to return (Takeuchi 1937, appendix, 12).

Although the East San Pedro Japanese acted as trans-Pacific residents, in their daily contacts with other racial groups, they inevitably realized their Japaneseness, albeit perhaps in a slightly different manner from their counterparts. The peculiar demographic makeup of East San Pedro, in which Japanese were the racial majority, reversed the racial demography then prevalent in the United States. In fact, in the early 1930s, one observer commented on this situation (Kawasaki 1931, 5–6):

> The social behavior patterns in this community are mainly Japanese, because the Japanese are the main inhabitants and only a small number of other races are represented in the community. I observed on many occasions that small white children spoke Japanese, sang the Japanese songs, and played some of the Japanese games. The reason for this is that all the children here attend the Japanese Christian Mission and play with groups of Japanese children.

This example demonstrates that the familiar narrative of immigrant assimilation into American society was not always the norm.

The high number of Japanese in East San Pedro was a result of many people being fishermen. Because of a high demand for their skills, Terminal Island Japanese were able to escape from some of the consequences of racial discrimination. Between 1919 and 1945, the Japanese Fishermen's Association tackled the problem of anti-Japanese fishing bills submitted to the California State Legislature. At least twenty-six bills were submitted during those years. Canning companies depended heavily on Japanese fishermen—one reason being that only the Japanese fished sardines around San Pedro—and therefore did not support those anti-Japanese measures. The Fishermen's Association led a movement against the bills and also pressured the Japanese Embassy and consulates to take action. In the end, only three bills passed the legislature, all of which were later ruled unconstitutional (Kawasaki 1931, 48–54; Chuman [1976] 1981, 227–231, 365–366nn5–10, 19; "Loss to Port Seen in Bill," 12).

In the world of commercial fishing, the Japanese saw themselves as equal to whites. At times, white fishermen became their rivals, but they could also be strong partners in confronting exploitative canning companies. Established in 1915, the Southern California Japanese Fishermen's Association became a primary ethnic organization in the area, with six hundred members in the late 1930s. The Japanese association dealt with conflicts between Japanese and white fishermen and their associations. Essentially created to protect the interests of Japanese fishermen, the association occasionally became a basis for interethnic solidarity, for example, when fishermen had standoffs with canning companies. One of the association's most important tasks was to negotiate the prices for fish with canning companies, which were their virtual employers.

Fishermen were able to earn good money, and their mind-set was potentially different from that of the typical working class. In the 1900s, a farmer earned approximately one and a half dollars per day, and a fisherman earned three to four dollars per day for his catch. Nevertheless, fishermen were not free from the control of canning companies. Most of them lived in small houses rented by canneries, and labor disputes frequently occurred when fishermen were dissatisfied with the prices for fish suggested by the companies. On such occasions, the Japanese Fishermen's Association joined hands with its counterparts in San Diego and Monterey as well as with white fishermen. When negotiations broke down, fishermen went on strike. In July 1925, for example, Japanese and white fishermen in San Diego went on strike to protest the canning companies' reduction of prices for fish. The strike lasted for two weeks, and the fishermen emerged victorious (Takeuchi 1937, 48–54; Ryono 1994, 7, 10–11; Kawasaki 1931, 54–55).

That apparent equality of the Japanese with whites was sustained by Japanese efforts to adapt to U.S. society. This meant, above all, trying to be accepted by whites. A "Fishermen's Hall" was completed in 1918 and served as a local community center, which purported "to illuminate fishermen's intellect, cultivate their character, and develop in them the habit of diligence and thrift so that canneries and white people in general will trust them more" (Takeuchi 1937, 51).

In Japanese immigrant narratives, rarely did Mexicans, Filipinos, or any other people of color appear. Although the Japanese in the Terminal section of the island might have had a different story to tell, no documentary evidence exists that reveals their views on race relations. Although Mexicans and Filipinos worked alongside Japanese female laborers at canneries, because they were primarily laborers and not fishermen, they did not occupy an important place in the minds of many local Japanese. It is understandable, then, that Japanese on Terminal Island were concerned more about being on friendly terms with whites than about developing solidarity with other peoples of color.

However, efforts to adapt to U.S. society did not mean complete assimilation or subservience to whites. Many Terminal Island Issei spoke in the dialects of Japanese villages, and few were fluent in English. Their children developed a unique identity as "Terminal Islanders" and used the dialect of Terminal Island, or *Tāminaru-ben,* calling each other *yū-ra, mī-ra* (you and us). The casual nature with which children spoke Japanese in classrooms led white American teachers to yell, "This is America. Speak English!" (Yukio Tatsumi, personal communication, March 4, 2011). However, the white teachers also tried hard to understand the Japanese. Both East San Pedro Public School and the multiethnic Terminal School hosted a program to celebrate Japanese Doll Day (*Hinamatsuri*). Japanese parents were particularly grateful to the principal of East San Pedro School, Mildred Obarr Walizer, who showed deep affection and understanding toward Japanese children. Furthermore, she helped their parents, who rarely spoke English, in forming the Fukei-kai (Parent-Teacher Association) and Fujin-kai (Women's Association). To repay her kindness, the Fukei-kai collected 3,700 dollars to sponsor her to take a tour of Japan and visit southern Wakayama

Figure 4.2   O. Walizer and Children at Taiji Elementary School, 1930
(Courtesy of Taiji Historical Archives)

in 1930. Walizer had been interested in Wakayama even before the trip was planned, as many of her students had roots in the prefecture. She visited towns and villages along the southern coast of Wakayama (such as Shingū, Ugui, Taiji, Tawara, Tanami, and Esumi) to see her former students (see Figure 4.2), then set sail to return to the United States after visiting the village of Mio, a famous *Amerika-mura* (American village).[8] Walizer may have had an exceptionally strong sense of mission as an educator, but her relationship with the Japanese can be taken as a reflection of the race relations in general on Terminal Island. The Japanese were not simply the victims of racism. At times learning from whites, they nonetheless asserted their autonomy and shared the happiness they found in interacting with local whites with their home villages across the Pacific (Takeuchi 1937, 72–74, 76, 118, 134; Wakayama-ken 1957, 456–460; Ryono 1994, 29; "San Pedro" 1932, 5; East San Pedro School 1937; Terminal School 1938).

Conclusion

The case of Taiji and Terminal Island shows the degree to which pre–World War II Japanese immigrants embraced a localism rooted in Japan and at the same time contributed to community development in the United States. In a sense, Terminal Island was an exception rather than the norm with regard to trans-Pacific localism and U.S. race relations. The majority of the population in East San Pedro was dominated by people who came from a relatively limited number of areas in Japan. That made it easier for residents not only to retain "village" mentalities brought over from Japan but also to re-create a sense of home in the new community by asserting a degree of autonomy. Although it is difficult to make generalizations about immigrant localism or race relations in Southern California based only on this case study of Terminal Island, the story of Taiji and Terminal Island demonstrates a type of localism and community formation that suggests one way of understanding the immigrant mentality. It exemplifies a close connection between multiple localities and shows a way of looking at immigrants as creators of a fluid community of trans-Pacific migrants and residents. At the same time, such an example sheds light on human relations that go beyond the "dominant whites" and "immigrant minorities" dichotomy and shows the possibilities of a new approach that explores in depth the power relations within peculiar occupational structures, such as those of fishing.

Notes

1. For exemplary works that look at both emigration and immigration contexts, see Ritsumeikan Daigaku Jinbun Kagaku Kenkyūjo (1964) and Yamada (2000). Fuminori Minamikawa, in his work on Japanese American community formation in Los Angeles, also discusses the significance of "translocal" connections for immigrants until the early 1910s. See Minamikawa (2007).
2. Kenkichi Iwasaki created the term "neighboring effect" to explain how emigration fever traveled from one village to another. According to him, overseas emigration from the southern coastal area of the Kii peninsula was initiated by economic needs as well as by chance and sustained by the neighboring effect and custom. See Iwasaki (1938a, 38–40) and Iwasaki (1938b, 77).
3. There is also a possibility that the characters for his personal name were read as "Hironosuke."
4. The figure becomes 27 if one includes a father who was always sailing to the South Pole for whaling.
5. From 1924 onward, it became impossible for legal residents in America to bring over their Japan-born children. Therefore, the students who went to the United States despite having registered domiciles in Japan might have actually been born in the United States. Or, if they were admitted into American universities, they would have been able to enter the United States as students.
6. In 1931, 3,175 people from four countries remitted a total of 1,876,327 yen to Wakayama Prefecture.
7. This is a quotation from Kanichi Kawasaki's 1931 MA thesis (p. 37). Curiously, although Kawasaki presents this quote as if it were from an American newspaper, his footnote suggests that it is from an interview with a Japanese immigrant who related the content of a newspaper article to him.
8. Mio has been called *Amerika-mura* for a long time, and the current town of Mihama (into which Mio was eventually incorporated) has been trying to attract tourists using this legacy. Mio was and is called an *Amerika-mura* because its emigrants flourished in Canada as fishermen and brought back wealth to the village. Hence, the *Amerika* in the phrase refers to North America.

References

Chuman, Frank F. [1976] 1981. *The Bamboo People: Japanese-Americans, Their History and the Law*. Chicago: Japanese American Research Project, Japanese American Citizens League.

海外旅券下付 (附与) 返納表進達一件 (含附与明細表) (Documents and Tables on Passports Issued or Returned). 1906. Archived material, Record Group 3.8.5.8.: Microform, reels 43–46. Diplomatic Archives of the Ministry of Foreign Affairs of Japan, Tōkyō, Japan.

East San Pedro School. 1937. おひなまつり (Doll Day). Pamphlet, File: East San Pedro School—Terminal School. Los Angeles: San Pedro Bay Historical Archives.

Fogelson, Robert M. [1967] 1993. *The Fragmented Metropolis: Los Angeles, 1850–1930*. 1st paperback edition. Berkeley: University of California Press.

Ichihara, Ryōhei 市原亮平. 1959. 移民母村の漁業構造と人口問題―和歌山県東牟婁郡太地町の実態調査報告(1) (Emigrants' Home Village (1)). *Economic Review of Kansai University* 8 (6): 28–50.

Iwasaki, Kenkichi 岩崎健吉. 1938a. 紀伊半島南海岸に於ける海外出稼移民の研究 (第3報) (A Study of Emigrants to Foreign Countries from the South Coast of Kii-Peninsula (3rd Report)). *Chirigaku Hyōron* 14 (4): 28–46.

———. 1938b. 紀伊半島南海岸に於ける海外出稼移民の研究 (第4報) (A Study of Emigrants to Foreign Countries from the South Coast of Kii-Peninsula (4th Report)). *Chirigaku Hyōron* 14 (6): 76–77.

Kawasaki, Kanichi. 1931. "The Japanese Community of East San Pedro, Terminal Island, California." MA thesis, Department of Sociology, University of Southern California.

Kodama, Masaaki 児玉正昭. 1992. 日本移民史研究序説 (An Introduction to the Study of Japanese Immigration History). Hiroshima: Keisuisha.

"Loss to Port Seen in Bill." 1927. *Los Angeles Times*, February 20.

Minamikawa, Fuminori 南川文里. 2007. 「日系アメリカ人」の歴史社会学：エスニシティ、人種、ナショナリズム (Historical Sociology of "Japanese Americans": Ethnicity, Race and Nationalism). Tōkyō: Sairyūsha.

移民ニ関スル統計及調査関係雑件 在外本邦人々員並送金額調査 第4巻 (Miscellaneous Records on Statistics and Surveys about Emigrants: Surveys of the Number of, and the Amount of Remittances Sent by, the Overseas Japanese, vol. 4). 1931. Archived material, Record Group J.1.2.0.J8–2. Diplomatic Archives of the Ministry of Foreign Affairs of Japan, Tōkyō, Japan.

Queenan, Charles F. 1983. *The Port of Los Angeles: From Wilderness to World Port*. Los Angeles: Los Angeles Harbor Department.

登録者カード (Registrants' Cards) 1909–1941. Archived material, Japanese American Research Project: Boxes 164–225. Charles E. Young Research Library, University of California, Los Angeles.

Ritsumeikan Daigaku Jinbun Kagaku Kenkyūjo 立命館大学人文科学研究所, ed. 1964. 湖東移民村の研究 (The Study of Emigrant Villages of Kotō). Special issue, *Memoirs of the Research Institute of the Cultural Sciences of Ritsumeikan University*, 14.

Ryono, Robert. 1994. *Although Patriotic, We Were Drydocked*. N.p.: n.p. Book, Permanent Collection, Japanese American National Museum, Los Angeles, CA.

サンピードロ (四日) 日本古典紹かいに大成功を収めたる公立学校雛祭 ("San Pedro [on the 4th]: The Public School's Doll Day Festival Makes a Great Success in Introducing Japanese Classics.") 1932. *Kashū Mainichi Shimbun*. March 5.

Taiji Chōshi Kanshū Iinkai 太地町史監修委員会, ed. 1979. 太地町史 (The History of Taiji Town). Taiji-chō: Taiji-chō Yakuba.

Taiji Jinjō Kōtō Shōgakkō 太地尋常高等小学校. Ca. 1902–1914. 性行録 (Records of Characters and Behaviors). Archived material, Taiji Historical Archives, Taiji, Wakayama, Japan.

———. Ca. 1923–1940. 寄贈賞品授与名簿 (The List of Donated Gifts Conferred). Archived material, Taiji Historical Archives, Taiji, Wakayama, Japan.

———. Ca. 1936–1940. 個性調査簿 (Records of Characters). Archived material, Taiji Historical Archives, Taiji, Wakayama, Japan.

Taijikō Takushokubu 太地校拓殖部. Ca. 1931–1933. 太地町海外発展状況調 (Survey of the Overseas Development of Taiji Town). Archived material, Taiji Historical Archives, Taiji, Wakayama, Japan.

Takeuchi, Kōsuke 竹内幸助, ed. 1937. サンピドロ同胞発展録 (Records of the Development of the Comrades in San Pedro). Los Angeles: Kōsuke Takeuchi.

Terminal School. 1938. 雛祭プログラム (The Doll Day Program). Pamphlet, File: East San Pedro School—Terminal School. San Pedro Bay Historical Archives, Los Angeles, CA.

U.S. Census. 1930. California. Los Angeles County. Population schedule. Ancestry Library Edition, ancestry.com.

Wakayama-ken 和歌山県. 1933. 和歌山縣統計書 昭和6年 (Statistical Periodical of Wakayama Prefecture, 1931). Wakayama: Wakayama-ken.

———, ed. 1957. 和歌山県移民史 (The History of Emigration from Wakayama Prefecture). Wakayama: Wakayama-ken.

Yamada, Chikako 山田千香子. 2000. カナダ日系社会の文化変容:「海を渡った日本の村」三世代の変遷 (The Cultural Transformation of the Nikkei Society in Canada: Three-Generational Changes in the "Japanese Village That Crossed the Ocean"). Tōkyō: Ochanomizu Shobō.

Zangs, Mary. [1991] 1999. *Terminal Island History*. 2nd ed. Special issue, *Shoreline* 19 (1).

CHAPTER 5

Vernacular Representations of Race and the Making of a Japanese Ethnoracial Community in Los Angeles

Fuminori Minamikawa

Vernacular Representations and the Translation of Racism

Translation is a critical factor in Japanese American studies, especially studies on first-generation immigrants (Issei) in the United States. Most Japanese immigrants lived in a world with two different languages: Japanese and English. Thus, the act of translation between two languages was a foundational part of their everyday practices. When we think of how they experienced American racism and found a collective identity as "Japanese" in the early twentieth century, the process of translation, interpretation, and accommodation should be considered from, among others, sociological and historical perspectives.

How did racism in the United States shape the immigrants' communal identification as "Japanese"? This chapter focuses on the cognitive aspect of immigrants' representations of their communities. The cognitive approach to culture, ethnicity, and race emphasizes that collectivity enters into immigrants' lives through frameworks that enable them to understand their social position in a foreign land (DiMaggio 1997). Japanese immigrants usually interpreted racism by drawing from the vocabulary they already had in their native, or vernacular, language. Racism, which deeply affected the immigrants, took the form of a denial of their human dignity, physical violence, and institutional restrictions. Therefore, racial minorities such as the Japanese sought phrases and vocabularies from different cultural repertories and combined them into new schema in order to explain, understand,

and fight against racial representations that negated their existence in the United States. Thus, the vernacular representations that Japanese immigrants created through their vocabularies usually had multiple, unstable, and transitive bases that existed across cultures, languages, and places. As is the case with Rogers Brubaker's term the "ethnic way of seeing," which describes the lenses through which ethnic minorities see the world, the "immigrant way of seeing" is constructed through translation between different languages, terminologies, and significations.[1]

The issue of translation also relates to a methodological question in Japanese American studies. Japanese American historiography developed on both sides of the Pacific. Although knowledge of the Japanese language is necessary for understanding the "immigrant way of seeing," many historical writings have not engaged in critical surveys of Japanese-language primary sources such as newspapers, organization materials, and personal narratives.[2] With the transnational turn in the study of Asian American history in the 1990s that was brought about by scholars who used their language abilities to interpret immigrants' vernacular language, dialogues between scholars on the Japan side and those on the American side have led to a revision of the account of early Japanese immigration history. Japanese-language newspapers such as *Rafu Shimpo* and *Nichibei Shimbun* have become the most frequently used materials in this new "transnational" historiography, and they have contributed to a deepening of our understanding of first-generation immigrants' experiences. Analyses of Japanese-language materials have provided us with access to the details of what was going on within the immigrant community and the variety of their reactions to their environments (Ichioka 1988; Hayashi 1995; Kumei 1995; Sakaguchi 2001; Azuma 2005).

However, how "deep" has this dialogue gone? A false assumption is that scholars in Japan can understand the vernacular world of Japanese immigrants through their native language. Historical analyses must start by recognizing that vernacular discourses surrounding Issei immigrants were very different from present-day understandings of race and ethnicity both in Japan and the United States. We must understand these discourses as things constructed in their respective contexts.[3] While from the outside it might appear that people who use a vernacular language are homogeneous and share a genuine group culture, vernacular languages are in fact entities that continually change in response to their temporal and spatial contexts. A gap also exists when translating vernacular words into their English counterparts. The translation often misses the creativity and multiplicity of the vernacular.[4] The contributions of scholars who can take advantage of Japanese-language sources are neither as "native informants" nor "translators" of the Japanese immigrants' vernacular world. If the role of language is not so simple, what purpose does trans-Pacific dialogue serve? If exact translation is impossible, why should we focus on vernacular discourses?

This chapter will serve as a reflexive intervention in this trans-Pacific dialogue by acknowledging such difficulties in dealing with vernacular vocabularies. This does not mean that efforts for dialogue are in vain. Rather, I hope to increase the critical ability of this dialogue to think about race, ethnicity, and nation in the trans-Pacific world. Vernacular representation is not a literal text through which scholars can find the "true" meaning of what Japanese immigrants wrote and spoke. It is a "social text" that must be understood in relation to a particular context (Spivak 2010). This chapter depicts the crystallization of a vernacular imagination based on Japanese immigrants' lived experiences of mobility and suffering as well as their reactions to them across nations. Through an analysis of this vernacular imagination, we will be able to more clearly understand the U.S. conception of race, its interpretation by Japanese migrants, and shared constructions of racisms in the two nations in the context of trans-Pacific imperial expansions in the early twentieth century.

Vernacular representation has been a classic topic in the study of immigration and adaptation (Viswanath and Arora 2000). The vernacular press provides immigrants with important information about the host society, facilitates their adaptation, and finally helps assimilate them into mainstream American society (Park 1922, 87–88). However, scholarship on the topic has underestimated the immigrants' ability to resist racist expressions that are found in the dominant language of a host society.[5] Self-representations in a vernacular language can produce discourses that counter stereotypes, prejudices, and biased images of minorities. However, as other theorists have noted, people's interpretations of their everyday lives in "racial terms" often reinforce the hegemony of race. Racial formation theory emphasizes that minorities' self-representation can lead them to "consent" to the social structure's racial order (Omi and Winant 2015, 132). This chapter shares those studies' understanding of the vernacular as being multifaceted and contradictory and seeks to understand how vernacular representations that were a reaction to American racism created a discursive space in the making of an ethnoracial community of Japanese immigrants in Los Angeles.

Japanese immigrants in the early twentieth-century United States were usually defined as an immigrant-based ethnic group as well as a non-white racial group.[6] Their vernacular representations were involved in the social formation of race and ethnicity in the country. This study deals with how the vernacular media portrayed Japanese people in American society. Histories of those media depictions portray the "Japanese" community in the United States as a product of contradictory and intertwining group formations. I use the term "ethnoracial formation" to highlight the process by which Japanese immigrants molded a collective self by reacting to their racialized image as a colored group in the United States and identifying themselves as an immigrant-based ethnic group (Minamikawa 2007, 2011). This production of vernacular representations involved interpretation, translation, appropriation, and articulation of the concept of "Japanese" as an ethnoracial group at the intersection of racism and migration in the early twentieth century.

Japanese immigrant leaders in business, religion, and politics argued over the nature of American society. Faced with the anti-Japanese campaigns, they came to understand the contradictions of Americanism and racism.[7] Furthermore, they attempted to mobilize their community members to counter this contradictory Americanism. These discussions, which sought to understand the state of Americanism and mobilize co-ethnics, were conducted mostly in Japanese in vernacular newspapers and at community meetings.

Japanese immigrant leaders produced various vernacular representations to interpret their daily experiences in a foreign country by using and modifying familiar frames and schemas that they brought from their homeland. Those representations were usually made and consumed by the leaders and members with education and interests. They did not always share interests of lower-class immigrants, women, and other powerless people in their community. Rather, as this chapter discusses, vernacular representation was a part of a mechanism to mobilize community resources and discipline co-ethnic members. Thus, the vernacular language itself was a medium in the making of an ethnoracial community in the face of racism.[8]

In the next two sections, I explore the kinds of vocabulary used in Japanese immigrants' vernacular representations of themselves in Los Angeles in the face of anti-Japanese racism from the late 1910s to the early 1920s. Here, I highlight two Japanese terms: *minzoku* and *jinshu*. After examining how Japanese immigrants' self-representation constructed an ethnoracial community of Japanese people, I consider how the vernacular imagination enriches the trans-Pacific dialogue in Japanese American studies.

Minzoku: Nation, Ethnicity, and Race Intertwined

"Jap" and *"Yamato minzoku"*

Los Angeles is a focal point of Japanese immigration history in the United States. Little Tokyo in Los Angeles was a center of politics, economy, and culture for Japanese immigrant communities on the West Coast. The increasing visibility of Japanese immigrants in the urban center as well as in the rural spaces of Southern California in the early twentieth century caused anti-Japanese campaigns to spread rapidly. Those campaigns sought the restriction of Japanese economic activities and an end to immigration from Japan through legal actions, legislative controls, boycotts, and even physical violence.

Many Japanese immigrants experienced the anti-Japanese campaign as one of being forced into the foreign category "Jap." The campaign brought adversity and suffering for those who did not yet possess a national identity as Japanese. For example, a Terminal Island fisherman interpreted the campaign as a competition with other racial groups in the same line of business, saying, "We compete for fish with other white fishermen, you see. They called us 'Japs,' so we kicked them and ran away" (Sarasohn 1983, 61). Another Japanese man, in the United States for just three days, expressed that he did not know what "Jap" and "Yellow" meant, but he realized that he was "Jap" and "Yellow" after experiencing such name-calling "many times" (Uono 1927, 101). For most Japanese immigrants, the first experience of American racism was in their encounter with the category "Jap" in their workplaces and on the streets. Such categorization was accompanied by restrictions of rights, limited opportunities, and obstruction of upward mobility for immigrant workers, the self-employed, farmers, and business leaders. Thus, the anti-Japanese movement led them to realize that they had a shared interest in protecting their livelihoods. Economic survival was their primary concern when they vernacularly represented American racism.

The counter-discourse in vernacular newspapers and community documents reflects how Japanese leaders expressed themselves in their native language amid anti-Japanese racism. The Japanese term *"minzoku"* or *"Yamato minzoku"* frequently appeared in these media to express their collective self-image.[9] *Yamato* was a name of the ruling dynasty in ancient Japan from which the emperors of Japan were thought to have descended. *Yamato minzoku* usually referred to the "Japanese nation," that shared the myth of such ancestry. For example, a resolution by the Japanese Association of Los Angeles in 1919 articulated the Japanese immigrant experience in America in terms of *minzoku:*

> In the gloomy environment of anti-Japanese campaigns, a still institutionally and psychologically flawed Japanese community is under siege. Solidarity and unity are indispensable for developing the foundation of the *Yamato minzoku* on American soil. In all cases, Japanese must demonstrate the character of their *minzoku*, which is based on justice and humanity, and achieve glorious triumph in all fields of economic battle. (Rafu Nihonjinkai 1919a, 152)

In that resolution, immigrant leaders understood *minzoku* to be essential for the economic survival of the Japanese in the United States. Why did they choose the term *minzoku* to represent themselves in the face of racism?

At the time, *minzoku* was used as a popular term that described the national identity of the Japanese, a political slogan of the new Meiji government, and a concept in social sciences, including ethnology (*minzokugaku* in Japanese), anthropology, and sociology, since the late nineteenth century. Usually accompanied by the prefix *Yamato* or *Nippon/Nihon* (Japanese), it was as a "conflation of phenotype, geography, culture, spirit, history, and nationhood" (Robertson 2002, 195). The flexibility and multiplicity of the meaning of *minzoku* is a key in interpreting the vernacular discourse of Japanese immigrant leaders.[10]

Multiple Significations of *Minzoku*

Japanese immigrant leaders usually explained events involving them using the term *minzoku* to refer to the nation of Japan. For example, they often expressed their struggles against the anti-Japanese campaigns as "a trial for *Yamato minzoku*." Especially after Japan's victory in the Russo-Japanese War in 1905, a reason given for their exclusion in the United States was the presence of the *Yamato minzoku* in international politics (*Rafu Shimpo,* September 7, 1920). The articles in vernacular newspapers described the Japanese as a people "who in the competition of civilizations are part of the top group of the Great World Powers" (*Rafu Shimpo,* July 27, 1919). The position of their homeland was a source of pride for immigrant leaders, who also believed that Japanese immigrants should be gentle and law-abiding representatives of their nation to promote "international understanding" between Japan and the United States (*Rafu Shimpo,* March 11, 1919). Such nationalistic attachment also enabled them to counter negative images of "Jap" with their collective self-identity as *Yamato minzoku.* All those who suffered from anti-Japanese racism could identify as such and see themselves as sharing common interests with fellow Japanese.

In addition to its nationalistic meaning, the term *minzoku* was used to represent an ethnic identity as a minority group in American society. *Rafu Shimpo* editorials shared a pluralistic interpretation of the United States:

> Because American society has always been like an assembly (*yoriai-setai*) of immigrants from nations all over the world, impartial consideration and amicability towards all is most important. . . . The United States has embraced people from different nations who have different natures, customs, languages, traditions, and so on. It has done a good job of Americanizing them while they have contributed to strengthening of Americanism. . . . You should not forget that demonstrating the unique virtues and strengths of our *minzoku* would further improve the already great nature of the American nation. (*Rafu Shimpo,* October 24, 1924)

This article defines the Japanese community as a part of "an assembly of immigrants from nations all over the world." That interpretation of the United States as a country of immigrants enabled them to envision an egalitarian pluralism in which Japanese formed a part of the national community. There were several articles that expressed Americanism in terms of "impartiality," "equal treatment," and "egalitarianism," even in the era of anti-Japanese campaigns (*Rafu Shimpo,* September 5, 1924). In addition to the discourse of a nation of nations, Los Angeles was a cosmopolitan city and was called "the New York in the West Coast," where immigrants came from all regions of the world.[11] Editorials in Japanese-language newspapers saw the development of the *Yamato minzoku* in the United States as something that would strengthen "the already great nature of the American nation." In this case, the *minzoku* ideology of Japanese nationalism was transplanted into the discourse of ethnicity in a nation of immigrants. Japanese immigrants were able to employ the idea of "cultural pluralism" at least in their vernacular discursive productions.

Finally, *minzoku* was connected with the ideology of race. An editorial in *Rafu Shimpo* discussed "racial" roots of the *Yamato minzoku* to support Ozawa Takao, who sought to redefine Japanese Americans' position in policies involving U.S. citizenship in the early 1920s:

> The United States . . . has categorized non-black races as being part of the white race. Japanese, Chinese, Mexicans, East Indians, Syrians and so on are categorized as being part of the white race. It is a clear fact that within people who are generally called white there are races that have mixed with Orientals. . . . According to ethnologists, the ancestors of the *Yamato minzoku* were the white *Ainu* tribe as well as Mongolian, Malaysian, and other tribes. . . . Therefore, the point at issue in the court cases relating to Japanese who have applied to be naturalized is whether or not the *Nihon minzoku* belongs to the white race or not. (*Rafu Shimpo*, September 13, 1922)

This article justifies Ozawa's claim that "the root stocks and the dominant strain of the Japanese are of the white race" in terms of ethnological understandings of race (*New York Times,* August 6, 1921, 7).[12] The author emphasizes the resemblance between Ainu, the indigenous inhabitants of Hokkaido, and Russians not only in appearance such as "bone structure, skin color, and hairiness" but also with regard to their "manners, customs and language" (*Rafu Shimpo,* September 13, 1922).[13] In this case, *minzoku* was understood in terms of the time's anthropological or ethnological interpretation of race.

Thus, in the era of anti-Japanese movements, Japanese immigrants' representations of their *minzoku* defined their group position and collective identity in multiple ways. Anti-Japanese hysteria taught them the contradictory character of Americanism. Its civic ideals allowed them to develop arguments against racist campaigns. Even in the vernacular newspapers, editorials and resolutions often cited phrases from historical documents such as the Declaration of Independence and the U.S. Constitution.[14] By combining the multiple ideological frames of the term *minzoku* with the civic ideals in the United States, Japanese leaders produced a vernacular self-representation against the racism that targeted them.

Embracing *Jinshu:* Racial Worldviews among Japanese Immigrants

Jinshu in Interracial Relations in Los Angeles

Minzoku was not the only term used by Japanese immigrants to address their experiences of racism in the United States. *Jinshu* (usually referred to as "race" in English) appeared in daily discussions and representations in the vernacular world of Japanese immigrants, though less frequently than *minzoku*. Several articles on the *jinshu mondai* (race problem) in *Rafu Shimpo* reported on the system of racial segregation in the South and efforts to improve conditions among blacks.[15] In many cases when they used the term *jinshu*, it was in reference to the "black-white problem" in U.S. society.

Jinshu referred to the "race problem" in U.S. history and was used to imply prejudice, discrimination, and conflicts based on color. The *Rafu Shimpo* published several articles titled *"Jinshu Kannen"* (The Concept of Race) that dealt with conflicts between Japanese and other racial minorities (*Rafu Shimpo,* January 24, 1922; May 9, 1923). One of them reported an arson attack on a Japanese school in Sacramento committed by Mexicans and African Americans. The author of the column was shocked at the fact that racial minorities, who must have had similar experiences of oppression due to American racism, were suspects in the fire. The column then called on Japanese readers to think of their treatment of those racial minorities instead of attacking the suspects:

> Many Japanese have a tendency to call Mexicans *meki* and blacks *kuronbo*. It goes without saying that it cannot be denied that in these words there is contempt. If you criticize exclusion and dislike being despised, why don't you respect these racial minorities like they are of the same race? (*Rafu Shimpo,* May 9, 1923)

In fact, many vernacular articles depicted blacks and Mexicans as mean and dangerous criminals. For example, the phrase *"meki-doro"* (Mexican robber) frequently appeared in the local-news pages of the *Rafu Shimpo* (June 25, 1924; July 22, 1924). Some stories referred to black criminals as *"niga"* (nigger), *"kokudo"* (black slave), and *"jū-jin"* (a beast of a man) (*Rafu Shimpo,* October 12, 1924; March 25, 1925). In addition, they often made a clear distinction between *"rettō"* (inferior) eastern and southern European newcomers such as Italians and Russians and other *"kōtō hakujin"* (high-class whites) (*Rafu Shimpo Sha* 1914). Those representations suggest that

Japanese immigrants internalized the basic racial worldview in the United States through their daily lives in Los Angeles. In the popular images shared by Japanese immigrants, "high-class" whites were on the top, "inferior" Europeans in the middle, and blacks and Mexicans on the bottom (also see Almaguer 1994).

At the same time, some editorials not only criticized Japanese immigrants' feelings of superiority toward blacks and Mexicans but also persuaded Japanese readers to eliminate racial prejudice in their neighbors.[16] Many articles insisted that their economic survival in Los Angeles depended on the patronage of other racial minorities. This was especially true for entrepreneurs, who were the main readership of *Rafu Shimpo*. For them, the shift of their customer base from Japanese to non-Japanese was an urgent issue in the 1920s. Japanese small businesses found new markets in the eastern and southern parts of downtown Los Angeles where Mexicans, Jews, and blacks lived (Minamikawa 2007, 82–83). Articles said that *ta-jinshu* (other races) or *gaijin* (foreigners; in other words, non-Japanese people) should be new customers and clients of Japanese businesses (*Rafu Shimpo*, September 26, 1924; December 8, 1924). In addition, Mexicans were also recognized as a potential workforce for small farms run by Japanese in the surrounding area (*Rafu Shimpo*, May 9, 1923). The expansion of Japanese immigrant businesses pressed the businessmen to change their attitudes toward their new clients and employees. In this way, their campaign against racial discrimination was a part of Japanese entrepreneurs' economic strategy.

Pride of the "Yellow" Race: Through the Lens of Global Racial Politics

Interestingly, Japanese immigrant leaders thought that racial conflicts were also international or global issues. They frequently cited the idea of *jinshu byōdō* (racial equality), which the Japanese delegation advocated in a proposal to the Paris Peace Conference in 1919 (*Rafu Shimpo*, May 9, 1923). The concept of *jinshu* provided a perspective through which they could understand local incidents in terms of international politics at the time. In the vernacular press, global geopolitics was interpreted as a competition among races. The Japanese identified themselves with the *yūshoku jinshu* (colored race) or *ōshoku jinshu* (yellow race) (*Rafu Shimpo*, September 7, 1920). That viewpoint allowed immigrants to connect anti-Japanese nativism in California with larger issues that stretched the trans-Pacific region from British Canada to China, Manchuria, and Russia (Akahori n.d.).

In their reactions to trans-Pacific anti-Japanese campaigns, Japanese immigrants insisted that they should embody the idea of "racial equality" first by eliminating their prejudice against, contempt for, and discrimination toward other racial minorities. Otherwise, they argued, they would render invalid their homeland government's appeal at the Paris Peace Conference. A *Rafu Shimpo* correspondent in Tokyo emphasized the equality of foreigners in Japan, reporting that "Japanese treat foreigners equally regardless of their *jinshu* and there is no exclusion of Koreans or Chinese" (*Rafu Shimpo*, August 1, 1924).[17] Those self-representations of Japanese as seekers of racial equality partially corresponded with the rhetoric of the Japanese government's propaganda that was used to claim its share as a great power in the Asia-Pacific. The American public also perceived Ozawa's petition for U.S. citizenship and Japanese immigrants' support of him as part of the Japanese government's effort to hold a position as a great power in global politics. According to the *New York Times*, Ozawa's appeal had attracted public attention because his theory was associated with the Japanese government's propositions in the Paris Peace Conference (*New York Times*, August 6, 1921).

However, Ozawa lost his case in 1922, and this changed the discourse surrounding racial issues among Japanese immigrants. In the case of *United States v. Bhagat Singh Thind* in 1923, the U.S. Supreme Court decided that "Asian" was a distinct race in U.S. society. An editorial in the *Rafu Shimpo* after the decision insisted that Japanese immigrants were proud of being yellow even though the court did not accept the view that the Japanese shared a common origin with the white race. It highlighted that the Japanese embodied "the essence of Eastern Civilization" in order to "contribute to the development of world cultures," and it went on to claim the Japanese race to be "more advanced than whites who have exaggerated the fruit of Western Civilization" (*Rafu Shimpo*, November 16, 1922).

Trans-Pacific cultural politics following the enactment of the Immigration Act of 1924 in the United States accelerated the "Easternization" of the construction of the Japanese race in the vernacular press. The *Rafu Shimpo* interpreted the first Conference of the Institute of Pacific Relations held in Honolulu in 1925 through the lens of white-yellow interracial politics (*Rafu Shimpo*, July 26, 1925). The Japan-based political pundit Yusuke Tsurumi visited the Japanese community in Los Angeles after participating in the conference and delivered a lecture titled "Reconstruction of Asian Civilization." His lecture reportedly emphasized Japan's leading role among the "colored races" against white Western Civilization (*Rafu Shimpo*, August 11,

1925; August 12, 1925). Thus, in the face of the reality of U.S. racism, the vernacular self-representation of the Japanese gradually shifted from that of optimistic seekers of racial equality to an ethnocentric and self-oriented identity as a representative of the colored races.

Social Theory of *Jinshu:* Assimilation and Racial Struggle

The concept of *jinshu* in vernacular representations of Japanese immigrants in Los Angeles in the early 1920s was based on academic knowledge of social sciences. Japanese immigrant leaders were actively interested in the sociological discussion surrounding assimilation and recognized that they were one of the "subjects" of such research.[18] In January 1924, Robert Ezra Park, a leading sociologist from the University of Chicago, visited Little Tokyo and met Jisaburo Kasai, the chief secretary of the Japanese Association of Los Angeles, to explain his academic project, "Survey of Race Relations on the Pacific Coast." An article reported the conversation between Kasai and Park as follows:

> When Mr. Kasai asked whether the Japanese problem was an economic problem or a race problem (*jinshu mondai*), Dr. Park said, "The Japanese problem is apparently a race problem, not an economic problem." Then, Mr. Kasai asked what he thought of the Negro problem in the South and the Japanese problem in the Pacific. The doctor told us, "Negroes are too large in number to assimilate. I have dealt with the problem. But it is very difficult to find a good solution for Negroes. In contrast, Japanese are small in number and are expected to assimilate in a few generations. It is thinkable that your physical appearances will change as you live longer in the United States." (*Rafu Shimpo,* January 20, 1924)

The article underlined that Japanese were a "race group" in the United States; however, it did not liken them to African Americans. Kasai and other leaders adopted the concept of race from sociology in order to identify themselves as an "assimilable" group in the United States and distinguish themselves from other racial minorities. For Japanese immigrant leaders, the "race problem" was a problem of assimilation both in a cultural and physical sense. The sociological theory of race relations by the Chicago school at the time defined racial conflict as the step that precedes accommodation and assimilation (Park and Burgess 1921, 738). The theory enabled Japanese leaders to cite changes and transformations in the Japanese immigrant community as a sign of their gradual assimilation. That understanding spread throughout the Japanese community through vernacular media such as the *Rafu Shimpo,* supporting Japanese immigrants' claims to membership in U.S. society.

Like the English-language concept of race in the early twentieth century, the concept of *jinshu* as it appeared in the vernacular media often provided a reductionist view of group relations (cf. Smedley 2007). Some articles used a social Darwinist idea of race to understand the situation of Japanese immigrants. For example, a series of articles written by Gyumu Usuda introduced concepts of "Aryanism" and *jinshu tōsō* (racial struggle), both of which had been proposed by the French ethnologist Joseph-Arthur Gobineau (*Rafu Shimpo,* December 24, 1924). Usuda had internalized a white supremacist worldview so deeply that he could not consider the possibility of a harmonious future among white, yellow, and black races (*Rafu Shimpo,* December 28, 1924). Therefore, the vernacular representations of *jinshu* at that time among Japanese immigrants inherited the contradictions of race in academic discourses. Although they shared fatalist and reductionist understandings of racial conflicts, many Japanese immigrant leaders did not abandon the idea proposed by sociologists that assimilation was possible.

In sum, the idea of *jinshu* in vernacular discourses did not simply burden Japanese immigrants. The translation of the concept of race through the compound *jinshu* gave Japanese immigrants a way to understand the oppression of U.S. racial minorities, or provided a source of pride as members of the yellow race, and it offered theoretical authority for claims for "assimilation." Those multiple and contradictory meanings of *jinshu* supplied Japanese immigrants with a sense of their group position in the racial structures of the time.

How Did Vernacular Representations Form the Communal Discourse of Japanese Immigrants?

Vernacularization and the Patchwork of *Minzoku* and *Jinshu*

In Japan, the immigrants' homeland, there was no clear distinction between the two terms *minzoku* and *jinshu,* even among intellectuals. Since the late 1880s, both terms had become entangled with each other and gradually spread into academic and popular discourses. During the pioneer period of Japanese anthropology in the Meiji era, scholars called people who lived in Japan *Nihon jinshu* (the Japanese race). While those anthropologists defined *jinshu* in biological terms, in the early Taishō era (1910s) the term *minzoku* was introduced as a subject for cultural and historical research on groups of people.[19] Nonetheless, the two terms were still intertwined and mixed in popular usages with no definite meanings in the mainstream media.

Generally, in vernacular representations in Southern California, Japanese immigrants seemed to use *minzoku* as a term for self-identification, and they represented *jinshu* as a category that they met in the foreign land. However, it is difficult to find a sharp distinction between the usages of the two terms. Immigrant intellectuals and leaders did not necessarily understand what those concepts meant academically in Japan. Rather, their vernacular discourse was formed as a "patchwork" or "bricolage," and thus terms with different meanings could be used interchangeably. With the reality of forced categorization and racialization, the expression, signification, and definition of their daily lives with terms and ideas readily available was more important than distinguishing between their precise meanings.

Such a vernacular patchwork of representations of *minzoku* and *jinshu* brought immigrants of different classes, local origins, and gender backgrounds into an ethnoracial "community" of Japanese people in Los Angeles. Fundamentally, this communal identification was a result of anti-Japanese racism, which lumped them together as "Jap."

Vernacular representations became a basis of resistance to the stigmatized category of "Jap." *Minzoku* ideology enabled Japanese immigrants to transform the appellation into a collective identity so they could survive in the restrictive opportunity structure of the local political economy. As part of the development of their *minzoku,* they took advantage of resources and networks to establish a solidarity that connected different sectors of the ethnic economy. They proclaimed themselves "pioneers of development" in vernacular narratives (*Rafu Shimpo,* New Year special edition, January 1, 1917; *Rafu Shimpo,* June 21, 1922; Fujioka 1927). However, this did not mean Japanese immigrants established a self-sufficient enclave in Los Angeles. In the early 1920s, their project of *minzoku* development necessitated new patronage from Mexicans, non-WASP European immigrant workers, and blacks in Los Angeles's multiracial neighborhoods. The vernacular interpretations of *jinshu byōdō* (racial equality) in the Japanese-language press were also part of the strategy of economic survival under the limited circumstances.

Vernacular vocabularies allowed Japanese immigrants to challenge the definition of race in a nativist, racist United States. Those vocabularies were shaped by the trans-Pacific formation of the nation and empire of Japan, as well as civic and racial America. Japanese immigrants translated theories of assimilation, racial struggle, and civic U.S. nationalism into a vernacular theory of *minzoku* and *jinshu*. They combined them with ethnological and popular discourses surrounding "Japaneseness" from their homeland. That melding was developed to resist the fixing of racial hierarchies by outsiders and to define their own group position in the hierarchical order of Southern California.

Adjustment, Accommodation, and Racialization

This vernacular discursive space for Japanese immigrants not only opposed racism but also allowed immigrants to adjust to the existing social order of U.S. racial structures. That resistance usually shared the racialized social images of the time. Even when they sought "racial equality" among minorities in Los Angeles, Japanese immigrants used the terminology of racial hierarchy, such as *rettō* (inferior) whites, *meki, kuronbo,* and other derogatory terms that referred to racial minorities. At the same time, their active appropriation of *minzoku* ideology did not contradict the mechanism of racial stratification in the United States. Japanese immigrant leaders were convinced that they, as pioneers in the development of the *Yamato minzoku,* were "civilized" and thus could be a part of American civilization. The Russo-Japanese War was thought to be a proof that Japanese immigrants could compete with at least "inferior" newcomers from Europe in the middle of the racial hierarchy. As will be discussed later in detail, *minzoku* ideology also helped them to differentiate themselves from the Chinese with regard to their moral superiority and civilized characteristics (*Rafu Shimpo,* June 10, 1919; July 27, 1919).

Those representations and practices did not fundamentally challenge the hierarchy based on racial categories that were determined in the discursive structure of whiteness (cf. Ngai 2004, 43). Their redefinition of Japanese within that hierarchy did not change one of the underlying measures that formed the basis of racial formation in the United States: the ability to learn, understand, and realize a civilized (American) way of life. Japanese immigrant leaders internalized the rules of racial formation in their production of vernacular articulations of *minzoku* and *jinshu*. While they believed that the ability to adapt to the American way of life was indispensable to eliminate racial prejudice against the "Jap," whites believed that only whites possessed that ability.[20] In the face of their predicament as a non-white immigrant group, the Japanese relied on the "international" discourse of *minzoku* and *jinshu*. The concepts of *minzoku* and *jinshu byōdō* evolved from the idea that white civilization was the standard of the social order in the post–World War I era and that among the colored racial groups only the Japanese could meet its requirements. In this case, racialization through *minzoku* and *jinshu* was an adaptation to the racialized ideology of international politics that their home country was eager to embrace. Thus, these vernacular representations taught every Japanese immigrant the rules of racism and nationalism.

Devices for Community Control to Discipline Immigrants

During the 1910s and 1920s, voices in the vernacular were dominated by Japanese immigrant leaders. Rarely were ordinary Japanese immigrants such as workers and immigrant women given the opportunity to participate in the production of vernacular discourses. Rather, they found themselves as the objects and targets of such male, immigrant leader discourses. In that way, the Japanese vernacular world was, like the social world, hierarchical in terms of class, gender, and sexuality.

As Andrea Geiger has shown (see chapter 6 in this volume), Japanese immigrant leaders already held hierarchical views that originated from the historical caste system in their homeland. Their vision of modernization usually negotiated the borders of "Japanese" through practices of inclusion and exclusion. The Japanese Association and the Japanese consulate in Los Angeles shared the urgent need to discipline and control what they considered to be pre-modern, non-civilized, and un-American features to build a model community of "Japanese." Vernacular representations became a means by which to educate its members and define who should be included and excluded from the community.

To fight against anti-Japanese campaigns, Japanese immigrants tried to prove that they embodied the ideas of modern values and moral integrity that derived from early twentieth-century progressivism in the United States. Community institutions such as Japanese associations and religious organizations teamed up with the vernacular media to conduct moral reform campaigns in Little Tokyo.[21] Terms relating to the concept of *minzoku* appeared in the headlines promoting reform in the vernacular press. Targeting "Chinese gambling houses in Little Tokyo," those forces featured anti-gambling as a central moral reform issue in their campaign. They held that gambling was a symptom of "Sinification," in which Chinese "vice" brought moral corruption to the Japanese immigrant community. Those appeals were grounded in *minzoku* discourse that emphasized the gap between "half-civilized" or "colonized" China and "civilized" Japan (*Rafu Shimpo*, June 10, 1919; July 27, 1919). Ultimately, the reformers forced Chinese owners to close their gambling houses and excluded them from Little Tokyo (Minamikawa 2007, 123).

In addition to that exclusion of Chinese gambling houses from the community, the campaigners forcibly tried to keep Japanese gamblers and loafers away from gambling houses, declaring that gambling addiction was a "shame of [their] *minzoku*" (Rafu Nihonjinkai 1919b, 18; *Rafu Shimpo*, June 10, 1919). The executive board members of the Japanese Association of Los Angeles picketed gambling houses to persuade gamblers to quit. After a shooting incident involving several Japanese gamblers in August 1919, the Japanese consulate and the Japanese Association in Los Angeles established an organization that sought to expatriate the "troublemakers" and gambling addicts "in order to clean up the Japanese community" (Rafu Nihonjinkai 1919a, 166). The vernacular *minzoku* and *jinshu* discourses aided in those campaigns, which aimed to distinguish among "Orientals" and to establish racial purity and moral discipline in their Los Angeles community.[22]

Immigrant women who worked in bars, bathhouses, and brothels were also the targets of the moral reform campaigns. They portrayed the job of *shakufu* (bar hostess) held by young, unmarried women and often called "a special profession" and "an attractive feature of [the] dark-side Little Tokyo" as immoral and the bars as a site of vice. Gangs and traffickers deceived *shakufu* and sold them to brothels (*Rafu Shimpo*, June 1–June 5, 1919; July 2, 1919). City authorities and anti-Japanese activists often inaccurately mixed up the phenomenon of "picture brides" with the human trafficking system that targeted people engaged in the "professional" jobs (Gardner 2005, 39). Reformers attacked the *shakufu* system as one that exploited poor immigrant women economically, morally, and sexually. As a result of that moral reform campaign by immigrant leaders in the late 1910s, *shakufu* disappeared suddenly from the Little Tokyo district (*Rafu Shimpo*, July 2, 1919; Rafu Nihonjinkai 1919b, 41). The anti-*shakufu* campaign complemented the "Americanization" movement, which established norms for the immigrant family in which the proper role of the woman was as a domesticized housewife (Nanka Chuo Nihonjinkai 1920, 203; *Rafu Shimpo*, August 30,

1919). Under that normative assignment of gender roles for women, unmarried "professional" women were excluded from the Japanese moral community as imagined by vernacular representations.

Modernization and discipline were critical to securing an economic base for the community. Japanese immigrant business associations utilized the vernacular-language press to control the community by severely sanctioning troublemakers. In 1921, a large network of *tanomoshi-kō* (rotating credit associations) patronized by Japanese immigrants in Los Angeles collapsed, with the damages reaching $200,000 (*Rafu Shimpo*, April 30, 1921).[23] As a result, the Japanese Chamber of Commerce and the Japanese Association of Los Angeles set guidelines to prevent a "great collapse" of those rotating credit associations. They dictated "social sanctions" for *tanomoshi* members who violated the guidelines and disrupted the ethnic economy. The sanctions included exclusion from business activities in the Los Angeles Japanese immigrant community, and the business associations often announced in the vernacular media the names of people who had broken the rules and were expelled from the *tanomoshi*.[24]

Those practices reached beyond the community in Los Angeles. Relevant articles and announcements were easily transplanted to vernacular newspapers in other areas in the United States. Furthermore, to secure the *tanomoshi-kō* created by the Japanese Chamber of Commerce of Southern California, the association ruled that the "same social sanctions must take effect in the homeland even when the troublemaker has returned to Japan." The association was supposed to transmit information regarding "troublemakers" to municipal governments, business associations, and local newspapers, which would then inform the general public in the perpetrator's hometown (Nanka Nihonjin Shogyo Kaigisho 1921, 93–95). That national and transnational network of the vernacular press allowed social sanctions to be enforced on both sides of the Pacific. Thus, the press itself functioned as a critical device for such transnational ostracism.

Vernacular representations played a significant role in the exclusion of "troublemakers" by enlightening ordinary co-ethnic community members and thereby establishing a disciplined community in the name of their *minzoku*. Those representations conveyed messages from immigrant leaders to community members, and they played a role in institutional arrangements to impose modern values on the daily lives of immigrants. In other words, vernacularization more likely served the interests of community leaders rather than working-class, female, and other powerless migrants.

Vernacular Imagination in Japanese American Studies

Racism produced a patchwork of vernacular representations that became a vehicle for immigrants to establish ethnoracial solidarity. As their flexible and multiple interpretations of *minzoku* and *jinshu* demonstrate, ethnic cohesion, assimilation, and racialization overlapped with and reinforced each other in a shared worldview of Japanese immigrants. Japanese immigrants found such flexibility not only in the discourse surrounding those concepts in Japan; they translated and used U.S. narratives of ethnicity, nation, and race to articulate and support their arguments against anti-Japanese racism in California. The terms *minzoku* and *jinshu* played a central role in the translation of those narratives. As shown in my analysis of that vernacular imagination, Japanese immigrants found themselves at the intersection of overlapping intergroup relations in Los Angeles, in the imagined space of Japan's imperial expansion, and in the global struggle of colored people.

Little Tokyo in Los Angeles was a place where Japanese immigrant leaders articulated an idea of a "Japanese" community. As part of their resistance to anti-Japanese racism, leaders disciplined community members so that they would be "civilized" and demonstrate the "excellence" of their *minzoku* when judged by the standards of Western civilization. The intersection of social forces that advanced racialization, ethnicization, and transnationalism transformed Little Tokyo from a district where ethnic institutions were concentrated to a community that represented the collective identity of the "Japanese" people by excluding "uncivilized" members such as gamblers, "professional" women, and non-Japanese.

The interpretation of Japanese historical materials created and left by Japanese immigrants leads us to the vernacular world in which they lived. That vernacular imagination can enrich a trans-Pacific dialogue among scholars of Japanese American studies because it reveals a lived world that is very different from the one found only in English-language materials. *Minzoku* and *jinshu* were lenses through which Japanese immigrants saw U.S. racism as well as Japanese nationalism. Scholars cannot understand vernacular vocabularies without understanding their interpretative schema, which is located in a particular time and space, and the immigrants' vernacular world cannot be reduced to concepts and ideas from the English language alone. This study underlines the richness, creativity, and flexibility of the vernacular space. Moreover, Japanese immigrants' vernacular discourses should not be interpreted solely through a nationalist framework, which forces us to determine whether or not the immigrants were Japanese nationals. Such a misinterpretation denies the richness, creativity, and flexibility of the vernacular imagination of transnational migrants. Japanese immigrants were agents who built their social worlds through vernacular terms.

Early twentieth-century Japanese immigrants lived in a period when concepts of race, ethnicity, and nation were being produced in both the United States and Japan. Those concepts were fluid and thus their representations were relatively open to mistranslation and appropriation. We cannot underestimate the process of translation: the vernacular imagination shows us that immigration and adaptation have never been a one-way process. Nonetheless, the fact that those Japanese immigrants' challenges failed to halt anti-Japanese campaigns shows how dominant racism and nationalism were at the time. Perhaps they failed because those acts of resistance were not a fundamental challenge to the rule of the powerful structures of race and nation. The power of racism and nationalism reached across nations, ethnic groups, and racial boundaries through imperial expansion on both sides of the Pacific. A trans-Pacific dialogue, accordingly, between scholars across national boundaries can strengthen a sensitivity to the transnational structuring of race, ethnicity, and nation as well as to the vernacular imagination of immigrants and their struggles throughout recent centuries.

Notes

1 The cognitive approach in ethnicity theory has used the phrase the "ethnic way of seeing" to draw attention to the schemata through which "people see the world, parse their experience, and interpret events" (Brubaker 2004, 74–79).
2 Early historical work on the Japanese American experience, including that of the Japanese American Research Project in the 1960s, did not fully take advantage of the Japanese-language documents and personal narratives that the project collected from Japanese American communities across the United States. See Wilson and Hosokawa (1980).
3 Just as Renato Rosaldo has pointed out in his critique of the concept of the "ethnographic present," in which anthropologists describe "social activities as if they were *always* repeated in the same manner by *everyone* in the group" (italics added by author), ethnic studies scholars should not look at vernacular vocabulary as ahistorical (Rosaldo 1988, 42).
4 Anthony D. Smith has emphasized that in the case of European countries, vernacular mobilization has been a central part of the national project because it induces people to adopt "an 'authentic' national culture based on

pre-existing commonalities and heritage." In contrast, this paper focuses not on processes of nationalization but on why the vernacular has been important in the mobilization of people and where its power comes from (Smith 2011, 234).

5 Yasuko Takezawa has highlighted "representation as resistance" as one inseparable part of racial representations (Takezawa 2011, 15–17). Furthermore, in communication studies, vernacular discourses are seen as critical in the production of self-identity among minorities (Ono and Sloop 1995; Holling and Calafell eds. 2011). Also, vernacular representations of race are sometimes seen as an important part of the "counter public sphere" in political philosophy (Fraser 1992). Last, I would like to note that "diasporic imagination" in immigration history is another version of vernacularization as a resistance (Jacobson [1995] 2002).

6 Immigration history mainly focusing on Euro-American immigrants played a considerable role in the invention of the concept of "ethnicity" in social sciences. However, since the 1990s, whiteness studies have focused on the process by which immigrants from Europe came to think of themselves as white Americans, thereby redefining immigration history as one of racialization. Asian immigration history has also sought to rethink the concepts of ethnicity and race based on Asian immigrants' experiences as both migrants and racial minorities (Okihiro 1994; Ngai 2011).

7 Gary Gerstle has discussed how universalism in American civic nationalism coexisted with the racial exclusions of nonwhite minorities in the twentieth century (Gerstle 2001).

8 The main historical resources for vernacular representation were articles in vernacular presses. *Rafu Shimpo,* a Japanese-language newspaper circulated within the Japanese immigrant community in Southern California, is one of the richest sources to grasp their production. In the early 1920s, *Rafu Shimpo* became a dominant vernacular press among Japanese in Los Angeles. Main writers at that time were Issei male leaders, professionals, journalists, and students. This study does not view the vernacular discourses as a "subaltern" text that represents voices of the most disadvantaged people. It focuses on how the production of vernacular representations constructed an ethnoracial community that catered to interests of immigrant leaders and involved powerless immigrants in such a project. For a brief history and social influences of *Rafu Shimpo,* see Azuma (2013).

9 I would like to emphasize that vernacular terms in Japanese do not necessarily have exact English equivalents, and thus I have chosen to leave certain important terms like *minzoku* and *jinshu* in Japanese instead of translating them.

10 Azuma (2005) has pointed out that the Japanese term *minzoku* can be translated as "race," "ethnicity," or "nation." In his book, Azuma analyzes from a social history perspective these terms' identification with *minzoku* ideology and its effect on the distinct forms they took in a transnational context.

11 The description of the demography of Los Angeles found in *Rafu Nenkan* highlights the city's different population groups with their distinctive racial characteristics and economic position (*Rafu Shimpo Sha* 1914, part 5, 25–26; Nanka Nihonjin Nenkan 1921, 70).

12 Ozawa's theory of "Japanese as a white race" was partly based on the ethnographic work of Scottish physician Neil Gordon Munro (Iwata 2003, 29).

13 According to Eiji Oguma, the notion that the Japanese people were of Caucasian origin spread in popular and academic discourse in the Meiji period (1868–1912) and the Taishō period (1912–1926) in Japan (Oguma 2002, 143–155).

14 For example, the *Rafu Shimpo* introduced a resolution to resist the revision of the Alien Land Law in 1920, citing "All men are created equal" to legitimate the rights of Japanese immigrants and their American-born children (*Rafu Shimpo,* September 3, 1920).

15 *Rafu Shimpo* reported on the organizational activities of the Tuskegee Institute and the NAACP as well as their philosophies. Article topics included arguments between Booker T. Washington and W. E. B. Du Bois (*Rafu Shimpo,* July 22, 1922; April 29, 1923; November 12, 1925; December 27, 1925).

16 An article told a story about a Japanese-owned bathhouse in White Point, Southern Los Angeles, that refused to allow non-Japanese customers to take a bath (*Rafu Shimpo,* September 2, 1922).

17 Of course, this report did not accurately reflect the historical facts of Japanese colonial rule. There was harsh racial discrimination against Koreans and Chinese in Japan, and some articles in *Rafu Shimpo* concluded that Japanese colonial rule could be justified and was even beneficial to Koreans (*Rafu Shimpo,* May 15, 1923; February 23, 1925).

18 Some articles reported the plan and results of such sociological research (*Rafu Shimpo,* September 27, 1923; September 28, 1923; March 29, 1925). Shakuma Washizu, a journalist and contributor to *Rafu Shimpo,* wrote special feature articles on the "survey of race relations" carried out by dominant sociologists in the early 1920s. He also translated some pamphlets and articles into Japanese (*Rafu Shimpo,* October 3–6, 1923; Washizu 1930, 199–217). On the influence of sociological theories of race on young Nisei, see H. Yu (2001).

19 On the history of *minzoku* concept, see K. Yu (1994, 38–46). On the shift of study subject from *jinshu* to *minzoku* in Japanese anthropology, see Sakano (2005, 104–108). See also Oguma (2002).
20 According to Gary Gerstle, the advocate group that opposed immigrant restrictions in the Immigration Act of 1924 insisted that southern and eastern Europeans were able to assimilate because of their superiority to and incompatibility with non-Europeans such as Japanese, Mexicans, and African Americans (Gerstle 2001, 120–121).
21 The moral reform campaign in 1919 had four aims: punctuality, the Anglicization of signboards, assembly reform, and antigambling. These reflected the core values of the Progressive Era (Rafu Nihonjinkai 1919a, 135–137, 142–143).
22 According to the records of the Japanese Association of Los Angeles, as a result of this campaign, in Little Tokyo twelve out of the fourteen Chinese gambling houses and three out of the ten Japanese houses closed. This shows the main target of this campaign was Chinese houses rather than Japanese ones (Rafu Nihonjinkai 1919b, 162).
23 On rotating credit associations, see Light (1972, 92).
24 In *Rafu Shimpo*, the Japanese Produce Dealer's Association announced that they never deal with a certain Japanese produce broker who does business at the 9th Street Produce Market because he damaged the trust between members of his trade (*Rafu Shimpo,* November 18, 1923).

References

Akahori, Masaru 赤堀最. n.d. 吾人の診たる排日病と血清療法 (My Diagnosis on Sickness of Anti-Japanese Campaigns and Serotherapy). In *Rafu Nichibei* in Clippings of Newspaper Articles Written in Los Angeles for Various Japanese Language Papers in California Circa 1919–23. Box 12, Folder 5. Akahori Family Papers, Special Collection, Charles E. Young Research Library, University of California, Los Angeles.

Almaguer, Tomas. 1994. *Racial Fault Lines: The Historical Origins of White Supremacy in California.* Berkeley: University of California Press.

Azuma, Eiichiro. 2005. *Between Two Empires: Race, History, and Transnationalism in Japanese America.* New York: Oxford University Press.

———. 2013. "*Rafu Shimpo* (newspaper)." Densho Encyclopedia. Retrieved on August 14, 2014. http://encyclopedia.densho.org/Rafu%20Shimpo%20%28newspaper%29/.

Brubaker, Rogers. 2004. *Ethnicity without Groups.* Cambridge, MA: Harvard University Press.

DiMaggio, Paul. 1997. "Culture and Cognition." *Annual Review of Sociology* 23: 263–287.

Fraser, Nancy. 1992. "Rethinking the Public Sphere: A Contribution to the Critique of Actually Existing Democracy." In *Habermas and the Public Sphere,* edited by Craig Calhoun, 109–142. Cambridge, MA: MIT Press.

Fujioka, Shiro 藤岡紫朗. 1927. 民族発展の先駆者 (Pioneers of the Minzoku Development). Tokyo: Dobunsha.

Gardner, Martha. 2005. *The Qualities of a Citizen: Women, Immigration, and Citizenship, 1870–1965.* Princeton, NJ: Princeton University Press.

Geiger, Andrea. 2016. "Negotiating the Boundaries of Race, Caste and Mibun: Meiji-era Diplomatic and Immigrant Responses to North American Categories of Exclusion." In *Trans-Pacific Japanese American Studies: Conversations on Race and Racializations,* edited by Yasuko Takezawa and Gary Y. Okihiro, 133–157. Honolulu: University of Hawai'i Press.

Gerstle, Gary. 2001. *American Crucibles: Race and Nation in the Twentieth Century.* Princeton, NJ: Princeton University Press.

Hayashi, Brian Masaru. 1995. *"For the Sake of Our Japanese Brethren": Assimilation, Nationalism, and Protestantism among the Japanese of Los Angeles, 1895–1942.* Stanford, CA: Stanford University Press.

Holling, Michelle A., and Bernadette Marie Calafell, eds. 2011. *Latina/o Discourse in Vernacular Spaces: Somos de una voz?* Lanham, MD: Lexington Books.

Ichioka, Yuji. 1988. *The Issei: The World of the First Generation Japanese Immigrants, 1885–1940.* New York: Free Press.

Iwata, Taro. 2003. "Race and Citizenship as American Geopolitics: Japanese and Native Hawaiians in Hawai'i, 1900–1941." PhD diss., University of Oregon.

Jacobson, Matthew Frye. [1995] 2002. *Special Sorrows: The Diasporic Imagination of Irish, Polish, and Jewish Immigrants in the United States.* Berkeley: University of California Press.

Kumei, Teruko 粂井輝子. 1995. 外国人をめぐる社会史: 近代アメリカと日本人移民 (A Social History of Foreigners: Modern America and Japanese Immigrants). Tokyo: Yuzankaku.

Light, Ivan H. 1972. *Ethnic Enterprise in the United States: Business and Welfare among Chinese, Japanese, and Blacks.* Berkeley: University of California Press.

Minamikawa, Fuminori 南川文里. 2007. 「日系アメリカ人」の歴史社会学:エスニシティ、人種、ナショナリズム (Historical Sociology of "Japanese American": Ethnicity, Race, and Nationalism). Tokyo: Sairyusha.

———. 2011. "The Japanese American 'Success Story' and the Intersection of Ethnicity, Race, and Class in the Post-Civil Rights Era." *Japanese Journal of American Studies* 22: 193–212.

Nanka Chuo Nihonjinkai 南加中央日本人会. 1920. 日曜は休め (Take a Rest on Sunday). In 南加中央日本人会記録 (Records of the Central Japanese Association of Southern California). August 1915–January 1934, 203. Box 229. Japanese American Research Project Collection, Special Collection, Charles E. Young Research Library, University of California, Los Angeles.

Nanka Nihonjin Nenkan. 1921. 南加日本人年鑑 (Southern California Japanese Year Book). Los Angeles: Teikoku Insatsujo, 70.

Nanka Nihonjin Shogyo Kaigisho 南加日系人商業会議所. 1921. 頼母子講ニ関スル集会 (A Meeting on Rotating Credit Association). In 南加日本人商業会議所記録 (Japanese Chamber of Commerce of Southern California Records), vol. 1, January 1918–January 1923, 93–95. Box 272. Japanese American Research Project Collection, Special Collection, Charles E. Young Research Library, University of California, Los Angeles.

Ngai, Mae M. 2004. *Impossible Subjects: Illegal Aliens and the Making of Modern America*. Princeton, NJ: Princeton University Press.

———. 2011. "Immigration and Ethnic History." *In American History Now*, edited by Eric Foner and Lisa McGirr, 358–375. Philadelphia: Temple University Press.

Oguma, Eiji David Askew, trans. 1994 [2002]. *A Genealogy of "Japanese" Self-Images*. Melbourne: Trans Pacific Press.

Okihiro, Gary Y. 1994. *Margins and Mainstreams: Asians in American History and Culture*. Seattle: University of Washington Press.

Omi, Michael, and Howard Winant. 2015. *Racial Formation in the United States*, 3rd Edition. New York: Routledge.

Ono, Kent A., and John M. Sloop. 1995. "The Critique of Vernacular Discourse." *Communication Monographs* 62 (1): 19–46.

Park, Robert E. 1922. *The Immigrant Press and Its Control*. New York: Harper and Brothers.

Park, Robert E., and Ernest W. Burgess. 1921. *Introduction to the Science of Sociology*. Chicago: University of Chicago Press.

Rafu Nihonjinkai 羅府日本人会 (Japanese Association of Los Angeles). 1919a. 羅府日本人会記録 (Records of the Japanese Association of Los Angeles), vol. 1, June 10, 152. Box 237. Japanese American Research Project Collection, Special Collection, Charles E. Young Research Library, University of California, Los Angeles.

———. 1919b. 羅府日本人会記録 (Records of the Japanese Association of Los Angeles), vol. 2, June 20, p. 18. Box 237. Japanese American Research Project Collection, Special Collection, Charles E. Young Research Library, University of California, Los Angeles.

Rafu Shimpo Sha 羅府新報社. 1914. 羅府年鑑 (Los Angeles Japanese Daily News Yearbook), No. 7. Los Angeles.

Robertson, Jennifer. 2002. "Blood Talks: Eugenic Modernity and the Creation of New Japanese." *History and Anthropology* 13 (3): 191–216.

Rosaldo, Renato. 1988. *Culture and Truth: The Remaking of Social Analysis.* Boston: Beacon Press.

Sakaguchi, Mitsuhiro 坂口満宏. 2001. 日本人アメリカ移民史 (History of Japanese Immigration in the United States). Kyoto: Fuji Shuppan.

Sakano, Toru 坂野徹. 2005. 帝国日本と人類学者 1884–1952 (Imperial Japan and Anthropologists, 1884–1952). Tokyo: Keiso Shobo.

Sarasohn, Eileen Sunada. 1983. *The Issei: Portrait of a Pioneer, An Oral History.* Palo Alto, CA: Pacific Book.

Smedley, Audrey. 2007. *Race in North America: Origin and Evolution of a Worldview,* 3rd ed. Boulder, CO: Westview Press.

Smith, Anthony D. 2011. "National Identity and Vernacular Mobilisation in Europe." *Nations and Nationalism* 17 (2): 223–256.

Spivak, Gayatri Chakravorty. 2010. "Can the Subaltern Speak?," rev. ed. In *Can the Subaltern Speak? Reflections on the History of an Idea,* edited by Rosalind C. Morris, 20–78. New York: Columbia University Press.

Takezawa, Yasuko. 2011. "Toward a New Approach to Race and Racial Representations." In *Racial Representations in Asia,* edited by Yasuko Takezawa, 7–19. Kyoto: Kyoto University Press.

Uono, Koyoshi. 1927. "The Factors Affecting the Geographical Aggregation and Dispersion of the Japanese Residences in the City of Los Angeles." MA thesis, University of Southern California.

Viswanath, K., and Pamela Arora. 2000. "Ethnic Media in the United States: An Essay on Their Role in Integration, Assimilation, and Social Control." *Mass Communication and Society* 3 (1): 39–56.

Washizu, Shakuma 鷲津尺魔. 1930. 在米日本人史観 (History of the Japanese in North America). Los Angeles: *Rafu Shimpo.*

Wilson, Robert S., and Bill Hosokawa. 1980. *East to America: A History of Japanese in the United States.* New York: William Morrow.

Yu, Henry. 2001. *Thinking Orientals: Migration, Contact, and Exoticism in Modern America.* New York: Oxford University Press.

Yu, Kŏn-ch'a 尹健次. 1994. 民族幻想の蹉跌：日本人の自己像 (The Stumbling of Minzoku Illusion: Self-Portrait of Japanese). Tokyo: Iwanami Shoten.

CHAPTER 6

Negotiating the Boundaries of Race, Caste, and Mibun
Meiji-era Diplomatic and Immigrant Responses to North American Categories of Exclusion

Andrea Geiger

In early 1908, just as the Gentlemen's Agreement into which Japan had entered with both the United States and Canada was to go into effect, a new question regarding information provided on Japanese passports threatened to upset the delicate diplomatic balance Japan had achieved by agreeing to restrict labor emigration to North America as part of a larger effort to forestall passage of race-based anti-Japanese legislation. U.S. immigration officers were convinced that Japanese passport officials were dishonest in recording the occupations of those to whom passports were issued to avoid the limitations agreed to under the terms of the U.S. Gentlemen's Agreement.[1] The arrival of the *Tosa Maru* in Seattle on February 20, 1908, appeared to confirm their suspicions that Japanese passports did not accurately reflect the intended occupation of Japanese immigrants: although 106 of the Japanese labor migrants on board told immigration officers that they intended to work as laborers in the United States, only eight passports stated that this was their intention, and just one passport described the bearer himself as a laborer.[2]

On March 9, 1908, the U.S. ambassador to Japan raised the U.S. government's concern regarding these discrepancies with Vice Minister of Foreign Affairs Kikujirō Ishii, questioning his government's compliance with the Gentlemen's Agreement into which Japan had entered with the United

States. Ishii hastened to assure the U.S. ambassador that the passports in question must have been issued prior to December 1907, when the agreement was finalized. Occupations recorded on passports were not intended to indicate the bearer's intended occupation in the United States, Ishii told the ambassador, but to denote the "bearer's social status" (*mibun*) based on the official categories utilized during the Tokugawa period to order social relations. According to Ishii, these "designations . . . were merely formal and referred to the old classification of Japanese society under the heads of soldier, farmer, artisan and merchant." A case in point was that of *tatami* makers, who were listed as such not because they proposed to make straw mats in North America, but because this was the work in which their family had traditionally engaged in Japan. The same was true of other designations, Ishii explained, including herder, shoemaker, bath house attendant, dyer, weaver, and blacksmith.[3]

Although U.S. immigration officials remained skeptical, officers posted in various North American port cities, including Montreal and Vancouver, responded in the affirmative to a query posed by the commissioner-general of immigration as to whether their practical experience bore out Ishii's claims.[4] The most detailed response regarding the significance of the occupational designations listed on Japanese passports was provided by Barnabas C. Haworth, an interpreter for the U.S. Immigration Service in Vancouver, British Columbia, who reportedly had lived in Japan for many years. Based on his examination of passports of immigrants entering the United States after landing in Canada, Haworth assured his superiors that Japanese passport officials intended no deceit. The occupations listed on Meiji passports, he agreed with Ishii, were intended not to describe the kind of work the bearer intended to do in the United States, but to flag for Japanese consular officials the status of the bearer's family within the context of the Tokugawa-era status system (*mibunsei*). By way of further explanation, Haworth provided his superiors with a brief history of that system, noting that it had, historically, included outcaste classes but that older status distinctions were gradually being replaced by new designations:

> Formerly there existed in Japan a clear line of demarcation, amounting almost to a rigid caste system, between the Aristocracy or Nobles, the Military, the Farmer, the Artisan and the *Eta* (outcast) classes. These distinctions have been largely obliterated or displaced by the simpler classification into Nobility and Common People, the latter ("Heimin") now

including all but the royal family and the nobility. In the older passports we can trace the influence of the old system of records by social class. More recent passports, however, either omit all reference to social class or insert simply the word "Heimin" for all sorts of people below the noble class.⁵

By noting the existence of former outcaste groups, Haworth's explanation also helped U.S. officials to resolve the more puzzling question of what the intended meaning of the occupational designation "laborer" was. After carefully evaluating the various contexts in which this designation was used in light of Ishii's explanation, U.S. officials concluded that when "laborer" followed "emigrant," it was intended to indicate that the bearer was not a member of "the classes known as farmers, artisans, soldiers, etc."⁶ Because those once categorized as outcastes were the only commoners not encompassed within other named status groups, the observation made by U.S. officials suggests that in at least some cases "laborer" was a designation used to denote descent from former outcaste groups.

Satisfied with Ishii's explanation, U.S. officials noted that the historical status categories in question had no significance whatsoever in the context of U.S. immigration law and considered the matter resolved. A curious thing happened, however, when the short history of the Tokugawa status system provided by Haworth to his superiors in the U.S. Immigration Bureau was passed on to higher authorities. For reasons that the historical record does not reveal, all reference to the existence of former outcaste groups had been erased by the time his report reached the office of the U.S. secretary of state.⁷

Although Ishii's candor and Haworth's acquaintance with Japan helped to avoid a more serious diplomatic incident, the brief furor over the apparent discrepancies in the information provided on Meiji passports illustrates the kinds of misunderstandings that can occur in translation or when information is filtered through differing cultural lenses. It also reveals that historical ways of understanding difference rooted in the Tokugawa-era status system (*mibunsei*) retained their salience decades after it was abolished early in the Meiji period as part of Japan's larger, determined effort to remake itself as a nation that would be recognized as modern and civilized by those of North America and Europe. Both Meiji-era diplomats and emigrants carried these ideas and associated ways of viewing the world with them when they went abroad. Particularly revealing in this context is the idea of outcaste status. Although it was abolished as a matter of law together with other status categories at the beginning of the Meiji period, social and cultural taboos associated with outcaste status persisted.[8] As such, it serves as a particularly poignant example of ways in which consideration of status issues internal to particular immigrant groups can illuminate their strategies with respect to the dominant society in the countries to which they travel.

Mibun in general, and perceptions associated with outcaste status in particular, not only shaped relations among Japanese immigrants but mediated their responses to both constraints and opportunities in the North American West. Choices made by Meiji-era Japanese immigrants regarding potential livelihoods were a product not only of economic restrictions imposed by Canada and the United States but also of their own association of certain kinds of occupations with specific status groups. Although *mibun* would come to be increasingly conflated both with economic class and with concerns about whether Japanese labor emigrants were Westernized enough not to undermine Japan's image as a modernized nation, a hierarchical worldview—at once shaped by and reflected in the Tokugawa status system—would continue to inform the responses of both Meiji diplomats and immigrants to white racism as they encountered it in North America. White racism was offensive not only because it relegated Japanese to the bottom of the race-based labor hierarchies that ordered social relations in both the United States and Canadian West but also because it failed to recognize status and caste differences to which Japanese continued to ascribe meaning. It is because Meji Japanese in all status groups equated their treatment by white racists with that historically meted out to outcastes in Tokugawa Japan that their efforts to respond to white racism can be fully understood only by taking *mibun* generally—and outcaste status in particular—into account. This short essay briefly presents a series of contexts in which culturally distinct ways of understanding difference rooted in Japan's own historical experience informed both the strategies of Meiji officials as they endeavored to refute the racist claims of anti-Japanese exclusionists and the responses of Meiji-era immigrants to conditions they encountered in North America.

Meiji Officials

Given the tremendous effort that Japan had made since the beginning of the Meiji era to restructure its economic, social, and political institutions based on Western models, Meiji diplomats were determined to defend its status as a civilized nation equal to those of the West, arguing that Japan's modernization set it apart from other Asian nations. Acutely conscious of the way in which Japanese migrants were perceived in North America at a time when the United States and Canada were engaged in parallel efforts to racialize their borders, the Meiji government was particularly concerned that its subjects not become the object of anti-Japanese legislation similar to the Chinese Exclusion Act passed by the United States in 1882—legislation they attributed less to white racism than to the Chinese themselves, much as they would persist in attributing anti-Japanese prejudice to their own purportedly "lower class" or "unworthy" migrants.[9] The assumption that the emigrants themselves were primarily responsible for anti-Japanese prejudice in North America and that differences between "the lowest section" and other Japanese explained white racism informed the attitudes of Japanese officials for a number of decades. In 1891, the Japanese consul in San Francisco expressly linked negative perceptions of Japanese labor migrants to Japan's standing in the world. The failure to check the migration of those he considered responsible for these perceptions, he warned his government, would "undoubtedly create a grave situation in the relationship between Japanese and Americans in this country which, sooner or later, [would] adversely affect the honor and reputation not only of the Japanese in this country but also of those in Japan."[10] As late as 1914, Kahei Otani, a former member of the House of Peers, attributed anti-Asian prejudice to the migrants at whom he believed it was really directed:

> Only the lowest section of the Japanese are being discriminated against or excluded in America. The more respectable classes of Japanese are well treated and respected by the Americans. It is a striking illustration of this fact that there has been no anti-Japanese movement in Chicago or New York. In California and other Pacific coast states only has unfriendliness been shown toward our people. This is because many Japanese in those regions are unworthy.[11]

What Meiji officials did not realize was the extent to which anti-Japanese elements in North America understood and would be able to turn to their own purposes both their concerns that Japanese emigrants did not adequately represent a newly modernized Japan and the status- and class-based distinctions that they drew between labor emigrants and themselves. A report prepared by U.S. Immigration Commissioner W. M. Rice in 1899, which would also be incorporated into the findings of Canada's Royal Commission on Chinese and Japanese Immigration in 1902, for example, accepted the contention that Japan's "immigrating class" was drawn "largely from the lower order," and that a "wide line of demarcation exists between this class and the better people."[12] U.S. witnesses invited to appear before the Royal Commission included San Francisco immigration inspector R. Ecclestone, who described the Japanese labor immigrants then arriving in San Francisco as members of "the very lowest class" in Japan, and T. M. Crawford of Portland, Oregon, who testified that those arriving in Oregon were also drawn from "the worst class of the Japanese," a "low type and an ignorant class" that "may be called the coolie class."[13]

The cultural lens through which Meiji diplomats viewed Japanese labor migrants also invoked fears that North Americans would fail to distinguish between themselves and the emigrants they characterized as "unworthy" in explaining white racism. In an effort to persuade North Americans to differentiate between Japanese and Chinese on the one hand, and among Japanese on the other, Meiji officials developed a two-pronged argument to counter anti-Japanese prejudice in North America. Rather than attacking racism directly, Japanese officials urged North Americans to distinguish between themselves and the labor migrants they regarded as the real object of white hostility. They then went on to draw a second distinction, arguing that even though immigrant laborers were of low status relative to Japanese like themselves, the same immigrants—as subjects of a modern, imperial nation—were higher in status than those from nations like China that had not made the same commitment to modernization as had Japan. In short, rather than reject anti-Asian prejudice out of hand, Meiji officials attempted to bridge the racial divide by recasting anti-Japanese sentiment in terms they regarded as acceptable because they were more closely aligned with the historical ways of ordering difference with which they were most familiar.

The dual nature of the Meiji government's response to white racism is apparent in remarks made by Seizaburo Shimizu, Japanese consul in Vancouver, British Columbia, during his visit to the coal mining community of Cumberland, British Columbia, in 1899. Even as Shimizu urged white Canadians not to discriminate against the Japanese laborers working in the coal mines in Cumberland, he was at pains to distinguish himself from the coal miners whose working conditions he had come to inspect. "It is generally the lower class of my countrymen who immigrate into this country," Shimizu told a reporter in Cumberland, "and it is hardly fair to judge all of us from a single type."[14] Although Shimizu was willing to concede that prejudice against the Japanese labor immigrants who worked in the mines was justified, he also argued that they were higher in status than migrant laborers from other nations. Shimizu pointed to, in particular, the years of compulsory education required in Japan, a policy instituted early in the Meiji period as part of Japan's quest to reconstruct itself as a modern nation. This, he declared, meant that even its lowest classes of laborers were literate, in contrast to those from other countries, particularly China.[15] In a pamphlet published in 1897, self-described Japanese-Canadian K. T. Takahashi expressly invoked the abolition of outcaste status in Japan in arguing against the proposed extension of the head tax to Japanese: Japan had "no outcast and no pauper class," in contrast—he asserted—not only to China but also to Western nations. The disingenuous nature of the advocates of the head tax, he declared, was evident in their failure to distinguish Japanese and Chinese—a deliberate strategy, in his view, intended to inflame anti-Japanese sentiment."[16]

Arguing against proposed exclusionary measures in 1899, Shimizu also invoked imperial hierarchies, pointing to Canada's status as a British dominion and contrasting its subordinate role within the British empire with Japan's own position as an imperial power that had begun to acquire colonies of its own. If the British Columbia legislature passed anti-Japanese legislation, he warned, his own government retained the option of appealing to the "Imperial authorities" to which the province was subject. Great Britain, he noted, had recognized Japan as a nation equal in status when it rescinded its unequal treaty with Japan in 1894. Canada, a dominion that remained subject to British imperial authority, was thus precluded from treating Japan as less than equal.[17]

Shimizu also pointed to Japan's 1895 victory over China as evidence that Japan was both the equal of European nations and superior to China. "Japan made wonderful progress before that," he declared, "but the Chinese war demonstrated to other peoples that we have taken our place among the great nations of the world, and our government is determined to uphold that honor." Given Japan's achievements, Shimizu concluded, it "would be an insult to our national dignity" to exclude Japanese from Canada in the same way that Chinese—who, in his view, had not made equivalent progress—had been excluded.[18] Shimizu had made the same point in a letter to Wilfrid Laurier one year earlier: "It is unfair and unjust to legislate, or even attempt to legislate, discriminately against the subject[s] of the country which I have the honour to represent here, whose progress in civilization has excited the admiration of the world, and who has been internationally recognized as the equal of any country, in the same way as against the Chinese."[19]

Shimizu's approach extended an argument made by his predecessor, Tatsugoro Nosse, in response to efforts by the British Columbia legislature to persuade the Canadian government to raise the head tax that applied to Chinese immigrants to $500 per person and to extend it to Japanese immigrants in 1898. Like Shimizu, Nosse had also urged Canadians to draw a distinction between Chinese and Japanese immigrants. The failure to distinguish the two, Nosse declared, "was a mistake which only extreme ignorance could make."[20] The Chinese in Canada were, in his words—"the lowest on the scale"—and Chinese migration amounted to little more than a "species of slavery." In an apparent effort to invoke white stereotypes about Chinese in order to position Japanese migrants more favorably, Nosse further argued that the low status of Chinese immigrants was demonstrated by the purported fact that "they smoke opium; they start gambling dens; they are unclean; they never assimilated with the population; [and] they take all they earn to China." In contrast, Nosse declared, Japanese immigrants were representatives of a "modern, civilized" nation and "highly civilized people." Nosse pointed to, in particular, the growing number of married women in Japanese immigrant communities in North America as evidence of both the stability and the civilized nature of Japanese immigrant society. A majority of the eight hundred Japanese then living in British Columbia were Christians, Nosse claimed, and at least sixty were also wives: "they are clean and frugal; they set up the family; they open churches."[21]

As would Shimizu one year later, Nosse also underscored Canada's status as a British dominion, contrasting its subordinate role within the British imperial order with Japan's position as an imperial nation in its own right. Because Britain had recognized Japan as an equal, Nosse argued, Canada, as a "colony," had no justifiable basis for discriminating against Japanese subjects:

> Now why should we be discriminated against? England was the first to recognize Japan as a modern, civilized nation. England gave to Japan, in the new treaty, which was made with her two years ago, the benefit of the most favored nation clause. We are in the East what England is in Europe. . . . Canada is the greatest colony in the British Empire. Why should this colony discriminate against that people the progress and civi-

lization of which England was the first to recognize. Thirty years ago I would not have complained if an attempt had been made to keep us out. We had no status then in the civilized world; but to discriminate against us now is most unfair."[22]

Meiji diplomats, in short, argued against racism in North America not by attacking it directly but by endeavoring to recast it in terms of relative status, whether on the part of nations or of individuals. By distinguishing between a modern Japan and "tradition bound" China, Meiji officials sought to explain anti-Asian prejudice not on the basis of race but as resulting from a failure to modernize. In so doing, they embraced a hierarchical view of national progress that mirrored in significant ways the hierarchical social structure around which difference continued to be organized in Meiji Japan.[23]

Meiji officials would undermine their own contention that admissibility to Canada and the United States should not be determined based on race, however, by simultaneously invoking race in other contexts to argue *for* the inclusion of Japanese. Aware that Canada was recruiting European immigrants to populate its western provinces, for example, Meiji consular officials argued that immigrants from northern Japan were racially better adapted to conditions on the Canadian prairies than were European immigrants. Nosse thus declared in 1897 that "Canada needs a thrifty, hardy population, which Japan can supply." Japanese from northern Japan, he argued, were especially well suited to settle Canada's Northwest based on physical characteristics that were a product of the fact that they had lived in parts of Japan where they had dealt both with harsh weather and tidal waves over the centuries. In Nosse's words, they were "hardy; they have strong bodies and a high stature; and they are accustomed to hardship," they "are thrifty; they are strong; they are peaceable; and they can endure both cold and heat."[24] Given these racialized characteristics, Nosse argued in effect, northern Japanese were better suited to Canada than those from more temperate regions who had not had to endure equivalent hardships.

Nosse also sought to invoke Canadian fears that the United States— an expanding imperial power in its own right—might incorporate parts of British Columbia into its own West, insisting that it would be less than genuinely Canadian to pass a head tax because the proposal was, "to a great extent, fathered by men who are not even British subjects." "Do you know," Nosse asked, "that in [British Columbia's] Kootenay district and the Fraser river district the country is flooded with Americans, who want all for themselves, and who would prevent any other people from participating in benefits which are all the time increasing in value?"[25] Takahashi had likewise invoked Canadian stereotypes of the United States to bolster his own argument against extending the head tax to Japanese. It was the Americans and not the Japanese, he insisted, who posed the greatest threat to Canadian interests. Not only that, but they were also the more transient:

> The real and most serious enemy to the bread-winners of British Columbia are today as it had always been, those predatory aliens other than Japanese who freely cross and recross the boundary line and carry all their earnings away into the American side. When prospects are better and wages rise on our side they promptly come swarming in and at once make themselves the competitors of the sons and daughters of our soil. As promptly they depart when the tide changes, leaving our own workers poorer by what they take away with them.[26]

On the one hand, Takahashi appealed to Canada's vision of itself as distinct from the United States and embodying the virtues of British society, arguing that anti-Japanese legislation would "be an act of undignified petulancy toward a friendly power—an act unworthy of British fair play and Canadian dignity." Canada, he urged, was principled in ways that the United States was not. On the other hand, he held up the United States—as an imperial power in its own right—as an example that Canada should follow. Despite the fact that there were several thousand Japanese immigrants in the United States, he wrote, it had passed no laws excluding Japanese from that country. The fact that the United States "had longer and larger experience with the Japanese" but had "not found any cause to object to the latter's immigration" made clear that there was no basis for extending the head tax to Japanese. British Columbians, he declared, had no reason to find fault with Japanese when Americans did not.[27]

Immigrants

Concerns about hierarchy and the implications of historical status categories similar to those that shaped the attitudes of Meiji officials also mediated the responses of Meiji-era Japanese immigrants to conditions they encountered in the North American West and provided an interpretive framework for the race-based hostility they confronted on both sides of the U.S.-Canada border. That cultural associations specific to Japan continued to frame Japanese immigrant responses to Euro-American cultural practices into the early decades of the twentieth century is reflected, for example, in the reaction of one newly arrived Japanese immigrant woman to sausages she saw hanging in a California butcher's shop, described in Akemi Kikumura's brave and honest book about her mother, *Through Harsh Winters: The Life of a Japanese Immigrant Woman*. Kikumura's mother, who arrived in the United States in 1923 at the age of nineteen, described the meat sausages she saw as food for what she called *yotsu*—a derogatory term meaning "four-legged" used to allude to people historically categorized as outcastes, which reflects the visceral nature of the prejudice directed at them.[28]

The extent to which Japanese immigrants equated their treatment by white racists with that directed at former outcastes in Japan is revealed by their use of language and animal imagery historically projected on those categorized as outcastes to describe how white racism felt. One immigrant who arrived in the United States in 1919, for example, later explained his feeling that those who called him "Jap" "must have thought of us as something like dogs."[29] The Japanese-language newspaper *Shin Sekai* stated the point in still more graphic terms, making explicit the perception that white racism rendered all those from Japan equivalent to outcastes in the context of North American society:

> Though we have been treated like *burakumin* (outcasts), our legal rights were still undecided [until recently]. Now, we are clearly branded as *burakumin* [in America]. Yet . . . even if [America] dealt with us as pigs, or perceived us as dogs or cats, we must focus on our work obstinately.[30]

White racism was offensive, in short, not only because it relegated Japanese to the bottom of the race-based labor hierarchies that ordered social relations in North America but also because it rendered all Japanese equivalent to outcastes regardless of their own family status and, in so doing, failed to recognize status distinctions to which they continued to ascribe meaning.

Traditional status biases were also reflected in the efforts made by early Japanese immigrants to avoid occupations historically associated with outcaste status or otherwise regarded as stigmatizing in Japan or, where such occupations could not be avoided, to deny their involvement in them. The aversion of Japanese immigrants to work they regarded as stigmatizing was reflected, for example, in attitudes toward coal mining, one occupation for which laborers were recruited from Japan after the Meiji government lifted its bar on labor emigration in 1884.

Whether it was because coal mining was perceived as an industry associated with those who had once been categorized as outcastes in some parts of Japan or because it was assumed that it was an occupation to which only the utterly impoverished would turn, coal mining gave rise to considerable concern about its impact on the perceived status of those who engaged in it. Masato Uyeda of Seattle, for example, later told Kazuo Ito that when he was asked what kinds of work he had done in North America by the Japanese crown prince during his visit to Seattle in 1960, he could not bring himself to admit that he had worked as a coal miner when he first arrived. "For us 'Meiji men,'" he told Ito, coal mining was a "job for criminals or the lowest of the low."[31] Other evidence suggests that when Meiji-era Japanese immigrants believed others had worked as coal miners in Japan, they were unwilling to associate with them. In April 1893, for example, Cumberland's *Weekly News*—the same town that Consul Shimizu was visiting when he urged Canadians to distinguish between himself and others—reported that a group of Japanese labor migrants who had recently arrived to work in Cumberland's coal mines had refused to accept aid from another group of Japanese laborers who had arrived the previous year, even though the new arrivals were unaccustomed to mine work and lacked both food and the warmer clothing needed in a colder climate, to the point where several were close to death. Unaware of the cultural concerns that might have triggered their refusal to associate with the earlier group given that it was composed of experienced coal miners who had been brought to Canada from Fukuoka Prefecture, the reporter declared, "Why they did not apply to their countrymen in the camp who were able to help them is a mystery."[32] Whether these miners actually had ties to former outcaste communities or not, the fact that they had worked as coal miners in an area in Japan where some significant percentage of those laboring in the mines were reportedly former outcastes appears to have been enough to trigger status-based concerns on the part of the new arrivals.[33] That Meiji consular officials also ascribed significance to such distinctions and differentiated between those who had worked as miners in Japan and other Japanese immigrants is reflected in the fact that records submitted to the Japanese consulate in Vancouver, British Columbia, by Japanese employment agents distinguished between "common immigrants" and "miners" and tallied each separately.[34]

That perceptions of difference rooted in historical status categories persisted among Japanese immigrants in North America is also reflected in the constitution of the *Nihonjin Kakō Dōmeikai* (literally Japanese Shoemakers Association but translated as Japanese Shoe Repairers Association),[35] established in San Francisco in 1893 in response to a boycott organized by white shoemakers to force all Japanese cobblers out of business after fifteen Japanese were hired to break a strike at a local shoe factory. At the time the association was organized, its leaders would later write, its members were the object not only of racial prejudice but also of caste-based prejudice. Other Japanese in North America, they explained, subjected them to insults and indignities because they regarded leatherworkers as the most "base and inferior of all laborers."[36]

Leaders of the *Nihonjin Kakō Dōmeikai* carefully negotiated the issue of status within the Japanese immigrant community, cognizant of the critical gaze of others and careful not to overstep their bounds. They explained that in organizing the *Nihonjin Kakō Dōmeikai,* they made no claim to status as Japanese immigrant leaders in the United States. Forced by the nature of their work to emigrate to a place thousands of miles away from their homeland, they continued, they had expected simply to take their place among other similar businesses in the United States; only after they arrived did they realize that they would also face discrimination and hostility there, albeit on race-based grounds and together with other Japanese.[37] Although they were members of a "yellow race" and spoke little English, they declared, they did not regard themselves as inferior to whites, but considered themselves fortunate to be members of the Yamato race (*minzoku*).[38] They chose not to dwell on the unanticipated disadvantages they had encountered because they were not white. Instead, they were determined to use the power of cooperation to address the problems that all Japanese immigrants faced, as well as to provide a framework within which members of the *Nihonjin Kakō Dōmeikai* would be able to ensure one another's success by mutual support and the provision of aid in the event of illness or unexpected calamity.[39]

In contrast to Meiji consular officials like Shimizu, who responded to the racial animus Japanese encountered in North America by distinguishing between themselves and other Japanese on class- and status-based grounds, leaders of the *Nihonjin Kakō Dōmeikai* saw in the racialized conflict with white shoemakers an opportunity to assert their common identity as Japanese subjects and, in so doing, a way to challenge the historical caste-based prejudices of other Japanese immigrants. Their purpose was not only to establish a base for organizing against white racism but also, through their effective resistance to white racism, to prove themselves to those of their fellow immigrants who disparaged them because of ancestry or their work with leather. The decision of the white Boot and Shoe Repairers Association to accept Japanese immigrants as members in 1920 stands as one measure of the success of the *Nihonjin Kakō Dōmeikai;* less clear is the degree to which its efforts led to the erosion of historical caste-based prejudices held by other Japanese immigrants.[40]

The determination of the *Nihonjin Kakō Dōmeikai* to confront white racism directly stands in contrast to the approach adopted by Meiji officals to counter racist allegations. In the course of asserting their own humanity against those whites who discriminated against them on racial grounds, members of the *Nihonjin Kakō Dōmeikai* simultaneously asserted their place as fully participating members of the broader immigrant community. The more ambivalent response of Meiji diplomats to racist claims, and particularly their conviction that it was the migrants they described as "lower class" or "unworthy" who were primarily responsible for white racism, on the other hand, undermined their efforts to counter racial prejudice and played directly into the hands of anti-Japanese exclusionists. By failing to see the extent to which critiques of Japanese immigrants in North America were a product—and not the cause—of white racism, they provided anti-Japanese exclusionists with a way to turn their own claims against them. As long as they conflated race- and caste-based ways of understanding difference, their efforts avoided—and thus could not resolve—the real issue.

Conclusion

Meiji-era Japanese diplomats and immigrants alike remained acutely conscious of *mibun* and associated status issues, which remained one factor shaping both rhetorical and occupational strategies in response to the racial animus they encountered in North America on both sides of the U.S.-Canada border. Although Meiji diplomats attempted to counter the arguments of exclusionists by turning the language of race back on North Americans, their efforts were undermined by persistent social and cultural biases rooted in Japan's own historical experience, which persuaded them that white racism was best explained by the status and behavior of their own labor emigrants. Ironically, the contradictory nature of their arguments, together with their willingness to condone both status- or class-based and anti-Chinese prejudice, weakened the position of Japanese immigrants abroad, aiding in the reproduction of Japanese as an excludable category by allowing anti-Japanese exclusionists to turn the same arguments against them.

Japanese immigrants, in contrast, had a stake in obscuring the same distinctions that Meiji passport officials sought to maintain by denoting *mibun* on the passports they issued, whether it was because these migrants believed their families would be shamed by the work they did in North America, or because they saw in this new environment an opportunity to distance themselves from historical forms of social categorization that exposed them to caste-based prejudice and, instead, to assert their newly articulated status as subjects of a modern imperial nation. What the strategies of both Meiji diplomats and immigrants reveal is that the process of negotiating identity in the North American West was never just a result of simple confrontations with white racism alone, but a product of far more complicated acts of positioning that also made reference to historical ways of understanding difference specific to Japan.

Notes

This essay is excerpted and adapted from *Subverting Exclusion: Transpacific Encounters with Race, Caste, and Borders, 1885–1928* and is republished here with the permission of Yale University Press. In *Subverting Exclusion*, I argue for the importance of taking into account cultural perceptions rooted in the Tokugawa status system (*mibunsei*) in addition to more familiar paradigms of race, class, and gender in analyzing Meiji-era Japanese immigration history.

1   John H. Sargent, Inspector in Charge, U.S. Immigration Service, Department of Commerce and Labor, Seattle, Washington, to Commissioner-General of Immigration, Washington, D.C., 2 May 1908; Walter E. Carr, Inspector in Charge, U.S. Immigration Service, Department of Commerce and Labor, Port of Winnipeg, Manitoba, to John H. Clark, U.S. Commissioner of Immigration, Montreal, Canada, 17 April 1908. Record Group 85: Records of the Immigration and Naturalization Service [RG 85], Series A, Subject Correspondence Files, part 1, Asian Immigration and Exclusion, 1906–1913, National Archives and Records Administration, Washington, D.C. [NARA].

2   U.S. Ambassador O'Brien, Tokyo, Japan, to U.S. Department of State, Washington, D.C., 9 March 1908 (quoting telegram from [U.S. Secretary of State] Root to the U.S. ambassador in Tokyo, Japan, dated 25 February 1908), RG 85, NARA.

3   U.S. Ambassador O'Brien, Tokyo, Japan, to U.S. Department of State, Washington, D.C., 9 March 1908; notes re conference with Mr. [Kikujirō] Ishii, Foreign Office, Tokyo, Japan, by P. A. Jay, U.S. Embassy, Tokyo, Japan, enclosed with Dispatch No. 231 from Ambassador O'Brien, Tokyo, Japan, to U.S. Department of State, Washington, D.C., 10 March 1908 and associated reports.

4   F. P. Sargent, Commissioner-General, Bureau of Immigration and Naturalization, Department of Commerce and Labor, Washington, D.C., to John H. Clark, U.S. Commissioner of Immigration, Montreal, Canada, 17 April 1908; and see, for example, Walter E. Carr, Inspector in Charge, U.S. Immigration Service, Department of Commerce and Labor, Port of Winnipeg, Manitoba, to John H. Clark, U.S. Commissioner of Immigration, Montreal, Canada, 17 April 1908. RG 85, NARA. U.S. and Canadian officials were aware that Japanese distinguished among themselves based on historical status categories. *Supplemental Report of W. M. Rice*, U.S. Commissioner on Immigration, to Commissioner-General on Immigration, Washington, D.C., dated 2 May 1899, in Canada, *Report of the Royal Commission on Chinese and Japanese Immigration, 1902*, 424–425.

5   Barnabas C. Haworth, Japanese Interpreter, to P. L. Prentis, Inspector in Charge, U.S. Immigration Service, Department of Commerce and Labor, Vancouver, British Columbia, 25 April 1908, RG 85, NARA. Stanford professor Yamato Ichihashi also noted that occupations listed on emigrants' passports were not necessarily those they intended to pursue once they arrived in North America, but that they were intended to "indicate from what classes the Japanese immigrants were drawn." Yamato Ichihashi, *Japanese in the United States: A Critical Study of the Problems of the Japanese Immigrants and Their Children* (Stanford, CA: Stanford University Press, 1932), 67. For a breakdown of occupations listed on Japanese passports per Immigration Commission Reports between 1901 and 1909 see H. A. Millis, *The Japanese Problem in the United States* (New York: Macmillan Company, 1915), 6. The Tokugawa status system comprised four major status categories or *mibun*—in descending order, *samurai*, farmers, craftsmen, and merchants (*shi-nō-kō-shō*). Not included in these official status categories but also integral to the functioning of the Tokugawa system were outcaste groups who provided the labor needed for tasks regarded as polluting by other Japanese ("*eta*" was the deeply pejorative term applied to the best-known group). Although some scholars have argued that outcastes were essentially unclassified people, they were subject to strict legal constraints in many parts of Japan throughout the Tokugawa period. Howell explains that the boundary between the four major status groups and outcaste groups was qualitatively far more significant than that which existed between the

four major status categories. David L. Howell, *Geographies of Identity in Nineteenth-Century Japan* (Berkeley: University of California Press, 2005), 4, 7, 20–44.

6 Barnabas C. Haworth, Japanese Interpreter, to P. L. Prentis, Inspector in Charge, U.S. Immigration Service, Department of Commerce and Labor, Vancouver, British Columbia, 25 April 1908, RG 85, NARA. Like race, caste is a socially and historically constructed phenomenon. George De Vos and Hiroshi Wagatsuma explains that race- and caste-based distinctions are rooted in different mythological constructs. "Racism," he explains, "is usually based on a secularized pseudo-scientific biological mythology," whereas "caste is often based on a pseudo-historical religious mythology." George De Vos and Hiroshi Wagatsuma, *Japan's Invisible Race: Caste in Culture and Personality* (Berkeley: University of California Press, 1966), xx. Although scholars regard caste and class (as it refers to economic groupings) as conceptually distinct categories, Japanese did not always differentiate between them when speaking in English, using "class" even where context makes clear that reference to *mibun* was intended (see, for example, Ichihashi's reference to classes, supra, n. 5). Such terms should therefore be read in context and the difference between them understood as one of emphasis and not rigid definition. The same is true of the word "status," used both to refer to the Tokugawa status categories (*mibun*) and to rank or social position more generally. Ambiguous though they often are, the context in which phrases like "low class" are typically used reflects a tendency to group people according to social hierarchy and to assume that they have certain innate qualities based on where they are positioned. For a discussion of the difficulties associated with accurately translating Japanese into English, see Edward Seidensticker, "On Miner on Translating Japanese Poetry," *Orient/West* 7, no. 1 (January 1962). See also Marleigh Grayer Ryan, "Translating Modern Japanese Literature," *Journal of Japanese Studies* 6, no. 1 (Winter 1980): 49–60. The inverse, of course, poses many of the same challenges.

7 John H. Clark, U.S. Commissioner of Immigration to Assistant Secretary of State, 13 May 1908. RG 85, NARA, file 51931. The deletion of the reference to outcaste groups is reminiscent of a similar pattern of erasure in the historiography of Japanese immigration. Largely written out of Japanese immigration histories though they have been, acknowledging the presence of former outcastes among those who emigrated to North America has the potential to contribute to a more complex and nuanced understanding of immigration history itself. Relatively small though their numbers may have been, including people in this category in Japanese migration history makes it possible to begin to raise questions about the extent to which individuals at all levels of society emigrated to avoid social constraints that persisted in

Meiji Japan. The fact that some Japanese also emigrated for social reasons makes it possible, in turn, to challenge the false convention that all Japanese immigrants were simply sojourners or transient laborers—as contrasted with European migrants who were purportedly more interested in permanent settlement—which has structured conventional histories of Asian and European immigration to North America. See Sucheng Chan, "European and Asian Immigration into the United States in Comparative Perspective, 1820s to 1920s," in Virginia Yans-McLaughlin, ed., *Immigration Reconsidered: History, Sociology, and Politics* (New York: Oxford University Press, 1990), 37–75. It also brings into focus the social complexity of prewar Japanese immigrant communities, which were composed of people from all levels of Japanese society, who differentiated among themselves and responded in varying ways to the issues of the day based on their own particular goals and reasons for settling in the North American West, and demonstrates anew the injustice of the forced relocation and incarceration of people of Japanese ancestry by both Canada and the United States during World War II.

8 Outcaste status was abolished in 1871 and other status categories were abolished soon after. David L. Howell, "Liberating and Killing Outcastes in Early Meiji Japan" (Princeton University, Department of East Asian Studies, 2001), 5.

9 In January 1907, for example, the Japanese consul general in Hawai'i called on F. P. Sargent, U.S. Commissioner General of Immigration, to assure him that "the general policy of his government was opposed to settlement of the mainland of any considerable number of Japanese labourers, such government wishing to avoid conditions regarding Japanese of a character similar to those which had, in 1882 and 1884, brought about the laws excluding the Chinese labourers." F. P. Sargent, U.S. Commissioner General of Immigration, to President of the United States, 2 January 1907, RG 85, NARA. See also Official Dispatch No. 14, Takahashi Shinkichi, Consul of Japan, New York City, to Yoshida Kiyonari, Vice Minister of Foreign Affairs, February 13, 1884, *Nihon gaikō bunsho* 18, 104–111, criticizing not the U.S. Congress but Chinese immigrants for passage of the Chinese Exclusion Act, as quoted in Donald Teruo Hata, Jr., "'Undesirables': Unsavory Elements Among the Japanese in America Prior to 1893 and Their Influence on the First Anti-Japanese Movement in California" (PhD diss., University of Southern California, 1970), 33. For characterizations of Japanese migrants as "unworthy" and "lower class" see note 12, infra, and associated text.

10 Robert A. Wilson and Bill Hosokawa, *East to America: A History of the Japanese in the United States* (New York: William Morrow, 1980), 114–115, quoting Consular Dispatch No. 6 from Chinda Sutemi, Consul of Japan,

to Foreign Minister Aoki Shuzo, 25 April 1891, *Nihon gaikō bunsho* 24, 463–466.
11 Hon. Kahei Otani, "America and Japan Always Friends," in Naochi Masaoka, ed., *Japan's Message to America: A Symposium by Representative Japanese on Japan and American-Japanese Relations* (Tokyo, 1914), 62–63. Baron Rempei Kondo, a peer and president of the *Nippon Yusen Kaisha,* a trans-Pacific shipping company with ports of call in Vancouver and Seattle, similarly declared that the "Japanese who go to America generally belong to the lower classes. When they suddenly make their appearance in America, it is no wonder that they do things the Americans do not like." Baron Rempei Kondo, "Japan Harbors no Ill Feeling toward America," *Japan's Message to America,* 39.
12 *Report of the Royal Commission on Chinese and Japanese Immigration, 1902,* 424, *Supplemental Report of W. M. Rice,* 2 May 1899.
13 Ibid., 387, 424.
14 "Japanese Consul in Cumberland, What He Thinks of the Alien Bill, Our City and Other Things," *The Weekly News* (Cumberland, British Columbia), 4 March 1899.
15 Ibid.
16 K. T. Takahashi, *The Anti-Japanese Petition: Appeal in Protest Against a Threatened Persecution* (Montreal: Gazette Printing Company, 1897), 7, 12. Although Takahashi emphasizes his status as a Canadian citizen, he expressly defends statements made by Consul Tatsugoro Nosse, based in Vancouver, British Columbia, to the Japanese government, and also adopts or reinforces arguments by other consular officials.
17 "Japanese Consul in Cumberland," [Cumberland] *Weekly News,* 4 March 1899.
18 Ibid.
19 S. Shimizu, Japanese Consul, Vancouver, British Columbia, to Sir Wilfrid Laurier, 14 March 1898, Canada, *Sessional Papers* 18, *Fourth Session of the Tenth Parliament of the Dominion of Canada, Session 1907–1908,* 7–8, Edward VII, no. 74b, A., 1909. North American officials recognized that the issue of equal status was of great importance to Japan. See, for example, testimony of Alexander R. Milne, C.R., Collector of Customs for Victoria, British Columbia, *Report of the Royal Commission on Chinese and Japanese Immigration, 1902,* 220.
20 "Nosse in Montreal: Japanese Consul Gives His Opinion on British Columbia and Oriental Immigration," *Victoria Daily Colonist,* 28 March 1897. For a general description of the head tax imposed on Chinese, see *Report of the Royal Commission Appointed to Inquire into the Methods by Which Oriental Labourers Have Been Induced to Come to Canada, 1908,* 61.

21 "Nosse in Montreal," *Victoria Daily Colonist*, 28 March 1897. Although some Japanese immigrants were converted to Christianity, especially in later decades, Nosse appears to have been exaggerating the percentage of such conversions in 1897 for rhetorical effect.

22 "Nosse in Montreal," *Victoria Daily Colonist*, 28 March 1897.

23 As Akira Iriye explains, in Meiji Japan "history was conceived of in terms of progress, and all societies were given status in the scale of civilization in accordance with the degree of progress they had achieved." Akira Iriye, "Minds Across the Pacific: Japan in American Writing (1853–1883)," *Papers on Japan from Seminars at Harvard University*, vol. 1, Albert Craig and J. K. Fairbank, eds. (Cambridge, MA: Harvard University, East Asian Research Center, June 1961), 28.

24 "Nosse in Montreal," *Victoria Daily Colonist*, 28 March 1897.

25 Ibid.

26 Takahashi, *The Anti-Japanese Petition: Appeal in Protest Against a Threatened Persecution*, 13.

27 Ibid., 15.

28 Akemi Kikumura explains that "*yotsu*" is intended to suggest the purportedly "subhuman attributes of this outcaste group." Akemi Kikumura, *Through Harsh Winters: The Life of a Japanese Immigrant Woman* (Novato, CA: Chandler & Sharp, 1981), 27, 112. Use of this term persisted well into the second half of the twentieth century: I first encountered both it and other prejudices associated with outcaste status not as an abstract concept in university but in the context of my own lived experience as a youngster attending a Japanese school while living in Japan with my parents.

29 Eileen Sunada Sarasohn, *The Issei: Portrait of a Pioneer, An Oral History* (Palo Alto, CA: Pacific Books, 1983), 61 (Shibata Munejiro interview). Another Japanese American later used the words of a character in an autobiographical novel to express a similar sentiment: "These *hakujin* think we are animals. They treat us like animals." Tooru J. Kanazawa, *Sushi and Sourdough: A Novel* (Seattle: University of Washington Press, 1989), 87. Audrey Kobayashi recounts a similar experience, reporting that "when, in 1981, I interviewed an elderly woman in Japan who had spent some years working as a domestic servant in Canada, she rapidly became upset, expressing anger and contempt for the woman who had treated her 'like an animal.'" Audrey Kobayashi, "For the Sake of the Children: Japanese/Canadian Workers/Mothers," in Audrey Kobayashi, ed., *Women, Work, and Place* (Montreal: McGill-Queen's University Press, 1994), 63.

30 *Shin sekai*, 20 November 1923, as quoted in and translated by Eiichiro Azuma, "Interstitial Lives: Race, Community, and History among Japanese

Immigrants Caught Between Japan and the United States, 1885–1941" (PhD diss., University of California, Los Angeles, 2000), 165. Immigrants in lower status categories, in particular, reported that higher status Japanese were those most stung by white racism because they had never experienced prejudice in Japan. See Sarasohn, *The Issei*, 67.

31 Kazuo Ito, *Issei: A History of Japanese Immigrants in North America* (translated by Shinichiro Nakamura and Jean S. Gerard, Seattle, 1973), 557; Kazuo Ito, *Hokubei hyakunen zakura* (Tokyo: Hokubei Hyakunenzakura Jikkō Inkai, 1969), 655.

32 *Weekly News* (Cumberland, British Columbia), 26 April 1893. More than five hundred Japanese immigrants found work in British Columbia coal mines between 1884 and 1900, for example, beginning with a group of 24 miners brought to Canada in 1889 to work in the Union Coal Mines near Cumberland, British Columbia, followed by a second group of about 130 in December 1891. A third group of experienced coal miners recruited in Fukuoka and Kumamoto prefectures on the island of Kyushu arrived in August 1892 and were followed by others over the next two decades. Michiko Midge Ayukawa, "Creating and Recreating Community" (PhD diss., University of Victoria, 1996), 51, 60–64. That many in this line of work moved on as quickly as they could is suggested by the Royal Commission finding that, by 1902, just 102 Japanese migrants were "employed at the Union Mines, as miners, helpers, runners, drivers, labourers, timbering, blacksmiths, and labourers above ground, 77 being employed underground and 25 above ground." *Report of the Royal Commission on Chinese and Japanese Immigration, 1902*, 372.

33 See, for example, Regine Mathias, "Female Labor in the Japanese Coal-Mining Industry," in Janet Hunter, ed., *Japanese Women Working* (New York: Routledge, 1993), 98–121, stating that a significant percentage of those working in the coal mines in northern Kyushu during the second half of the nineteenth century were *burakumin* (people descended from former outcaste groups). Shigesaki Ninomiya also reports that a majority of miners in the Fukuoka coal mines were "*eta*." Ninomiya, "An Inquiry Concerning the Origin, Development, and Present Situation of the 'Eta' in Relation to the History of Social Classes in Japan" (MA thesis, University of Washington, 1931), 106. Mikiso Hane, in contrast, reports that some mining companies in Japan refused to employ "*eta*" until well into the Meiji period based on the belief that they would pollute the mines. Mikiso Hane, *Peasants, Rebels and Outcastes: The Underside of Modern Japan* (New York: Pantheon, 1982), 242. For attitudes to miners at the time, see Shidzue Ishimoto, "Are Miners Human Beings?," in her autobiography, *Facing Two Ways: The Story of My Life* (Stanford, CA: Stanford University Press, 1984),

158–164 (originally published in 1935). Shidzue Ishimoto, herself a convert to Christianity, provides a compassionate account of the conditions she observed in a coal mine in southern Japan during the early twentieth century, which highlights the harsh and dehumanizing conditions in which coal miners, male and female, worked. Although Ishimoto recognizes the essential humanity of the miners, she invokes the same kind of animal imagery historically associated with outcaste status to describe their daily lives. Ishimoto says, for example, that "it would be hard to tell the difference between the life of pigs and the life of these miners. Certainly the human beings were living like animals in barns." Ibid., 315–316. Emiko Ohnuki-Tierney, in turn, makes reference to Natsume Sōseki's book, *Kōfu (The Miners)* in the following terms: "to ask if there is an occupation more inferior (*katō*) than mining is like asking if there are any days in the year after December 31." She also describes a conversation in which "an educated miner, who had also 'fallen,' tells the young man, 'If you are a Japanese, get out of the mine and find an occupation that is good for Japan." Emiko Ohnuki-Tierney, *Rice as Self: Japanese Identities through Time*, trans. Megan Backus (Princeton, NJ: Princeton University Press, 1993), 104–05. See also Edward Norbeck, "Little-Known Minority Groups in Japan, " in George De Vos and Hiroshi Wagatsuma, eds., *Japan's Invisible Race: Caste in Culture and Personality* (Berkeley: University of California Press, 1966), 193, describing mineworkers as a low-status group only slightly less inferior than the most lowly regarded outcaste group termed "*eta.*"

34 *Report of the Royal Commission Appointed to Inquire into the Methods by Which Oriental Labourers Have Been Induced to Come to Canada, 1908*, 42, 48, citing records provided to the Japanese consul in Vancouver, British Columbia, by the Canadian Nippon Supply Company in 1907. The antipathy to coal mining meant that the labor contractors struggled to meet their contractual obligations to mining companies. S. Gotoh, a labor contractor and head of the Canadian Nippon Supply Company reported, for example, that although he had recruited 135 migrants to come to Canada to work as miners, he had "been unable to supply more than forty, as the men when they landed on this side of the Pacific declared that they preferred to work on the railways and he had no way of compelling them to go into the mines." For that reason, he had given up on trying to recruit miners in Japan altogether. Ibid.

35 That historical sensitivities about the meaning of leatherwork persist is suggested by the decision to avoid using the word "shoemaker" when translating the name of the *Nihonjin kakō dōmeikai* into English even today. Although *kakō* is the word used for shoemaker in Japanese, it was translated as "shoe repairers" because shoe repair was regarded as a less

polluted job, since those engaged in it were not directly involved in processing the leather used to make shoes. The Japanese word for "shoe repairer" is *shūrikō*. Andrew Nelson, *Japanese-English Character Dictionary*, 2nd ed. (Rutland, VT: Charles E. Tuttle, 1974), 952. Seizo Oka, director of the Japanese American National History Archives in San Francisco, explained that "shoe repairers" and not "shoemakers" remains the preferred translation for "*kakō*." Seizo Oka, conversation with author, San Francisco, 23 July 2002.

36 Kenji Ōshima, "On the Hardships Leading to the Founding of our Shoemakers League," *Kakō dōmeikai kaihō*, 1 January 1911, 9–14, Japanese American National History Archives [JANHA]. Also see De Vos and Wagatsuma, *Japan's Invisible Race*, 35 (shoemaking and leatherwork were occupations reserved to those categorized as *eta* within the context of the Tokugawa status system). Ohnuki-Tierney explains that "it is the lower parts of the body, including the feet, that are seen to be most defiling. Therefore, things representing that area—footgear, floor, and ground—are all dirty, and require no contact or immediate healing." Emiko Ohnuki-Tierney, *Illness and Culture in Contemporary Japan: An Anthropological View* (Cambridge: Cambridge University Press, 1984), 31.

37 Minutes of Meetings, *Nihonjin kakō dōmeikai*, 14 January 1908. JANHA.

38 The notion that there exists a unique Japanese race (*Yamato minzoku*) that is infused with a spirit that is quintessentially Japanese (*Yamato damashii*) and has its origins in Japan's mythical past was invoked during the Meiji period to facilitate the development of a strong sense of national identity. See, for example, Shimpei Goto, "The Real Character of the Japanese Race," in Naoichi Masaoka, ed., *Japan's Message to America: A Symposium by Representative Japanese on Japan and American-Japanese Relations* (Tokyo, 1914), 12–13, 17; T. Iyenaga and Kenosuke Sato, *Japanese and the California Problem* (New York: G. P. Putnam's Sons, 1921), 18–10. See also Carol Gluck, *Japan's Modern Myths: Ideology in the Late Meiji Period* (Princeton, NJ: Princeton University Press, 1985), 136.

39 *Nihonjin kakō dōmei kiyaku oyobi saisoku, dai 6 jō* (Constitution and By-laws, Article 6) and *Kakō dōmei setsuritsu no shui* (Establishment Manifesto), 1893. JANHA.

40 Seizo Oka, Japanese American National History Archives, conversation with author, San Francisco, 23 July 2002, noting that many members of the *Nihonjin kakō dōmei* eventually moved away from San Francisco.

References

Ayukawa, Michiko Midge. "Creating and Recreating Community." PhD diss., University of Victoria, 1996.

Azuma, Eiichiro. "Interstitial Lives: Race, Community, and History among Japanese Immigrants Caught Between Japan and the United States, 1885–1941." PhD diss., University of California, Los Angeles, 2000.
Canada. *Report of the Royal Commission on Chinese and Japanese Immigration*, 1902.
———. *Report of the Royal Commission Appointed to Inquire into the Methods by Which Oriental Labourers Have Been Induced to Come to Canada*, 1908.
———. *Sessional Papers 18*. 10th Parliament, 4th sess., 1907–1908, 7–8 Ed. 7, no. 74b, 1909.
Chan, Sucheng. "European and Asian Immigration into the United States in Comparative Perspective, 1820s to 1920s," in Virginia Yans-McLaughlin, ed., *Immigration Reconsidered: History, Sociology, and Politic*. New York: Oxford University Press, 1990, 37–75.
[Cumberland] *Weekly News*, "Report," April 26, 1893.
———. "Japanese Consul in Cumberland, What He Thinks of the Alien Bill, Our City and Other Things," March 4, 1899.
De Vos, George, and Hiroshi Wagatsuma. *Japan's Invisible Race: Caste in Culture and Personality*. Berkeley: University of California Press, 1966, 329.
Geiger, Andrea. *Subverting Exclusion: Transpacific Encounters with Race, Caste, and Borders, 1885–1928*. New Haven, CT: Yale University Press, 2011.
Gluck, Carol. *Japan's Modern Myths: Ideology in the Late Meiji Period*. Princeton, NJ: Princeton University Press, 1985.
Hane, Mikiso. *Peasants, Rebels and Outcastes: The Underside of Modern Japan*. New York: Pantheon, 1982.
Hata, Donald Teruo Jr. "'Undesirables': Unsavory Elements Among the Japanese in America Prior to 1893 and Their Influence on the First Anti-Japanese Movement in California." PhD diss., University of Southern California, 1970, 33.
Howell, David L. *Geographies of Identity in Nineteenth-Century Japan*. Berkeley: University of California Press, 2005, 4, 7, 20–44.
———. "Liberating and Killing Outcastes in Early Meiji Japan." Princeton University, Department of East Asian Studies, 2001, 5.
Ichihashi, Yamato. *Japanese in the United States: A Critical Study of the Problems of the Japanese Immigrants and Their Children*. Stanford, CA: Stanford University Press, 1932, 67.
Iriye, Akira. "Minds Across the Pacific: Japan in American Writing (1853–1883)." *Papers on Japan from Seminars at Harvard University*, vol. 1, edited by Albert Craig and J. K. Fairbank. Cambridge, MA: Harvard University, East Asian Research Center, 1961.
Ishimoto, Shidzue. *Facing Two Ways: The Story of My Life*. Stanford, CA: Stanford University Press, 1984.

Ito, Kazuo. *Hokubei hyakunen zakura*. Tokyo: Hokubei Hyakunenzakura Jikkō Inkai, 1969, 655.

———. *Issei: A History of Japanese Immigrants in North America*. Translated by Shinichiro Nakamura and Jean S. Gerard. Seattle: Japanese Community Service, 1973.

Iyenaga, T., and Kenosuke Sato. *Japanese and the California Problem*. New York: G. P. Putnam's Sons, 1921.

Kanazawa, Tooru J. *Sushi and Sourdough: A Novel*. Seattle: University of Washington Press, 1989.

Kikumura, Akemi. *Through Harsh Winters: The Life of a Japanese Immigrant Woman*. Novato, CA: Chandler & Sharp, 1981.

Kobayashi, Audrey, ed. *Women, Work, and Place*. Montreal: McGill-Queen's University Press, 1994.

Masaoka, Naochi, ed. *Japan's Message to America: A Symposium by Representative Japanese on Japan and American-Japanese Relations*. Tokyo, 1914.

Mathias, Regine. "Female Labor in the Japanese Coal-Mining Industry." In *Japanese Women Working*, edited by Janet Hunter. New York: Routledge, 1993.

Millis, H. A. *The Japanese Problem in the United States*. New York: MacMillan, 1915.

Nelson, Andrew. *Japanese-English Character Dictionary*, 2nd ed. Rutland, VT: Charles E. Tuttle, 1974.

Nihonjin kakō dōmeikai (Japanese Shoe Repairers Association) Collection, Japanese American National History Archives, San Francisco, California. *Nihonjin kakō dōmeikai kiyaku oyobi saisoku* (Constitution and By-laws), 1893a.

———. *Kakō dōmei setsuritsu no shui* (Shoe Repairers Association Establishment Manifesto), 1893b.

———. Minutes of Meetings, 1908.

———. *Nihonjin kakō dōmeikai kaihō* (Japanese Shoe Repairers Association Bulletin), 1911.

Ninomiya, Shigesaki. "An Inquiry Concerning the Origin, Development, and Present Situation of the 'Eta' in Relation to the History of Social Classes in Japan." MA thesis, University of Washington, 1931.

Norbeck, Edward. "Little-Known Minority Groups in Japan." In *Japan's Invisible Race: Caste in Culture and Personality*, edited by George De Vos and Hiroshi Wagatsuma. Berkeley: University of California Press, 1966.

Ohnuki-Tierney, Emiko. *Illness and Culture in Contemporary Japan: An Anthropological View*. Cambridge: Cambridge University Press, 1984.

———. *Rice as Self: Japanese Identities through Time*. Translated by Megan Backus. Princeton, NJ: Princeton University Press, 1993.

Ōshima, Kenji. "On the Hardships Leading to the Founding of our Shoemakers League." *Kakō dōmeikai kaihō* (1 January, 1911): 9–14, Japanese American National History Archives [JANHA].

Rice, W. M. *Supplemental Report of W. M. Rice, U.S. Commissioner on Immigration.* Washington, DC, 1899.

Ryan, Marleigh Grayer. "Translating Modern Japanese Literature." *Journal of Japanese Studies* 6 (1) (Winter 1980): 49–60.

Sarasohn, Eileen Sunada. *The Issei: Portrait of a Pioneer, An Oral History.* Palo Alto, CA: Pacific Books, 1983.

Seidensticker, Edward. "On Miner on Translating Japanese Poetry." *Orient/West* 7 (1) (January 1962): 17–20.

Takahashi, K. T. *The Anti-Japanese Petition: Appeal in Protest Against a Threatened Persecution.* Montreal: Gazette Printing Company, 1897.

United States, National Archives and Records Administration. Record Group 85. *Records of the Immigration and Naturalization Service, Series A, Subject Correspondence Files, Part I, Asian Immigration and Exclusion,* 1906–1913.

Victoria Daily Colonist. "Nosse in Montreal: Japanese Consul Gives His Opinion on British Columbia and Oriental Immigration," March 28, 1897.

Wilson, Robert A., and Bill Hosokawa. *East to America: A History of the Japanese in the United States.* New York: William Morrow, 1980.

Yans-McLaughlin, Virginia, ed. *Immigration Reconsidered: History, Sociology, and Politic.* New York: Oxford University Press, 1990, 37–75.

PART IV

INTERSECTIONS

CHAPTER 7

Americanization and Beika
Gender and Racialization of the Issei Community in California before World War II

Yuko Matsumoto

Introduction

Japanese scholars tend to study history of Japanese immigrants before World War II as a discrete academic area of historical studies rather than considering it in the broader context of U.S. history. They describe how Japanese immigrants, in isolation from the rest of society, constructed their community and contributed to the U.S. economy while they were excluded from the nation-state because of racism. In this chapter, I reexamine the correlation between U.S. society and Japanese immigrants before World War II, focusing on qualifications for full membership in the U.S. nation-state.

Full membership in the Constitution's "we, the [American] people" should guarantee the recognition, respect, and protection as an American citizen in addition to the legal entitlements associated with U.S. citizenship (Glenn 2002, 1). From the start of the U.S. nation after independence from Britain, not everyone within the U.S. border was granted full membership in the nation-state. For instance, American Indians were considered aliens without rights, and enslaved African Americans were considered property.

After the Civil War, African Americans were included in the category of citizenship, albeit without full rights. The Americanization movement in the early twentieth century tried to redefine the qualifications for full membership in the nation. Throughout U.S. history, the comprehension of American values such as freedom and democracy as well as fluency in

English have been the fundamental components in becoming "American." In addition, the Americanization movement tried to inculcate newcomers with "the American way of life," which promoted hygiene, efficiency, and the consumption of home appliances and furnishings. Those were modern, new values for both immigrants and U.S. citizens of the time. Social movements, including the home economics movement, promoted those modern ideas, and industrial capitalism and mass production encouraged mass consumption, which prominently featured home appliances and furnishings for the home. U.S. women were the primary targets. Such changes in early twentieth-century America should be analyzed against the background of the Progressive Era.[1]

In the same period, the nativistic movements against "new immigrants" from southern and eastern Europe and the anti-Asian movement flourished. The ideologies behind those movements, however, did not necessarily conflict with ideas of Americanization. My analysis of the discourses of the anti-Japanese (and Asian) movements in this chapter shows that the Americanization movement and movements for exclusion were two sides of the same coin in the process of defining membership in the U.S. nation-state.[2] By enumerating the reasons it was impossible to Americanize Japanese (and Asian) immigrants, activists revealed the limits and boundary of the U.S. nation.

From the standpoint of European immigrants who arrived in the early twentieth century, the boundary between "we, the American people" and "others" was fluid, flexible, and often multifarious. For other immigrants, by contrast, the border was not so fluid or free. In California, for instance, the Americanization movement aimed at integrating Mexican immigrants into U.S. society at its lowest levels, that is, as laborers (Garcia 2001). Almost simultaneously, the racialization of Mexican immigrants and Mexican Americans proceeded. In that way, Mexican immigrants in the early twentieth century stood on the dividing line between "we" and "others."

Those immigrants who were put on or outside the boundary between "we" and "others" believed that there was room for negotiation, and they proposed alternate visions for full membership in the U.S. nation-state. Although race was a decisive element, the categorization of race fluctuated in the early twentieth century. As whiteness studies reveal, for instance, southern and eastern European immigrants negotiated with American society regarding racial boundaries' becoming white.

Japanese immigrant leaders also assumed that there was room for negotiation even though they were regarded as ineligible for legal citizenship because of race. Responding actively to the discourses of anti-Japanese (and Asian) movements, Japanese immigrants tried to prove their eligibility for full membership in the U.S. nation by following their own interpretation of Americanization, or Beika (米化). One can understand the negotiation between American society and Japanese immigrants by examining how Japanese immigrant leaders interpreted the qualifications for full membership in the Americanization discourses and developed their own ideas of Beika.[3]

To appreciate the discourses of Americanization and those of Beika, it is necessary to pay attention to gender. Because "the American way of life" was to be pursued in the "private sphere," the Americanization movement put emphasis on women's roles. Women should be managers of their homes, "scientific" mothers, and the standard-bearers for an American way of living. For instance, an activist of the Americanization movement stressed the necessity of Americanizing the homes of Mexican immigrants with the slogan "Go after the Women" (White 1923, 34–35). Anti-Japanese (and Asian) movements criticized the gender relations of immigrant communites and regarded Japanese and other Asian immigrant women as "exotic others" who represented the impossibility of Americanization of Asian immigrants. Recognizing the significance of women's roles for Americanization, Japanese immigrant leaders also stressed the importance of gender roles in their perception of Beika.

In this chapter, therefore, I focus on the gender discourses of Beika, comparing those discourses with the ideas of Americanization and the propaganda of anti-Japanese (and Asian) movements. I also show how those views shed light on the process of becoming full members of the U.S. nation-state. That history demonstrates how the struggles of Japanese immigrants before World War II have affected the subsequent experience of Japanese Americans.

Gender Discourses in the Anti-Japanese (Asian) Movement

Picture Marriage and the American Home

Since the nineteenth century, immigration laws and immigration controls have protected the image of the American family. Immigration officers suspected European immigrant women who landed alone of having "immoral purposes" or "likely to be public charges." Concern over "white slavery" or prostitution was linked to racialized categories. Chinese women, in particular, were believed to have come to the United States for immoral purposes. According to the historian Martha Gardner, this sexualized image of Chinese women affected Japanese and other Asian women who arrived later (Gardner 2005, 54, 58–60; Lee and Yung 2010).

In the 1910s, there arose a vehement campaign against the picture marriages of Japanese immigrants. In the beginning, picture brides were suspected to have the same purpose as Chinese "slave girls." Gradually, however, the anti–picture brides campaign shifted its concern from prostitution to labor problems. Anti-Japanese propaganda accused the picture brides of breaching the "Gentlemen's Agreement" because they immigrated to the United States in order to become laborers in the fields (Benedict 1920, 3). Japanese scholars have tended to emphasize these economic problems concerning labor in order to rationalize the anti–picture bride campaign.

While the anti–picture bride propaganda did mention economic problems, its main contestation was around morality. The agitators and media characterized the practice of picture marriages as "immoral" and "undemocratic" because it differed from what they presumed to be legitimate marriage. In the early twentieth century, activists for Americanization inculcated immigrants with the significance of "the home" and premised that the American way of life should be based on companionate marriage between an earning husband and an economically dependent wife and their nuclear family (Dixon 1916, 120–122). At Angel Island in San Francisco Bay, immigration authorities asked Japanese women whether they could be loyal to and economically dependent on their husbands, demanding that the husbands in question submit various papers that ensured employment and economic stability (Gardner 2005; Lee and Yung 2010).

That discourse about morality in the anti–picture marriage campaign racialized Japanese immigrants. Anti-Japanese propaganda asserted that the practice of picture marriages proved the "barbaric" characteristics of "Oriental customs" of Japanese immigrants. As the term "Oriental customs" indicates, Japanese immigrants were not the unique target of such criticism. Hindu marriage, Chinese marriage, and polygamy were also labeled as Asian "uncivilized customs" that undercut American values (Shah 2011, 176). Those discourses concerning marriage in the early twentieth century therefore racialized Asian immigrants as a homogeneous group. They also confirmed the stereotype of Japanese women, and of Asian women in general, as those who were so submissive that they could not oppose "coerced" marriages. Those stereotypes might have had their origin in an American image of the "Orient" or Asia. Nevertheless, the racialization of immigrants from various areas of Asia as "Oriental" or Asians on the grounds of customs of marriage in the early twentieth century confirmed those stereotypes, which survived until at least the 1960s.

While the anti–picture marriage campaign gained steam, Japanese immigrants could not persuade themselves that the custom of picture marriage was "immoral." One Japanese immigrant, for instance, denounced the condemnation of picture brides as a violation of the rights of marriage in an article in *Zaibei Fujinn no Tomo*[4] (Niisato 1924, 16–17). Nonetheless, people who were concerned about the problem of picture marriage in both Japan and the United States strived to make immigrants and future brides comply with American ideals of "home" and the Western style of life. In 1920, a representative of the Japanese Association of America reported its intention before a committee of the U.S. House of Representatives: "We consider it most important and necessary that the Japanese in America should marry and settle down in domestic life, because the home is not only essential to the wholesome existence of individuals, but also the foundation of a stable national and social structure" (U.S. House of Representatives 1921, 719). In this committee, Japanese immigrant leaders repeatedly testified to their efforts to make immigrants adopt a Western style of marriage.

Despite these efforts, opposition did not weaken or decrease. As a result, Japan ended picture marriages in 1920, although the Los Angeles Japanese Association and the Japanese Association of Southern California protested the abolition on behalf of Japanese single men in the United States (Fujioka 1940, 14, 30). Even though they were abolished within a short time frame, the controversy over picture marriages created a persistent stereotype that the Japanese immigrant community itself was complicit in solidifying. According to recent studies conducted by Japanese researchers, many Japanese picture brides were highly educated and chose to live in the United States of their own volition. Nonetheless, the Japanese and American YWCA instilled in the community the idea that these women were from Japan's lower classes and that they were "vain, immoral and uncivilized." It was also reported that some Issei women felt "ashamed" of being a picture bride.[5]

The American Home and Women's Labor

After settling in California, Japanese immigrant women continued to be the target of anti-Japanese propaganda, which accused them of working on family farms for long hours and even on Sundays without pay. This accusation was a well-worn explanation for the causes of anti-Japanese agitation.

The real cause of such propaganda might have been economic competition, as Japanese men were also criticized for working long hours. Nonetheless, the discourse of anti-Japanese propagada argued that Japanese women's work in the fields constituted "immoral" conduct because wives neglected their homes and mothers failed to take proper care of their children.

Anti-Japanese propaganda utilized the same discourses that Americanizers advocated regarding proper women's roles. Harry A. Millis, an economics professor at the University of Kansas, who in 1915 conducted research on the "Japanese problem" under the authority of the Federal Council of the Churches of Christ in America, claimed that Japanese women neglected household duties for work in shops and fields, while the "average American" assumed that wives should not "work regularly at the chief gainful pursuit of the family" (Millis 1915, 194, 256–257). Milton Esbero, a member of San Francisco's Chamber of Commerce, emphasized the significance of the division of labor based on gender. "Anti-Japanese agitation in California is largely due to the non-adoption of American standards of living, working, and working hours, together with the fact that there seems to be no discrimination on the part of the Japanese as to whether the men or the women do the work, as the same basis seems to apply for both sexes" (Harada 1922, 14).

In reality, that so-called norm concerning women's labor had not fully permeated American society. For instance, white American farm women worked both in and outside their homes. In 1919, the Department of Agriculture surveyed the lives of 10,044 farm women all over the country and showed that they were productive workers on the farm, and 24 percent of them worked in the fields (Ward 1920, 437–457). In the same period, the federal government and agricultural colleges advocated the necessity of modernizing farm life, and agents of the national Home Extension System visited rural areas and demonstrated to American farm women the "modern" kitchen and clean bathroom (Holt 1995). Indeed, the American way of life that Americanizers and anti-Japanese campaigners advocated was not necessarily practiced all over the country. The campaign against Japanese immigrant women's labor in the fields in California represented not an abiding American value but the ideal of the new "modern" way of life that some urban, middle-class reformers promoted.

Agitators in California and other West Coast areas, however, claimed that women's labor in the fields was "immoral," as if the practice violated a universal value. In fact, they assigned "immorality" to racial characteristics such as the so-called Oriental patriarchal structure and the "submissiveness" of traditional Japanese women. As the historian Nayan Shah points out, the contrast between "white women's release from manual labor" and "nonwhite women's servitude" established the racial boundary of full membership in the U.S. nation-state (Shah 2011, 41).

Some Japanese immigrants thought that such accusations against women's labor were undeserved because it was natural for women to help their husbands in the fields or stores (Survey of Race Relations 1925b, 3). Leaders of the Japanese immigrant community, however, recognized that the issue of women's labor was significant because it related to American virtues or morality concerning gender relations and family lives. One Japanese-language paper reported that from the American point of view, women's work in the fields symbolized "abusive husbands" who forced battered wives to work (*Nikka Noho* 1919, 9–10). Various articles on Americanization in a special issue of *Zaibei Fujinn no Tomo* in 1919 identified women's labor as one of the major causes behind anti-Japanese campaigning. Both male and female contributors charged that women could not develop good family lives or bring up children properly if they worked outside the home all day. In the same year, the Central Japanese Association declared a ban on women's labor on Sundays for the sake of "the happiness of the family" and "clean homes" (*Zaibei Fujinn no Tomo* 1919). In 1920, Tsuneko Yamauchi, the wife of the editor of *Zaibei Fujinn no Tomo,* undertook field labor as research for an article she was writing because of the continued controversy over such work. She wrote that working in the fields was a "disgrace for women" and exerted a bad influence on children, thus supporting the proposal of the Central Japanese Association (Yamauchi 1920, 16–24).

Thus, the leaders of the Japanese immigrant community recognized that maintaining gendered and separate spheres were moral codes that should be observed, but they could not accept the idea that the problem of women's labor constituted the racial boundary of full membership in the U.S. nation-state. They believed that the problem would be solved when Japanese immigrant women stayed at home. Just as Japanese society and the Japanese immigrant community's elite intensified the stereotypical image of the "picture bride," male and female leaders of the Japanese immigrant community lent their support to constructing the stereotype of submissive Japanese immigrant women by criticizing women who continued to work outside the home.

Racialization and Self-Racialization

The Japanese immigrant community fully understood that they did not belong to the "white race." Along with African Americans and Mexican Americans, Japanese immigrants and their descendants were refused admission to public swimming pools and found it was the "unwritten rule" that they were unwelcome in restaurants other than Chinese and Japanese eating places (Wada 1986–1987, 3–20). The secretary-general of the Central Japanese Association characterized the cause of the anti-Japanese campaign as racism, which was "the prejudice that every race inherited congenitally" (Kondo 1919, 2). The general statement of the *Biographical Dictionary of Japanese in the United States,* published in 1922, described racism as "a kind of patriotic activity for American people" (Nichibei Shimbun-sha 1922, 16–17), thereby linking race with citizenship.

Racialization is a reciprocal process. Facing up to the wall of race, members of various organizations, Buddhist temples, and churches strengthened their ties and developed measures for mutual aid. Because most Japanese immigrant organizations were male centered, Japanese immigrant women organized auxiliaries to male organizations or founded their own women's organizations. Through those organizations, Japanese immigrant leaders advocated the necessity of solidifying the consciousness of the "Japanese race," or "Yamato race," as different from the "white race." At the same time, as the scholar Fuminori Minamikawa argues in his chapter in this book, they advocated their superiority to other nonwhites and eastern and southern European groups. In other words, they fought against white racializations by racializing themselves.

Gender was significant in that process of self-racializing. As Lisa Lowe (1996, 71) has pointed out, it is impossible to isolate race from gender. To strengthen the ties of community and to demonstrate their adaptability to American society, Japanese immigrant leaders tried to put their members under strict social control. This social control put pressure on the lives of Japanese immigrant women and underscored the gender imbalance, particularly concerning morality. For instance, women were more often blamed for marital problems than men. The Reverend Paul Tamura remembers how marital difficulties were publicized in the early twentieth century: "It seemed that every day the papers would have three or four notices concerning runaway wives. The picture and description of the woman would appear with a reward offered for finding her" (Survey of Race Relations 1925c, 2). Kannichi

Niisato wrote three books on the lives of Japanese immigrants in Los Angeles during the 1930s. Although his descriptions are full of exaggeration, rumors, and gossip lacking credibility, his writing reveals an unequal attribution of morality and immorality when writing of women instead of men. For instance, in *Immigrant Elegies: Family Tragedy,* a collection of his articles published in *Zaibei Fujinn no Tomo* during the 1920s, Niisato introduces cases of "immoral" behavior such as divorce, infidelity, and prostitution and warns female readers to behave themselves (Niisato 1933).

Beika

Americanization Programs and Japanese Immigrants

At the turn of the century, missionaries, volunteer organizations, and some sociologists tried to Americanize Japanese and Chinese immigrants even though they were ineligible for legal citizenship. Soon thereafter, Asian immigrants became marginalized. George Warren Hinman, district secretary of the American Missionary Association, suggested in 1920 that the Americanization activities of federal and state organizations did not extend their concern for Japanese and Chinese immigrants. Kiichi Kanzaki, general secretary of the Japanese Association of America, charged in 1920 that the California Commission of Immigration and Housing had never published any book or booklet on Americanization in Japanese, although such books were translated into Spanish, Italian, and other languages (U.S. House of Representatives 1921, 552, 645).

This indifference toward Asian immigrants, however, was not commonly seen in every locality. In the interior states, according to historian Eric Walz, corporate organizations often encouraged the Americanization of Asian immigrant laborers (Walz 2012, 108). In Hawai'i, the Americanization movement reached out to Japanese immigrants and Japanese Americans, but it did not target Japanese immigrant women. During the 1910s, for instance, 44 percent of all Japanese females ten years and older worked outside the home (Tamura 1990, 57). Accordingly, it was difficult to associate women's labor outside the home with "immorality." Rather, the Americanization movement in Hawai'i focused on the Nisei. According to sociologist Evelyn Nakano Glenn, Americanization programs in Hawai'i aimed at constraining Nisei ambitions for upward mobility and keeping them in agricultural labor through vocational education (Glenn 2006, 308–312; Tamura 1990).

Recognizing this fluidity and multiplicity of the Americanization programs, Japanese immigrant leaders tried to propose alternative visions to prove their qualifications for full membership in the U.S. nation-state. In Los Angeles, Japanese immigrant leaders asserted that Japanese immigrants should pursue American middle-class values in order to acquire equality. They did not follow the example of Americanization programs for Mexican immigrants, recognizing that the main objective of such programs was to make good laborers. Sei Fujii argued that if Japanese immigrants were good workers, white people would accept them, but when they tried to socialize with white people on an equal basis, they would be rejected (Fujii 1940, 82). In 1921, the newsletter of the Japanese American Association pointed out that farm labor was "disgraceful" and recommended that the children of the laboring classes receive vocational education and acquire a higher level of skills (North American Association of Japanese Language Schools 1930, 168).

Leaders of Japanese immigrants acknowledged that the primary objective of the Americanization programs was to attain the American standard of living and the American way of life. Even though major societies of their community were all male centered, leaders still recognized correctly the significance of women in the Americanization programs. Various types of organizations, including the churches of Japanese immigrants, Buddhist temples, and Japanese-language schools prepared Americanization programs, many of which targeted women.

At the same time, Japanese immigrant women were not just the passive targets of Beika but also its active agents. Japanese immigrant women's organizations, Buddhist temples, and churches organized classes on home economics, hygiene, milk consumption, and other knowledge and skills considered essential to pursuing the American way of life.[6] In a *Zaibei Fujinn no Tomo* special issue on Americanization, for instance, Chiyo Fujioka, the wife of the president of the Central Japanese Association, and Tatsuko Kondo, the wife of the secretary-general of the Central Japanese Association, emphasized the importance of Americanization. Both women accentuated the responsibility of mothers and the significance of the companionate family in which male members should not exert their authority too much (*Zaibei Fujinn no Tomo* 1919, 24–36).

Americanization Programs and Beika

Japanese immigrant leaders interpreted correctly what was required of membership in the nation-state. Nevertheless, they appended their own values to their interpretation in promoting Beika. Being racialized in American society, Japanese immigrant leaders needed to claim that they and their descendants were deserving of U.S. citizenship and full membership in the nation as "an exceptional race." In 1919, Choei Kondo, the secretary-general of the Central Japanese Association, for instance, asserted that Beika meant maintaining characteristics such as love and duty (*girininnjou*), which were "unique" to Japanese culture, and grafting those onto American values, such as enjoying leisure and comfortable lives or taking good care of wives (Kondo 1919, 2–5).

There are some nuanced but significant differences between Beika and Americanization. First, while Japanese immigrant leaders understood the significance of Americanizing their homes, they did not, or would not, recognize the difference between the notion of the American home and their concept of home (*ie*). The American home was supposed to consist of a companionate family in which a woman was the "manager" of the household. The concept of *ie* had a rigid patriarchal structure and a seniority system within the family. One Nisei high school student critically observed relations between her parents in 1924: "The man was everything and his wife had to do just as he said. The wife had to work so hard . . . when he came in from work in the evening she was supposed to have his supper ready for him" (Survey of Race Relations 1925a, 3).

In fact, Japanese immigrant leaders believed that the Japanese *ie* was superior to the American home and would make a better foundation for the U.S. nation because the Japanese home had "strong family ties." Interviewed by a researcher participating in the Survey of Race Relations in 1925, Mrs. K. Iseri, a Nisei, praised the family ties of Japanese immigrants: "Like the Jews, the family tie is very strong among the Japanese. The children have more respect for their parents than is true of many of the people of southern European countries and there seems to be much less disharmony in the homes resulting from the Americanization of the children" (Survey of Race Relations 1925d, 1). In the 1930s, Shinnichiro Hasegawa, vice president of the Los Angeles Japan America Society, asserted that the Japanese should teach "familism" to Americans. Emphasizing the "superiority" of the homes of Japanese immigrants, he asserted that the "Yamato race" was exceptional among non-white racial groups and deserved to be accepted as full members of American society (Hasegawa 1937, 229–255).

The second significant difference is that Japanese immigrant leaders believed Japanese immigrants could attain the American standard of living within a short period. Anti-Japanese movement agitators denounced the everyday lives of Japanese immigrants, commenting on their poor housing and meager furnishings, which, they maintained, did not and could not reach "the American standard of living." Sociologist Ralph Burnight, who analyzed "the Japanese problem" in 1920, pointed out that "the Japanese farmer spends practically nothing on the luxuries, which almost every American family counts as a necessity" (Burnight 1920, 5–7).

Theoretically, it was possible for anyone, including Asian immigrants and other racial minorities, to attain the American standard of living. Agitators of anti-Japanese movements, however, argued that biological differences between races determined their standard of living. Describing how low the Japanese immigrants' standard of living was, newspaperman V. S. McClatchy concluded, "The Japanese seems to stand this sort of life without strain on the nervous system.... The white race as educated in the American environment not only will not do it, but perhaps cannot do it" (McClatchy 1921, 53). Protesting the construction of this racial boundary, Japanese immigrant leaders asserted that it was highly possible for Japanese immigrants to reach the American standard of living in the near future. In 1920, Kiichi Kanzaki refuted such assumptions at the Committee on Immigration of the U.S. House of Representatives: "Japanese immigrants' standards of living are not inferior—as a matter of fact, they are superior—when compared with those prevailing among other immigrant races" (U.S. House of Representatives 1921, 648).

At the same time, some Japanese immigrants criticized the American standard of living as measured by consumption. The report of the Southern California Japanese Christian Churches Association in 1931 criticized "the pleasure and materialism" of "western civilization" and pointed out that because Japanese immigrants and their descendants had the special ability to absorb different cultures, Japanese immigrants could fuse "Japanese civilization" with "western civilization." This report also introduced the opinion of a Japanese scholar who argued that Japanese values such as "a sense of honor and loyalty" could be "the antidote against the materialism of American civilization" (Nannka Nihonjin Kirisutokyo Kyokai Renmei 1932, 115).

Beika and *Yamatonadeshiko* (Women of the Yamato Race)

Among the differences between Americanization and Beika, disagreement over the idea of womanliness was conspicuous. Although Japanese immigrant women were expected to learn the skills and knowledge of the American way of life, Japanese immigrant leaders claimed that the primary role of women was the reproduction of the "Yamato race" and maintaining the virtues of the *Yamatonadeshiko*. In 1919, an article in a special issue of the *Zaibei Fujinn no Tomo* about Beika argued that immigrant women should maintain the virtues of Japanese women such as "gentleness and chastity" while acquiring "the intelligence and physical strength of western women" (Hara 1919, 22).

Most of the articles in *Zaibei Fujinn no Tomo* propagated the virtue of *Yamatonadeshiko* while criticizing white American women. An article in 1924 denigrated "new women" who demanded equality and freedom and declared that the strength of Japanese women lay in "love, sympathy, patience, modesty, and motherhood" (Takaoka 1924, 2–7). Both male and female contributors supported the virtue of *Yamatonadeshiko*. In 1920, Tayoko Sakamoto, a women's leader in the YWCA of Los Angeles, asserted that the mission of women was to "spiritually" guide men, who tended to pursue material gains, and criticized the "new women" who demanded "complete equality" between men and women (Sakamoto 1920, 2–4). An Issei woman pointed out in a 1925 article in the same journal that imitation of "the flaws of American women" was not the first step toward Americanization. These flaws were the "predominance of women, vanity, and individualism" (Yanase 1925, 9–14).

In the interviews conducted during the Survey of Race Relations in the mid-1920s, multiple answers given by Japanese immigrants identified "freedom" or the demand for equal rights as one of the main causes of family difficulties. A Japanese male immigrant argued that it was "undesirable" to "let a woman stand above a man" and concluded that "women's freedom" made wives "selfish and willful" (Survey of Race Relations 1924, 5–13). At the meeting of the Women's Association of the Los Angeles Japanese Methodist Church in 1931, a Japanese pastor warned that because demands for equal rights would endanger the foundation of any nation, Japanese immigrant women had to maintain Japanese feminine virtues, such as patience (Los Angeles Japanese Methodist Church 1931). *Yamatonadeshiko* was required to offer "obedience" not only to their family group but also to the entire Japanese immigrant community, because this entire community was regarded as an extended family (Kikumura 1981, 125).

As studies on the history of white American women fully prove, American women did not achieve complete freedom or precedence in gender relations during that time. That observation of Japanese immigrant leaders about American women and American gender relations simply reflected stereotypes about American society that they had created.

Male and female leaders of Japanese immigrants also constructed negative stereotypes about American youth culture. They became anxious about the influence of American culture on young people, although they promoted educating them in the English language and American customs and values. Concerns regarding the influence of American culture on the Nisei also demonstrated gender bias. *Zaibei Fujinn no Tomo*, for instance, published various articles that criticized "modern girls" who had short hair and wore "too much make-up." Another article denounced "modern girls" for desiring only the pleasure of the moment.[7] Kannichi Niisato's book dealing with "the Nisei problem" claimed that Nisei women had more "immoral problems" than their male counterparts because of "liberal education and lack of discipline at school and at home" and "the precedence of women in American society" (Niisato 1934, 14).

Those norms of "womanliness" continued to be deeply rooted in the Japanese immigrant community. According to historian Valerie Matsumoto, Nisei women in particular confronted the tensions between "Japanese ways" and the values of American mainstream culture involving love and marriage (V. Matsumoto 1994). This emphasis on *Yamatonadeshiko* is also one of the causes of the contradiction between racial solidarity and sexism in the Asian American movement in the 1960s (which Matsumoto analyzes in her chapter in this book).

In sum, Japanese immigrant leaders expected that Japanese immigrants could Americanize themselves based on the virtues of the Yamato race and *Yamatonadeshiko*. From the viewpoint of most researchers in Japan and the United States, Beika based on the consciousness of the "Yamato race" and programs of Americanization cannot be reconciled. Researchers on the history of Japanese immigrants often analyze Beika as merely an "external" or "superficial" type of assimilation. Yuji Ichioka, for instance, argued that Americanization was the promotion of a superficial assimilation, akin to making Japanese immigrant women wear dresses instead of kimono (Ichioka 1988). Some scholars point out that Japanese immigrants placed priority on their sense of belonging to Japan, as demonstrated by their emphasis on retaining consciousness of the "Yamato race" (Hayashi 1995).

Was Beika then mere rhetoric? The answer might hinge on the meaning of "superficial," but it appears that the activities of Japanese immigrant associations in promoting Beika were sincere and substantial. Japanese immigrants did not just look to Japan, either. The leaders of the Japanese immigrant organizations tried to prove painstakingly that they were exceptionally capable of crossing the racial boundary of U.S. citizenship.

It seems that for Japanese immigrant leaders prior to World War II, Beika and Americanization were not in conflict with each other. The education provided in Japanese-language schools demonstrates some of the typical aspects of Beika. Although state and federal governments attacked them as being anti-American, Japanese-language schools kept teaching the virtues of the "Yamato race" to Nisei for the purpose of making them into good U.S. citizens (Kumei 1998). As the Japanese publisher Kyutaro Abiko argued, "*Yamatodamashii*," the soul of the Yamato race, made children into better American citizens (North American Association of Japanese Language Schools 1930, 310–311). A Japanese textbook published in 1933 described pledging allegiance to the U.S. flag as equivalent to the loyalty of the samurai to their masters (Kawamura 1933). Even at the end of the 1930s, Sachiko Furusawa, president of the Federation of Women's Organizations, encouraged young Nisei soldiers to be loyal to the United States as representatives of the "Yamato race" at their send-off ceremonies (*Rafu Shimpo* 1941).

Discourses of Beika and the Daily Lives of Japanese Immigrants

It is difficult to prove whether the discourses of Beika really influenced the lives of Japanese immigrant laborers and farmers. As the historian Eiichiro Azuma pointed out, we can assume that the masses did not fully conform to the admonitions of Japanese men and women leaders (Azuma 2005). Indeed, an article in the radical newspaper *Dōho* claimed that the activities of Japanese immigrant women's organizations were simply opportunities for socializing among upper-class women (Ihara 1938).

In the rural areas, Beika was distant from Japanese immigrants' everyday lives. The anthropologist Akemi Kikumura recalled the life history of a Japanese woman (her mother) in the countryside. The account reveals a harsh life, isolated both from Japanese immigrant organizations, which were centered in urban areas, as well as from American society (Kikumura 1981). Leaders in Japanese immigrant organizations realized the necessity of reaching Japanese immigrants in rural areas. In 1919, *Shin Sekai,* a San Francisco Japanese-language newspaper, proposed reforming the lives of Japanese immigrant women in rural areas. According to the editors, Japanese women worked from dawn to night in the fields with men and lived in shacks without any leisure or interaction with neighbors or kin. Accordingly, the newspaper proposed the adoption of Beika and the introduction of work suitable for women (*Shin Sekai* 1919, 7–9). *Nikka Noho,* a Los Angeles agricultural newspaper, pointed out that if Japanese immigrants in rural areas were indifferent to Americanization, efforts to promote Beika in Los Angeles were useless (*Nikka Noho* 1919, 9–10). Those articles illustrated the distance between farm areas and the urban-centered activities of Beika.

As previously noted, discourses of anti-Japanese movements alleged that the submissiveness of farm women represented the impossibility of Americanizing Japanese immigrants. As many studies on Japanese immigrant women have pointed out, however, these women were far from passive and instead played active roles in community life (Shimada 2009). Not only were Japanese women leaders active participants in women's organizations, but they were also historical agents in the sphere of everyday work. Although Japanese immigrant leaders advocated that women should not work outside the home, necessity was given priority over social norms. According to Susan M. Kataoka, who interviewed around 270 Issei women in the 1970s, 83 percent of them did both housework and outside work, such as labor in fields, before World War II (Kataoka 1977, 228). And as Eileen Sunada Sarasohn, an editor of the Issei Oral History Project, points out, the Issei women who worked for survival were not necessarily passive or battered wives. They managed and supported their families while carefully protecting the image of their husband as the head of their household (Sarasohn 1998). Even when placed in oppressive situations, they asserted themselves. Among the 292 divorce cases filed by Japanese people in Los Angeles County between 1921 and 1930, for instance, 81 percent of them were filed by women (Fujisaka 2005, 138–144).

Thus, Beika represented a top-down social norm in the Japanese immigrant community, and it did not take root deeply in the everyday lives of Japanese immigrants who struggled for survival. Nonetheless, the gender structure or the norm of gender relations outlined by Beika persisted even after World War II. Although immigrants who struggled for survival might not have cared about norms and standards set by the Japanese immigrant community, when Japanese immigrants could afford "decent" lives and participate in social activities in the immigrant community, the norms of gender relations and other issues of morality in the discourse of Beika played pivotal roles.

Conclusion

Japanese immigrant leaders who advocated Beika were not submissive assimilationists. When the need arose, they challenged the racism and made an appeal that anti-Japanese (and Asian) laws and activities were in conflict with American principles. At the same time, Japanese immigrant leaders perceived the necessity of proving that Japanese immigrants were qualified for full membership in the U.S. nation-state.

The anti-Japanese (and Asian) movements claimed the impossibility of Americanizing Japanese immigrants. Responding to this propaganda, Japanese immigrant leaders interpreted the qualifications for full membership that the Americanization movement proposed in their own way, that is, Beika, and tried to promote Beika among Japanese immigrants. The ideas of Beika were based on idealized Japanese virtues, as well as on what was required by the Americanization movement. Through the efforts of Beika, leaders claimed that Japanese immigrants were qualified for full membership in the U.S. nation-state because of the virtues of the "Yamato race." In other words, they asserted that Japanese immigrants should be regarded as exceptional despite their non-white skin color because of Beika.

In this process, discourses of gender played a significant role. Americanization programs and anti-Japanese propaganda delineated that women's roles at home, the nuclear family as a fundamental unit of society, and the American way of life were siginificant criteria for full membership in the U.S. nation. Advocates of Beika also recognized those criteria. Even though they used parallel terms in ideas of Beika, however, the gender discourses such as virtues of *Yamatonadeshiko* and the definition of family highlighted the difference between the views of Americanization and those of Beika despite their similar intentions.

Beika ended in failure. Attempts to prove the exceptionality of Japanese immigrants ultimately racialized them and led to an adverse effect. Nevertheless, comparing the views of Americanization and Beika reveals how the qualities required for full membership and the boundary of the U.S. nation were perceived by marginalized groups.

The gap in perception between the two views also demonstrates how ideas of Beika have affected the subsequent history of Japanese Americans. Discourses of Beika conveyed Japanese social norms that were idealized to conform to American society. Yet as their criticism against white American women and American youth culture demonstrated, the ideas of Beika might have hampered a deeper understanding of the reality of American society among Japanese immigrants. This gap in perception might have reinforced the racialized and gendered stereotypes on both sides and hindered mutual understanding.

Notes

1 I could not discuss the Americanization movement fully here. See Nuys (2002); Ziegler-McPherson (2009). Also see my argument about Americanization and citizenship in Y. Matsumoto (2007).
2 There was even a significant overlap between activists who promoted the inclusion of newcomers in the Americanization movement and those who supported exclusion of immigrants from Asia in early twentieth-century California, which I could not discuss in this chapter. See Y. Matsumoto (2007).
3 To illuminate the meaning of Beika, I focus on the discourses of leaders of various Japanese immigrant organizations and also voices of immigrants interviewed in the Survey of Race Relations (1924–1926), Hoover Institute, Stanford University. This material is now digitized. I used the microform of Survey of Race Relations, located in the library of the University of California, Los Angeles. Concerning the project of the Survey of Race Relations, see Yu (2001). It is possible that what Japanese immigrants said during interviews did not represent the reality. Nevertheless, I used this source to illuminate how Japanese immigrants presented themselves to American society.
4 This journal, written in Japanese, was published from 1918 to 1930 [?] in Los Angeles and was reprinted in 2012 by Bunnsei Shoin, Tokyo. The title can be translated literally as *The Monthly Magazine of Japanese Women Living in the United States*. Male and female writers of this journal targeted Japanese immigrant women and Nisei women, especially in urban areas, as readers and discussed social norms for women while they offered various information about everyday lives and social activities, including information on women's organizations. In this chapter, I use several articles from this journal to analyze opinions of leading Japanese immigrant men and women about Americanization.
5 For instance, Smith (2005); Hassell (1987). Concerning studies of Japanese researchers, see Yasutake (2000); Yaguchi (2000); Tanaka (2000).
6 See, for instance, Ogura (1932, 25); Yugi (1935, 16–19); Kojima (1924, 76–79).
7 For instance, see Miho (1927); Nemoto (1925).

References

Azuma, Eiichiro. 2005. *Between Two Empires: Race, History, and Transnationalism in Japanese America*. New York: Oxford University Press.
Benedict, H. Stanley. 1920. California and the Japanese. *Grizzly Bear* 27 (4).

Burnight, Ralph F. 1920. "The Japanese in Rural Los Angeles County." *Studies in Sociology* 4 (4).

Dixon, Royal. 1916. *Americanization*. New York: MacMillan.

Fujii, Sei 藤井整. 1940. 米国に住む日本人の叫び (The Voice of Japanese in the United States). Los Angeles: Kashumainichi Shinbunsha.

Fujioka Shiro 藤岡紫朗. 1940. 米国中央日本人会史 (History of U.S. Central Japanese Association). Los Angeles: Beikoku Chuo Nihonjin Kai.

Fujisaka, Kyoko Kakehashi. 2005. "Japanese Immigrant Women in Los Angeles, 1912–1942: A Transnational Perspective." PhD diss., University of Wisconsin–Madison.

Garcia, Matt. 2001. *A World of Its Own: Race, Labor, and Citrus in the Making of Greater Los Angeles, 1900–1970*. Austin: University of Texas Press.

Gardner, Martha. 2005. *The Qualities of a Citizen: Women, Immigration, and Citizenship, 1870–1965*. Princeton, NJ: Princeton University Press.

Glenn, Evelyn Nakano. 2002. *Unequal Freedom: How Race and Gender Shaped American Citizenship and Labor*. Cambridge, MA: Harvard University Press.

———. 2006. "Race, Labor, and Citizenship in Hawaii." In *American Dreaming, Global Realities: Rethinking U.S. Immigration History*, edited by Donna R. Gabaccia and Vicki L. Ruiz. Chicago: University of Illinois Press.

Hara, Kosaku 原耕作. 1919. 新しく渡米した従妹の母に送る手紙 (A Letter to the Aunt Whose Daughter Came to the United States Recently). *Zaibei Fujinn no Tomo* 2 (10): 20–24.

Harada, Tasuku. 1922. The Japanese Problem in California: Answers to Questionnaire. San Francisco: Private circulation. Reprint, San Francisco: R & E Research Associates, 1971.

Hasegawa, Shinichiro 長谷川新一郎. 1937. 在米日本人の見たる米国と米国人 (America and Americans Seen by the Japanese in the United States). Tokyo: Jitsugyo no Nihonsha.

Hayashi, Brian Masaru. 1995. *'For the Sake of Our Japanese Brethren': Assimilation, Nationalism, and Protestantism among the Japanese of Los Angeles, 1895–1942*. Stanford, CA: Stanford University Press.

Hassell, Malve Von. 1987. "Issei Women Between Two Worlds: 1875–1985." PhD diss., New School for Social Research.

Holt, Marilyn Irvin. 1995. *Linoleum, Better Babies, and the Modern Farm Woman, 1890–1930*. Albuquerque: University of New Mexico Press.

Ichioka, Yuji. 1988. *The Issei: The World of the First Generation Japanese Immigrant, 1885–1924*. New York: Free Press.

Ihara, Kikuyu 井原きくよ. 1938. 戦争と婦人団体 (The War and Women's Organizations). *Dōho*. Los Angeles: Dohosha, March 20.

Kataoka, Susan M. 1977. "Issei Women: A Study in Subordinate Status." PhD diss., University of California, Los Angeles.

Kawamura, Yusenn 河村幽川. 1933. アメリカ日本語読本 (Japanese Reader). North American Council of Japanese Children Education, Japanese American Research Project (JARP). Research Library of University of California at Los Angeles: Box 321.

Kikumura, Akemi. 1981. *Through Harsh Winters: The Life of a Japanese Immigrant Woman*. Novato, CA: Chandler & Sharp.

Kojima, Haruko 小島治子. 1924. 女子青年会の仕事の一端 (Work of Japanese YWCA). *Zaibei Fujinn no Tomo* 7 (9): 76–79.

Kondo, Chouei 近藤長衛. 1919. 排日運動と米化 (Anti-Japanese Movement and Beika). *Zaibei Fujinn no Tomo* 2 (7): 2–5.

Kumei, Teruko 粂井輝子. 1998. 国民の創生――在米日本人移民の第2世教育と米化運動 (Creation of the Nation: Education of Nisei and Beika). *Journal of Shirayuri Women's University* 34: 119–144.

Lee, Erika, and Judy Yung. 2010. *Angel Island: Immigrant Gateway to America*. New York: Oxford University Press.

Los Angeles Japanese Methodist Church. 1931. 羅府美以週報 (Bulletin of Los Angeles Japanese Methodist Church), July 7. JARP: Box 292.

Lowe, Lisa. 1996. *Immigrant Acts*. Durham, NC: Duke University Press.

Matsumoto, Valerie. 1994. "Redefining Expectations: Nisei Women in the 1930s." *California History* 73 (1): 44–53.

Matsumoto, Yuko 松本悠子. 2007. 創られるアメリカ国民と「他者」 (Boundaries of Citizenship in the Age of Americanization). Tokyo: University of Tokyo Press.

McClatchy, V. S. 1921. *Japanese Immigration and Colonization*. Washington, DC: Government Printing Office.

Miho, Shizuko 美保静子. 1927. モーダンガールに就いて (Modern Girls). *Zaibei Fujinn no Tomo* 10 (10): 56–58.

Millis, Harry Allen. 1915. "Some of the Economic Aspects of Japanese Immigration." *American Economic Review* 5: 787–804.

Nanka Nihonjin Kirisutokyo Kyokai Renmei 南加日本人基督教教会連盟. 1932. 在米日本人基督教五十年史 (History of the Christian Japanese Activities in the United States, 1882–1932). Tokyo: Shinseido.

Nemoto, Fuji 根本ふぢ. 1925. 断髪は不賛成 (Against the Short Hair). *Zaibei Fujinn no Tomo* 8 (4): 64.

Nichibei Shimbun-sha 日米新聞社. 1922. 在米日本人人名辞典 (Biographical Dictionary of Japanese in the United States). Nichibei Shimbun-sha. JARP: Box 352–356.

Niisato, Kanichi 新里貫一. 1933. 移民地哀話――家庭悲劇編 (Immigrant Elegies: Family Tragedy). Tokyo: Shinposha.

———. 1934. 移民地哀話――第二世編 (Immigrant Elegies: The Nisei). Tokyo: Shinposha.
Niisato, Suikin 新里翠琴. 1924. 在米同胞婦人に與ふ (Toward Japanese Women in the United States). *Zaibei Fujinn no Tomo* 7 (9): 15–17.
Nikka Noho 日加農報. 1919. 同胞の婦人虐待 (The Abuse of Women by Our Brethren). *Zaibei Fujinn no Tomo* 2 (7): 9–10.
North American Association of Japanese Language Schools 北米日本語学園協会. 1930. 日本語学園沿革史 (History of Japanese Language Schools in California). North American Association of Japanese Language Schools. JARP: Box 328.
Nuys, Frank Van. 2002. *Americanizing the West: Race, Immigrants, and Citizenship, 1890–1930.* Lawrence: University Press of Kansas.
Ogura, Kosei. 1932. "Sociological Study of the Buddhist Churches in North America." MA thesis, University of Southern California.
Rafu Shimpo 羅府新報. 1941. 応召兵壮行会 (Send-off Party for the Nisei Selectee). May 11.
Sakamoto, Tayoko 坂本太代子. 1920. 婦人の一大使命 (A Great Mission of Women). *Zaibei Fujinn no Tomo* 3 (5): 2–4.
Sarasohn, Eileen Sunada. 1998. *Issei Women: Echoes from Another Frontier.* Palo Alto: Pacific Books.
Shah, Nayan. 2011. *Stranger Intimacy: Contesting Race, Sexuality, and the Law in the North American West.* Berkeley: University of California Press.
Shimada, Noriko 島田法子. 2009. 写真花嫁・戦争花嫁のたどった道 (Crossing the Ocean). Tokyo: Akashi Shoten.
Shin Sekai 新世界社説. 1919. 職業及生活の改良 (Reform of Work and Life). *Zaibei Fujinn no Tomo* 2 (7): 7–9.
Smith, Susan L. 2005. *Japanese American Midwives: Culture, Community, and Health Politics, 1880–1950.* Chicago: University of Chicago Press.
Survey of Race Relations: A Register of Its Records in the Hoover Institution Archives. 1924. "Chotoku Toyama: The Life History as a Social Document."
———. 1925a. "Interview with Miss Chiyoe Sumi."
———. 1925b. "Mr. Nitta, Santa Ana."
———. 1925c. "Life History of Reverend Paul Tamura."
———. 1925d. "Interview with Mrs. K. Iseri and Mrs. Takeyama."
Takaoka, Imahei 高岡今平. 1924. 女性の強み (Strength of Women). *Zaibei Fujinn no Tomo* 7 (9): 2–7.
Tamura, Eileen H. 1990. "The Americanization Campaign and Assimilation of the 'Nisei' in Hawai'i, 1920–1940." PhD diss., University of Hawai'i.
Tanaka, Kei 田中景. 2000. 20世紀初頭の日本・カリフォルニア「写真花嫁」修業 (Education of 'Picture Brides' in Japan and California in the Early Twentieth Century). *Journal of Doshisha University Institute for Study of Humanities and Social Sciences* 68: 303–334.

U.S. House of Representatives. 1921. *Japanese Immigration: Hearings before the Committee on Immigration and Naturalization. House of Representatives.* 66th Congress, 2nd sess., July 15–20, 1920.

Wada, Yori. 1986–1987. "Growing Up in Central California." *Amerasia Journal* 13 (2): 3–21.

Walz, Eric. 2012. *Nikkei in the Interior West.* Tucson: University of Arizona Press.

Ward, Florence E. 1920. "The Farm Woman's Problems." *Journal of Home Economics* 12 (10): 437–457.

White, Alfred. 1923. *The Apperceptive Mass of Foreigners as Applied to Americanization of the Mexican Group.* Los Angeles: University of California Press.

Yaguchi, Yujin 矢口祐人. 2000.「ピクチャーブライド」のポリティックス (Politics of "Picture Brides"). *Rikkyo American Studies* 22: 117–146.

Yamauchi, Tsuneko 山内常子. 1920. 婦人の屋外労働に就いて (Women's Labor in the Fields). *Zaibei Fujinn no Tomo* 3 (6): 16–24.

Yanase, Shiyou 簗瀬紫葉. 1925. 在米婦人の長所・短所 (The Advantage and Disadvantage of Japanese Women in the United States). *Zaibei Fujinn no Tomo* 8 (4): 9–14.

Yasutake, Rumi 安武留美. 2000. 北カリフォルニア日本人移民社会の日米教会婦人たち (Women of Japanese-American Churches in Northern California). *Studies of Christianity and Social Problems* 49: 46–76.

Yu, Henry. 2001. *Thinking Orientals: Migration, Contact and Exoticism in Modern America.* New York: Oxford University Press.

Yugi, Shojiro 湯木庄次郎. 1935. 羅府日本人美以教会四〇年史 (40 Years of Los Angeles Japanese Methodist Church). Los Angeles: Los Angeles Japanese Methodist Church.

Ziegler-McPherson, Christina A. 2009. *Americanization in the States: Immigrant Social Welfare Policy, Citizenship, and National Identity in the United States, 1908–1929.* Gainesville: University Press of Florida.

CHAPTER 8

Sansei Women and the Gendering of Yellow Power in Southern California, 1960s–1970s

Valerie J. Matsumoto

In July 1973, Peggy Miyasaki, a Sansei woman student at California State University, Long Beach, wrote a letter to her father trying to explain her newly awakened sense of the importance of ethnic culture. Published in *Gidra,* an Asian American movement newspaper, the letter examined the values transmitted by her parents, values forged in hardship. Postwar race relations framed her own sensibility as she recounted the childhood difficulties she had faced when her family moved from the west Los Angeles community of Culver City, a largely Japanese American area, to Montebello, a predominantly Chicano town east of Los Angeles. In order "to avoid being made fun of because of my slanty eyes," she said, "I would try to become more white so that everyone would like me" (Miyasaki 1973, 4). Feeling pressure to change from the time she entered elementary school, Miyasaki wanted to have friends and to belong: "I couldn't change my physical features so I began to reject all that you taught me on how a 'good Japanese girl' should be." Instead of wearing "oxford shoes" and "Sunday school dresses" to school, she persuaded her mother to buy her "black leather boots and a hip hugger skirt." Wanting to wear her hair long like her friend Lupe, she refused to have "a neat bowl-shape" haircut. When she became involved in high school club meetings, dances, and parties, her father, who had "previously encouraged extracurricular activities," criticized her, saying, "You go out too much, you're running wild with your Mexican friends." Although Miyasaki maintained the good grades expected (but not acknowledged) by her father, clearly her growing independence and choice of non–Japanese American friends threatened his ideal of a good Sansei daughter.

As a college student, Miyasaki's notion of what it meant to be a Japanese American daughter shifted when she took an Asian American studies class that she said "opened my mind."[1] She wrote, "The white Americans say the Japanese have made it. They hold us up as examples to other minorities. They speak of our success in assimilating to their society, but it really isn't much of a success when you must give up your cultural identity and become 'white.' What we have succeeded in doing is adopting white values and attitudes. First we had to reach the standards set by the dominant white American society before we were able to assimilate or even be considered good enough to become an American" (Miyasaki 1973, 5). Miyasaki's words echo the earlier prewar struggles for social acceptance discussed by Yuko Matsumoto in this book. In her chapter in this book on gender and the racialization of Japanese immigrants in California, Matsumoto illuminates the attempts by Issei leaders to develop Beika, a way to gain acceptance in U.S. society while maintaining Japanese cultural identity. She further reveals how women's roles became a prominent and contested feature of this endeavor. During the 1970s, a number of the Issei's grandchildren, like Peggy Miyasaki, also struggled to define themselves and the roles of women within the ethnic community and mainstream society. However, coming of age in an era when people of color and women had begun to challenge the status quo, Sansei activists aspired not to gain acceptance in the larger society but to transform it.

In this chapter I examine how third-generation Japanese American women in Southern California began to challenge gendered racializations in both the ethnic community and the larger society. As activists in the Asian American movement (and influenced by other liberation movements of the time), they criticized stereotypical images of Asian/Americans, utilizing the arts to create new representations as they drew inspiration from Asian women engaged in revolutionary struggle. Many Sansei women became activists motivated to "serve the people," working alongside men in movement organizations. Like the Issei women of whom Yuko Matsumoto writes, they too contested the gendered conventions stressed by male leaders. And, like their mothers and grandmothers, they organized women's groups to address the needs of their peers and community; their efforts included developing social service programs to tackle childcare accessibility, seniors' health, workers' rights, and drug abuse among youth (to name a few). In the process of defining themselves, Sansei women not only assessed their position in U.S.

society but also debated their relationship to Japan. Their experiences reflected the persisting significance of gender in the racialization of Japanese Americans as well as the ways in which women's critique of gender expectations helped to shape the Asian American movement.

I use the term "Japanese American" to refer to people of Japanese descent in the United States, and "Japanese/American" when discussing Japanese and Japanese Americans together. "Asian Americans" refers to people of Asian descent in the United States. When I use the term "Asian," I refer to people in Asia. I have used "Asian/American" when speaking of Asians and Asian Americans together.

Growing Up Sansei in Southern California

The social climate in which the Sansei grew up differed significantly from that of their Nisei parents, a majority of whom were teenagers on the eve of World War II. The rebuilding of Japanese American communities in Southern California after wartime uprooting and incarceration required continuing struggle. However, as the historian Charlotte Brooks has documented, shifting international geopolitics altered the racialization of Japanese Americans and other Asian Americans in ways that increased their residential mobility and socioeconomic opportunities. The status of Japanese Americans rose in tandem with the importance of Japan as a U.S. ally during the Cold War and the need to solidify America's position as a world leader by countering criticism of domestic race relations (Kurashige 2002, 123–125). As Naoko Shibusawa stated, "The way Americans treated racial minorities—including the recently interned Japanese Americans—became not just a matter of moral conscience, but one of foreign policy and national prestige as the United States sought to win over newly decolonized nations into its orbit" (Shibusawa 2006, 7). One manifestation of this political shift was the movement into white (and Mexican) communities by Japanese Americans and other Asian Americans during the 1950s; white Californians still viewed them as fundamentally foreign, though now desirable neighbors (Brooks 2009, 221–22). In this period, Japanese American enclaves grew in suburban areas of Los Angeles County, including Gardena and Torrance in the South Bay, the Sawtelle and Crenshaw areas, and Boyle Heights and Pasadena in east Los Angeles (Kurashige 2008, 234–258; Allen and Turner 1997, 127–129).

The Sansei women who took part in the Asian American movement in Southern California were both urban and suburban, some middle class, others working class (Kao 2009, 112–38; Omatsu 1994). In this chapter, I draw primarily on articles, letters, poetry, and art from *Gidra*, the aforementioned monthly newspaper, which became a major organ for Asian American movement activities in Southern California. Because *Gidra* was first established by undergraduates at the University of Southern California, Los Angeles, many, though not all, of the women I write about were middle-class students. What most had in common were Japanese immigrant grandparents and second-generation parents whose early lives had been severely disrupted by World War II incarceration. These Sansei were the baby boom daughters of gardeners and plant nursery operators, seamstresses, factory workers, engineers, clerical workers, and teachers. As in Peggy Miyasaki's home, Nisei parents stressed the importance of education and hard work as the keys to social acceptance and economic success. Some Sansei joined Japanese American Girl Scout troops and church-sponsored clubs established by Nisei mothers who had enjoyed similar girls' clubs in their youth (Matsumoto 2003, 172–87; Matsumoto 2014).[2] And, like urban Nisei young women in the 1930s, many Sansei loved to dance, but instead of foxtrots and waltzes, they grooved to the soulful sounds of artists such as the Delfonics and to rock bands like The Midnighters and Chicago. Like Miyasaki, many Sansei also participated in multiracial school organizations and activities frequently denied to prewar Nisei youth.

The largest group of third-generation Asian Americans in Southern California, the Sansei came of age in an era marked by the emergence of liberation movements that would have far-reaching impact, including opposition to U.S. involvement in the Vietnam War and a resurgence of feminism. Disillusioned by the broken promises of government officials and limited gains, the African American youth vanguard of the civil rights movement turned to black nationalism, drawn by the vision of Malcolm X and the Nation of Islam. By the mid-1960s, rather than seeking integration, they called for African American community self-determination and self-reliance: black power (Jones et al. 2003, 883–84). The black power movement particularly inspired Chicano/Latino, Native American, and Asian American activists. As Amy Uyematsu wrote in 1969, "Within the last two years, the 'yellow power' movement has developed as a direct outgrowth of the 'black power' movement," which had "caused many Asian Americans to question themselves" (Uyematsu 1969, 8). Asian Americans also looked to the ideology of third world revolutions in Africa, Asia, Latin America, and the Middle East for guidance (Omatsu 1994, 26).

The Asian American movement, composed of many organizations addressing different needs in different regions, arose on the West and East Coasts and in Hawaiʻi, areas with a substantial Asian American population. Japanese American students and others began to form groups such as Sansei Concern, which organized an "Are You Yellow?" conference at UCLA to discuss issues of "yellow power, identity, and the war in Vietnam" during the summer of 1968 (Ling 1989, 53).[3] Glenn Omatsu has identified the 1968 San Francisco State strike, the first campus protest in which Asian Americans participated as a collective group, as the birth of the Asian American movement (Omatsu 1994, 25–26; Umemoto 1989, 3–42).[4] Beginning in November 1968, several Asian American student organizations joined with African American, Chicano/Latino, and Native American students as part of the Third World Liberation Front, calling for "open admissions, community control of education, ethnic studies, and self determination" (Omatsu 1994, 26). Although most of the strikers' demands went unmet, they succeeded in not only securing the establishment of the first ethnic studies program in the country but also in forging "a new vision for their communities, creating numerous grassroots projects and empowering previously ignored and disenfranchised sectors of society" (Omatsu 1994, 25). Chinese, Filipino, Japanese, and Korean Americans took part in a wide array of campaigns to provide housing and social services, transform education, oppose martial law in the Philippines, deal with drug abuse, organize unions, and celebrate ethnic cultural arts. Men and women of all ages and diverse backgrounds participated in the movement, including low-wage workers, small-business owners, educators, and veterans—but students became particularly visible, especially with the growth of Asian American studies on college campuses.

A vital organ of the Asian American movement in Southern California, *Gidra* was a monthly newspaper founded by five undergraduates at the University of California, Los Angeles: Dinora Gil, Laura Ho, Mike Murase, Tracy Okida, and Colin Watanabe. With the support of the fledgling Asian American Studies Center and a $100 contribution from each of the founders, the first issue of *Gidra* appeared in March 1969. Run by a volunteer staff of men and women, many of whom were Japanese American, *Gidra* reported on community concerns, movement developments, and international issues and also provided a venue for creative writing and art. As Mike Murase recounted, "*Gidra* gradually changed its focus from the campus to the community, from Asian identity to Asian unity, and from 'what happened' to 'what can we do'" (Murase [1974] 1976, 312). Throughout the newspaper's five-year life span, women contributed articles, poetry, drawings, photographs, interviews, comics, and recipes.[5] *Gidra* aired women's concerns about the gender dynamics of the movement and even produced a special women's issue in January 1971.

Yellow Power, Americanization, and Self-Definition

Like the Issei leaders of whom Yuko Matsumoto writes, Sansei activists of the sixties and seventies hotly debated the meaning of acceptance in mainstream American society, but within a very different context. The impact of liberation movements, particularly the ideology of black power, led them to question both the desirability and possibility of Americanization. In her influential 1969 essay "The Emergence of Yellow Power in America," Amy Uyematsu contended that Chinese Americans and Japanese Americans, then the largest groups of Asian Americans, had received "the token acceptance of white America" because of their middle-class status and relatively small populations. Yet, Uyematsu pointed out the racial disparity between the income of whites and those of more educated Japanese Americans and Chinese Americans: "White America praises the success of Japanese and Chinese for being the highest among all other colored groups . . . but they should not step out of place and compare themselves with whites."[6] More pessimistic than the Issei leaders who sought Beika, she argued that "the American capitalistic dream was never meant to include non-whites." Despite their embrace of European American values, "the subtle but prevailing racial prejudice that 'yellows' experience restricts them to the margins of the white world" (Uyematsu 1969, 8).

For Asian Americans, Uyematsu asserted, the cost of seeking elusive social acceptance proved too steep: "In the process of Americanization, Asians have tried to transform themselves into white men—both mentally and physically. . . . They have adopted the 'American way of life' only to discover that this is not enough" (Uyematsu 1969, 8). She charged that Asian Americans had rejected their "physical heritages" and wished instead to "be tall with long legs and large eyes."

Though affecting both sexes, women experienced particular pressure to alter their appearance and conform to a white ideal. "This self-hatred," Uyematsu wrote, "is . . . evident in the yellow male's obsession with unobtainable white women, and in the yellow female's attempt to gain male approval by aping white beauty standards" (Gil 1969, 2, cited in Uyematsu

1969, 8). Applauding the model of black cultural nationalism, she concluded, "The 'Black is Beautiful' cry among black Americans has instilled a new awareness in Asian Americans to be proud of their physical and cultural heritages. Yellow power advocates [view] self-acceptance as the first step toward strengthening personalities of Asian Americans" (Gil 1969, 2, cited in Uyematsu 1969, 8). Indeed, yellow power, like black power, emphasized the importance of defining "our own image" and thus curtailing the power of stereotypes.

Asian American women activists began to define themselves in ways that linked local and international struggles. On page 2 of the *Gidra* women's issue, the fifteen contributors (three Chinese Americans, twelve Japanese Americans) identified themselves as "Third World, Asian sisters uniting in the struggle for liberation." Rather than associating themselves with an ethnic-specific heritage, they signaled a broader pan-Asian affiliation. Their claim to third world status not only suggested a sense of solidarity that transcended national borders but also reflected the unequal position of racial minority people in the United States.

As their declaration of purpose revealed, these "Asian sisters" viewed the task of redefining themselves as intertwined with challenging sexism and racism. They vowed to

1. oppose this capitalistic society which confines the role of women to a cheap labor force, or to mindless bodies completely influenced by Madison Avenue propaganda;
2. resist the degrading images that a racist society has imposed on both ourselves and our brothers;
3. struggle with our brothers against male chauvinism and join in constructing new definitions for self-determination in the revolutionary society.

Their aims reflect their sense of facing the intertwined "triple oppression" of race, class, and gender, in what Mary Uyematsu Kao termed "the three-step boogie" (Kao 2009, 112–138).

"In the Movement Office": Sansei Women Critique Sexism

Sansei women decried sexism in both American and Asian cultures. Activist Merilynne Hamano charged, "Sexism makes sisters *believe* that they are weak, dependent, powerless . . . incomplete without a male figure. . . .

Sexism makes sisters feel passive, guilty, ashamed." Relying on a structural analysis, she asserted that "the sexism we know has been taught to us from the time we are born and reinforced by the institutions of family, school, church, media, government" (Hamano 1972, 8).

Activists such as Yvonne Wong Nishio were dismayed to encounter sexism within the movement as well. In *Gidra* (January 1971) she wrote, "The Asian American movement is for human liberation, but many males' idea of women's liberation is something for their girlfriends to do to other women while they're [the men are] busy in decision-making. Group organizing, leading meetings, and using revolutionary rhetoric seem to be the males' role in the movement. Because of their constant visibility and verbal encounters, men are given feedback and rewards. Little recognition is given to women who actually do the work. Can you remember who did the typing, who ran the office machines, who did the telephoning, and who did the tedious research?" Women's discontent was not confined to the Asian American movement: Chicanas in *el movimiento*, for example, also expressed dissatisfaction at being relegated to doing the behind-the-scenes work of planning events and providing food (Ruiz 1998, 118). Wong Nishio noted that the Asian American movement remained fettered to the stereotypes found in mainstream society: "It is essential that Asian American men and women interchange roles in working within the movement. But many men have argued that Asian women prefer supportive roles; they cannot reason or argue logically; and they are dependent on male initiative." She concluded, "These stereotypes of Asian women are the same ones used to justify oppression of Third World people" (*Gidra,* January 1971, 6).

A biting critique of sexism appeared in the special 1971 women's issue of *Gidra* in the form of a one-page play, "In the Movement Office," by a woman who used the pseudonym Killer Fawn (Killer Fawn 1971, 13). The play features three unnamed characters: a "sister" and two "brother" activists. The play opens with the sister asking the men what they think of women's liberation, to which one responds by glibly quoting Chairman Mao: "Unite and take part in production and political activity to improve the economic and political status of women." Displaying their failure to take this injunction seriously, the men immediately begin to discuss plans for an upcoming conference. Instead of regarding the woman as an equal participant, they treat her as a secretary, expecting her to bring them coffee, type materials for the conference, and contact people for a general meeting. Leaving her to do all the work of putting together the conference, they blithely depart to attend a meeting and to do unspecified "people's work." The play ends with the woman activist, angry and alone, saying, "What the fuck's going on! I got a goddamn meeting, too! The people's work. . . . What the hell do they think this is?" (Killer Fawn 1971, 13).

Women's frustration with sexism in the movement also found expression in verse. In her famous poem "from a lotus blossom cunt," Tomi Tanaka blasted the sexual exploitation of women in the Asian American movement by their "brothers." The provocative title drew attention to the stereotyping of Asian/American women as exotically foreign, sexually available bodies. The poem suggested that Asian American male activists had also stereotyped Asian American women, viewing them as "a legit lay for the revolutionary" and expecting them to provide sex. Tomi Tanaka noted a significant shift in the consciousness of women activists: "we chronic smilers/ asian women/ we of the downcast almond eyes/ are seeing each other/ sisters now, people now/ asian women." She affirmed her continuing support of the men, adding pointedly, "But I'm so damned tired/ of being body first, head last/ wanting to love you when all/ you want is a solution to glandular discomfort. . . ." She further warned male activists, "We are women, we are Asian/ We are freeing ourselves/ Join us/ Try to use us,/ and you'll lose us/ Join us" (Tanaka 1971, 14).[7]

Despite their frustrations, most of the Asian American women activists remained committed to working with their brothers in the movement. Like Chicana feminists, Asian American women activists were alienated from the European American women's movement (Ruiz 1998, 110; Pulido 2006, 183–184).[8] One Sansei woman wrote that she "found the white women's liberation movements mildly intimidating" and, though disgruntled by patronizing, chauvinistic brothers in the Asian American movement, she retained "strong comradely feelings" toward them (Mochizuki 1971, 6).[9] Quoting Mao's admonition to "unite and take part in production and political activity to improve the economic and political status of women," she affirmed that men and women should "work together" (Mochizuki 1971, 6). Linda Iwataki proposed that instead of separating themselves from or fighting with movement men, women should direct their energy to giving the brothers constructive criticism: "If they refuse to listen and continue to interfere with our right to be self-determining human beings, then we'll be forced to use other means to bring this to a halt. At all times we should try to set an exemplary example of the type of women we are advocating: self-determining, strong, sensitive human beings" (Iwataki 1971, 12).

The emergence of an Asian American women's movement did not occur without some male resistance. As Linda Iwataki observed, "Sometimes even in the movement for social change, when we [women] try to make our oppression heard, we are told we're taking away energy from the 'main' struggle. . . . But when we question this attitude, we're isolated and told, 'Sexism is *not* the primary contradiction.' Well, . . . it sure as hell is a big part of the contradiction." She concluded, "The Woman Question is a fundamental part of the building of a better society—just as Asian people are a fundamental part of the Third World revolutionary movement" (*Gidra,* February 1974, 3).[10]

Sansei men's responses varied. Some, as women's writings indicate, balked at relinquishing their privilege. As participants in a liberation movement, others might have felt political pressure to express support for their Asian American sisters but did not immediately accept the redefinition of female roles: "I'm for women's liberation," said one man. "The only thing that bothers me, is that women would lose a lot of their femininity" (*Gidra,* January 1971, 11). Other men strove to change their own thinking and behavior. For example, Mike Yamamoto, in an essay titled "Male Perspective," stated, "As men, we are all faced with the proposition that we must not only give up the cozy master-servant relationship to which we have been so long accustomed, but also the sexual roles which have served to perpetuate and entrench sexual inequality throughout history." Yamamoto posited, "It will take a revolutionary change of direction, an open-minded redefinition of the traditional male and female roles to bring about sexual justice; and history has proven that this achievement will not come from the voluntary relinquishment of control by the cadres of men. It will come from the clamoring counterstrokes of organized women" (*Gidra,* January 1971, 13).

Sansei Women Take Action

Women's organizational activities across generations constitute a strong thread in Japanese American history. As Yuko Matsumoto related, the early Japanese immigrant community was highly organized, with most of the groups organized by gender. Separated from their networks of female kin in Japan, immigrant women founded their own organizations, as well as female auxiliaries of men's groups. Urban Nisei daughters also formed and joined numerous prewar girls' clubs in the 1920s and 1930s (Matsumoto 2003, 172–187; Matsumoto 2014). These clubs offered young urban women a place of belonging during an era of racial discrimination, gave them opportunities to push the boundaries of female behavior in the ethnic enclave and socialize with young Nisei men, provided access to recreational and cultural activities, channeled their energy into community service, and helped them to claim and demonstrate American identity. During World War II incarceration and postwar resettlement, girls continued to seek camaraderie and recreation in clubs. Sansei activists also established women's organizations and similarly provided social services for the ethnic community, but they did so with a highly critical stance on mainstream American society. As citizens by birth who came of age during the ferment of the sixties, the Sansei activists did not strive for social acceptance but sought to transform the larger society.

While remaining active in the Asian American movement, a number of Sansei women began to form their own groups. Many of their Chicana sisters, as Vicki Ruiz pointed out, similarly maintained involvement with *el movimiento Chicano*, while simultaneously forming organizations such as the Chicana Action Service Center (Ruiz 1998, 112; Pulido 2006, 184–185). The Los Angeles Women's Group offers an example of how early organizations coalesced. In 1971, several Asian American activists organized "casual meetings on Saturday mornings, not only to discuss the women's place in the movement but also to add new direction by setting up various projects, such as the women's presentation (of slides and skits) and the car wash to fund the Vancouver women's delegation." They also formed work groups to educate themselves about childcare, U.S. women's history in America, and "women in struggle all over the world" (Mochizuki 1971, 6).

This process brought rewards, from peer support to leadership training. One female activist said of the women's group, "It has been the one positive thing that helps me keep my sanity." A sense of friendship and sisterhood grew among women working together on projects. As in most group dynamics, conflicts arose. Members also faced the challenge of balancing organizational involvement with personal needs. Not surprisingly, participation stimulated changes in members' perceptions; for example, some began to "analyze their own hang-ups of competitiveness with other sisters and brothers." Of importance, as Mochizuki reported, women began "learning to deal with the subtle forms of male chauvinism which pervade the movement and establishing effective feminine leadership roles within the movement hierarchy" (*Gidra*, June 1971, 6).[11]

In the 1970s, these Southern California Asian American women developed a range of projects to provide much-needed social services to their local communities. For example, they established the Little Friends Playgroup in Chinatown to meet the need for childcare (Ling 1989, 57–59).[12] In 1972 at UCLA, Karen Ito Chan and May Ying Chen inaugurated a course on Asian American women subtitled "a thousand burdens" in reference to the racial, economic, and gender discrimination faced by women of color (Chan and Chen 1972, 14).[13] Women also rallied in response to the alarming rate of drug abuse, ignored by traditional leaders, noting, "California schools lead in drug use (seventy-five percent of the students are into drugs), many of them young Asian brothers and sisters who continue to overdose on barbiturates or 'reds'" *(Gidra,* January 1973, 15). In 1972 a Japanese American women's group, Asian Sisters, obtained funding from the Department of Health, Education and Welfare to start a drug abuse program for women. Believing that the funding should be used to begin programs in other Asian American communities as well, they formed an advisory committee composed of women representing different ages and ethnic backgrounds. Together they founded the Asian Women's Center (AWC), with the primary goal of developing "a viable alternative for Asian women through our program areas, and to provide women with the tools to organize for change" *(Gidra,* January 1973, 14).[14] In 1973, the AWC's first year, organizers focused on five program areas: education, drug abuse, counseling, child development, and health.

The opening statement by the AWC in *Gidra* illustrates their analysis of the damaging effects of gendered and racial stereotypes on Asian American women and the ways in which they sought to counter them. While they cited several systemic causes of drug abuse, the AWC staff also noted that narcotic overdoses by Asian American women outnumbered those of "males by three to one," and they linked this gendered drug problem in part to sexism in U.S. society and Asian culture: "In a male-oriented [U.S.] society, it is even easier for a sister to feel weaker and dominated—a feeling reinforced by an Asian culture which places both men and women in strict and mutually oppressive roles or stereotypes" *(Gidra,* January 1973, 15). The activists believed that a new vision of women, rooted in understanding the past, was vital to addressing the issue of drug abuse. They declared, "We, as Asian women and sisters and as a part of the Asian community feel the need to organize and develop a positive self-image as women by studying our history collectively and sharing experiences in weekly rap/education sessions." They aimed to combine study with action, "working together cooperatively in creative youth activities" and "building a sense of a real community through coordination and participation with other groups involved in the area of drugs and youth, such as the Drug Offensive and Asian Sisters, etc." (*Gidra,* January 1973, 15). Within organizations like the AWC, Asian American women worked to "serve the people" and to pursue self-determination for themselves as well as their communities.

Contesting Stereotypes and Creating New Representations

One aspect of self-determination and a core goal of the Asian American women's movement, declared in the *Gidra* women's 1971 statement of purpose, was resisting "degrading images." During the 1960s and 1970s, activists in the Asian American movement and other activists of color vigorously protested demeaning stereotypes, particularly as reinforced by the media. In 1972, Karen Ito Chan wrote, "The true racist and sexist attitudes of America towards Asians is no more cruelly apparent than in [television] commercials. Men are impotent, silly, or karate fiends. Women are sexy teasers" (Chan 1972, 4).

As Yuko Matsumoto asserted, Issei women and their female descendants have all faced persisting stereotypes of Japanese women as passive, submissive, superfeminized, and exotic. The image of the Japanese woman as the nonthreatening, sexually available geisha "has been used to both feminize and dominate Japan in ways that obscure the imperializing impulses of the West" (Yamamoto 1999, 60).[15] Because mainstream society tends to conflate Asian and Asian American women, as well as Asian ethnic groups, these stereotypes have affected Japanese American and other Asian American women (Yamamoto 1999, 65). Yasuko Takezawa's research on Japanese Americans in Seattle also indicates that the stereotypes of exotically attractive Asian women and "wimpy" Asian men "created serious tension" between Sansei men and women during the sixties and seventies (Takezawa 1995, 142–143).

Karen Ito Chan presented a withering analysis of the media imagery of Asian/American women, portrayed as the "Professional Handmaiden," the "ever supplicant, willing helpmate" (Chan 1972, 4). According to Ito Chan, three "white, male oriented media images and fantasies of Asian women" predominated:

1. the Geisha—who represents soft sex,
2. the Dragon Lady/Suzi Wong image—who represents hard sex,
3. the Housekeeper—the comforting, all-understanding mother image.

Ito Chan warned of the pernicious effects of these stereotypes: "The Geisha and Suzi Wong fantasies become the basis for many Asian women 'kept' as mistresses or viewed as prostitutes. The housekeeper becomes the good wife: quiet, hard-working, self-effacing and modest. The housekeeper image is also transformed into the professional worldly stereotype of the efficient and trustworthy secretary or teacher" (Chan 1972, 4). The character of "Mrs. Livingston," played by Miyoshi Umeki in the television series *The Courtship of Eddie's Father*, furnished an example of the maternal Japanese housekeeper.

Sansei activists were concerned not only with how stereotypes affected the mainstream public's perceptions of Asian/American women but also how Asian American women had been influenced by media imagery and "Madison Avenue propaganda."

Sansei activists decried the way in which Asian American women strove to meet Western standards of beauty, often using a range of commercial products. A two-panel comic by Yuri Kurahashi poked fun at women's reliance on such beauty aids: The first panel shows a large lump in bed under a blanket at night. A brief dialogue below reveals that beneath the blanket is a heterosexual couple having sex. While the male's only remark is heavy breathing ("PANT . . ."), the female is thinking, "Thank you magic tape, Revlon, Max Factor, Tab, Maidenform, Slender, Ban, Colgate 100, Dentyne . . ." (*Gidra*, January 1971, 15). This litany of brand names reflected her use of makeup, diet soda to stay slender, deodorant, undergarments to shape the figure, toothpaste, and chewing gum advertised to brighten the teeth; her expression of appreciation conveyed the belief that these products enabled her to attract her male partner. The fact that the first product mentioned is "magic tape" indicates that she is an Asian American woman using tape to achieve the effect of a more white-looking double eyelid. The second panel shows the couple the next morning, lying on opposite sides of the bed and still covered by the blanket. The "dialogue" is even briefer: The woman is asleep, indicated by "Zzzzzz"; in the daylight the man has caught a glimpse of what she looks like after the cosmetics have worn off, and he shouts with dismay, "YIPES!!!" This comic panel draws attention to—and mocks—women's use of commercial products to attain fleeting, superficial beauty, but it does not criticize the sexual double standard, which places emphasis on female physical appearance while valuing men for a wider range of attributes.

Though both sexes were affected, women felt particular pressure to alter their appearance and conform to a mainstream ideal of beauty. Comparing Asian American and African American practices in the pursuit of a whiter appearance, Amy Uyematsu noted that "yellow females" used "peroxide, foam rubber, and scotch tape to give them light hair, large breasts, and double-lidded eyes" (Gil 1969, 2, cited in Uyematsu 1969, 8). As a poem about her high school days suggested, this description partially mirrored personal experience: "I had that mature look—/ imitated sansei chicks with ratted hair,/ glued on eyelashes, shiny adhesive slivers/ taping eyelids round like blackeyed lacquer dolls" (Uyematsu 1992, 4). Inspired by the black power movement's slogan "Black is beautiful," Sansei and other Asian American women activists stopped putting tape on their eyelids and cultivated pride in their own "physical and cultural heritages" (Uyematsu 1992, 4). In this process of self-definition, they faced the opposition of large geopolitical forces fueled by war.

The Gendered Racialization of Asian/American Women during the War in Vietnam

America's involvement in the war in Vietnam affected Asian Americans in multiple ways. Protests across class and ethnicity raged on hundreds of college campuses as President Richard Nixon escalated the war—invading Cambodia and Laos and continuing to bomb North Vietnam—while beginning a slow removal of U.S. troops that ended in 1973. As Evelyn Yoshimura stated, "The drafting of our brothers into the military, and the taxes that we must pay for this war are two very concrete ways in which we are touched" (Yoshimura 1971, 4). But "the ugliness of that war," she contended, was also felt in the way that the U.S. military used the image of Asian women as sexual objects.

Yoshimura's analysis sheds light on the gendered racialization of Asian/American women during the war. Drawing on the experiences of Asian American male veterans, she described how the U.S. military portrayed Asian women as sexual objects as a tool to "psychologically break down GIs so they can instill the values and mentality that is necessary to become effective killers." During boot camp training, one "Asian American brother" explained, the drill instructors would begin classes with a dirty joke, "usually having to do with prostitutes they had seen in Japan or in other parts of Asia while they were stationed overseas." These jokes conveyed a sense of the "Asian woman being a doll, a useful toy, or something to play with" and "not quite as human as white women." Asian women were denigrated as physically different from white women: "For instance, . . . the instructor would talk about how Asian women's vaginas weren't like a white woman's, but rather they were slanted, like their eyes. Some guys really believed this shit too" (Yoshimura 1971, 4).[16] Citing Wilhelm Reich's psychological theory of sexual suppression, Yoshimura argued that the stereotype of the Asian woman was utilized to inculcate in soldiers submission to authority, as well as to encourage racism against Asians: "The image of a people with slanted eyes and slanted vaginas enhances the feeling that Asians are other than human, and therefore much easier to kill." She also charged that the sexual objectification of the Asian female helped sustain the elevated position of white women (Yoshimura 1971, 4).[17]

This sexualized stereotype of the Asian woman also affected Asian American women. Because most non-Asian people in the United States saw "little if any difference between Asian Americans and Asians in America," Yoshimura asserted that Asian Americans were "either being lumped with Asians, and therefore considered 'foreigners,' or we are invisible" (Yoshimura 1971, 15). A Sansei GI's experience illustrated this: During basic training, a (presumably white) drill instructor confiscated photos of the soldier's friends—Asian American girls with whom he'd gone to high school—and kept them, while making derogatory comments about their looking like whores he knew in Japan. The drill instructor further harassed him by insisting that the soldier's older sister was a prostitute he had encountered in Japan (Yoshimura 1971, 15). Linda Iwataki also commented on the insidious effects of these stereotypes, citing the attitudes of U.S. soldiers returning from Vietnam: "Every Asian woman who's been accosted by brothers who have been brainwashed by the military, knows that the hate and sexism produced by the war has not ended" (*Gidra*, February 1974, 3). Yoshimura viewed the perpetuation of such stereotypes as part of U.S. militarization: "As long as there are U.S. troops in Asia, as long as the U.S. government and the Military wage wars of aggression against Asian people, racism against Asians will serve the interest of this country" (Yoshimura 1971, 15). For these reasons, she declared, "We as Asian American women cannot separate ourselves from our Asian counterparts. Racism against them is too often racism against us." She called for action: "We must destroy the stereotypes of Asian women, and Asian people, as a whole, so we can define ourselves, and be free to realize our full and total potential" (Yoshimura 1971, 15).

New Female Role Models and Imagery

The women involved with *Gidra* challenged both the stereotype of exotic, submissive Asian/American women and their own invisibility as subjects by both stern verbal critiques and dynamic self-representations. In the process, they linked the oppression they faced as racial/ethnic women in the United States with that of Asian women. The third page of the January 1971 women's issue of *Gidra* (see Figure 8.1) made this explicit: The top half of the page features a leaflet sent to U.S. servicemen advertising a booklet to help them meet Japanese immigrant and American-born "girls and ladies" in the United States and Canada. The ad promises, "Here's your chance to end loneliness, to enjoy the companionship of a loyal, considerate, and thoroughly pleasant lady and to find a suitable wife." Men not seeking a girlfriend or spouse could learn how to obtain "maids, domestics, female servants, social housekeepers, cooks, and household workers." In the upper right corner, the *Gidra* caption states that the leaflet "exemplifies the exploitation of Asian women and perpetuates their stereotype."[18] Both identifying with Asian women and claiming Americanness, the *Gidra* writers proclaim, "We, as Amerasian women, will continue to resist this exploitation in our struggle for liberation." They underscored their resistance by juxtaposing the ad with a dramatic photo on the lower half of the same page. In the picture, ten women who had contributed to the issue confront the viewer with serious, unsmiling gazes; in their midst, Mary Uyematsu raises her middle finger in a striking gesture of defiance.[19]

Rejecting the U.S. media stereotypes of "Suzy Wong" and "Madame Butterfly," Asian American female activists also turned to women involved in third world liberation movements as role models. Because the artists who produced the drawings, photos, and comics that appeared in *Gidra* were only sporadically identified, it is difficult to analyze separately images produced by women and men. However, Cyndy Fukugai's full-page drawing in May 1971 of six Southeast Asian women leaders offers a sense of the qualities Asian American women activists admired (*Gidra,* May 1971, 9). Beneath the phrase "SOLIDARITY WITH OUR INDOCHINESE SISTERS AND BROTHERS," Fukugai depicts delegates from the Laos Patriotic Women's Union, the Vietnam Women's Union of North Vietnam, and the Women's Union for the Liberation of South Vietnam, whose experiences were the focus of the anti-imperialist Indochinese Women's Conference, held in Vancouver, Canada, in April 1971.[20] These women made a deep impression on the Asian American women who attended. According to attendee Kiku Uno, "Their physical presence had tremendous impact on the hundreds of Third World and white women" (*Gidra,* May 1971, 12).[21] Fukugai's picture focuses on the faces of the six Southeast Asian women, whose torsos

Figure 8.1   Women on Gidra Newspaper Staff
A special women's issue of *Gidra* (January 1971, page 3) criticized a stereotypical advertisement that promised to help men find Japanese wives and female servants, juxtaposing it with the photo of ten women who worked on the issue. Front row, from left to right: Candice Ota, Melinda Quan Berg, Mary Uyematsu Kao, and Evelyn Yoshimura. Back row: Chizuko Nishimura Endo, Carol Hatanaka Ono, May Chen, Patti Iwataki, Vivian Matsushige, and Miya Iwataki.
(Photo courtesy of Mike Murase)

are barely suggested by minimal outlines and a little shading. The viewer's eye is drawn to their faces, each conveying individual personality, strength, humor. A caption on the lower left side of the page explains that these women are able to "unite a great diversity of women from the western United States while educating them about the war and its atrocities. This conference . . . played an important role in determining the potential of women in the struggle against capitalism, racism, and imperialism" (*Gidra,* May 1971, 9). Highlighting women's involvement in political struggle in Southeast Asia, *Gidra* included the account of one of the six leaders, Dinh Thi Huong, who searingly described the years of imprisonment and torture that spurred her to join the liberation movement in South Vietnam *(Gidra,* May 1971, 11).

In her poem "My Friend," Chris Murakami contrasts the heroic figure of the Vietnamese woman soldier with that of a Sansei friend whose values she no longer shares: "you speak of becoming/ a Nisei Week queen . . . / a cheerleader . . . / a typical amerikan youth." Formerly idealized aspirations, such as winning a beauty pageant, came under fire by feminists in the 1970s. Murakami expressed impatience with her friend's weeping over romantic woes, which appeared trivial compared with the wartime suffering of the Vietnamese people: "i speak of the/ Vietnamese soldier/ who looks like you/ who is the same age/ as you—/ the young fighting sister / who cannot think/ of pleasures" *(Gidra,* October 1971, 3).[22] Inspired by the struggle of the Vietnamese people, the poet vows not to cry but to fight. On one level, the victory she seeks is to end the war; on another level, the victory may be tied to a changing consciousness of liberation.

Striking images of the armed Asian woman soldier, usually Vietnamese or Chinese, recur in *Gidra*.[23] For example, the cover art for the March 1970 issue depicts a woman carrying a baby and rifle while reading a small book, possibly Maoist precepts. The appeal of this image for Asian American activists might have paralleled the appeal of the soldadera [female soldier] image among Chicana/o activists. As Vicki Ruiz pointed out, the figure of "La Adelita" of the Mexican Revolution did not challenge Chicano nationalists but rather suggested the supportive female comrade (Ruiz 1998, 111). Likewise, the Asian woman fighter served as a representation of strength and action, while also affirming commitment to maternal nurturing and nationalist struggle in solidarity with men.

Sansei Perspectives on Japan

In the late 1960s and 1970s, Sansei activists not only looked to the revolutionary struggles in China and Vietnam for inspiration but also became interested in their ancestral homeland. Critical of what they viewed as the high price of acceptance in the dominant white society, they turned to Japan as a symbol of ethnic culture and pride. "As Japanese people growing up within racist America," Evelyn Yoshimura wrote in 1972, "many of us begin to look toward Japan for some of our roots—for some meaning to our lives. . . . Tired of the plastic culture of America, we idealize Japan as a place where rich eastern culture oozes out of everything and everyone." Yoshimura warned that Japanese Americans, like non-Japanese Americans, tended to perceive Japanese society "in terms of images and fantasy" *(Gidra,* May 1972, 6).

In analyzing the appeal of Japan for Japanese Americans, Yoshimura contrasted equally problematic fantasy and reality through striking gendered figures: the medieval male warrior and the contemporary urban woman. She argued that, tired of the passive powerless images of Japanese/Americans in U.S. media, Sansei tried "to relate to the image of the supermacho Samurai in the flicks we see: the strong, spiritual stoic, who is also a bad motherfucker." Deflating the fantasy, Yoshimura pointed out that this masculine icon "is as out of place in urban, westernized Japanese society as he would be walking down Crenshaw Blvd. in L.A." She asserted that Japan's position as the third-strongest capitalist nation and an imperial power, like the United States, shaped Japanese society. As an example of the idealization of western standards of beauty in Japan, Yoshimura stated, "it is a common sight to see Japanese women walking down the streets of the cities with bleached hair, and surgically rounded eyes and breasts." Extending an Asian American movement critique to Japan's embrace of Western culture, she charged, "Young people in the cities feel this cultural imperialism in the forms of alienation, drugs and crime—sound familiar?" *(Gidra,* May 1972, 6).

Travel to Japan sometimes produced ambivalent reactions in Sansei from the continental United States. Japan's shifting status, heralded by the 1964 Tokyo Olympics and the 1970 World Expo in Osaka, attracted increasing numbers of tourists, including Japanese Americans. Literary scholar Traise Yamamoto has discussed these journeys as an important part of the "process of disentangling Japanese American identity and subjectivity from racist configurations that elide the differences between Japanese Americans and Japanese" (Yamamoto 1999, 82),

Lack of language skill was a key problem for many of the Nisei and Sansei visiting Japan, who, the *Hokubei* reported, "often speak the language imperfectly, if at all" (Yamamoto 1999, 82). Commenting on Japanese people's differential expectations of proficiency for Japanese Americans and European Americans, one Sansei remarked, "If you don't speak Japanese well, it's better to be white" (Yamamoto 1999, 82). In a letter to *Gidra*, Linda, a Sansei woman who spent several weeks in Japan in the fall of 1971, said ruefully, "I sure wish I had studied harder in Japanese school. It really makes me sad that there's such a heavy barrier between me and my brothers and sisters in Japan" *(Gidra*, November 1971, 3).[24]

Social issues, such as gender inequality, that concerned Japanese American activists in the United States also drew their attention when they visited Japan. Linda further reported, "One of the things that disturbs me the most in Japan is the men and women situation. . . . In Japan the men are superior and the women inferior. Everyday actions, employment, movies, television, and advertisements reflect this attitude. The women are portrayed as weak and servile. . . . Japan is definitely a man's country" *(Gidra*, November 1971, 3). This realization dispelled Sansei women's idealized visions of their ancestral land.

Nor did visiting Japan offer an escape from issues of social stratification by race and ethnicity. Evelyn Yoshimura compared ethnic/racial discrimination in Japan and the United States, viewing it as more alike than not. She contended, "Japanese cities are becoming archetypes of American cities—complete with ghettoes where national minorities, like the Koreans and Chinese, are forced to live." She likened their position to the status of racial minorities in the United States, identifying many as "second and third generation Japanese residents who are victims of the same kind of racism that Third World people in America are subjected to" *(Gidra*, May 1972, 6).

Some Sansei also experienced discrimination that they had not expected to face, and both men and women reported disappointment. Agnes Moriuchi, an English teacher, found it difficult to make friends and said, "I've encountered more discrimination here than anywhere in the United States" *(Gidra*, November 1973, 2).[25] At a seminar held at the International House of Japan, third-generation attendees criticized Japanese prejudice toward Japanese Americans, "citing the widely accepted view that most Japanese who emigrated were 'farmers who couldn't make it' in their overcrowded rural communities" *(Gidra,* November 1973, 2). This stereotype about the class and perhaps weak character of the Issei and their descendants stung the Sansei.

For Sansei who visited Japan in the 1970s, such journeys could elicit complicated emotions. In her letter to *Gidra,* Linda expressed both appreciation and frustration. She extolled the beauty of the countryside and the hardworking rural folk who, to her, epitomized the spirit of Japan; by contrast, she found the city people cold and rude. Her letter conveys the novelty of being in a place where her physical appearance marked her as belonging, rather than as a foreigner: Linda noted that she and a Japanese American friend could "blend really well into the crowds and remain quite inconspicuous until we open our mouths and then it's all over." She lamented her limited ability to speak Japanese, saying, "Because of this language barrier I feel alienated many times, but other times I feel such an affinity for the land, people, culture and heritage" *(Gidra,* November 1971, 3).[26] Whether in Japan or the United States, the third generation faced issues of gender, culture, and belonging.

Conclusion

After leaving home, presumably to attend college, Peggy Miyasaki thought she had escaped "from all the 'Japaneseness'" of her parents: the sounds of koto[27] music, home cooking, her father's words of Japanese. But soon she began to call her mother for directions on how to prepare rice and okazu. Both familial distance and an Asian American studies class gave her fresh perspective. Although conscious of her internalization of Western values, Miyasaki wrote joyfully of a new cultural awakening: "I'm also more aware of the efforts being made by many Sansei and other Asian American people to regain the old culture and build a new one which is a mixture of our heritage from Asia and our experience in America" (Miyasaki 1973, 5).[28] Involvement with the Asian American movement fostered in Sansei both ethnic pride and a sense of pan-Asian American bonds, rooted in understandings of shared history and struggle. In this vein, Miyasaki declared her determination to "see my children growing up with knowledge of the traditions and beauty of the Japanese culture and the Asian American experience."

For some Sansei women, founding and joining movement organizations represented the beginning of a lifelong commitment to community service and social transformation. Merilynne Hamano Quon described her involvement as "a pivotal turning point in my life. The Asian American student movement brought together all the elements of my personal identity and experiences as a woman, a Japanese American, and as a member of the Third World" (Quon 2001, 209). After graduating from the University of California, Los Angeles in 1971, Hamano Quon made the decision not to enter graduate school but instead dedicated her life to "making change in America!" (Quon 2001, 209). In 1972, she wrote for Asian Sisters the $100,000 federal funding proposal that would give rise to the Asian Women's Center. She was also active in the UCLA Asian American Studies Center, *Gidra*, the National Coalition for Redress and Reparations, Communications Workers of America, and other groups. In 2001 Hamano Quon noted the success of grassroots drug abuse organizations such as Asian Sisters as well as the women activists' productivity in building careers and families. "Asian Sisters was proof positive that sisterhood is powerful!" (Quon 2001, 213).

Sansei women activists in Southern California followed in the footsteps of their urban mothers and grandmothers as they organized women's groups and provided social services in (and beyond) the ethnic community. Working together with "sisters" and "brothers," they challenged sexism in both the larger society and the Asian American movement. Drawing inspiration from their peers as well as women engaged in third world liberation movements, they developed alternative images of female power, strength, and self-determination. Community organizations, cultural arts programs, and Asian American studies classes continue to reflect their enduring efforts to "serve the people."

Notes

1 Peggy Miyasaki wrote that she had stereotyped other Japanese American youth as either quiet, studious "bookworm types" or "rowdy outspoken" types. She attributed her attitude partly to her experiences with her peers and partly to her father's pressure to date Japanese boys, who he insisted were all "the best kind . . . intelligent, polite, clean boys." Because the few Japanese American boys who asked her on dates seemed only to be interested in "the next dance, getting drunk, or their new car," Miyasaki came to reject "all Japanese people, myself as Japanese," and her father.
2 In the difficult period of postwar resettlement, as before the war, urban Nisei clubs provided camaraderie and a place of belonging for youth who were often excluded from mainstream white organizations. The persistence of ethnocultural youth clubs may reflect both racial tensions faced by Japanese Americans and the continuing significance of ethnic ties in their lives. See chapter 5 of my book *City Girls: The Nisei Social World in Los Angeles, 1920–1950* (Oxford University Press, 2014).

3 As Susie Ling notes, wanting to attract diverse members, Sansei Concern changed its name twice, first to Oriental Concern, and in 1969 to the Asian American Political Alliance.
4 The five-month strike was the longest student strike in U.S. history.
5 Despite the staff's efforts to create a "self-sufficient progressive media," financial instability appears to have been a key factor in *Gidra*'s demise. Mike Murase, one of the founders, offered thoughts on *Gidra*'s history and ending in the essay "Toward Barefoot Journalism" in the final issue in April 1974. Murase noted that other movement organizations such as the Yellow Brotherhood were also experiencing turmoil. Among a number of issues, the "problem of money" was "a constant source of concern and apprehension for the staff," particularly after they graduated from college; during the life span of *Gidra,* not one staff member "received a single payroll check." "Toward Barefoot Journalism" was reprinted in *Counterpoint: Perspectives on Asian America,* edited by Emma Gee (Murase, 1976, 307–319). In a short video about *Gidra* made by the Japanese American National Museum for its 2011–12 exhibition "Drawing the Line: Japanese American Art, Design & Activism," Mike Murase, Evelyn Yoshimura, and Doug Aihara talk about the challenges of publishing the newspaper. See https://www.youtube.com/watch?v=OYwPTNtuhhc&index=10&list=PLE4C2713B1F34BDE4.
6 Drawing on 1965 California state statistics in *Californians of Japanese, Chinese and Filipino Ancestry,* Uyematsu listed the median annual income of Chinese men ($3,803), Japanese men ($4,388), and white men ($5,109).
7 See also the similar "Poem," by anonymous, which begins "Sister/ Para nuestra hermanas" (*Gidra,* April 1974 [final issue], 24).
8 It is not clear from the *Gidra* reportage what kinds of alliances might have been forged by Asian American women with other minority women's groups between 1969 and 1974. Laura Pulido has suggested that Chicana/o and black activists in Southern California tended to overlook Japanese American activism and to dismiss Asian Americans as a "nonoppressed group" (2006, 154–162). In her essay "The Mountain Movers: The Asian American Women's Movement in Los Angeles," Susie Ling quoted an Asian American woman activist who said regretfully, "I wish we had made more contact with other women's groups throughout the city—White and Asian" (Ling 1989, 66).
9 This column was written by Carol Mochizuki, but since it is written in the third person, it is not clear if she was reporting her own experience or someone else's.
10 Iwataki gave this statement as the representative of the Asian Coalition at a Dump Nixon Coalition rally on January 20, 1974.
11 This article was written by Carol Mochizuki in the third person. Presumably, the experiences and observations she details were her own, but the relationship is not completely clear.

12 As Ling has pointed out, a number of Asian American movement groups, such as Asian American Hardcore and Yellow Brotherhood, focused on men's drug problems, but women's problems were different.
13 The course attracted more than seventy students.
14 The AWC closed in 1976; see Ling (1989, 59–63).
15 See also Yamamoto (1999, 22–27).
16 Traise Yamamoto cited "the inanity, circulated and widely believed during World War II, that Japanese women's vaginas, like their eyes, were horizontal slits" (1999, 58).
17 Yoshimura pointed out that white women were also in an oppressive situation.
18 A year later, *Gidra* featured another similar ad for mail-order brides, mostly Japanese, with a lengthier critique by Patty Iwataki.
19 Laura Pulido (2006, 210) noted the unusualness of this photo, included in her book *Black, Brown, Yellow, and Left: Radical Activism in Los Angeles;* her photo shows nine of the original ten women, in the same pose. According to Pulido, other ethnic women activists in Southern California rarely documented themselves in this way.
20 Regarding the participation of Asian American women in the 1971 Indochinese Women's Conference in Vancouver, Canada, see Judy Tzu-Chun Wu (2013, 219–265), *Radicals on the Road: Internationalism, Orientalism, and Feminism during the Vietnam Era*.
21 Nisei Kiku Uno reported that 200 women of color attended the conference, including 120 Asian Americans, among whom were "many Sanseis, two Niseis, and one Issei."
22 Laura Pulido has noted the proliferation of gun images in *Gidra*.
23 See, for example, the issues of January 1971 (pp. 10, 12) and November 1971 (p. 3).
24 Linda's last name was not included with her letter.
25 Reprinted from an article in San Francisco newspaper *Hokubei Mainichi* (October 1973). Moriuchi was from New Jersey.
26 Linda did not identify her friend Nach as Japanese American, but, in context, this seems likely.
27 The koto is a stringed instrument.
28 It is not known whether Miyasaki became a member of any Asian American movement organizations, but, as her letter reflected, taking an Asian American studies class had a significant effect on her.

References

Allen, James P., and Eugene Turner. 1997. *The Ethnic Quilt: Population Diversity in Southern California*. Northridge, CA: Center for Geographical Studies, Department of Geography, California State University.

Brooks, Charlotte. 2009. *Alien Neighbors, Foreign Friends: Asian Americans, Housing, and the Transformation of Urban California.* Chicago: University of Chicago Press.

Chan, Karen Ito. 1972. "The Asian American: Caught in a Media Massage." *Gidra: The Monthly of the Asian American Experience,* April.

Chan, Karen Ito, and May Ying Chen. 1972. "A Thousand Burdens." *Gidra: The Monthly of the Asian American Experience,* April.

Gil, Dinora. 1969. "Yellow Prostitution." *Gidra: The Monthly of the Asian American Experience,* April.

Hamano, Merilynne (see also Quon, Merilynne Hamano). 1972. "Thoughts of Remembrance for Clara." *Gidra: The Monthly of the Asian American Experience,* May.

Iwataki, Linda. 1971. "Women's Herstory." *Gidra: The Monthly of the Asian American Experience,* January.

Jones, Jacqueline A., Peter H. Wood, Thomas Borstelmann, Elaine Tyler May, Vicki L. Ruiz, eds. 2003. *Created Equal: A Social and Political History of the United States.* Vol. 2 (from 1865). New York: Longman.

Kao, Mary Uyematsu. 2009. "Three-Step Boogie in 1970s Los Angeles: Sansei Women in the Asian American Movement." *Amerasia Journal* 35 (1): 112–138.

Killer Fawn. 1971. "In the Movement Office." *Gidra: The Monthly of the Asian American Experience,* January.

Kurashige, Lon. 2002. *Japanese American Celebration and Conflict: A History of Ethnic Identity and Festival in Los Angeles, 1934–1990.* Berkeley: University of California Press.

Kurashige, Scott. 2008. *The Shifting Grounds of Race: Black and Japanese Americans in the Making of Multiethnic Los Angeles.* Princeton, NJ: Princeton University Press.

Lee, Shelley Sang-Hee. 2014. *A New History of Asian America.* New York: Routledge.

Ling, Susie. 1989. "The Mountain Movers: Asian American Women's Movement in Los Angeles." *Amerasia Journal* 15 (1): 51–67.

Maeda, Darryl Joji. 2012. *Rethinking the Asian American Movement.* New York: Routledge.

Matsumoto, Valerie J. 2003. "Japanese American Girls' Clubs in Los Angeles during the 1920s and 1930s." In *Asian/Pacific Islander American Women: An Historical Anthology,* edited by Shirley Hune and Gail M. Nomura, 172–187. New York: New York University Press.

———. 2014. *City Girls: The Nisei Social World in Los Angeles, 1920–1950.* New York: Oxford University Press.

Miyasaki, Peggy. 1973. "Dear Dad, From Your Sansei Daughter." *Gidra: The Monthly of the Asian American Experience,* July.

Mochizuki, Carol. 1971. Untitled column. *Gidra: The Monthly of the Asian American Experience,* June, 6.

Murase, Mike. 1974. "Toward Barefoot Journalism." *Gidra: The Monthly of the Asian American Experience,* April. Reprinted in *Counterpoint: Perspectives on Asian America,* edited by Emma Gee. Los Angeles: Asian American Studies Center, University of California, 1976.

Omatsu, Glen. 1994. "The 'Four Prisons' and the Movements of Liberation: Asian American Activism from the 1960s to the 1990s." In *The State of Asian America: Activism and Resistance in the 1990s,* edited by Karin Aguilar-San Juan, 19–69. Boston: South End Press.

Pulido, Laura. 2006. *Black, Brown, Yellow, and Left: Radical Activism in Los Angeles.* Berkeley: University of California Press.

Quon, Merilynne Hamano. 2001. "Individually We Contributed, Together We Made a Difference." In *Asian Americans: The Movement and the Moment,* edited by Steve Louie and Glenn Omatsu, 207–219. Los Angeles: UCLA Asian American Studies Center Press.

Ruiz, Vicki L. 1998. *From Out of the Shadows: Mexican Women in Twentieth-Century America.* New York: Oxford University Press.

Shibusawa, Naoko. 2006. *America's Geisha Ally: Reimagining the Japanese Enemy.* Cambridge, MA: Harvard University Press.

Takezawa, Yasuko. 1995. *Breaking the Silence: Redress and the Japanese American Ethnicity.* Ithaca, NY: Cornell University Press.

Tanaka, Tomi. 1971. "From a Lotus Blossom Cunt." *Gidra: The Monthly of the Asian American Experience,* July.

Umemoto, Karen. 1989. "'On Strike!' San Francisco State College Strike, 1968–69: The Role of Asian American Students." *Amerasia Journal* 15 (1).

Uyematsu, Amy. 1969. "The Emergence of Yellow Power in America." *Gidra: The Monthly of the Asian American Experience,* October.

———. 1992. "To All Us Sansei Who Wanted to Be Westside." *30 Miles from J-Town.* Brownsville, OR: Story Line Press.

Wu, Judy Tzu-Chun. 2013. *Radicals on the Road: Internationalism, Orientalism, and Feminism during the Vietnam Era.* Ithaca, NY: Cornell University Press.

Yamamoto, Traise. 1999. *Making Selves, Making Subjects: Japanese American Women, Identity, and the Body.* Berkeley: University of California Press.

Yoshimura, Evelyn. 1971. "G.I.'s and Asian Women." *Gidra: The Monthly of the Asian American Experience,* January, 4, 15.

PART V

BORDERLANDS

CHAPTER 9

Nakayoshi Group
Postwar Okinawan Women's Articulation of Identity in America

Wesley Ueunten

Proclaimed a journalist about overseas Okinawan immigrants in America in 1926: "If we had much of anything in Okinawa that was worthy of national pride, then it would have the power of changing other people when we openly engaged our 'national customs'; unfortunately, that is not the case.... So... we must be careful not to make a display of our most striking and unique customs." (As cited in Kobashigawa 2000) He joined a chorus of educated male Okinawan voices that intoned shame and embarrassment over how Okinawans were seen by their Japanese countrymen and by Americans. A year earlier, also writing about overseas Okinawans, a leading educator in Okinawa criticized the tattooing of women's hands and other body parts as "shameful" and wondered if there was a way for Okinawans over the age of thirty-four or -five to hide their tattoos (Kobashigawa 2000).

Reinforced by Japanese government efforts to assimilate Okinawans into Japanese culture these top-down voices rang loud in the Okinawan diaspora. Burned in the memories of countless Okinawan schoolchildren is the punishment meted by schoolteachers in Okinawa for speaking the Okinawan language. A common practice before World War II was to hang a wooden tag around the neck of a student who spoke in the Okinawan language. On the tag, the word "*hogen* (方言)," or "dialect," was written in bold letters. The student could pass on the tag to another student who spoke in Okinawan. The practice created a stigma toward speaking the Okinawan language that was carried over to the diaspora and fortified by the litany of voices from above that admonished Okinawans from displaying their "Okinawanness"; my own parents, like most Nisei Okinawans in Hawai'i and other parts of the diaspora, were discouraged from learning to speak Okinawan by their parents because it was a marker of inferiority and backwardness.

More than eighty years after Okinawan male elites were deriding anything visibly or audibly Okinawan by overseas Okinawans, I received a package in the mail from Michiko,[1] who immigrated to California in the 1960s. In the package were a cassette tape recording and the handwritten Okinawan lyrics of a song she had written called "Fūchibā jushī no uta." Upon first reading of the lyrics, I only found a song about the humdrum topic of making a porridge with the insignificant mugwort. However, upon more reflection, I was struck with the realization that this seemingly unimportant song raises the possibility of reimagining identity, culture, and community in ways that scholars are usually not comfortable with. This reimagining involves considering resistance to hegemonic power structures in forms other than publicly observable "heroic" and "dynamic" acts that are carried out largely by privileged males. The argument here is that "Fūchibā jushī no uta," as commonplace as it may seem to many scholars, is part of a longer tradition of resistance to hegemonic power. Important to this tradition of resistance is the emotional medium of music.

"Fūchibā jushī no uta"	"The *Fūchibā* Porridge Song"
Fūchibā niui ya kabasaibin	The fragrance of *fūchibā* (mugwort[2]) is nice
Jushīmē du tsukuyabitan	I made *fūchibā* porridge
Chumakai wanne ajisakutu	I had one serving of it
Tamakai mimakai fūsaibin	I wanted to have two and three servings
Anshi māsaru jushīmē	A delicious porridge!
Mē nu nukuinu aibīnē	When there is leftover rice
Umibushi tu fūchibā shi jushīmē	I add *ume boshi* and *fūchibā*
Katsuo tu shōyu shi aji chikiti	I give it some flavor with *katsuo bushi* and *shōyu*
Usaga misōchi ajiubiti	Partake and remember the taste
Ippē māsaru jushīmē	A very delicious porridge!

Dushi nu chā tu suritōti	My friends and I get together
Ashibi tanushimi sōyabitan	To enjoy ourselves
Asaban jibun naibindo	It's lunchtime now!
Chunu asaban nūyaibīga	What's for lunch?
Jushīmē du yaibindo	It's *jushīmē*!
Wattā uchinānchu ya	We Okinawans
Kugatō amerika ni chabitan	Have come to this faraway America
Fūchibān ītuyabin	*Fūchibā* has also prospered
Ippē fusagati uibindo	It is a very strong Okinawan plant![3]
Fūchibā ya washiyabiran	Never forget *fūchibā*

Michiko is part of a small group of about ten Okinawan immigrant women above the age of sixty-five scattered in the Bay Area who have been meeting at least once a month for more than fifteen years to share one another's company in singing, eating, and talking. They call themselves Nakayoshi Group, where "*nakayoshi*" can be roughly translated as "getting along together" or "being friendly to each other." Over the past several years, I have gotten to know the Nakayoshi Group as they have invited me to some of their monthly gatherings at de facto leader Dolly's home, where they share food and sing Okinawan and Japanese songs to karaoke. I also asked them to join my Okinawan *sanshin*[4] group when we performed at a ceremony to open an exhibit on the Battle of Okinawa in January 2011 and to commemorate the Battle of Okinawa in June of the same year.

Michiko had carefully handwritten the Okinawan words using the *katakana* phonetic system used by Japanese for writing "foreign" and onomatopoetic words. Using *kanji* (Chinese characters) and *hiragana* (the phonetic system for "Japanese" words), she provided a translation in "standard" Japanese, which I translated into English above. Taking the time to see beyond the seemingly quaint or mundane topic of preparing mugwort porridge with leftover rice for visiting friends, one can understand the song as part of the process in which Nakayoshi Group members maintain culture as a healthy expression of their unique identity as both Okinawans and immigrants to America. This understanding is especially important if one remembers that Okinawan culture has been struggling to survive the assimilationist policies that were imposed on Okinawa following its reversion by Japan in 1879. Getting to the last verse of the song, which uses the hardy *fūchibā* as a metaphor for Okinawans surviving and thriving in an unfamiliar land,

I am struck at how identity production and "reproductive labor" are woven together through song.

The song is even more meaningful when one remembers that most of the Nakayoshi Group members directly experienced the bloody Battle of Okinawa or were schoolchildren separated from their families and evacuated to mainland Japan soon before the American forces landed on Okinawa. The fabric of Okinawan culture was torn to shreds and indelibly stained by the blood and tears of the Okinawan population that experienced an estimated one-fourth to one-third decimation in less than three months of intensive ground and air fighting. Regardless of where they were during the Battle of Okinawa, the members of Nakayoshi Group all experienced at least part of the chaotic postwar period in Okinawa when it was administered and occupied by the U.S. military from 1945 to 1972. Consequently, they bring to us an increased understanding of how war and military occupation shape immigration to the United States and to the rest of the Americas[5] and, more significantly, how experiences of war and military occupation shape the identity of Okinawans in the United States and the rest of the Americas.

A closer examination of Nakayoshi Group also reveals provocative ironies and raises challenging questions for those of us with *fūchibā*-like cultural practices and identities and for scholars who seek to study these practices and identities. "Fūchibā jushī no uta" is representative of such ironies as it exemplifies how Japanese assimilationist efforts, the Battle of Okinawa, and American occupation in Okinawa and persistent Orientalism and racism in the United States have not completely stamped out Okinawan cultural practices and identity. The military, economic, political, and cultural strength of both American and Japanese empires has succeeded in creating embarrassment, shame, stigma, and often self-loathing toward things "Okinawan" both at home and in the diaspora, but like the seemingly simple *fūchibā*, certain cultural practices and identities seem to keep regenerating themselves. At this point, I would like to express my desire for this study to contribute to the agency and voices of the people who carry out those practices and hold those identities.

In doing so, there are some other provocative ironies that begin to emerge. For instance, Nakayoshi Group members seem to be accommodationist, but are oppositional. Their practices seem to be transitory and even randomly trivial, but are rooted in an ontology that precedes the structures of power that have historically encroached on Okinawa since the seventeenth century. The women and their practices seem to be innocuous, but challenge the very ideological framework of empire.

These ironic juxtapositions of power are inspirational for those of us who have stood in the path of imperial expansion (and contraction) and who have desperately struggled to hold on to our identities in the process of surviving the weight and pain of oppression, exploitation, and violence. As scholars who identify with the subjugated and subaltern, perhaps our work is to document and bring to light the everyday lives and practices of the people we study, taking inspiration from French sociologist Michel de Certeau, who urges us to shift our focus away from the obsession of scientific institutions on analyzing systems that repress individuals to one that examines the practices that take place within and against these systems. The former type of analysis is privileged because scientific institutions study the very system of which they are a part and "conform to the well-known genre of the family story." Certeau writes,

> Seeing this elucidation of the apparatus by itself has the disadvantage of *not seeing* practices which are heterogeneous to it and which it represses or thinks it represses. Nevertheless, they have every chance of surviving this apparatus *too,* and, in any case, they are *also* part of social life, and all the more resistant because they are more flexible and adjusted to perpetual mutation. When one examines this fleeting and permanent reality carefully, one has the impression of exploring the night-side of societies, a night longer than their day, a dark sea from which successive institutions emerge, a maritime immensity on which socioeconomic and political structures appear as ephemeral islands. (Certeau 1984)

Certeau's words are inspiring for allies of subalterns, underdogs, and the "wretched of the earth." They also push Japanese American studies toward painting more complete pictures that include the finely detailed brushstrokes that represent the lives of people that large "grand narrative" brushstrokes cannot, such as "war brides" and "GI brides"; immigrants from Korea and other former Japanese colonies in Japantowns; mixed-race, LGBT, and "radical" Japanese Americans; and Burakumin, Zainichi, Okinawans, and other Japanese minority groups. In other words, Certeau's breathtaking vision enables our imagination community of "Japanese American" to embrace and engage with a larger collection of people.

However, as rousing as Certeau's words are, the use of similes and metaphors from nature to analyze the lives of ordinary people in structures of power can also be risky. One potential problem is the reinscription of binaries and the rearticulation of teleologies through the assumption of the natural triumph of "our side" over the "other side"—whether it is the "low" over the "high," "good" over "bad," or "chosen" over "unchosen." Such an assumption can be seen in some of the very ideas that Japanese American studies has resisted such as Manifest Destiny, Orientalism, and the assimilationist paradigm. Even my own appropriation of *fūchibā* as a simile for subaltern resiliency reinforces the hypothetical assumption that the oppressed and exploited will win in the end.[6] The assumption of the eventual victory of the subordinated over the dominant is similar to other teleological notions such as the triumph of communism over capitalism.

A second potential problem is in regard to agency; by using similes and metaphors taken from nature to analyze the lives of people we invite the possibility of taking away the life, breath, feelings, thoughts, and actions of our "subjects" and, instead, empowering their practices, identities, and cultures. That is, the scholar's constructions of practices, identities, and cultures are given agency while the actual people who carry out these practices or create and maintain these identities and cultures can and are robbed of agency. For example, while it is definitely true that the Nakayoshi Group members themselves and their cultural practices are persistent survivors, it is important to make sure that I do not indiscriminately represent both of them together with the hardy *fūchibā*. In getting caught up in the aesthetics of simile and metaphor or the elegance of theoretical abstraction, one can deemphasize the agency of the people we purportedly study—to the point that they become seen as primitives from the past who live on instinct for survival or quaint exotics who follow "ancient" tradition. The following is an example in Japanese American studies of a metaphor taken from nature to talk about norms:

> Probably the one outstanding characteristic of Japanese norms is their *adaptiveness* to fixed positions and to external realities. Rather than a stream making its own course, the stream follows the lines of least resistance—their norms *emphasize* duty and obligation; their values *include* conformity and obedience. (Kitano 85; italics mine)

In the quote above and in the following, agency exists not with Japanese Americans, but with abstract concepts such as norms and culture:

> The bond that held the Japanese community together was its *culture*—that is, everything that was brought over from Japan, and the subsequent development, maintenance, and change of that *culture* in the new country. It would include its economic, political, social, family and religious structures, its institutions, and its norms, values, personality, and behavior. (Kitano 83; italics mine)

The subject of the foregoing quotes is culture. That is, culture is the bond that holds the Japanese community together, rather than the people themselves. Where are the people in Japanese American studies? What are they doing? How do they imagine and create community?

In Search for the People

In September 2011, I called Dolly to explain that I wanted to write a paper on Nakayoshi Group. I told her that I thought it was important to document the experience of Okinawan women who came to the United States after the war as well as the activities of cultural groups such as Nakayoshi Group. A few days later on September 30, I went to eat with the Nakayoshi Group at one of their favorite restaurants, the New Chinese Buffet in San Leandro. After eating, we went to Dolly's house for the group's usual monthly karaoke session. Below is a description of the events of that day with excerpts of the audio recording I made of group conversations. I also add information from oral history interviews that I did later as well as my own recollections and reflections from previous encounters with Nakayoshi Group members.

September 30, 2011

In Dolly's living room, surrounded by the eight women, ages sixty-seven to eighty-one, I turned on my audio recorder. To warm them up, I asked them to tell me their names. Dolly took the lead and said each member's name out loud. As mentioned earlier, to keep the women anonymous, I have changed their names. I have also blocked out their last names below, but five of the women have "American" last names and three have "Japanese" last names. Dolly and Kathy use "American" first names as well. Because it is a group conversation (in a mixture of Japanese, Okinawan, and English), I cannot identify all the voices that appear, but I try my best to capture and translate the spirit of the group, which bubbles over frequently into laughter and humorous comments.

Wesley: What's the date again?
[Different voices at once:] September 30.
Wesley: [Into microphone] This is a Nakayoshi Group gathering. [To the women] Say whatever you feel like. *Yuntaku*[7] is fine.
Dolly: Yoroshiku onegai shimasu.
[Unidentified voice]: Yuntaku hantaku.
Wesley: Well, maybe we could start off with you all telling me your names.
Dolly: [Says everyone's name in room, including her own and then mischievously says, ". . . and Wesley san!"]
[Everyone laughs]
Dolly: Yoroshiku onegai shimasu!
Wesley: Today's gathering is a monthly event?
Dolly: Yes, yes.
Wesley: Who lives the farthest?
Gladys: That's us. We come from Richmond.
[Unidentified voice:] She's really good at driving.
Wesley: Do you drive fast?
[Everyone laughs]
Gladys: Well, there are times when I drive fast. When I go to the casino, I drive fast.
Wesley: Is that so?
[Everyone laughs]

The humorous banter and laughter is infectious. It lifts my spirits while bringing me down to earth as I am a target of their jokes. Singing Okinawan love songs toward me, the women succeed in embarrassing me. One of the women says, "It was Michiko-san's dream to marry a *samisen*[8] player and singer." Another echoes in, "Yes, that was her dream!" The women all giggle as they look at me, forcing me to apologize for being born too late. They laugh loudly as Dolly says, "Ueunten-san, you should have come around earlier! Michiko-san would have taken good care of you!"

At that moment, the women clearly do not fit into the stereotypically shy, demure, and obedient geishalike Japanese wife as represented by Tae in *Japanese War Bride* (1952) and Hanaogi and Katsumi of *Sayonara* (1957). More important, they live a story that is oppositional to the Japanese American "grand narrative." Roughly speaking, in that grand narrative, Japanese male Issei come to the United States before World War II. Issei women follow them or are called over as "picture brides." Their Nisei children are caught between Japanese and American cultures but succeed in becoming loyal Americans while retaining such Japanese cultural values as *giri* (duty), *on* (obligation), and *gaman* (perseverance) while achieving upward mobility despite discrimination, especially during World War II. Their (assumed monoracial) Sansei children have integrated into American society, and so there seems to be a collective loss as to how to tell the story to include Yonsei and later generations and mixed-race Japanese Americans. The story also inelegantly excludes postwar Japanese immigrants.

The Nakayoshi Group members were on the "Japanese side" during World War II. They represent the "enemy race" image that Japanese Americans were trying to escape. The inclusion of postwar Japanese immigrants in the grand narrative is prevented by the fact that they have married white or African Americans and have had mixed-race Japanese children.

Being Okinawan also makes a big difference, as this fact placed many in the middle of the Battle of Okinawa and subjected all of them to U.S. occupation after World War II. Both the Battle of Okinawa and the subsequent occupation from 1945 to 1972 were cases in which Okinawans were sacrificed for the rest of Japan.

Under the surface of the laughing, eating, and singing, the Battle of Okinawa always looms large for the members of Nakayoshi Group. Earlier in the day of my visit, at the all-you-can-eat buffet, I was surprised at how the women could eat so much. They made repeated trips to the buffet to get servings of dim sum, spring rolls, fried chicken, ribs, desserts, and other rich foods. When I remarked to the women how surprised I was at the amount they ate, Gladys told me that she loves food because during the Battle of Okinawa there was little to eat besides grass.

A few years earlier, I had brought my teenage daughter to a Nakayoshi Group gathering. While my daughter and I were feasting on the Okinawan, Japanese, and American food that the members had prepared, one of the members asked my daughter how old she was. When my daughter replied her age, the woman remarked that it was around the same age that her older sister died during the Battle of Okinawa.

My understanding of the Battle of Okinawa, which is shallow because my family had immigrated to Hawai'i decades before World War II, was deepened when I asked Nakayoshi Group to perform with my *sanshin* group for the opening of the Battle of Okinawa exhibit that I curated in San Francisco from January to August 2011. Even after sixty-six years, some of the members found the memories of the battle too painful and refrained from participating.

At the opening of the Battle of Okinawa exhibit, Dolly cried when she saw the replica of the cave shelter that Okinawan civilians took refuge in during the battle. She explained that she had been orphaned during the battle as a young child. After the war, a couple that had returned from mainland Japan adopted Dolly. When she was still a child, Dolly was taken to meet a younger sister who was said to have been born in a cave shelter during the battle and was adopted by a family of relatively affluent background on Okinawa, but because they were raised apart, they had no mutual affinity. In 1979, when Dolly went back to Okinawa for the first time after coming to the United States, she learned from a woman who had returned from Saipan[9] after the war that they might have been related, because the woman had heard about a relative's child that was passed from cave to cave during the battle.

With Dolly's closest kin torn apart by the war, her cultural upbringing was also shattered and disrupted. Soon after adopting her, Dolly's parents took her back to Miyako, an island southwest of the main island of Okinawa. The Sakishima Channel, which lies between Okinawa and Miyako, has resulted in the two areas of the Ryukyu Archipelago developing different cultures and languages. Dolly lost the ability to speak the language of the main island of Okinawa while acculturating to Miyako. Further, Dolly became a live-in nanny after the childless couple later had their own child. From as early as she can remember, Dolly carried the baby on her back while her parents ran a restaurant. She was not allowed to go to school and acquired rudimentary Japanese reading skills by reading comic books.

It has been through the Nakayoshi Group that Dolly has relearned the language of the main island of Okinawa by picking up words and phrases that some of the other members use. Impressively, music was how Dolly greatly improved her Japanese reading skills: reading the subtitles of her favorite songs while singing karaoke with Nakayoshi Group members allowed her to learn many of the *kanji* that she never had the opportunity to study as a child. Most important, however, the camaraderie, warmth, and playfulness of the Nakayoshi Group gatherings return a childhood that was cut short.

Lingering Effects of Japanese Imperialism

> *Wesley:* Who thought of the name "Nakayoshi"?
> *[Multiple voices:]* Everyone did . . .

> *[Unidentified voice:]* Nakayoshi dakara, nakayoshi ni shiyou ka (We figured that since we get along well, we should call ourselves "nakayoshi") . . .
> *[Unidentified voice:]* Everyone is good at singing, but when we stand on stage, we get nervous. . . . If only we had self-confidence . . .
> *[Unidentified voice:]* Dolly is the only one who doesn't get stage fright.
> *[Unidentified voice:]* Meeting once a month is our enjoyment.

My rudimentary life history of Dolly reveals just a glimpse of the complex real lives of the many women who experienced the Battle of Okinawa and came to the United States married to American men. It also shows the tenacious efforts of people like Dolly to put themselves back together again. Okinawan music—albeit in the commodified form of VHS and DVD karaoke recordings—has been an important medium in this effort. As will be seen below, however, the Nakayoshi Group members make even the commodified music their *own* music as they re-create their identity as well as build a community in the lingering shadows of Japanese discrimination against "Okinawan" as "quasi-Japanese" that belies the recent popularity of Okinawan culture.

Soon after I started recording our conversation, the women said that they wanted to sing karaoke, and so Dolly turned on the television set and the DVD player. The women began taking turns singing their "*jūhachiban*" songs, or the songs that they "own." In between Okinawan songs, they also sang Japanese *enka*. I noticed that a few of the women actually sang *enka* with more confidence and skill than they did Okinawan *minyo*. In fact, most of the women did not learn to sing Okinawan songs (aside from children's songs) until after coming to the United States. One reason is that Okinawan *sanshin* music was seen as improper for women in Okinawa when they were growing up. Women who played the *sanshin* and sang were associated with *juri*, or courtesans. The other reason is the stigmatization of Okinawan culture as a result of the forced assimilationist policies that were imposed in Okinawa following annexation in 1879. Some of the women were old enough to have gone to school in Okinawa before World War II, where they were punished for speaking Okinawan and made to feel as if they were "inferior Japanese." Even after World War II when Okinawa was under direct U.S. occupation, Okinawan teachers who had been educated before the war continued to discourage students from speaking Okinawan. Some of the women even remembered the common practice of teachers hanging a tag with the words *hogen fuda,* or "dialect tag," around the necks of schoolchildren who spoke in Okinawan. The student could be released from wearing the tag if he or she found another who spoke in Okinawan.

While Japanese knowledge of Okinawa has increased greatly since Okinawa's reversion to Japanese control in 1972, the cultural chasm between Japan and Okinawa is still deep in Japanese America. Seen as only quasi-Japanese because of Okinawa's late entry into Japan in 1879 and direct U.S. control from 1945 to 1972, many Okinawan women experienced marginalization in the larger postwar Japanese immigrant community. However, because Nakayoshi Group refrains from speaking negatively about anyone as their emphasis is on *nakayoshi,* or "getting along," I seldom hear any personal stories of marginalization. In other contexts, the common story of Okinawan women is that of being told by other postwar Japanese immigrants, "I'm surprised how well you speak Japanese!" Another common assumption by other Japanese is that Okinawan women speak English well because of the U.S. occupation of Okinawa.

Okinawan women immigrants in the Bay Area usually belong to circles and networks that are not necessarily Okinawan. The Nakayoshi Group members are no exception, as individual members belong to different groups such as religious organizations, exercise groups, and karaoke clubs. However, Okinawan women immigrants seem most comfortable with other Okinawans. Perhaps paralleling the Asian American fatigue over having to explain why we speak English, the Okinawan women find it refreshing not having to explain to other Japanese why they speak Japanese. They also feel less threatened by other hints of their inferior status among Japanese, such as comments over the "interesting" Okinawan accent or "exotic" features, which include deeper facial features and darker skin.

> *Wesley:* Did you all meet after coming here?
> *[Multiple voices:]* Yes, yes.
> *Wesley:* Where did you all meet? Did it happen spontaneously?
> *[Unidentified voice:]* We met at Okinawan—
> *[Unidentified voice:]* Kenjinkai gatherings.
> *Kazuko:* We did meet at kenjinkai gatherings, but we didn't get that close.
> *[Unidentified voice:]* It was *samisen.* It was when we met at Kazuko's place.

> *[Unidentified voices:]* The first people to meet were these four: Dolly, Michiko, Minako, and Hiromi . . .
> *Dolly:* Then Kathy and I became friends. Saito-san came later. . . . Kathy was in Japan, but her husband lived in the United States, so that's why she's here.
> *Michiko:* We're *Uchinaanchu* (Okinawan) and so, one by one we bring other into the group.
> *Hisako:* Yes, it's by word of mouth.
> *Michiko:* That's why the Nakayoshi Group will always be *nakayoshi*.

According to stories from other Okinawan women in the Bay Area, the Japanese American community was not welcoming to postwar Japanese women in general for various reasons. One was that they were reminders of the Japaneseness that Japanese Americans had strove so hard to distance themselves from. Another was the connection made between "war brides" and Japanese women in the sex industry in U.S.-occupied Japan. I recall one Okinawan woman telling me that a Japanese American Nisei woman told her that she had "stolen" American men from other American women.

Music and Identity

> It must have been about twenty years ago when my two-year stay in America had ended. As the tedious sea voyage was coming to an end, from a radio in the ship's cabin I suddenly heard an Okinawa folk song sung to the *samisen*. At that instant, I gasped and stopped in my tracks. I guess one could even say that my blood was "stirred up." My body was moved by unspeakable emotion. My colleagues were also similarly affected as they suddenly stopped the conversations that they had been engrossed in. There were even those who shed tears. From that moment onward, I have constantly asked myself "What was that emotion?" Perhaps the question can be rephrased as "What am I?" In turn, the question leads inevitably to the other question of "What are Okinawans?" (Ōta 1985)[10]

Masahide Ōta, a Battle of Okinawa survivor who would become governor of Okinawa, writes about returning from the United States to Okinawa in the preface of his book *Okinawajin to wa nanika* (What Is an Okinawan?). In the absence of any formal religion that was linked to Okinawan identity (such as Catholicism for Filipinos, Protestant Christianity for Koreans, and Shinto and Buddhism for Japanese), Okinawans have reaffirmed their identity through music.

Okinawan music has been a crucial vehicle through which Okinawans have reproduced their identities through upheavals of invasion, occupation, war, annexation, forced assimilation, and diasporization. In other words, Okinawans have had a degree of independence from regimes of power because they have created and re-created identities that refuse to be completely assimilated by those regimes. Music flows from the past into the future as a vehicle for Okinawan identity. The women of Nakayoshi Group are part of the flow of Okinawan music when they gather monthly to sing Okinawan songs in front of Dolly's television screen. I came into Okinawan music as an identity-seeking Sansei (third generation) Okinawan from Hawai'i who has been a student of traditional Okinawan *sanshin* music for more than half my life.

It goes without saying that the emotions that I have in relation to being Okinawan are not necessarily the same as those of the Nakayoshi Group members. Nor can I assume that the Nakayoshi Group members share the same emotions ascribed to being Okinawan among themselves. While we share ancestral connections to Okinawa, a myriad of factors have no doubt shaped our emotional attachment to being Okinawan, including gender, age, education, place of birth, religious affiliations, economic background, and political views, just to name a few. However, music is an important medium of emotion through which we can claim, create, and perpetuate a shared Okinawan identity despite our arguably tenuous connections to each other.

As a scholar rooted in Japanese American studies, which shares a genealogy with ethnic studies, Asian American studies, women's studies, and other fields rooted in the desire to work toward social justice, music is where "insights into the workings of power" are revealed.

The perspective from which I both experience and analyze music as a medium of emotion in the Okinawan diaspora is rooted in "Tinsagunu Hana," a song that came to me through imperfect understandings, interpretations, and conveyance of meanings. I grew up hearing from my Nisei mother about how her mother, my Issei grandmother, sang a song called "Chinsagu[11] nu Hana" often at home. She told me about how her mother explained that the song was about dyeing everything that one's parents say into one's heart as one would dye the color of the *chinsagu* flower on one's fingernails. Needless to say, because the song had to traverse an ocean, generations, and languages, my understanding of the song was far from perfect. Further, because my mother had grown up being self-conscious of her stigmatized Okinawan background, she never learned to sing the song. All I understood about the song was that it was one of the very few "Okinawan" things that were passed down to me. Much later in life, when I was trying to find my "roots" as a Sansei who had been inspired by the identity politics during the 1980s, I learned to play the *sanshin*. "Tinsagunu Hana" was one of the songs that I learned early in my Okinawan music education. I learned to sing three verses of the song:

Tinsagunu hana ya	Dye the tips of your fingernails
Chimisachi ni sumiti	With the petals of the *tinsagu* blossom
Uyanu yuushi gutu ya	Dye the teachings of your parents
Chimu ni sumiri	Onto your heart
Tin nuburi bushi ya	If you tried, you could
Yumiba yumarishiga	Count the stars in the sky
Uya nu yushi gutu ya	But you cannot count
Yumi ya naran	What your parents teach you
Yuru harasu funi ya	A ship sailing at night
Ninufaa bushi miati	Gets its bearings from the North Star
Wan nacheeru uya ya	My parents who gave me life
Wan du miati	Get their bearings from me

It is from this ontological and epistemological position that I argue that the Okinawan diaspora cannot be understood completely without including analyses of emotive aspects such as yearning to find one's "roots," pride for Okinawan culture, sadness over a lost past, and unresolved trauma. Renato Rosaldo critiques the "manly" ethic in social sciences, which is literate, male centered, "rational," and detached from emotion and subjectivity or what Max Weber would call "passionate detachment." While Weber actually advocated for researchers to be emotional, whatever emotions they had were to be relegated to the passion one carried in approaching the research. For Weber, the researcher should be disciplined enough to carry both "warm passion (that) emanates from devotion to a cause" and "a cool sense of proportion (that) derives from the detachment that clarifies reality" (Rosaldo 1993). Consequently, a researcher has the impossible task of being "warm" and "cool" at the same time. Rosaldo writes,

> Weber's "manly" ethic should be loosened because its androcentrism has suppressed valuable sources of insight deemed unworthy by bearers of the high standard. This ethic underestimates the analytical possibilities of "womanly weaknesses" and "unmanly states," such as rage, feebleness, frustration, depression, embarrassment, and passion. Victims of oppression, for example, can provide insights into the workings of power that differ from those available to people in high positions. . . . Why narrow one's vision to a God's-eye view from on high? Why not use a wider spectrum of less heroic, but equally insightful, analytical positions? (1993)

The early parts of this chapter were written on the third floor of the newly renovated Faculty and Graduate Student Reading room in the San Francisco State University library overlooking the "Quad," where students protested during the Third World Liberation Front strike for ethnic studies back in 1968. Looking over to my left, I saw the Cesar Chavez Student Center, which was, according to an original student striker and now a senior Asian American studies faculty member, built after the strike by a construction company that specializes in building prisons. Noticing the network of railed walkways and platforms that are perched as high as the tallest trees on campus, making them vantage points for armed police in case of large gatherings of people, I do see the resemblance of SFSU to a penitentiary with guard towers.

I included in this chapter a personal account at the risk of again being seen as, among other things, self-indulgent, overly subjective, and inadequately academic. However, these are some of the very same criticisms that such oppositional fields as ethnic studies, Asian American studies, and women's studies have been enduring since at least as early as those days of protest in 1968. I ask rhetorically, hopefully in the voice of my predecessors, "How different are the physical structures that tower over SFSU and the structures of academia that serve as platforms for surveillance and silencing?"

In "Crafting Ethnic Studies," Gary Okihiro points out that "ethnic studies, like women's studies, sees experience as crucial to the recovery of voices and perspectives missing or distorted in the master narratives written mainly by white men" (2001, 44). The ethnic studies approach counters the "race relations" model that assumed the triumph of U.S. modernity and democracy and treated groups that did not follow the path to equality, integration, and assimilation into the mainstream, such as African and Asian Americans, as deviants or "problems" for not succumbing to the master narrative.

Okinawan emotion is, of course, preserved and conveyed through media other than music. I have not talked about traditional Okinawan dance, which perhaps has a larger population of people who study it formally in the Okinawan diaspora than traditional music does.[12] I also leave out formal genealogies[13] and Okinawan food.[14] However, music is central to my discussion on Okinawan emotion and identity for various reasons. On a personal note, my connection to music is not only through "Tinsagunu Hana" but also through my mother's learning Okinawan dance when she was pregnant with me. Ever since I can remember, Okinawan music has simultaneously stirred my emotions while providing a sense of comfort.

This personal story leads to the larger importance of Okinawan music as a medium of identity: Music has been able to travel Okinawan diasporic space and time easily. It travels in such forms as audio recordings and musical notation and through performances by diasporic Okinawans. Further, it travels with dance, the other important medium of Okinawan emotion and identity. In my own case, my mother, who had earlier been ashamed of being Okinawan, underwent a reawakening to her Okinawan culture when she joined my father, who had been stationed in Okinawa during the Korean War in the early 1950s. When she became pregnant with me, she took the opportunity to learn Okinawan dance from a woman who had immigrated to Hawai'i from Okinawa after the war. The dance lessons took place in our family home using a phonograph to play the music over and over again, giving me the opportunity to be immersed in their sounds.

The evolution of sound media has only made Okinawan music more accessible in the diaspora. As a teenager interested in Okinawan dance, I traveled across my island of Kaua'i to learn from an Issei Okinawan who had settled there with his family after coming from Peru via a U.S. Department of Justice internment camp in Crystal City, Texas.[15] Over and over again, we practiced Okinawan dance to the Okinawan music on cassette tapes. One need not mention that in more recent years, Okinawan music has become available with a few finger strokes on handheld devices.

Like all music, Okinawan music bears the imprint of past social formations. Music and dance had an important place in ritual, which was originally controlled by women in traditional Ryukyuan society up to the increasing influence of patriarchal culture, especially after 1609. Beyond ritual, however, music and dance were no doubt integral to everyday life as evidenced by the older generation of Okinawans, such as my grandmother and other Okinawan relatives both in Hawai'i and Okinawa, who break into impromptu song and/or dance frequently.

Consequently, the persistence of music and dance in Okinawa and the overseas diaspora could probably be attributed to the strong undercurrent of music and dance in the everyday life of Okinawans since ancient times. However, another development in Okinawan music needs examination in order to understand it as a medium of Okinawan identity. Because the small Ryukyuan Kingdom could not resort to military force to deal with Japan and China, its diplomacy relied largely on music and dance. As a tributary of China, Ryukyuans were required to accommodate periodical visits of Chinese envoys who came for months at a time to install each new Ryukyuan king. The Ryukyuan Kingdom put enormous resources into entertaining the Chinese envoys, including preparing elaborate performances of music and dance. These performances were not merely to entertain the Chinese and to impress them with Ryukyuan high culture, but were ways to hide the fact that the Ryukyuan Kingdom was actually controlled by Japan via Satsuma.

Music and dance were also important when Ryukyuan envoys made periodical visits to the Tokugawa court. The Ryukyuan entourage would travel through Japan from Satsuma to Edo and were expected to perform music and dance along the way and at Edo.

Because of their importance in diplomacy, music and dance were under the auspices of the Ryukyuan Kingdom. Probably rivaling the proportion of American resources going to the military, the amount of Ryukyuan resources spent on music and dance was substantial, as officials were assigned to preserve and produce music and dance pieces and to train the best performers possible.

Aside from the prestige that music and dance have because of their importance in past Ryukyuan diplomacy, the abolishment of the Ryukyuan Kingdom led to a dynamic hybridization of the high court music with the music of the commoners. This happened as former court musicians and dancers were forced to make a living by performing in public. To appeal to wider audiences, the former court musicians and dancers combined the slower and heavier songs and dances of the court with the faster and lighter songs and dances of the commoners. Thus, the postannexation period is characterized by a flowering of music and dance creativity in Okinawa. Further, formal training in court music and dance was actually more accessible than ever as the former court musicians and dancers began taking students from the former commoner class.

The *sanshin*, the three-stringed plucked instrument with roots in China, was the main instrument in Ryukyuan court music. Whereas *sanshin* playing was limited to relatively few commoners before the abolishment of the kingdom, the accessibility of training in court music led to *sanshin* playing being propagated much more widely in Okinawa. Among the Okinawans who emigrated overseas were those who had former training in *sanshin*. Further, as Okinawan immigrants achieved relative economic affluence, many used their newfound money to buy *sanshin* to bring back to their overseas homes.

Okinawan Gumbo

Back to Dolly's living room. The women have warmed up and are singing songs back to back. Somehow, through their travels back and forth to Okinawa and Japan or through friends and relatives, they obtain videotapes and DVDs of a large repertoire of songs. Interestingly, many, if not most of the songs that the women sing were composed in Okinawa or Japan after they immigrated to the United States. These are not "traditional" songs, but rather are songs that they learned in the United States. In other words, the songs are transnational songs in that they are shared with other Okinawans in other parts of the world.

An example of this transnational exchange network and the importance of music and emotion were revealed to me a few months later when I went to do an oral history with Gladys at her home on November 25, 2012. She fed me a meal of leftover gumbo she had made for Thanksgiving dinner the day before and shared her experiences of coming to the United States as the wife of an African American man from New Orleans.[16] When I asked her what feelings she had when she sang Okinawan songs, she said, "When I sing Okinawan songs, I remember Okinawa and growing up there. . . . Shall I sing for you?" She stood up and walked over to her ancient karaoke machine to put in a cassette tape. As she rewound the tape, she explained that her older sister had sent the tape from Okinawa before she died several years ago. After finding the beginning of the tape, the sound of her sister's voice suddenly came out of the speakers. Her sister speaks in Okinawan that is unmixed with Japanese. In her message, her older sister expresses concern because she heard the news of forest fires in California. After the message, her sister sings Okinawan songs on her own karaoke machine. Gladys solemnly sings along with the well-worn tape of her departed sister singing karaoke. The analog technology of this network contrasts with the cut-and-dried digital technology of CDs, DVDs, iPods, and YouTube through which the transnational spreading of Okinawan music has accelerated in the past ten years.

Because of its analog nature, I imagine that Gladys's cassette tape will eventually wear out, but the emotions and memory attached to it will be carried forward in some form or another by her, her family, friends, and others who have heard it or have heard her sing its songs. Gladys's cassette tape will transmit an analog "signal" that can either fade or increase its intensity and will be either "corrupted" or "creatively enhanced"—depending on how one looks at it. For good or bad, emotion cannot be digitalized.

Summary

Unna machishita ni   Under the pine trees at Un-na
Chiji nu fe nu tachushi   A sign commands: No Rendezvous!
Kuishinubu madinu   Did they really expect it would
Chi ya nesami   Stay the flow of our love?[17]

It may be informative to locate the Nakayoshi Group members in a genealogy that stretches back to the priestesses who held high rank in every level of society, from the family and village, to the Ryukyuan Kingdom. According to Okinawan historian Matsuda Mitsugu, women were influential in the society and government of the Ryukyuan Kingdom even after Chinese Confucian thought entered Okinawa from the fourteenth century. In 1609, however, the militaristic southern Japanese feudal domain of Satsuma invaded Okinawa. Under Satsuma's influence, the religious authority of women was challenged as Ryukyuan government officials imposed Confucianism as the dominant ideology. It was then that the chief priestess, known as *chifijin* or *kikoe ogimi,* was demoted in official rank and the practice of handing official documents to the king via women priestesses was abolished (Matsuda 1967).

Likely because of their exclusion from governance, women in Okinawa have continued to be voices of dissent. For example, the words to the version of the song "Unna Bushi" at the beginning of this section are attributed to a poem by Unna Nabī, a woman of commoner background from the "backwoods" northern region of Okinawa in the early 1700s. "Unna Bushi" is a rhetorical question that critiqued the post-Satsuma invasion of the Ryukyuan Kingdom, and Satsuma attempts to prevent lovers from meeting as well as to prohibit traditional ceremonies, rituals, and other gatherings in public places (Hateruma 2008).

While the women throughout the Ryukyuan archipelago had traditionally prayed and passed down traditions and stories through ritual song and dance, male court officials eventually gained official supremacy over music and dance. Ironically, this version of "Unna Bushi" is widely sung by *koten* (classical) Okinawan musicians, who are mostly male and whose repertoire and singing styles are rooted in the court of the former Ryukyuan Kingdom. The song is perhaps an echo of a voice that questioned the legitimacy of an imposed male-centered hierarchy that the court symbolized.

I do not mean to imply that resistance through music is solely an enterprise of disenfranchised Okinawan women. Further, I do not want to portray the Nakayoshi Group members as "freedom fighters" who represent a natural-born Okinawan mission to fight for an independent Okinawa. We share music, but we do not necessarily share political positions regarding such issues as Okinawa's role as the site of a large U.S. military presence and Japanese resorts. I do propose, however, to reimagine Okinawan identity, culture, and community by also reimagining Okinawan history as containing a tradition of opposition to hegemonic power through the emotional medium of music. In other words, notwithstanding my aforementioned apprehensions regarding using simile and metaphor in studying and representing people, I believe that music is an apt representation for the often subtle and subdued, but tenacious and dogged struggle to resist the dehumanizing effects of externally imposed structures of power and, most important, to carve out and maintain spaces—both metaphorical and physical—for meaningful interaction.

This is a good segue to talk about my stakes in Japanese American studies. Thanks to my esteemed colleagues who have supported me by allowing me to write about Okinawan music and to include my own subjectivity, I feel a strong investment in Japanese American studies. Namely, I feel a commitment to carving out a space for both intellectual and subjective interaction that can lead to mutual understanding. My being as a Sansei born and raised in Hawai'i shapes both my subject position and intellectual approach. However, to return to the music metaphor, I would like Japanese American studies to be a space for the type of call-and-response that happens in music.

I take to heart the words of Sachiko Kawakami, who writes about post-1965 immigrants and their descendants in San Francisco's Japantown. Based on exhaustive ethnography, Kawakami writes about the complex context of the everyday commercial practices of these immigrants, most of whom are Korean but include other immigrants with postcolonial affinity to Japan. I am greatly inspired by her attention to the everyday practices in her study, which enables her to make such a perceptive comparison of our works. She points out that the Nakayoshi Group members are "conditioned to connect their everyday practices to their self-image and identities," while postcolonial immigrants in Japantown "are conditioned to disconnect their everyday practices from their self-image and identities." This comparison opens up new ways of contextualizing Okinawans within Japanese American studies, especially when I recall that Nakayoshi Group members and I have sung on different occasions in San Francisco's Japantown. What does it all mean when we have occupied the same space but have had little interaction?

From Kawakami's work, I take the following quote: "Although it might not be the most common or comfortable choice of topic in this conference, the ultimate purpose here is to search for 'common ground' for transnational, cross-generational, and inter-ethnic collaborations to resist against all sorts of imperialisms" (Kawakami 2011).

I hope that this discussion can be a part of an ongoing call-and-response. I am, of course, not narrowing this to a literal definition of call-and-response in terms of music, but one must consider the metaphor of music as way to connect on a more emotional level even if it is not something that scholars find the most "common or comfortable choice of topic."

Notes

1. I have changed the names of the Nakayoshi Group members to protect their privacy.
2. "*Yomugi*" in Japanese.
3. The song does not include any reference to the plant being Okinawan, but the translation into Japanese provided by the composer refers to it as a "strong Okinawan plant."
4. The *sanshin* is a three-stringed plucked instrument that is derived from the Chinese *san hsien* and the predecessor of the Japanese *samisen* or *shamisen*. Traditionally, the *sanshin* has been meant to be subordinate to singing as there are very few *sanshin* pieces that are without singing.
5. Postwar Okinawan immigration to the United States must also be seen in relation to the postwar migration of Okinawans to American-friendly countries in South America due to the expansion of U.S. military bases, which left insufficient land for Okinawans to farm. In countries such as Argentina, Bolivia, and Peru, Okinawans make up the majority of the Japanese populations there.

6   It is important to note that while the song compares Okinawans coming from far away to establish themselves in America with the *fūchibā,* using it as a simile for subaltern resistance is my own doing.
7   *Yuntaku, yuntaku hintaku,* or *yuntaku hantaku* [Okinawan] refers to the practice of "shooting the breeze," or what is referred to in Hawai'i as "talk story."
8   Okinawans who came of age before the 1990s tend to use the Japanese word *samisen.* It was in the 1990s that the more "authentically" Okinawan word *sanshin* began to be more widely used by Okinawans as Okinawan music became more popular and accepted in Japanese mainstream society.
9   Okinawans made up a large portion of the settlers in Japan's South Pacific territories. After the end of the war, most of them were repatriated to Okinawa.
10   The original Japanese text is as follows: もう、かれこれ二十年余も前のことになりましょうか、二カ年のアメリカ留学を終えて帰国するさいのこと、退屈な船旅もようやく終わりに近づいたとき、突然、船室のラジオから三味線に乗って沖縄の民謡が聞こえてきました。その瞬間、私は思わず息を呑み、その場に立ちすくんでしまいました。「血が騒ぎ立つ」とでもいえばよいのでしょうか、私は言い知れぬ感動に身を震わせたものです。他の同僚たちも同様だと見え、おしゃべりに夢中になっていたのが一瞬、押し黙ってしまい、涙を浮べている者さえいました。あの感動は、一体何だったのか、そのとき以来、私は自問しつづけずにはいられませんでした。その意味を問うことは、いってみれば「私は何者か」を問うことであり、ひいては「沖縄人とは何か」を解き明かすことに他なりません。
11   The standard pronunciation for the song's title in Okinawa is "*tinsagunu hana,*" but perhaps in my grandmother's dialect it was pronounced "*chinsagunu hana.*" The other possibility is that "*chinsagu*" represents a Nisei Okinawan pronunciation of *tinsagu,* because Nisei Okinawans were encouraged to learn standard Japanese rather than Okinawan by their parents. Because standard Japanese does not have a "*tin*" sound, "*chin*" would be the closest sound.
12   Dance is an effective medium for Okinawan emotion as it involves the whole body in the tangible expression of Okinawan identity. Futher, the performances of dance are usually done with costumes that are recognizably "Ryukyuan" or "Okinawan" and thus have the potential to evoke emotions associated with being Okinawan.
13   The recovery of formal genealogies is also rooted in emotional ties to the past. In the days of the Ryukyuan Kingdom, there was a class system in which society was roughly divided between those with genealogies (*chiimuchi*) and those without genealogies (*muchii*). This class structure has roots in the seventeenth century when the Ryukyuan Kingdom, very likely conforming to the militaristic hierarchichal structure of Japan that was being imposed through Satsuma, set up an office of genealogies. In Okinawa

itself, many families have recovered or attempted to recover the official genealogies of the kingdom period, most of which had been destroyed during the Battle of Okinawa. In the diaspora, especially among Sansei and Yonsei in Hawai'i, there has been a similar effort to recover genealogies. Simultaneously, many Okinawans in Hawai'i have attempted to find their "mon" (*kamon*) or family crest. However, unlike in mainland Japan where virtually every family was required to have a family crest during the Tokugawa period, in the Ryukyuan Kingdom, only those with genealogies had such a family crest. Consequently, not every person of Okinawan descent can clearly claim a formal genealogy or family crest. However, the search for a formal genealogy and family crest among many Okinawans in the diaspora, even when not entirely fruitful, must be seen as rooted in strong emotive ties to the past.

14 Certain dishes and cooking styles have survived in various degrees outside of Okinawa such as stir-frying vegetables and the liberal use of pork and vegetables not usually found in Japanese cooking, such as bittermelon (*gōya*), sweet potato leaves (*kandabā*), and loofah (*nābērā*). From personal experience as an Okinawan Sansei growing up in Hawai'i, I recall knowing which houses were Okinawan by the smell of pork that had permeated the premises through years of frying and boiling various parts of the pig, including the feet, ribs, ears, and intestines.

15 Toshio Yamasato was taken forcibly to the United States as part of a program of "hostage exchange" in which Japanese from Latin America were rounded up to barter for Americans held in Japanese territory after the attack on Pearl Harbor. After the war ended, the Japanese Latin Americans who were taken to the United States under this program were informed that they were illegal aliens in the United States and were compelled to leave. Peru, which had provided the bulk of the internees, refused to accept the Japanese back. Many returned to war-torn Japan and Okinawa, and many others worked at Seabrooke Farms in New Jersey under oppressive conditions. Some, like Yamasato's family, were fortunate to have relatives that could sponsor them to live in the United States.

16 The rich contents of that conversation would take more space than this paper can contain.

17 B. Taira. *My Favorite Okinawan Songs* (4th ed.). (Japan: Author, 1969).

References

Certeau, M. de. 1984. *The Practice of Everyday Life*. Berkeley: University of California Press.

Hateruma, E., ed. 波照間永吉. 2008. 新編 沖縄の文学 (Okinawan Literature), rev. ed. Okinawa, Japan: Okinawa Jiji Shuppan.

Kawakami, S. 2011. "What Brings Korean Immigrants to Japantown? Commodifying Racial Differences in the Age of Globalization." Paper presented at Japanese and Asian Americans: Racializations and Their Resistances, October 13 and 14, 2011, at UCLA.

Kitano, H. H. L. 1976. *Japanese Americans: The Evolution of a Subculture.* Englewood Cliffs, NJ: Prentice-Hall.

Kobashigawa, B. 2000. "Antinomies of Okinawan Immigrant Identity: Ethnic Pride and Shame within a Double Minority." In Uchinanchu Diaspora International Scholars Forum, Waipahu, U.S.A.

Matsuda, M. 1967. "The Government of the Kingdom of the Ryukyu, 1609–1872." PhD diss., University of Hawai'i.

Okihiro, G. 2001. "Crafting Ethnic Studies." In *Ethnic Studies Research,* edited by Timothy Fong, 35–57. Lanham, MD: Altamira Press.

Ōta, M. 大田昌秀. 1985. 沖縄人とは何か (What Is an Okinawan?). Okinawa: Green Life.

Rosaldo, R. 1993. *Culture & Truth: The Remaking of Social Analysis,* rev. ed. Boston: Beacon Press.

Taira, B. 1969. *My Favorite Okinawan Songs,* 4th ed. Japan: Author.

CHAPTER 10

What Brings Korean Immigrants to Japantown?
Commodifying Racial Differences in the Age of Globalization

Sachiko Kawakami

Splash: Is there any Koreatown in San Francisco?
Johnny Ma: Best Answer—Chosen by Asker
there are actually many Koreans that live near Japantown in SF. Ever notice how many korean karaoke bars there are? It's true there's no formal organized K-town in SF, there are Koreans . . . Another observation-
 many if not most of the japanese Sushi places in the East Bay are Korean run . . .

From: YAHOO ! ANSWERS

Introduction: How Can We Approach Invisible Racism?

As Yasuko Takezawa has stated, racism today "often disguises itself, making it difficult for us to pinpoint and loudly claim: 'this is racism'" (Takezawa 2011a, 2). In fact, "difference" has come to no longer only have meaning in the political context of articulating a collective identity for resistance and community activism, but also in the commercial context of creating economic value for business and marketing activities. As the global economy shaped by neoliberalism has become part of the common sense of everyday life, "difference" has been increasingly perceived as a competitive advantage that is a marketing resource to differentiate oneself from other competitors in the market. Thus, in such a market-oriented, color-conscious, and color-blind society as the United States, some commercial forms of racism and racial hierarchies that operate within and support structures of white supremacy tend to be less problematized and hence naturalized, blurring the ethical divide between "discrimination" and "differentiation." The former needs to be fought against, while the latter is sometimes deemed empowering and progressive for the lives of racial minorities.

In these conditions, while Asian Americans have continuously fought against the ideas of Asians as "unassimilable aliens, "model minorities," and "perpetual foreigners" by engaging in political actions to mobilize themselves as a community, they have simultaneously faced market realities in which perceived foreignness can be manipulated and reproduced by people of any color and nationality to make a profit. In the meantime, some people, especially foreign-born immigrants, have silently been involved in the community of others without calling for recognition of their presence.

Furthermore, these practical dimensions of racialization have not always been clearly articulated; rather, those who engage in the economic activities within the community of others do so quietly. Also, among ethnic studies scholars, there is an underlying assumption that antiracist activism is only made possible through the examination and construction of collective political subjectivity. In fact, recent studies on San Francisco's Japantown mainly focus on urban renewal projects and preservation movements emphasizing collective identity formation and politics (Lai 2006; Sugiura 2007; Sugiura and Oda 2009; Tsukuda 2009, 2011).

However, as mentioned, in today's society, racial hierarchies are (re)created and naturalized in subtle, invisible ways in the privatized sphere. For this reason, in this chapter, I focus on Korean immigrants' spatial practice primarily revolving around individual daily commercial and consumption activities in San Francisco's Japantown.

As shown in the above excerpt from a question and answer website, it is a well-known fact among people living in San Francisco that some Korean immigrants work, live, and socialize in Japantown, also known as Nihonmachi. Since the mid-1980s, elderly Korean immigrants have occupied the senior housing complexes as tenants, and their merchant children have purchased properties to engage in business activities there (Kotani 2008). These property sales and the increased visibility of Korean-language store signs (see Figure 10.1) have induced emotional reactions that impel some Japanese American community members to express, "Why don't they go to Koreatown?" or "What brings Korean immigrants to Japantown?" By seeking to answer these questions from the standpoint of Korean immigrants

Figure 10.1 Korean-language Store Signs in Nihonmachi
Korean-language signs and displays are part of everyday landscape in Nihonmachi.

who live and work around Nihonmachi, I explore the invisible and complex realities of contemporary Asian American racism and racialization.

This chapter draws on my research in an anthropological study based on fourteen and a half months of ethnographic fieldwork in the Korean immigrant communities of Oakland and San Francisco between 2003 and 2006 (Kotani 2008; Kawakami 2014). I spent many hours interacting particularly with elderly Korean immigrants at both Japanese American and Korean American community institutions. I also visited homes, businesses, community meetings, family gatherings, various ceremonial parties, informal gatherings, karaoke events, festivals, Korean-language schools and churches, and elections in the Korean immigrant community. In this portion of the current study, I focus on the following two groups of people who migrated to the United States from South Korea after the 1965 Immigration Act: (1) Japanese-literate male and female Korean seniors who grew up during the colonial period (1910–1945) and (2) Korean immigrant small business owners (predominantly male) who spoke little English and mainly used Korean. I conducted personal interviews with them in Korean, Japanese, and English.

Perspective: From Articulated Identity to Silent Affinity

In my study, Japanese American community activists were inclined to emphasize their strong ethnic identity and articulate their connection to Nihonmachi as a symbolic community (Tsukuda 2009, 2011). Korean immigrant respondents who live, work, and socialize in Nihonmachi, to the contrary, have not attempted to represent the place as their community, repeating the phrase "Japantown is Japantown."

To highlight this particular position and subjectivity of Korean immigrants in Nihonmachi, I propose the concept "silent affinity." By this I mean a subtle, practical sense of belonging that is formulated on an individual basis. Independent of the notions of lineage, silent affinity can be developed toward many particular entities, including places, groups of people, languages, ideologies, and lifestyles. But in this chapter, I particularly focus on Korean immigrants' place-based silent affinity with Nihonmachi. In this particular context, I pay attention to their postcolonial subjectivity formed through participating in the lives and communities of others to satisfy their practical needs.

It should be noted that unlike the notion of identity formation, silent affinity as a concept is fairly unstable and elusive, and for this reason, it usually neither mobilizes people to collective action nor leads to multicultural alliances. It is discreet and rarely articulated in public, and represents a choice in an individual's life.

Silent affinity as a concept has limitations. First of all, just like many other abstract ideas, it is not objectively tangible and measurable. For some, silent affinity remains an elusive epistemological state that deserves no attention. However, the idea of silent affinity is useful in understanding cultural diversity from a different angle, beyond the discussions of identity politics or multicultural alliances. It allows us to approach a kind of ambiguous, unorganized, and unarticulated state of "difference" that is found commonly in everyday life but often regarded as too trivial in public scenes (see Figure 10.2).

Moreover, it helps us to reexamine an academic act of representation that relies heavily on an assumption that cognitive coherence is necessary. As racial categories are complex with diverse meanings that criss-cross the boundaries of historical periods, different languages and disciplines, public and private sectors, the local and the global, and different ethnic communities, what is needed in academic studies now is not only to make order out

Figure 10.2 Korean-language Community Information Available in front of a Korean-owned Restaurant in Japan Center
Nihonmachi provides links with and information on resources for the Korean immigrant community.

of chaos but to create opportunities for contradictive multilingual narratives to emerge.

I examine the silent affinity of Korean immigrants in Nihonmachi as a source of their livelihoods as well as a source of their racial struggles. By using the term "livelihood," I refer to acts of building more convenient, easier lives both financially and materially. By emphasizing the conflicting contexts within Korean immigrants' subjectivity in Nihonmachi, I suggest that their difference is made invisible by the Korean immigrants themselves. To save face as Koreans, to protect their livelihoods, and sometimes due to language barriers, many Korean immigrants choose to be silent about their affinity to Nihonmachi.

San Francisco's Japantown as a Subject of Silent Affinity

San Franciscans began to move to an area known as the Western Addition in the 1870s. The neighborhood that is now Japantown (Nihonmachi) emerged in this area after the devastating 1906 earthquake and fire. A number of people emigrated from Japan, moved from Chinatown, and began settling in this area for mutual support. They built churches, shrines, and newspaper companies, as well as opened shops and restaurants. The neighborhood took on ethnic Japanese characteristics, and before long became a Nihonjin-machi, or Japanese town. By 1940, the neighborhood was home to more than five thousand Japanese residents and two hundred Japanese businesses (Kawaguchi and Seigel 2000).

During World War II, the Japanese Americans in San Francisco and in other West Coast communities were suddenly uprooted and sent to the concentration camps. The neighborhood became empty during the war years, and African Americans who migrated from the South started settling there. After the war, many of the original Japanese American residents returned to the neighborhood. However, because of their forced uprooting during the war and the urban redevelopment projects that followed in the 1960s and 1970s, the character of the area changed significantly.

As a study found (Lai 2006), the postwar period was characterized by a shift from Nihonjin-machi as a space of "use" value to a place of "exchange" value—that is, it was a lived space and then, commercialized. The former served as Nihonjin-machi (a Japanese town), and the latter as Nihonmachi (Japantown). Despite local opposition, that transformation was justified and initiated by city officials and transnational corporations, which commodified and "hyperorientalized" the area (Lai 2006). In the meantime, the first Korean business in Nihonmachi was a Korean restaurant that opened in 1954. When this restaurant first moved there, surrounding businesses were not particularly welcoming of their new Korean neighbor. Yet, the business endured, and by the 1970s, it had become a gathering place for local Korean Americans (Japantown Task Force 2005).

In 1968, the three-square-block Japan Center (originally the Japanese Trade and Cultural Center), which included a hotel and two malls, was completed. This centerpiece development "symbolized and served as an encapsulated space for San Francisco's trade orientation toward the Pacific Rim, and the entire center itself was designed as a space of tourism, a sight/site for voyeuristic experiencing of things Japanese" (Lai 2006, 9). It seemed that cultural commercialization and consumption could be replicated by anyone for the mass public (see Figure 10.3). That was the context for an influx of immigrants from East Asia.

Nihonmachi has functioned as a geographical base for Korean immigrant communities in San Francisco since the 1970s. In the beginning, Korean immigrants mainly came to Nihonmachi to buy Asian specialty

Figure 10.3 Periphery Location of Korean Businesses in Nihonmachi
Korean specialty stores and medical offices concentrate at the back of the Japan Center building.

goods such as rice. For example, a woman who immigrated in 1975 recalled that she went to Nihonmachi to buy Japanese-style mochi (sticky rice cake) because there were no shops that made Korean-style mochi in San Francisco at the time. Other than the restaurant, there were only two other Korean-owned businesses at the time: a travel agency and a Korean herbal doctor's office.

According to local residents, Korean-language signs started to increase from the middle of the 1980s.[1] In 1984, Chinese and Japanese businessmen built a new building next to the restaurant; Korean businesses increased over the years as the landlords rented space to Korean immigrant tenants who started beauty salons, cafes, video stores, gift shops, and a karaoke store. There were also professional offices, including medical, accounting, and legal services. By 2006, 80 percent of the business tenants in the building were Korean immigrants.

In the meantime, since the late 1990s, Japanese American community leaders in the area had been working toward preserving Japantown as a unique cultural and economic district to symbolize an appreciation for Japanese American culture. Similar projects of cultural reclamation had been taking place simultaneously in the other two official Japantowns, in Los Angeles and San Jose, under the California Japantown Preservation Pilot Project (Japantown Task Force 2005). The historic legislation authorizing the project (California Senate Bill 307) was passed in 2001 to recognize the cultural significance of the Japantowns as ethnic neighborhoods and publicize the diversity of the state. It provided grants to Los Angeles, San Jose, and San Francisco to promote the preservation of their neighborhoods. As a result, representatives from all three communities worked together to secure funding from the state to preserve the Japantown legacy.

Since then, Nihonmachi has served as a culturally unique platform for a diverse group of people, including old-timers and newcomers. According to the 2000 census, whites account for 44 percent of the area's population, 30 percent are Asian, 17 percent are black or African American, and 5 percent identify as "two or more races." Among the Asian population, 31 percent self-identified as Chinese, 30 percent as Japanese, 21 percent as Korean, 7 percent as Filipino, 6 percent as South Asian, 1 percent as Pacific Islander, and 1 percent as "other Asian."

Silent Affinity as a Source of Livelihoods

For Elderly Korean Immigrants

Nihonmachi has attracted a large number of the elderly. According to data compiled by a local community organization in 1999, the average age of the residents was 45 while the city average was 38.8.[2] According to other demographic data, in 2005, 24 percent of the 11,613 Japantown residents were 65 years old or older, and 25 percent of residents were in the 25–34 age group.[3]

Korean immigrants who are 65 years or older were born during the Japanese colonial rule of Korea (1910–1945). They were forced to study Japanese language and history instead of Korean language and history at school. As a result, during their schooling years, many spoke better Japanese than English. However, after Korea's liberation from Japan, many had not used their Japanese-language skills. But they started using Japanese again due to the linguistic challenges presented by English after their immigration to the United States, which often happened at later stages in their lives. As I showed in my master's thesis on elderly Korean immigrants in Oakland,

California, watching Japanese television news and reading Japanese newspapers were common practices among Korean seniors (Kotani 2001). By doing so, some found jobs, business partners, and information on religions (e.g., Soka Gakkai, Kofuku no kagaku). Others used Japanese to converse with neighbors from Taiwan.

Most of the elderly Korean residents moved to the United States from Korea after retirement, invited by their children who had immigrated earlier for business, to study, or to reunite with family members. Upon arrival, most of the seniors lived with their children for a certain period of time, ranging from a few months to several years. However, eventually most of them moved out of their children's homes in the suburbs to live alone or as couples in subsidized senior housing in urban neighborhoods such as Nihonmachi. There are more than twenty senior housing complexes in the Nihonmachi area, and each apartment has maintained a long waiting list of Korean immigrant applicants since the end of the 1980s.

What brought elderly Korean immigrants to Nihonmachi was their practical needs for the goods and services available there. More concretely, I have identified three main reasons that Nihonmachi remains such a popular destination for elderly Korean immigrants in the San Francisco Bay Area.

1. Convenience: The elderly choose to live or visit Nihonmachi primarily for reasons of convenience. First, the location is convenient for them because it is easily accessible by public transportation. There are buses going directly to Chinatown and downtown, and there is no need to depend on their children for transportation needs. Second, many things are within walking distance. The area provides easy access to daily necessities like rice and kim-chi, medicine, doctors, and haircuts. In addition, the purveyors of those items and services usually speak Korean or Japanese.
2. Entertainment: Retired Korean seniors not only use Nihonmachi to fulfill their basic needs; they gather in Nihonmachi to seek entertainment and socialization. They frequently visit the place because it provides them with entertainment opportunities. They meet with friends and enjoy karaoke or coffee together. Some go regularly to fitness gyms early in the morning, and others enjoy drinking at pubs or lounges at night. There are free shuttles during the annual Korean Folk Festival, as well as tour buses run by Korean travel agencies from Nihonmachi.

Figure 10.4   Japanese-style Hot Lunch Program for Japantown Seniors
Immigrant seniors from Japan, Korea, and China have a chat over lunch at a community center in Nihonmachi.

3. Welfare services: Nihonmachi is well known among local seniors as a hub for special social services for the elderly. The largest organization is Kimochi, which the Japanese American media has described as "the largest senior center in the Bay Area caring for the Japanese/Korean elderly population."[4] Kimochi began to provide culturally sensitive care for Japanese American seniors in 1971, and Korean seniors have been using the services since the 1980s. Since 1999, a Korean-speaking social worker has been employed by the organization.

To fulfill their practical needs (see Figure 10.4), some elderly Korean immigrants have used their knowledge of the Japanese language. As noted earlier, many of the elderly Korean immigrants I met in Nihonmachi spoke Japanese better than English, mainly because of the Japanese colonial legacy.

For Korean Immigrant Merchants

Those who run small businesses in Nihonmachi are sometimes the children of elderly residents. Unlike their parents, most of them were not directly affected by Japan's historical colonization of Korea. However, I have found that linguistic and cultural familiarity with Japan have been passed to the next generation through business activities. For example, a Korean restaurant owner who advertised his restaurant through a television commercial on a local Japanese-language broadcasting station did not speak Japanese himself, so his father-in-law, who spoke fluent Japanese, acted as an interpreter in making the arrangements with the broadcasting station.

In addition to the high self-employment rate, the statistics show that the majority of Korean immigrants attend church. The merchants of Nihonmachi are no exception, and the majority are associated with Christian churches of various Protestant denominations.

While the strategies of identity politics emphasize ethnoracial differences of values, Orientalism in a commercialized context has obscured the boundaries between "Japanese-ness" and "Korean-ness." Although Asian American activism has fought against images of the exotic "other" created and manipulated by the Western imagination, when it comes to Korean American merchants conducting business in the mainstream market, they often face the need to accommodate themselves to situations where these exotic images are potential sources of creating profit. Their priority, therefore, shifts from cultural resistance to economic profit.

In Nihonmachi, for instance, a karaoke shop owner has utilized the ambiguity of Asianness to do business. While emphasizing the image of the Japanese cultural authenticity of karaoke by putting up Japanese-language signage, the Korean immigrant owner maintains an ambiguous Oriental image and widens the potential target of his customers by having a music selection that includes songs from Japan, Korea, China, and the Philippines. Pan-Asianism is strategically utilized to generate profits.

Silent Affinity as a Source of Struggle

Silent affinity not only provides a source of livelihoods but also brings struggles. Except for a few tenants who have larger capital and stronger connection with the Japantown business community, Korean immigrant businesses are concentrated along the outskirts of the commercial center of Nihonmachi, indicating the peripheral position of Korean businesses there. In

2006, there was only one Korean immigrant business located in the Japan Center, the landmark shopping center. A Japanese American social worker in the neighborhood told me that there were many Korean immigrant business owners who wished to get into the Japan Center, but it was usually very difficult for them to rent space there because of high rental cost and internal politics.

Resistance can recede into the background for those who show silent affinity. Despite the disadvantaged position of doing business in Nihonmachi, the focus was placed on their privatized place-based practices, and few collective actions were attempted by Korean immigrant merchants. In fact, the Korean immigrant merchants I interviewed all emphasized their self-effort and achievement.

The Korean immigrants developed silent affinity to Nihonmachi because they perceived Nihonmachi as a community of others. Their interest was neither the symbolic territorialization of Nihonmachi nor the acquisition of political power within it; rather, their interest was in the available resources. For example, as a way of coping with the shortage of Korean-speaking social workers and services, Korean seniors utilize their Japanese-language skills to use the Japanese-language services available in Nihonmachi.

Yet, why did the Korean immigrants perceive Nihonmachi as the community of others? American civic ideology emphasizes the ethics of participation, and following this inclusive principle, most of the community meetings in Nihonmachi are open to all the interested individuals and parties. Also, some community efforts have already been made to create an inclusive atmosphere. For example, some of the community notices have been translated into Korean, and Korean American bilingual or trilingual interns and social workers have been at Japanese American organizations since the end of the 1990s.

It is true that various community efforts have been made to include Korean American residents to represent the Nihonmachi community. However, as is expressed in the question "How can effective collaborations occur when worldviews and interactive styles differ?" (Kikumura-Yano, L. Hirabayashi, and J. Hirabayashi 2005, viii), the differing epistemologies and priorities, plus the English dominance of communication, seemingly have hindered the Korean immigrants in their participation in public dialogues. Consequently, in contrast to the Japanese American business community members, who are actively involved in the politics and governance of

Nihonmachi, Korean immigrant entrepreneurs are situated as "perpetual foreigners," regardless of their actual citizenship status.

In addition to these political struggles, Korean immigrants have struggled against economic racial hierachies. In many countries, products associated with Japan can be sold at a higher price than those associated with Korea or China. For example, in the U.S. market, Japanese cuisine is usually more expensive than Korean or Chinese cuisine. Similarly, in the global market, Japanese manga is more popular than Korean "manhwa."

People tend to take this hierarchy for granted, but it is important to note that it has shaped our perceptions of particular races, ethnicities, and interethnic relationships, both locally and globally. For example, Nadia Kim has discussed Japan's global power as seen in Japanese Americans' greater visibility and recognition in the United States. That power "has been affirmed by the low levels of immigration from Japan, hence, Japanese Americans' predominantly native-born populace, their higher socioeconomic levels, and their higher rates of citizenship and English fluency" (Kim 2008, 117). Thus, the lives of Korean immigrants are "shaped not only by the social location of their group within the United States but also by the position of their home country within the global racial order" (Kim 2008, 2). Korean immigrants are conditioned to commodify and consume goods and services due to their silent affinity toward Nihonmachi, which is now fashioned in "the United States-led global economic order" (Kim 2008).

Conclusion

Korean immigrants' silent affinity to San Francisco's Nihonmachi reveals their colonial legacy in Korea under Japan and racialization in the United States, which stresses their otherness, foreignness, and invisibility. However, it does not mean that they are mere passive subordinates. Their multilingual hybrid activities as consumers and merchants testify to their own local and global ethnic network, their creativity to make lived space within capital-based conceived space, and their resistance against English-centered American (global) civic ideology.

It is true that imperial Japan remains a political force to fight against in the lives of Korean Americans in the United States. However, in the everyday lives of Korean immigrants in Nihonmachi, the meaning of Japan is not so political. Rather, it has commercial connotations because they need to prioritize their daily survival to make a daily living. As a result, within the same community and even in the same person, Nihonmachi signifies conflicted meanings. On the one hand, Nihonmachi remains one of the most culturally familiar neighborhoods for Korean Americans in San Francisco as well as the place where they frequently experience isolation and otherness. On the other hand, Nihonmachi simply means another market opportunity or access to resources and services. In this way, the elusiveness and "boundarylessness" of the silent affinity transform racial hierarchies and inequalities into mere daily routines of making use of "differences" as resources.

Finally, the findings outlined in this chapter call attention to the complex realities of the marginalized within contemporary Asian America and beyond. In fact, in the United States, most of the working-class, post-1965 immigrants from Asia and Latin America spend many hours working in the communities of others. The everyday landscape of Japantown is supported by these people, including Korean immigrant small business owners whose stores are located at the outskirts of Japantown, Mexican American chefs making takoyaki, Brazilian part-time floor staff at a yakiniku restaurant, and a number of other foreign-born workers in the kitchen. They are visible in Japantown; all local people know about their presence.

Sadly, they are invisible in too many academic contexts. This is because previous studies have focused on the identity formation of ethnic groups and limited their discussions of invisibility to the context of social participation as citizens.

However, as this study shows, as the by-product of globalization, contemporary immigrants are expected to Americanize themselves in two conflicting ways. While they learn to insert themselves into mainstream U.S. politics and culture in one way, their lives are simultaneously shaped by the Americanized global politics and culture in another way. In other words, American civic ideology encourages American-born minorities to claim and preserve their differences in English in the public political sphere, but American and global mainstream forces exploit their differences in the private commercial sphere by targeting foreign-born immigrants who have less competency to articulate themselves in the dominant language. This is why third-generation Japanese American community leaders and first-generation Korean immigrants experience their racial struggles differently in Japantown, making it difficult for them to understand each other. I believe that understanding such diverse complexities is a step toward creating a common ground for a more inclusive way of representing Asian America (Kikumura-Yano, L. Hirabayashi, and J. Hirabayashi 2005; Okihiro 2001).

Notes

Epigraph. http://answers.yahoo.com/question/index?qid=20090122084620 AAucJkO.

1. A similar trend is observed in Los Angeles's Little Tokyo (Befu 2002). According to Julie Ha, senior editor for *KoreAm Journal* and former reporter for the English section of *Rafu Shimpo* (Murakami 1997, 172), nearly 30 percent of the small businesses in Little Tokyo were Korean-run. Moreover, the waiting lists for the area's two major low-income senior housing complexes were dominated by Korean Americans (Ha 2008).
2. Japantown Planning Preservation and Development Task Force 1999, *Demographic Data,* submitted to the San Francisco Redevelopment Agency, July 26, 1999. Table IV is available at http://www.japantowntaskforce.org/studies/AND%20-%20CCDDC%20report/and-ccdc.jppdtf.report.htm.
3. Japantown Task Force 2005, *Senate Bill 307, Neighborhood Cultural Preservation Report for San Francisco's Japantown.* http://www.japantowntaskforce.org/studies/sb307_report/web_files/web_full_report.htm
4. *Nishibei Times,* August 19, 2004.

References

Befu, Harumi ベフハルミ. 2002. 変貌するリトルトーキョーと二世ウィーク (Changing Little Tokyo and Nisei Week). In 日系アメリカ人の歩みと現在 (The Footsteps of Japanese Americans and Today), edited by Harumi Befu. Kyoto: Jimbun Shoin.

Ha, Julie. 2008. "Neighborhood Watch." *KoreAm Journal.* http://expo.newamericamedia.org/winners/stories/race_and_interethnic_relations.

Japantown Task Force Senate Bill 307 Committee. 2005. *Defining Cultural Preservation: Methodology.* Report. http://japantowntaskforce.org/studies/sb307_report/web_report/methodology.htm.

Kawaguchi, Gary, and Shizue Seigel. 2000. "San Francisco's Prewar Japantown: The Shaping of a Community." *Nikkei Heritage* 12 (3): 4–7, 15.

Kikumura-Yano, Akemi, Lane Ryo Hirabayashi, and James A. Hirabayashi. 2005. *Common Ground: The Japanese American National Museum and the Culture of Collaborations.* Boulder: University Press of Colorado.

Kim, Nadia. 2008. *Imperial Citizens: Koreans and Race from Seoul to LA.* Stanford, CA: Stanford University Press.

Kotani (Kawakami), Sachiko 小谷 (河上) 幸子. 2001. "Life Histories of Elderly Korean Immigrants: Place Attachment and Japanese Imperialism." Master's thesis, Department of Geography and Environmental Studies, California State University, Hayward.

———. 2008. 在米コリアンのサンフランシスコ日本町：マルチカルチャーのエスニックタウン (San Francisco's Japantown for Korean Americans: Ethnic Town of Multicultures). PhD diss., Graduate University for Advanced Studies. Hayama, Japan: Sokendai.

———. 2014. 在米コリアンのサンフランシスコ日本街：境界領域の人類学 (Korean Immigrants in San Francisco's Japantown: Affinity and Liminality). Tokyo: Ochanomizu Shobo.

Lai, Clement. 2006. "Between Blight and a New World: Urban Renewal, Political Mobilization, and the Production of Spatial Scale (April 24, 2006)." Institute for the Study of Social Change. ISSC Fellows Working Papers. Paper ISSC_WP_09. http://repositories.cdlib.org/issc/fwp/ISSC_WP_09.

Murakami, Yumiko 村上由見子. 1997. アジア系アメリカ人：アメリカの新しい顔 (Asian Americans: A New Face of America). Tokyo: Chuko Shinsho.

Okihiro, Gary. 2001. *Common Ground: Reimagining American History.* Princeton, NJ: Princeton University Press.

Sugiura, Tadashi 杉浦直. 2007. サンフランシスコ・ジャパンタウン再開発の構造と建造環境の変容：活動主体間関係に着目して (The Structure of Redevelopment and Changing Built Environment of San Francisco Japantown: Focusing on the Interactions of Local Actors). *Kikan Chirigaku* 59 (1): 1–23.

Sugiura, Tadashi, and Takashi Oda 杉浦直・小田隆史. 2009. エスニック都市空間における場所をめぐる葛藤：サンフランシスコ・ジャパンタウンの一事例から (The Struggle over Place in an Ethnic Urban Space : An Example from San Francisco's Japantown). *Kikan Chirigaku* 61 (3): 157–177.

Takezawa, Yasuko. 2011a. "Introduction." In *Racial Representations in Asia,* edited by Yasuko Takezawa, 1–6. Kyoto: Kyoto University Press.

Tsukuda, Yoko 佃陽子. 2009. "Place, Community, and Identity: The Preservation Movement of San Francisco's Japantown." *Tokyo Daigaku Amerika Taiheiyo Kenkyu* (9): 142–159.

———. 2011. 移民史を「場所」に刻印すること：サンフランシスコ日本町保護運動を事例として (Inscribing the Immigration History in a "Place": The Case of the Preservation Movement of San Francisco's Japantown). *Kyoyo Ronshu* (23): 49–65.

PART VI

REORIENTATIONS

CHAPTER 11

The Making of a Japanese American Race, and Why Are There No "Immigrants" in Postwar Nikkei History and Community?
The Problems of Generation, Region, and Citizenship in Japanese America

Eiichiro Azuma

Racial formation in Japanese America is highly slanted in terms of generation, citizenship status, and geography. Take this writer as an example. Professionally, I am a historian of Japanese America. Racially, I am of Japanese ancestry (Nikkei).[1]

I would be nonetheless hard pressed to claim the Japanese American community or its corporate identity as my own. Unlike other Asian communities that thrive on the inclusion of postwar immigrants, contemporary Japanese America has virtually no place for someone like me, who arrived in the United States after 1945.[2] I am technically a "Shin Issei"—literally, a "new first-generation immigrant." When I am outside California or Hawai'i, I tend to encounter fellow Shin Issei and other newcomers from Japan (like postwar Kibei) more frequently than U.S.-born Nikkei—"Nisei," "Sansei," and so on. They can be small business owners, sushi chefs and restaurateurs, spouses of native-born citizens, or students-turned-engineers. Even according to a conservative estimate, the number of these post–World War II immigrants exceeded 250,000 by 2000 (U.S. Department of Homeland Security 2006, table 2).[3] One would reasonably expect that the Japanese American community, and its representation, should reflect its tremendous diversity within, and so should a scholarly analysis of manifold racial formation processes.

Yet, despite the notable exceptions of Toyota (2012) and Ueunten (in this volume), few historical accounts of Japanese Americans, academic or popular, discuss the experience of Shin Issei, as though they never existed. If anything, postwar immigrants are mentioned only in passing, or are occasionally depicted as part of "foreign" capital from corporate Japan intent on taking over "ethnic" Little Tokyos of California or "local" Hawai'i for redevelopment or tourism (Kurashige 2002, 190–196; Okamura 1994, 165–169). Deemed perpetual outsiders, albeit of the same lineage, postwar Japanese immigrants have suffered a lack of historical representation, and it is deeply intertwined with the corporal exclusion of Shin Issei and other "misfits" from community membership consisting solely of native-born U.S. citizens. Combined, the basic definition of race in Japanese America offers no room for newcomers colored by foreignness. Furthermore, the formation of such restrictive group boundaries is also accompanied by a long-standing slight of locations "east of California" as legitimate sites for historical unfolding and community developments. Conventional ethnic narratives have compounded a spatially compartmentalized approach to historical research, and vice versa, which automatically binds the Japanese American experience to the Pacific Coast states, especially California, and Hawai'i. Because the non-Western locations encompass a large portion of postwar immigrants, they have become invisible under the influence of this regional bias, too.

It is important to note that the making of Japanese America in public representation and as racial collectivity entails multifaceted instances of exclusion, which serves to privilege descendants of pre-1924 immigrants to Hawai'i and the Pacific Coast states who hold birthright citizenship and share specific sets of racial experiences. The integrity and oneness of the Japanese racial category in America, which most existing studies seem to elucidate, would look dubious when considering such intraracial formation that divides rather than unites the constituent members of the racialized ethnic group. Asian Americanists, including myself, share a major responsibility for helping perpetuate the omissions to narrow and flatten the public understanding of Japanese American people and community at the cost of its diversities and complexities.

This study specifically investigates and unravels the intricate, mutually reinforced relations between the orthodox mode of history writing and the skewed process of community building in Japanese America. Despite the impressive volume of scholarship on Nikkei history, it has created—and cemented—only a particular understanding of the ethnic group and its experiences. The aforementioned partialities largely stem from four major strains of historical contrivance in the past scholarship, which ironically mirrored the Nikkei's varied—and often desperate—responses to white racism. In the context of discursive formation and political agitation against early Japanese immigrants in the American West, white exclusionists and antiracists compiled books, pamphlets, manifestos, commentaries, and editorials (Boddy 1921; Gulick 1914; Ichihashi 1932; Kawakami 1921; Millis 1915). While this first strain of contrivance helped plant certain images of Issei and solidify the meanings of Japaneseness in the American mind, ethnic intellectuals also took part in the production of historical knowledge, albeit usually in the vernacular language, to rebut discursive denigration (Azuma 2003, 1401–1418). Produced by white and Asian American writers, the post–World War II scholarship on the incarceration of West Coast Issei and Nisei (and tangentially their military service) constitutes the third strain of historical scholarship—one that tends to be fixated on the questions of national loyalty, citizenship, and civil rights (Azuma 2005b, 102–104). From the 1960s on, the narrow scope of storytelling in the internment studies intersected with the fourth strain—the Japanese American Research Project and subsequent endeavors in ethnic studies—which has sought to unveil the reasons and consequences of the mass incarceration as well as the achievements of Japanese American citizens before and after that event. These strains of history making—popular and scholarly, old and new—have been mutually imbued to corroborate the production of historical knowledge that prioritizes racial formation of certain categories of Japanese in the West Coast and Hawai'i.

The rest of this discussion explains how various writers and academicians—while fighting or supporting racial exclusion at different times—have inadvertently helped perpetuate a historical "unconsciousness" about actual regional and demographic diversities in Japanese America. It has naturalized doubly contrived narrations of Japanese American experiences and rendered them normative, thereby causing the public to (mis)recognize a partial story as a complete one. That historical unconsciousness has specifically exalted Nisei birthright citizenship as well as their loyalty and total assimilation to white America. It was to the detriment of postwar newcomers along with the locations relatively unaffected by prewar and wartime anti-Japanese racism. Based on the accumulated effects of discursive omission, the established notions of community, identity, history, and indeed race in contemporary Japanese America have affirmed and even encouraged the corporal exclusion of anomalous individuals as perpetual foreigners within.

Regional Focus and Divergence: California and Hawai'i as Separate and Only Stories

The first concerted efforts to construct systematic knowledge about Japanese immigrants date back to 1905 and the rise of exclusionist agitation in California. White intellectuals, journalists, and political activists were involved in a lively debate on "the Japanese problem," wherein negative images of the hitherto excluded Chinese were superimposed upon another horde of "coolies" and "prostitutes" from the "Orient." The early 1910s witnessed the emergence of two clearly defined sides on the issue, each entrenched in differing racial thought and political positions regarding Asians. The fierce agitation against Issei, which increasingly "drew a color line," still confronted formidable oppositions from anti-exclusionist groups until the passage of the alien land laws in California and other western states and the 1924 Immigration Act by the U.S. Congress (Daniels 1966). During this turbulent political development, many publications emerged to present "the truth" about California's Japanese immigrant population. Authored by white social scientists and missionaries-turned-"experts," most studies of the 1910s revealed a common tendency to focus deliberately on Issei's (un)assimilability through the interpretation of statistical data, analyses of their cultural practices, and an overview of their history in the state (Ichioka et al. 1974, 4–7; Chan 1996, 364–366). Whether such studies offered support for the antiracist or exclusionist cause, the basic political thrust that informed them served to restrict the regional scope of analysis to California (and occasionally its neighboring states).

Of those numerous books and pamphlets, Harry A. Millis's *The Japanese Problem in the United States* (1915) was the most important, with an aura of scholarly objectivity; it illustrates the manner in which Japanese immigrant experience was reduced to a mere California story. The University of Kansas professor examined many aspects of the Issei experience, including immigration processes, demographic changes, economic activities, labor, racial discrimination, group characteristics and mentality, and assimilation. A trained economist, Millis predicated his careful analysis on the statistical data collected by the U.S. Immigration Commission as well as information supplied by local Japanese organizations and diplomats. The vast majority of his data originated from California, and his discussion of racial discrimination concentrated on the first alien land law in that state. Sympathetic to the cause of anti-exclusionist white clergy, Millis supported Issei naturalization rights and vouched for their assimilability. But since his "objective" study was designed to refute the charges and conclusions made by *California*'s white supremacists, this first major academic treatise on Issei inescapably set a regional parameter of research on the Golden State.

Whereas the epistemological nexus between "California" and "Japanese immigrants" was being established in nascent academic discourse in conjunction with ongoing exclusionist politics in that state, Hawai'i largely escaped such a politicized regional association. With no comparable organized movement against the local Japanese population, only a handful of writers bothered to produce substantive accounts of English-language Issei history in the islands (Adams 1924; Wakukawa 1938). Yet, the California-centered mode of analysis sometimes exploited selected dimensions of Hawai'i's Issei experience as derogatory examples relative to the central question of their racial assimilability. With a longer history of settlement and a larger population than in the continental United States, the Japanese of Hawai'i were exploited by California exclusionists as a convenient historical reference. This reference was used to predict what might happen in California should its own "Japanese problem" be similarly left unchecked (McClatchy 1919, 26–30; Scharrenberg 1922, 742–750).

According to a common argument, Hawai'i's Issei remained exceedingly parochial and traditional, with a negligible degree of "Americanization" in their cultural practices. The residents were also depicted as low-class plantation workers whose moral qualities were incommensurate with white American standards. Added to this list of negatives was the allegation that the Issei of the islands and their Nisei children held an uncompromised allegiance to imperial Japan, making them an alien menace to the white republic. Thus, the political debate of the 1910s was characterized by the notions of Hawai'i as "a lost territory" and of California as the next victim of a Japanese takeover (McClatchy 1919, 27–28). Masquerading as a historical crystal ball foretelling the eventual doom of white hegemony in California, such a contrived story of the Hawai'i Issei experience played a supportive role in forging a metanarrative of Japanese immigrant invasion into the U.S. Pacific Coast. Indeed, as one Issei writer observed, "No Californian, arguing against the Japanese, fails to . . . warn that his state must never become a second Hawai'i (Kawakami 1921, 1).

To counter the racist attacks, some Issei writers fluent in English made important interventions into this politicized process of knowledge production. Their refutations, however, did not lead to the dissolution of the inherent California focus in the emergent historical discourse. Instead, the immigrants validated the California-Hawai'i divide in their counterargument, since they clearly and deliberately distinguished between the qualities of California Issei and their Hawai'i counterparts. Their rhetorical strategy accounted for the deeply seated class biases that the mainland ethnic leaders held against their islands compatriots, as well as the expedient and reactive nature of their history writing. In no uncertain terms did the California immigrant writers contend that the Japanese of the two locations shared little in their historical experience and moral character.

Kiyoshi K. Kawakami of San Francisco played a central role in the production of such English-language counterdiscourse, because he served as one of the official publicists for the immigrant community (Azuma 2009, 28–29, 32–34). After publishing two books, Kawakami authored *The Real Japanese Question,* which dedicated the first two chapters to discussions on "the 'Japanization' of Hawai'i" and "the 'Hawai'ianization' of the Pacific Coast." After reviewing the unique historical circumstance under which "low class" plantation laborers were brought over to the islands, this Issei writer declared, "The so-called Japanization of Hawai'i is entirely due to conditions peculiar to the islands—conditions that do not exist at all on the Pacific Coast" (Kawakami 1921, 20). Rather than absolving all Japanese immigrants, Kawakami opted to concentrate on the allegedly higher cultural quality of his immediate "community" for the purpose of rehabilitation. As the Issei writer suggested, Japanese in California should be considered to be "American," or at least well on their way to becoming "American," whereas those in Hawai'i had markedly lagged behind in that respect (Kawakami 1921, 1–40).

Moreover, Kawakami twisted the meaning of "Japanization" by detaching it from the popular theme of racial invasion. His brief rendition of the Hawai'i Issei experience revolved around the principle of racial harmony, for "if the term 'race problem' is used in the sense of 'race hatred,' certainly Hawai'i has reason to be proud of its absence" (Kawakami 1921, 8). In this manner, Kawakami not only rejected the notion of Hawai'i as an allegory for the exclusionist narrative of the Japanese colonization of California, he also generated the contrasting histories of Japanese immigrants in the two locales: as beneficiaries of racial tolerance and as victims of racist hostility, respectively. Drawing on the contemporary progressive theory of assimilation and race relations, the Japanese immigrant writer turned around the rhetoric of causation and ascribed the origin of "the Japanese problem" to the erroneous thinking of white supremacists. Whatever deficiencies the immigrant group might have, he suggested, the Issei should not have been considered a race problem. Without racist agitation against them, California Japanese, much like their Hawai'i counterparts, should be able to coexist with the local white population harmoniously, as they made a slow but steady stride toward assimilation, albeit at a different pace. Designed to convince white Californians to reconsider their relations with Issei from a liberal academic perspective, Kawakami's idealization of Hawai'i's racial landscape foreshadowed how others would later tell the story of the island Japanese experience as exemplifying a "multiracial paradise" (Adams 1937; Fuchs 1961; Lind 1946; Lind 1961; Okamura 1998, 265–266).

Authored by Stanford University professor Yamato Ichihashi, *Japanese in the United States* widened the rifts between California Japanese and their Hawai'i counterparts, albeit in a different manner. Based on his Harvard dissertation, the four-hundred-page study was "the accepted standard work on the Japanese immigrants" before the 1970s (Ichioka et al. 1974, 7). Even though it was published in the decade after the height of anti-Japanese political agitation, the book still displayed the persistent influence of the lingering exclusionist discourse that dwelled on Issei assimilability as well as regional differences in the group's experience. In a highly scholarly manner, *Japanese in the United States* argued that California Issei had no significant relationship to Hawai'i Issei in terms of their class background, immigration process, and overall history. First, as Ichihashi explained matter-of-factly, most immigrants who came directly to the U.S. Pacific Coast were not of "the laboring classes," whereas "the Japanese seeking Hawaii . . . were mostly laborers under (plantation) contract" (Ichihashi 1932, 67–68). Thus, the mainstay of California's Issei population supposedly consisted of "merchants" and "students"—that is, an educated class of permanent settlers that differed from the "birds of passage" in Hawai'i, who "were decidedly inferior in their educational and financial status" (Ichihashi 1932, 65, 68, 81–82).

Challenging the earlier exclusionist claims about an inferior cultural and intellectual standard of California Issei, this differentiation also implicitly drew a parallel between middle-class white Americans and West Coast

Japanese on grounds of their compatible dispositions, not the color of skin (Ichihashi 1932, 207–227). Viewed from this formulation, Japanese residents in California certainly would be good additions to American society. By suggesting the divergent trajectories of community formation in California and Hawaiʻi, Ichihashi's study cleansed his West Coast compatriots of the undesirable qualities that those in the islands purportedly embodied. It is important to note that, like Kawakami, Ichihashi did not—and could not—engage in the wholesale critique of dominant racial discourses that rendered certain (or all) aspects of Japaneseness inferior, if not injurious, to white America. Such emphasis on intragroup differences based on their collective class attributes crystallized the potency of hegemonic racial ideas and categories—even in progressive thought of the time. In an attempt to repudiate the most perilous biological racism, Issei writers opted to exploit the liberal classist definitions of American identity to elucidate their cultural/moral assimilability in their racial (self-)representation.

Deemed the most authoritative scholarly work for decades, Ichihashi's *Japanese in the United States* had two important consequences of historical mythologizing. First, the volume provided academic legitimacy for the theory that there was little connection between California Issei and Hawaiʻi Issei—one that reflected a particular vision of Ichihashi and other educated Japanese more than actual differences.[4] Another legacy of Ichihashi's influence in historiography was a tendency to contain the Issei story within the episode of anti-Japanese agitation between 1905 and 1924. Indeed, insofar as he devoted much of his analysis to debunking the exclusionist myths, Ichihashi's narrative offered little room for other discussions. It is for this reason that after detailing the process leading to Japanese exclusion up to 1924, the Issei scholar abruptly shifted his narration to the "problem of the second generation Japanese." Consequently, the historical presence and agency of the "immigrant" generation were firmly encapsulated in a single block of the pre-exclusion years in Japanese American history—a pattern of historical representation that later works have inherited. In the context of their struggle against racial exclusion, thus, Issei intelligentsia inadvertently compartmentalized the meaning of Japanese American "race" according to generational differences, where the constituent members held clearly distinguished temporal markings. Simply put, the "immigrant" era came to mean the pre-1924 years in the typical periodization of Japanese American experience.

Issei History Making: Mythologizing Japanese Pioneer Past in the American West

Following the triumph of the exclusionist movement, white American deliberations on Japanese immigrants lost their very political raison d'être. Nonetheless, the crafting of ethnic historical narrative still continued after the mid-1920s, but mainly among Issei writers and community leaders in their native tongue.[5] Building on discursive partialities, dozens of their publications included additional historical inventions, which had tremendous ramifications for how Americans now understand the Nikkei experience. The most notable myth they created was the "Issei pioneer thesis"—a narrative that valorized the centrality of California and agriculture in the group's history in the language of the U.S. popular discourse on frontier conquest. In 1927, Shiro Fujioka of Los Angeles published a Japanese-language treatise entitled *Pioneers of Japanese Development* (*Minzoku hatten no senkusha*), which helped set the basic tone and direction of subsequent historical construction. Tracing the trajectory of the anti-Japanese movement up to 1924, Fujioka's work aimed at providing a "correct" understanding of the Issei's struggle against California racism and their contribution to America. The author depicted his fellow immigrants as "the pioneers of Japanese development, [who] have endured poor living conditions, patiently fought exclusion and persecution day and night, and still established the basis for social progress" in that state (Fujioka 1927, 3).

Compared with the precedence of white frontiersmen, the collective Issei past was presented as a glorious story of pioneer settler colonists who also conquered wilderness for the benefit of the California economy. Fujioka and other amateur Issei historians challenged the Anglo-American monopoly of frontier expansionism, arguing for their own relevance in the settling of the western lands. The racially prescribed nexus between the mastery of the frontier and the agency it entailed was reworked to include Japanese pioneers as legitimate participants in their storytelling. Thus, the Japanese immigrant past came to claim a place, as one Issei writer expressed, "in the annals of American literature and history." As this man declared staunchly, their chronicle would be "surely worth preserving along with the story of the white man's advance to this frontier land" (Miyazaki 1938, 54). White settlers still played a key role in overall frontier history, but Japanese were rendered as an indispensable partner.

Issei's vernacular history of the 1930s all celebrated their "contributions" to the western agricultural industry. Compiled jointly by San Francisco Issei writers and community leaders, *Zaibei Nihonjinshi* (1940, 147) aptly summarized this aspect of the pioneer thesis:

> Back in 1849, California was an importer of foodstuff, which totaled over $10 million. . . . By 1919, it was an exporter with the income of $750 million. In the same year, Japanese farmers grew approximately one tenth of the net export. Our total population was smaller than one twentieth of the three million Californians, but we were responsible for that much produce. It is a product of Japanese diligence and superiority in [farming] skills. Despite the alien land laws, Japanese have always kept their farms green and supplied the produce of higher quality. That even anti-Japanese legislation has failed to divorce us from California farms crystallizes our exceptional ability and talent.

By placing the story of their illustrious contribution in direct contrast to the unjustness of exclusion (often described as "tribulations and triumphs"), Issei writers not only discredited white racism but also discursively empowered themselves vis-à-vis racial otherization. From inassimilable Orientals to respectable mainstream Americans, Issei's history making managed to spin their racial/national identity. Just as Ichihashi did, Issei historians put forth a sanitized collective self-identity, evoking the image of European settler-colonists in deeds and dispositions (Azuma 2005a, 98–105). Exposited in the emergent master narrative, this immigrant search for whiteness characterized a common pattern of racial formation in the 1930s—and beyond.

The legacies of this race history were far-reaching. Indeed, its articulation of the romanticized American national past and white racial traits explains why the Issei pioneer thesis still underpins the present-day narratives of early Nikkei history. Because parts of the immigrant publications have been translated into English, many postwar writers have nonchalantly adopted key concepts of "Issei pioneer/frontier spirit," their "superiority in [farming] skills" and agricultural "contribution," and their "tribulations and triumphs" (Kikumura-Yano 1992; Iwata 1990; Spickard 2009). In a fundamental sense, Issei history writing was tied to the political context of their responses to the institutionalized exclusion and denial of their worth as Americans, which they sought to repudiate through the emphasis on their outstanding racial character (Azuma 2005a, 96–97, 111–112, 184–185). This crucial constitutive context was lost on postwar authors, rendering the problematic narrative schema of Issei history immune from critical historicized scrutiny. The first generation of Japanese American studies scholars—many of whom participated in the Asian American movement—offered a major corrective to the lopsided identity of California Issei as quintessential settler-colonists by redefining their experience as a "labor history" (Ichioka 1988, 2).[6] This class-based intervention counterbalances the particular vision of history proposed by Issei authors, but the other pivotal concepts and themes have generally survived in academic and popular representations of the Japanese immigrant past. Even as they lost their original function as a rhetorical weapon against racial exclusion, the Issei-produced concepts, like superior group fortes, are now accepted at face value and often utilized as ubiquitous analytical categories in writing "the story of Americans with Japanese faces"—whether it refers to prewar Issei or postwar Nisei experience (Hosokawa 1969, 494–496).

Moreover, insofar as all these concepts derived from the basic premise of Japanese bond with the frontier land, the geographically restricted interpretation has persisted in the postwar scholarship. The standard narrative scheme still focuses mainly on the subject of California (or western) agriculture; Issei "pioneers" are depicted as having quickly risen from field hands to farmers before California's alien land laws marred their success. Yet, other immigrants, for example, urban intellectuals and rural merchants of the western states, international traders and struggling artists in New York, and domestic service workers in Chicago, are denied their historical due. Meanwhile, Hawaiʻi's Japanese had been removed from virtually any and all narratives of the race history produced in the mainland.[7] Hence, remnants of the old Japanese-language literature have reinforced the built-in western focus in the historiography with a decidedly farming slant. Now, in our common historical understanding, the "immigrants," or the people called "Issei," are almost synonymous with Pacific Coast agriculturalists, whose experience is largely locked up in the pre-1930s period.

Postwar History Writing: the Extolment of Birthright Citizenship and the Nisei Model Minority

The post–World War II scholarship added two important strains of historical construction: internment studies and the Japanese American Research Project (JARP). Since before the end of the Pacific War, internment studies have dominated a major portion of academic research on Japanese Americans. Placing Nisei citizens as the protagonists, this literature ushers in a brand-new era of Japanese American history writing. Its basic political thrust, however, has shared much in common with the antiracist undercurrents of the prewar scholarship. After all, internment studies, too, generally scrutinize the negative impact of white racism and examine various forms of Japanese American resistance to it during and after the war. It also means that these studies continue to discourage scholars from confronting the aforementioned flaws in the predominant narrative scheme.

Ever since legal scholar Eugene Rostow defined the incarceration of Japanese Americans as "our worst wartime mistake" in 1945, most writers have been preoccupied with a single question: "Why could such a gross violation of civil rights happen in democratic America?" (Rostow 1945, 193–201). The search for plausible explanations characterizes a dominant liberal orientation in academic analyses of the internment and its aftermath, which has striven to pinpoint major culprits—individuals/groups and the ideas that they represented—who allegedly tarnished the Constitution of the United States.[8] At the same time, with an eye to illuminating the peril of wartime racism, some scholars, especially Asian Americanists, turn their attention especially to the plight and anguish of Nisei citizens, as well as their exemplary efforts as loyal Americans to correct the wrongs. They find that most of the youngsters managed to overcome the enormous injustice wrought by their own government through uncompromised patriotism and enduring faith in American citizenship (Daniels 2004; Gruenewald 2005; Ishizuka 2006). Many works on a subfield of internment studies, Nisei male military service and heroism, also emerged out of the same scholarly and popular interest in Japanese American loyalty and dedication to color-blind democracy.

Intended to highlight the profound consequence of the "failure of government leadership" in protecting Nisei citizenship, internment studies also sympathetically discuss the contrary choices that some Japanese Americans made. After the infamous loyalty test, several thousand Nisei, including many Japan-educated Kibei, were officially categorized into the "disloyal" group and subsequently segregated in Tule Lake, while others refused to serve in the U.S. armed forces when their draft status was reinstituted (Irons 1983; Muller 2003; Weglyn 1976). Whether they were "loyal," "disloyal," or "draft resisters," the second-generation citizens collectively occupied a central place in the narrations of wartime Japanese American history. Because of their legal status as "enemy aliens," Issei internees were summarily placed at the fringe in the internment studies that focused on the central question of Nisei citizens' constitutional rights. If they are mentioned at all, the immigrants are merely presented as an additional factor to accentuate the centrality of the Nisei's victimization, predicaments, and heroism (Ichioka 2006, 293–294).[9] And with a focus on the wartime and postwar "resettlement" experiences of Japanese American citizens, internment studies painted Nisei with temporal markings of the 1940s and 1950s, rendering those decades a "Nisei era" in the orthodox periodization of race history. It is important to note, however, that the story of Nisei's "tribulations" and "triumphs" did not allow for the inclusion of *postwar* Kibei—a group almost completely ignored in the existing scholarship—whose birthright citizenship and patriotism looked and remained dubious due to wartime residence in Japan or renunciation and repatriation.

As the second generation replaced the immigrant generation as the key agent of historical changes and developments after December 7, 1941, internment studies have continued to leave intact the long-standing West Coast focus. In the existing historiography, the wartime history of Japanese Americans is equated almost entirely with the saga of the mass incarceration. And because the 120,000 Nisei and Issei internees came exclusively from the Pacific Coast states and a part of Arizona, their collective experience remains figuratively and realistically a story of West Coast Nikkei, albeit in the inland internment camps where the population was *temporarily* imprisoned. The resettlement of many internees in the midwestern and eastern states resulted in a large-scale population dispersal outside the Pacific Coast states for the first time. Except for a casual mention of this fact, however, little scholarly attention has been given to the subject of Japanese American experience outside the American West. Several studies on resettlement "east of California," as well as the national student "relocation" program, tend to examine only the decade following the internment, with a focus on Nisei citizens (Austin 2007; Austin 2004; Austin 2003; Brooks 2000; Harden 2003; Okihiro 1999; Robinson 2005; Sawada 1986–87). Despite their historical importance, such studies likewise fail to delve into how the newcomers released from the camps interacted with longtime local Nikkei residents as they jointly reshaped their communities. Instead of asking these questions, scholars generally move their focus back to California after the so-called resettlement phase, because "eighty percent of the entire [mainland] ethnic population in 1950 had resumed their concentrations in Washington,

Oregon, and especially California," as one author rightfully justifies such a shift (Kurashige 2002, 111). But consequently, other than the short period of temporary dispersal, Japanese American life "east of California" still holds little attention in the story of the postwar Japanese American experience.

The story of the JARP is another important chapter in postwar history writing. Initiated in 1959 by the Japanese American Citizens League (JACL) for the purpose of compiling an "authoritative definitive history," the JARP became perhaps the first collaborative endeavor between the minority community and academia (Miyakawa to Fahs 1961, 3).[10] It existed several years before Asian American studies formally emerged as a discipline and an institution at the University of California, Los Angeles—the future academic sponsor of the project. While exerting considerable influence over the ensuing scholarly research in ethnic studies, the JARP continued to authenticate many of the preexisting partialities and myths in the historiography. The initial objectives of the Nisei-led project reflected the Nisei rendition of racial collectivity and identity, rooted in an idealized understanding of their parents' generation. Fundamentally, Nisei history writing aspired to reclaim a prewar immigrant past in order to make sense of the rehabilitation and ascent after the internment of the Japanese "model minority," who supposedly overcame not only the foreign "enemy" but also domestic "racial prejudice." The community-wide enterprise of historical research, publication, and archival development under the JARP represented an important aspect of the ethnic group's ongoing quest for acceptance as full-fledged "model citizen" Americans (Wu 2013, 162–180).

This quest reveals both an interesting divergence from and convergence with Issei's representational strategies. Rather than using the trope of frontier colonialism, the American-born generation opted to embrace their legal national membership. This practice constituted an extension of what many internment studies attempted to do in highlighting the evil of "blood will tell" racism of the wartime United States: the extolment of birthright citizenship as the basis of a color-blind American identity, and hence Nikkei identity. Yet, while loudly asserting their "Americanness" on the basis of legal national membership, Nisei also strove to elucidate their outstanding group dispositions and civic values acceptable to white America, just as Ichihashi did. In line with Cold War pluralist racial discourse, this argument was designed to inflate the meaning of the Nisei's cultural heritage—their prized monopoly, bestowed by Issei frontiersmen—which purportedly enabled their exemplary behavior as Americans par excellence. Through historical studies of the first-generation past and legacies, many Nisei expected the JARP to explain why they had been able to reach the status of "model citizens" so quickly despite, or indeed because of, their Japanese background in the aftermath of the internment experience. In the end, four major historical monographs emerged directly from the JARP; those books faithfully followed its central mandate to narrate Nikkei experience as "part of the American history in which Issei and Nisei had a significant role" (Miyakawa to Fahs 1961, 3; Miyakawa to Allport 1962, 2; Miyakawa to Raushenbush 1962, 2).[11]

Under the aegis of Nisei leadership, the JARP forged regimented definitions relative to the basic character that the first and second generations had supposedly possessed, and the specific temporal space that they could occupy in race history. Before UCLA became the formal sponsor in 1962, JACL leaders and JARP social scientists had already compiled "a list of virtually all the Issei in the U.S. and their places of residence." JACL local affiliates conducted over 820 interviews in accordance with a JARP guideline (Japanese American Research Project [n.d.], 1–3, esp. 2). These data, and the method of data collection, inherited many of the partialities and contrivances that had been implanted in past writings of Japanese American history. Echoing the Issei's own characterization three decades earlier, a 1966 JARP report summarized its interpretation of the immigrant past:

> The record is remarkable: for despite denial of citizenship and of land ownership, exclusion from certain occupations, frequent exposure to hate campaigns, identification as agents of a foreign power, the impossibility of further immigration and military removal from their habitats with its consequent losses, Japanese Americans have surmounted these obstacles. (Japanese American Research Project 1966, 4)

Clearly, the "tribulations" and "triumphs" still underpinned the Nisei's mode of storytelling.

Whereas the initial—and most crucial—phase of the JARP's community survey concentrated on the prewar first generation, its ultimate purpose was to explain the "dominant pattern of achievement differentiating the children of the Japanese immigrants from some other minority groups" in contemporary American society (Japanese American Research Project [n.d.], 1). In keeping with the nascent national discourse on the model minority, members and advisers of the JARP research team hypothetically ascribed the successful assimilation of postwar Nisei to their "value system," "cultural identity," "in-group cohesion," "family upbringing," "heritage," and "a strongly supportive belief system (e.g., a belief in their ethnic superiority)" (Japanese American Research Project 1966, 4). Purportedly, all these attributes originated from the culture and mores of their immigrant parents, and hence the JARP's general emphasis on "the relation of the Issei culture and family life to the Americanization of the Nisei" (Miyakawa to Rostow 1962, 1).

Based on the idea of group culture as the bridge, the generational categories of "Issei" and "Nisei" thus embodied coded meanings from the beginning. First, because the immigrants had to be the bearer of all positive traits that presumably allowed for the current rise of their American-born sons and daughters since the internment, JARP scholars and ethnic community leaders carefully finessed the chronological purview of the Issei generation. They officially decided to restrict the first-generation Japanese immigrants exclusively to "those who came to the United States on or before July 1924" [sic]—the month when the exclusionary immigration law became effective (Miyakawa to Morizono 1964, 2; also Minamikawa 2007, 214). Thus, post-1924 immigrants were altogether disqualified from the grouping of "Issei," and by extension, from the identity of the parents of assimilated Nisei. Since many of the prewar Issei entered the United States through some unlawful means after July 1924, these individuals did not fit the image of outstanding, law-abiding members of American society. Their "value system" could not have been presented as something that had positively influenced their "Nisei" children—the model citizens. Considering the paramount goal of the JARP as envisioned by JACL Nisei, it is understandable why they had to whitewash the Issei identity from any notion of criminality through such delicate chronological artifice. Yet, its effect was still manifested in the form of intragroup exclusion in Nisei history writing.

Furthermore, the JARP's Issei definition completely excludes postwar newcomers from Japan, including "war brides" and other "Shin Issei." Not only discursively but also numerically was it no insignificant matter, since their aggregate number had reached as high as 82,584 between 1946 and 1969 (Gaimushō Ryōji Ijūbu 1971, 144–145). And their exclusion leads to another omission pertaining to second-generation Japanese Americans. Interracial children of Japanese war brides, for example, would have little chance for community inclusion as normative Nisei, because they are not sons and daughters of the authentic Issei couples. The JARP's lexicography of generational categories simultaneously promoted a pure-blooded ethnic identity in Japanese America—a type of internal racism that has become a subject of fierce debate in recent years. It is important to note the JARP's artifice of the ideal immigrant type did not take place solely in the realm of scholarly survey. It was intertwined with concurrent ethnic group practice, one that denied Shin Issei presence and enforced racial purism. It is for this reason that the JACL, and its weekly newspaper, *Pacific Citizen*, declared only the exclusive JARP definitions acceptable in community affairs by "reserv[ing] Issei [status] to those who came prewar" in the public usage of the term (Honda 1967; Masaoka 1967).

The regional bias remained unchallenged in the JARP's method of data collection. First, Hawai'i was never within the scope of research, since the "authoritative definitive history" it desired to produce was supposed to "concentrate on the mainland United States" from the beginning (Miyakawa to Fahs 1961, 2). Furthermore, when the JARP asked JACL local affiliates to locate surviving pre-1924 immigrants in their jurisdictions, its survey guideline specified those who "have lived in America (anywhere in the [continental] U.S)" (Miyakawa to Morizono 1964, 2). From a practical standpoint, it is understandable that they kept Hawai'i out, since there was no local JACL chapter in the islands at that time. It also meant that no significant donations came from Hawai'i Nisei to the endeavor. The inevitable result, nonetheless, was that the JARP's production of a synthetic race history failed to rectify the long-standing regional divides. JARP publications make only cursory references to Hawai'i Nikkei.

Second, even though the JARP did not formally designate the West Coast as its main focus, the actual process of data collection revealed a consistent emphasis on that region at the expense of other areas within the continental United States. Fundamentally, the problematic methodology stemmed from the arbitrary definition of Issei, which resulted in the disowning of so many individuals—especially postwar newcomers, who tended to reside east of California. In 1963, when the Issei survey was barely under way, anthropologist Richard Beardsley called into question correlations between the JARP's West Coast focus and its restrictive immigrant category. Specializing in the cultural anthropology of Japan, the University of Michigan professor did not share the particular goal that Nisei leaders assigned to the scholarly project—that is, an analysis of early Issei culture as a means to explain the exceptional character and quintessential American identity of their U.S.-born children. Oblivious to the Japanese American race-based agenda, the white scholar was unable to comprehend why the JARP's survey fell short of covering the more ubiquitous recent immigrants—carriers of less-diluted Japanese culture and hence an ideal research subject for the themes of acculturation and cross-cultural negotiations from his essentialist standpoint (Beardsley to Miyakawa 1963; also Minamikawa 2007, 213–214).

Beardsley urged the research team to extend its coverage, especially to Japanese war brides, who composed a good majority of the newcomers during the 1950s and early 1960s. Wedded mainly to non-Japanese GIs, many of these women settled outside the West Coast or Hawai'i since their husbands came from all over the United States. Beardsley (1963, 3) thus argued, "These girls, to an important degree, represent Japanese immigrants in a unique and new position, and their experiences—generally in isolation from other Japanese unless by coincidence—adds a new dimension to the relationship of Japanese with American culture." Essentially, his advice was to make the Issei survey more inclusive in terms of both chronology and geography so that the study of cultural negotiation and transformation would be more comprehensive.

Although out of a different concern, Min Yasui of Denver echoed the white scholar's reservations about the omissions in the JARP's research. This Nisei's criticism was more extensive and fundamental. In his letter to JARP director Miyakawa, Yasui (1963) named five different groups of non–West Coast Issei he thought were missing in a supposedly comprehensive survey. Under a rubric of "the off-beat Japanese experience," he first directed attention to the histories of "urban Japanese away from the West Coast" and "rural Japanese away from the West Coast" before the 1920s. After discussing many and diverse examples of early Japanese activities in Colorado, Texas, Illinois, and other nonwestern states, Yasui underscored the incompleteness of the ongoing community survey and interviews that precluded much of the United States. In addition, not only "the 'Mik[k]o-Nin' (illegal entrants)" but also "the 'loners'" should be seen as legitimate members of prewar Japanese America, he argued. According to Yasui, the latter ranged from "an alcoholic bum" to "these trim, spare, neat old Issei men who were 'gentlemen's gentlemen' and who worked for wealthy [white] families in St. Louis, or in Colorado Springs . . . in places like New York, and possibly in Boston and elsewhere" (Yasui 1963).

Yasui also cast his critical eye on the JARP's disregard for the postwar years. Citing from the 1960 U.S. census, he pointed out that a more-than-fivefold increase of the Japanese population in Texas between 1950 and 1960 was due chiefly to the influx of Japanese war brides, and not "Issei" and "Nisei" as defined by the JARP. "And there is a story here to be told too," he continued (Yasui to Miyakawa 1963, 4). "It has always impressed me that it either took desperation or a great deal of courage for these women to come thousands of miles into an alien land, without even the rudiments of language—in the expectation of making a home and raising a family." The Denver Nisei leader also advocated the inclusion of their "half-Japanese children who [would] undoubtedly color the acceptance of my own children into the [white] community at some future times" ([Yasui] to Miyakawa 1963).

The challenge that Beardsley and Yasui posed fell on deaf ears because their voices of dissent never induced a serious intellectual debate; their letters were simply kept in the project correspondence files. Neither the "offbeat Japanese experience . . . away from the West Coast" nor the war brides and their interracial children were included in the chronologically and regionally skewed structure of the JARP survey. Even Yasui soon reversed his stance and went on to subscribe to the formal definition of Issei, which restricted the immigrants to the pre-1924 period (Minamikawa 2007, 213–214).[12] However, T. Scott Miyakawa, JARP director and Boston University sociologist, seemed to have taken portions of Yasui's earlier advice seriously—if only privately. To his Nisei colleagues, he expressed a desire to keep at least "the documents collection . . . national and all inclusive" after receiving the letters from Beardsley and Yasui (Miyakawa to Honda 1963). The JARP head then instructed that he wished to get his hands on "everything from everywhere and of every period, from the first Issei background to present day, and NOT just pre-1914 [sic] ones" (Miyakawa to Honda 1963). Having lived in New York and Boston for a few decades, Miyakawa especially felt that the experience of East Coast Issei was "in some ways as important as those of the West Coast Issei in understanding the overall history" (Miyakawa to Masaoka 1967).[13] Although his intervention allowed the JARP archives to acquire valuable primary source collections from New York and other eastern locations as well as Hawai'i, his vision of "an inclusive national study" ended as an unfulfilled possibility in rectifying the regional partialities that had been so thoroughly entrenched in the Nikkei historiography since the 1910s.

Historical Orthodoxy and Community Formation in Contemporary Japanese America

Since the 1970s, Asian Americanists have made remarkable discursive interventions into the conventional narrative scheme, effectively mitigating the all-too-flowery characterizations of Issei as settler-colonists and of Nisei as the model minority. Yet, it is also true that some critical remnants of past history making and writing have survived in Japanese American history and community. Those legacies are responsible for limited thematic choices and the inadvertent effacing of many historical agents and their heterodox experiences from ethnic narrative and knowledge. Missing almost altogether from mainstream Japanese American history is also the story of "east of California," where many of the Nikkei newcomers have dispersed.

Consequences were manifested most strikingly in the day-to-day process of community formation after the 1950s, as well as the meaning of race in Japanese America. In the post-internment years, partial historical representations often crystallized into *actual* practices of internal border making—that is, politics of intragroup exclusion. As previously explained, history writing always constituted expressions of Nikkei's assertions for national inclusion. Since they were so focused on rebutting the racist notion of otherness, both Issei and Nisei writers glossed over certain aspects of the Japanese American experience and ignored dissonant historical agents in their narrations to draw a parallel between Japanese America and white America. In the prewar years, however, immigrant leaders did not—and could not—actually purge the heterodox presences from the community body, because Japanese of all backgrounds were forced to cling together in the face of all-encompassing legal discrimination. It made no exception for any class or segment of the vilified race, making it possible for idiosyncratic Issei to remain connected to or physically within the ethnic community.

Contrarily, in tandem with partial historical representations, postwar Nisei generally managed to dissociate their community from new immigrants and other misfits, like postwar Kibei, in actuality—a practice that the third generation has largely inherited. This "Nisei exclusionism" in community building still explains a salient form of Japanese American response to marginalization—the continuous burden of race—but postwar racial liberalism enabled U.S.-born Japanese to claim a national identity and honorary whiteness on account of their birthright citizenship and its constituent patriotism. In postwar America, these attributes make up the most fundamental yardsticks for American identity, and they are what newcomers from Japan cannot claim. For many Nisei, the meaning of being Japanese therefore split into two polarized notions: those who belong to a domestic ethnic group and hence are admissible into their community, and those who are alien and cannot be considered "real" Americans. This intraracial differentiation accounts for their survival strategy in an ostensibly antiracist society that still sustains the principle of conditional inclusion for nonwhites.

Seen from this perspective, it is not difficult to understand why the JACL went as far as to actively deliberate on the "problem" of war brides at its national convention in the late 1950s—just as California exclusionists half a century earlier had discussed "the Japanese problem" as a foreign menace (Fifteenth National Convention Minutes 1958, 31–35; IDC 1956, 2; IDC 1957, 3). Many Nisei leaders felt that these women embodied the failure of acculturation due to a high divorce rate and frequent reports of their becoming public charges. Rather than extending a helping hand, many Nisei citizens were inclined to consider the war brides as co-ethnic outsiders who allegedly tarnished the good reputation of assimilated Japanese Americans—a stigma of foreignness that was subsequently extended to other postwar newcomers. Therefore, the JARP's reluctance to heed Yasui's criticism was not incidental; it was illustrative of Nisei's constant policing of group boundaries against alien elements, albeit of common racial background. For this reason, the "absent presence" of war brides and Shin Issei at the crossroads of actual practice and representation persists even to this day.[14] Racial membership in Japanese America is now defined primarily in terms of the native birth and the ties that the constituents hold to the prewar Issei era and the Nisei war/internment experience.

In all fairness, it is important to note that it takes both sides to keep them divided. Indeed, many Shin Issei—especially educated ones—carry strong anti-*dekasegi* emigrant biases passed on from prewar Japan, and thus consciously have distanced themselves from descendants of prewar "Issei" (Azuma 2005a, 99–100). Yet, what matters here is not so much about individual likes or dislikes as about the question of who holds the authority to represent the racial collectivity, its identity, and its experience. Shin Issei have no comparable political or discursive power to define Japanese America for themselves or for outside audiences. Therefore, whether in the area of historical representation or in the form of community membership, an initiative for inclusion must come from the dominant community of Nisei and Sansei. In 2000, for example, a group of war brides—now in their sixties and seventies—urged the Japanese American National Museum to tell their story as a part of race history. Although the Los Angeles museum held a small symposium in response, it has yet to feature experiences of any postwar immigrants in its exhibitions (Yasutomi 2002, 64–66). With the exception of Evelyn Nakano Glenn (1988), published studies of war brides, including Simpson (2001, 147–185), treat them as an object of white racial discourse rather than as historical agents in Nikkei history.[15] Nor does their story or that of other Shin Issei get meaningfully integrated in synthetic group history yet.

This study has traced the origins and major types of particularities in Japanese American history and racial formation. Contributed by white experts, Issei intellectuals, Nisei community efforts, and Asian Americanists in the last centenary, the different strains of historical scholarship have implanted those particularities into the current structure of knowledge and the orthodox form of racial representation in Japanese America. To turn a story of Nikkei experience into a more inclusive and less geographically bound one, it would take the thorough reworking of the preexisting categories, thematic choices, regional parameters, and periodization. In particular, decentering—but not disregarding—the anti-Japanese exclusion movement (1910s to mid-1920s) and the incarceration of West Coast Japanese (early 1940s) would be one effective means to dismantle conventional generation-based analyses and spatially circumscribed interpretations. In established storylines, these episodes signify decisive historical identities for the two generations of Japanese Americans and dominate the understanding of the respective period with a common focus on the West Coast. In the master narrative of Japanese American history in Hawaiʻi, which is not as systematized as in the mainland, the comparable historical marks for "local" Japanese Americans seem to be prewar plantation work, as well as the attack on Pearl Harbor and the rise of Nisei political power in the 1950s (Kotani 1985). As long as these discrete schemes dictate how we understand historical unfolding and racial formation, Shin Issei, war brides, and all other "foreignized" others within have little chance to play a meaningful role as full-fledged participants in group history and community life that inherently privilege native-born descendants of the pre-1924 Issei. And informed by the ongoing legitimization of lopsided historical knowledge, racial representation in Japanese America continues to serve not only as a poignant reflection but also as a powerful mechanism of internal exclusions and omissions.

Notes

1. In this essay, when appropriate, I deliberately use "race" and "racial," rather than "ethnicity" and "ethnic," because various instances of internal exclusions and omissions in Japanese America have taken place in the context of Japanese Americans' struggle against white racism. Being racialized as national others by whites provides a crucial background for the lopsided ways in which Japanese Americans, especially Nisei, have represented themselves as acceptable Americans, only to the detriment of postwar newcomers from Japan. In this sense, the whole process should be deemed fundamentally an act of racializing vis-à-vis white America instead of simple ethnic formation. Thus, I also refer to the group history of Japanese Americans as "race history" and their collective identity as "racial identity."
2. The omission of postwar immigrants from the ethnic community and history is unique in comparison with other groups of Asians in the United States. Not only does Japanese America have a longer history than other groups (except Chinese America), its demography is tilted toward the native-born population despite the post-1965 immigration, which has changed the compositions of other Asian groups in an opposite way. But these reasons alone do not suffice to explain the pervasiveness of internal exclusion in contemporary Japanese America.
3. The figure only includes those who entered the United States with an "immigrant" visa. The actual number of newcomers must have been much larger, because more Japanese, especially after 1965, initially came as "non-immigrants" (for example, students) before adjusting their status to permanent residence.
4. Only recently did a few scholars discuss the need for bridging the Hawai'i-California divides in the study of Japanese Americans; see Ichioka (2006, 294–295); Asato (2005); and Tamura (2000, 70).
5. On examples of Japanese-language immigrant history, see Nakagawa (1932); Nichibei Shimbunsha (1931); Tōga (1927); Washizu (1930); and Zaibei Nihonjinkai (1940). From the mid-1920s, most English-language works on Japanese Americans looked at the Nisei children for the purpose of testing the assimilation theory developed by the Chicago School of Sociology, especially its thesis on the "Marginal Man." See Strong (1934).
6. The same leftist thrust explains a comparable tendency after the 1970s to treat Hawai'i Issei experience as a working-class plantation story.
7. It is important to note that a few dozen vernacular histories of Hawai'i Japanese came out in the 1920s and 1930s in the islands. Although this essay does not delve into the narrative schemes of these works, due to the limitation of space, I would point out that the twin themes of plantation labor and the

fight against race-based exploitation constituted their story of "tribulations" and "triumphs." Though bearing striking similarities to the mainland frontier thesis, Issei history making in Hawai'i remained oblivious to it, thereby keeping the concurrent formation of historical narratives almost completely detached from one another. This divergent development would continue in the postwar years. Consequently, to date, there is no synthetic historical work that brings together the experiences of Hawai'i Japanese and mainland Japanese.

8   On representative works that illuminate the racist thinking of military and government officials as well as the American public, see Conn (1964, 115–149); Daniels (1971, 42–73); Grodzins (1949); tenBroek et al. (1954); Irons (1983); Robinson (2001, 120); Weglyn 1976; and Commission on Wartime Relocation and Internment of Civilians (1997, 18). Tangential to the problem of Nisei citizenship is another popular theme of Nisei "democratic" education in the camps. See James (1987); Pak (2002).

9   One notable exception is Brian Masaru Hayashi's historical study (2004), which provides equal attention to the Issei and Nisei. His research nonetheless seems to be incongruent with the kind of conclusive statements that he makes in his book. Instead of using Japanese-language sources produced by immigrant internees, Hayashi relies primarily on the English-language reports on Issei produced by monolingual white camp researchers. In this respect, despite his conscious effort to include Issei into internment history, Hayashi's work may well fall short of satisfactorily uncovering their camp experience from their vantage point.

10 The Japanese American Citizens League (JACL) first became interested in compiling an official history of Issei around 1948. In late December, its organ, *Pacific Citizen,* published a "Special Holiday Edition" entitled "These Are Our Parents." Adopting the scheme of Issei's own history writing, many articles referred to the immigrants as "pioneers." In 1954, the JACL formed a preparatory committee for an Issei history project, which culminated in the Japanese American Research Project five years later. Concurrently, Nisei community leaders launched another history project with a focus on past activities of the JACL. See *Pacific Citizen,* December 25, 1948; January 28, 1950; Japanese American Citizens League (1959); Intermountain District Council (IDC) (1959); Alice Kasai Papers (AKP) (1948); and Masaoka (1960). The official history of the JACL was published in *JACL: In Quest of Justice* (Hosokawa 1982). On the establishment of JARP, see also Minamikawa (2007, 205–212).

11 The official JARP publications include Wilson and Hosokawa (1980); Iwata (1990); Chuman (1976); and Hosokawa (1982). Predictably, they examine

early immigration and community development in the American West, Issei's agricultural contribution, a series of legal discriminations and the resistance to them, and the growth of Nisei. Though not part of the initial publication plan, a number of major sociological studies also took advantage of freshly collected JARP data. See Bonacich and Modell (1980); Modell (1977); and Montero (1980).

12 Judging from a trail of documentary evidence, Yasui changed his stance within a matter of three months between May and August 1963.

13 See also Miyakawa (1964) and *Study of the United States-Japan Trade and of the East Coast Japanese Americans* [n.d.]. Later, independent of JARP, Miyakawa began writing his own scholarly monograph on East Coast Issei based on the collected historical material. After his death, the incomplete manuscript was donated to the JARP collections. See also Miyakawa (1972).

14 With modifications, I borrowed the notion of "absent presence" from Simpson (2001). Michael Cullen Green (2010, 84) unveils the practice of gradated Nisei discrimination against Japanese war brides. The women wedded to black soldiers "were routinely shunned by other Japanese Americans," suggesting the wives of white citizens fared better. It reflected Nisei's assimilationist racism that favored whiteness over other colors and ethnicities.

15 Even Glenn (1988) looks at war brides in the San Francisco Bay Area only. The omission of newcomers other than war brides is even more striking. Spickard's general history (2009, 154, 164–165) spares one short paragraph for war brides and one page for postwar immigrants in general.

References

Adams, Romanzo. 1924. *The Japanese in Hawai'i: A Statistical Study Bearing on the Future Number and Voting Strength and on the Economic and Social Character of the Hawaiian Japanese.* New York: National Committee on American-Japanese Relations.

———. 1937. *Interracial Marriage in Hawai'i: A Study of the Mutually Conditioned Processes of Acculturation and Amalgamation.* New York: Macmillan.

Alice Kasai Papers (AKP). 1911–2007. Marriott Library. University of Utah, Salt Lake City.

Asato, Noriko. 2005. *Teaching Mikadoism: The Attack on Japanese Language Schools in Hawai'i, California, and Washington, 1919–1927.* Honolulu: University of Hawai'i Press.

Austin, Allan W. 2003. "'A Finer Set of Hopes and Dreams': The Japanese American Citizens League and Ethnic Community in Cincinnati, Ohio, 1942–1950." In *Remapping Asian American History,* edited by Sucheng Chan, 87–105. Walnut Creek, CA: AltaMira Press.

———. 2004. *From Concentration Camp to Campus: Japanese American Students and World War II.* Urbana: University of Illinois Press.

———. 2007. "Eastward Pioneers: Japanese American Resettlement during World War II and the Contested Meaning of Exile and Incarceration." *Journal of American Ethnic History* 26 (2): 58–84.

Azuma, Eiichiro. 2003. "The Politics of Transnational History Making: Japanese Immigrants in the 'Western Frontier,' 1927–1941." *Journal of American History* 89 (4): 1401–1430.

———. 2005a. *Between Two Empires: Race, History, and Transnationalism in Japanese America.* New York: Oxford University Press.

———. 2005b. "From Civil Rights to Human Rights: Reinterpreting the Japanese American Internment in an International Context." *Reviews in American History* 33 (1): 102–110.

———. 2009. "Dancing with the Rising Sun: Strategic Alliance between Issei and Their 'Home' Government." In *The Transnational Politics of Asian Americans,* edited by Christian Collet and Pei-te Lien, 25–37, 188–190. Philadelphia: Temple University Press.

Beardsley, Richard K. 1963. Beardsley to T. Scott Miyakawa. JARP: Box 511, April 11.

Boddy, E. Manchester. 1921. *Japanese in America.* Los Angeles: E. Manchester Boddy.

Bonacich, Edna, and John Modell. 1980. *The Economic Basis of Ethnic Solidarity: Small Business in the Japanese American Community.* Berkeley: University of California Press.

Brooks, Charlotte. 2000. "In the Twilight Zone between Black and White: Japanese American Resettlement and Community in Chicago, 1942–1945." *Journal of American History* 86 (4): 1655–1687.

Chan, Sucheng. 1996. "Asian American Historiography." *Pacific Historical Review* 65 (3): 363–399.

Chuman, Frank F. 1976. *Bamboo People: The Law and Japanese-Americans.* Del Mar, CA: Publisher's Inc.

Commission on Wartime Relocation and Internment of Civilians. 1997. *Personal Justice Denied: Report of the Commission on Wartime Relocation and Internment of Civilians.* Seattle: University of Washington Press.

Conn, Stetson. 1964. "Japanese Evacuation from the West Coast." In *The United States Army in World War II: The Western Hemisphere,* 115–149. Washington, DC: Government Printing Office.

Daniels, Roger. 1966. *The Politics of Prejudice: The Anti-Japanese Movement in California and the Struggle for Japanese Exclusion.* Gloucester, MA: Peter Smith.

———. 1971. *Concentration Camps U.S.A.* New York: Holt, Rinehart and Winston.

———. 2004. *Prisoners Without Trial: Japanese Americans in World War II.* New York: Hill and Wang.

Fifteenth National Convention Minutes. 1958. AKP: Box 47, Folder 6. August 22–25.

Fuchs, Lawrence H. 1961. *Hawai'i Pono: A Social History.* New York: Harcourt, Brace.

Fujioka, Shirō 藤岡紫朗. 1927. 民族発展の先駆者 (Pioneers of Japanese Development). Tokyo: Dōbunsha.

Gaimushō Ryōji Ijūbu 外務省領事移住部. 1971. 我が国民の海外発展：移住百年の歩み (資料篇 (Overseas Development of Our Nation: Footsteps of Hundred-Year Migration). Tokyo: Gaimushō.

Glenn, Evelyn Nakano. 1988. *Issei, Nisei, War Brides: Three Generations of Japanese American Women in Domestic Service.* Philadelphia: Temple University Press.

Green, Michael Cullen. 2010. *Black Yanks in the Pacific: Race in the Making of American Military Empire after World War II.* Ithaca, NY: Cornell University Press.

Grodzins, Morton. 1949. *Americans Betrayed.* Chicago: University of Chicago Press.

Gruenewald, Mary Matsuda. 2005. *Looking Like the Enemy: My Story of Imprisonment in Japanese American Internment Camps.* Troutdale, OR: New Sage Press.

Gulick, Sidney L. 1914. *The American Japanese Problem: A Study of the Racial Relations of the East and the West.* New York: Charles Scribner's Sons.

Harden, Jacalyn D. 2003. *Double Cross: Japanese Americans in Black and White Chicago.* Minneapolis: University of Minnesota Press.

Hayashi, Brian Masaru. 2004. *Democratizing the Enemy: The Japanese American Internment.* Princeton, NJ: Princeton University Press.

Honda, Harry. 1967. *Pacific Citizen* memo, re: JACL Style Sheet. JARP: Box 125, Folder 1, May 4.

Hosokawa, Bill. 1969. *Nisei: The Quiet American, The Story of a People.* New York: William Morrow.

———. 1982. *JACL: In Quest of Justice.* New York: William Morrow.

Ichihashi, Yamato. 1932. *Japanese in the United States: A Critical Study of the Problems of the Japanese Immigrants and Their Children.* Stanford, CA: Stanford University Press.

Ichioka, Yuji. 1988. *The Issei: The World of the First Generation Japanese Immigrants, 1885–1924.* New York: Free Press.

Ichioka, Yuji, Eiichiro Azuma, and Gordon H. Chang. 2006. *Before Internment: Essays In Prewar Japanese American History.* Stanford, CA: Stanford University Press.

Ichioka, Yuji, Yasuo Sakata, Noboya Tsuchida, and Eri Yasuhara. 1974. *A Buried Past: An Annotated Bibliography of the Japanese American Research Project Collection*. Berkeley: University of California Press.
Intermountain District Council (IDC). 1956. Meeting minutes. AKP: Box 15, Folder 1. June 24, November 25.
———. 1957. Meeting minutes. AKP: Box 15, Folder 2. April 14.
———. 1959. Meeting minutes. AKP: Box 15, Folder 4.
Irons, Peter. 1983. *Justice at War: The Story of Japanese-American Internment Cases*. Berkeley: University of California Press.
Ishizuka, Karen L. 2006. *Lost and Found: Reclaiming the Japanese American Incarceration*. Urbana: University of Illinois Press.
Iwata, Masakazu. 1990. *Planted in Good Soil: A History of the Issei in the United States Agriculture*. New York: P. Lang.
James, Thomas. 1987. *Exile Within: The Schooling of Japanese Americans, 1942–1945*. Cambridge, MA: Harvard University Press.
Japanese American Citizens League. 1959. National Board Meeting Minutes. AKP: Box 33, Folder 5.
Japanese American Research Project. 1966[?]. Report. JARP: Box 509.
Japanese American Research Project. n.d. Guideline. Section II: Privileged Communication. JARP: Box 507.
Japanese American Research Project Collection (JARP). n.d. Department of Special Collections. Young Research Library. University of California, Los Angeles.
Kawakami, K. K. 1921. *The Real Japanese Question*. New York: MacMillan.
Kikumura-Yano, Akemi. 1992. *Issei Pioneers: Hawai'i and the Mainland, 1885–1945*. Los Angeles: Japanese American National Museum.
Kotani, Ronald. 1985. *The Japanese in Hawai'i: A Century of Struggle*. Honolulu: Hochi.
Kurashige, Lon. 2002. *Japanese American Celebration and Conflict: A History of Ethnic Identity and Festival, 1934–1990*. Berkeley: University of California Press.
Lind, Andrew W. 1946. *Hawai'i's Japanese: An Experiment in Democracy*. Princeton, NJ: Princeton University Press.
———. 1961. *Hawai'i's People*. Honolulu: University of Hawai'i Press.
Masaoka, Mike M. 1960. Masaoka to Mrs. Sam J. Tobin. AKP: Box 46, Folder 12, May 6.
———. 1967. JACL Style Sheet. JARP: Box 125, Folder 1, May 1.
McClatchy, V. S. 1919. *The Germany of Asia*. Sacramento.
Mike M. Masaoka Papers. n.d. Marriott Library, University of Utah, Salt Lake City.

Millis, H. A. 1915. *The Japanese Problem in the United States.* New York: Macmillan.

Minamikawa, Fumisato 南川文里. 2007. 日系アメリカ人の歴史社会学 (Historical Sociology of Japanese Americans). Tokyo: Sairyūsha.

Miyakawa, T. Scott. 1961. Miyakawa to Charles Burton Fahs. JARP: Box 512, July 3.

———. 1962. Miyakawa to Eugene Rostow. JARP: Box 513, May 4.

———. 1962. Miyakawa to Gordon W. Allport. JARP: Box 512, May 7.

———. 1962. Miyakawa to Winifred Raushenbush. JARP: Box 513, May 9.

———. 1963. Miyakawa to Harry Honda. JARP: Box 512, August 18.

———. 1964. Miyakawa to Katsuyo L. Takeshita. JARP: Box 510, February 26.

———. 1964. Miyakawa to Mike Morizono. JARP: Box 511, December 16.

———. 1967. Miyakawa to Joe Masaoka. JARP: Box 510, July 20.

———. 1972. "Early New York Issei Founders of Japanese American Trade." In *East across the Pacific: Historical & Sociological Studies of Japanese Immigration & Assimilation,* edited by Hilary Conroy and T. Scott Miyakawa, 156–186. Santa Barbara, CA: ABC-CLIO.

Miyazaki, C. S. 1938. "To Our American Sons and Daughters." In 央華日系市民写真 (Pictures of Japanese [American] Citizens in Oregon and Washington), edited by Sosuke Kawai. Tacoma, WA: Takoma Shūhōsha.

Modell, John. 1977. *The Economics and Politics of Racial Accommodation: The Japanese of Los Angeles, 1900–1942.* Urbana: University of Illinois Press.

Montero, Darrel. 1980. *Japanese Americans: Changing Patterns of Ethnic Affiliation over Three Generations.* Boulder, CO: Westview Press.

Muller, Eric L. 2003. *Free to Die for Their Country: The Story of the Japanese American Draft Resisters in World War II.* Chicago: University of Chicago Press.

Nakagawa, Mushō 中川無象. 1932. 在米闘士録 (Records of Japanese Strugglers in America). Los Angeles: Rafu Shimpōsha.

Nichibei Shimbunsha 日米新聞社. 1931. 日米大鑑 (Cyclopedia of Japanese American Relations and Community). San Francisco: Nichibei Shimbunsha.

Okamura, Jonathan Y. 1994. "Why There Are No Asian Americans in Hawai'i." *Social Process in Hawai'i* 35: 161–178.

———. 1998. "The Illusion of Paradise." In *Making Majorities: Constituting the Nation in Japan, Korea, China, Malaysia, Fiji, Turkey, and the United States,* edited by Dru C. Gladney, 264–284. Stanford, CA: Stanford University Press.

Okihiro, Gary. 1999. *Storied Lives: Japanese American Students and World War II.* Seattle: University of Washington Press.

Pacific Citizen. 1948. December 25.

———. 1950. January 28.

Pak, Yoon K. 2002. *Wherever I Go I Will Always Be a Loyal American: Seattle's Japanese American Children during World War II*. New York: Routledge.

Robinson, Greg. 2001. *By Order of the President: FDR and the Internment of Japanese Americans*. Cambridge, MA: Harvard University Press.

———. 2005. "Nisei in Gotham: Japanese Americans in Wartime New York." *Prospects: An Annual of American Cultural Studies* 30: 581–595.

Rostow, Eugene. 1945. "Our Worst Wartime Mistake." *Harper's* 191: 193–201.

Sawada, Mitziko. 1986–1987. "After the Camps: Seabrook Farms, New Jersey, and the Resettlement of Japanese Americans, 1944–47." *Amerasia Journal* 13: 117–136.

Scharrenberg, Paul. 1922. "The Japanese in Hawai'i." *American Federationist* 29 (11): 742–750.

Simpson, Caroline Chung. 2001. *An Absent Presence: Japanese Americans in Postwar American Culture, 1945–1960*. Durham, NC: Duke University Press.

Spickard, Paul R. 2009. *Japanese Americans: The Formation and Transformations of an Ethnic Group,* rev. ed. New Brunswick, NJ: Rutgers University Press.

Strong, Edward K., Jr. 1934. *The Second-Generation Japanese Problem*. Stanford, CA: Stanford University Press.

Study of the United States-Japan Trade and of the East Coast Japanese Americans. n.d. Mike M. Masaoka Papers: Box 69, Folder 8.

Tamura, Eileen H. 2000. "Using the Past to Inform the Future: An Historiography of Hawai'i's Asian and Pacific Islander Americans." *Amerasia Journal* 26 (1): 55–85.

tenBroek, Jacobus, with Edward N. Barnhart and Floyd W. Matson. 1954. *Prejudice, War and the Constitution*. Berkeley: University of California Press.

"Tenth National Convention Minutes." 1948. AKP: Box 47, Folder 5.

Tōga, Yoichi 藤賀與一. 1927. 日米関係在米国日本人発展史要 (Chronological History of U.S.-Japan Relations and Japanese in America). Oakland, CA: Beikoku Seisho Kyōkai Nihonjinbu.

Toyota, Tritia. 2012. "The New Nikkei: Transpacific Shin Issei and Shifting Borders of Community in Southern California." *Amerasia Journal* 38 (3): 2–27.

U.S. Department of Homeland Security. 2006. Office of Immigration Statistics. *2004 Yearbook of Immigration Statistics*. Washington, DC: Government Printing Office.

Wakukawa, Ernest K. 1938. *A History of Japanese People in Hawai'i*. Honolulu: Toyo Shoin.

Washizu, Shakuma (Bunzō) 鷲津尺魔(文三). 1930. 在米日本人史観 (Perspective on the History of Japanese in America). Los Angeles: Rafu Shimpōsha.

Weglyn, Michi. 1976. *Years of Infamy: The Untold Story of America's Concentration Camps.* New York: William Morrow.
Wilson, Robert A., and Bill Hosokawa. 1980. *East to America: A History of the Japanese in the United States.* New York: William Morrow.
Wu, Ellen D. 2013. *The Color of Success: Asian Americans and the Origins of the Model Minority.* Princeton, NJ: Princeton University Press.
[Yasui, Min]. 1963. To T. Scott Miyakawa. JARP: Box 511, May 15.
Yasutomi, Nariyoshi 安富成良. 2002. 戦争花嫁と日系コミュニティ (III) (War Brides and Japanese [American] Community [III]). *Kaetsu University Research Review* 44 (2): 55–82.
Zaibei Nihonjinkai 在米日本人会. 1940. 在米日本人史 (History of Japanese in America). San Francisco: Zaibei Nihonjinkai.

CHAPTER 12

Reorienting Asian American Studies in Asia and the Pacific

Rika Nakamura

At the Asian American Studies in Asia: An International Workshop, held at Academia Sinica in Taipei in 2010, Viet Thanh Nguyen, a U.S.-based Vietnamese American scholar, posed this question: How does Asian American studies in the United States translate in Asia? Two years later at the Nikkei Studies and Beyond: Dialogue between Scholars in Japan and the U.S. conference, held in Tokyo, Gary Okihiro, a renowned U.S. historian of Japanese ancestry, challenged his audience with a similar question: What is your investment in engaging in Asian American studies in Japan? I understand that with the second-person plural, Okihiro addressed the Japanese scholars, who constituted a majority of his audience.[1]

This chapter intends to respond to their questions about what it means to engage in Asian American studies in Japan/Asia and will later explore the relations between those two locations. What Nguyen and Okihiro posed is not the kind of question "we" Japan-based Japanese scholars often ask in our own land, where it is taken for granted that "we" have the "right" to study Asian American, especially Japanese American, experiences. In addition, in Asia and Japan, our positionalities are rarely challenged.

This, however, is not to deny the voices *within Asia* that have interrogated the meanings of Asian American studies in this location. The workshops in Taipei and Tokyo demonstrate two such attempts. Their organizers, Chih-ming Wang and Yasuko Takezawa, invited the participants to explore the shifting significance of the discipline within their respective locations. The meetings served as bridges enabling constructive dialogue across the Pacific and across Asia. In that context, Yoshiyuki Kido has critiqued the "epistemological violence" (Kido 2002, 29) of an uncritical sense of identification that Japanese historians often claim with Nikkei experience.

This chapter is my attempt to respond to those U.S.-based and Asia-based scholars' challenges and efforts as I explore the possibility of a more trans-Pacific, and possibly inter-Asian, Asian American studies.[2] I submit that a reoriented Asian American studies can and must be a place of deconstruction, conversation, and mutual learning among scholars based in various American and Asian locations. Toward that end, I ask the following questions: What happens when U.S. racial minority studies are relocated to a place where Asians do *not* constitute racial minorities? How does this new location and perspective help transform the existing U.S.-based knowledge structure in which the discipline currently arises? What do we learn from this perspective, the project of "Asian American Studies in 'Asia,' " with our heterogeneities and (neo)colonial relations?

This chapter argues that the intellectual encounter between Asia and Asian America encourages U.S.-based minority studies to interrogate its complicities with U.S. imperialism. As Viet Nguyen stated, the U.S. minority's "new burden" of "revised double consciousness" reveals how Asian Americans are "not exempt" from the problem of being "implicated in the exercise of US power" (Nguyen 2012, 929). The critical act of looking at Asian American studies from Asia can help explore the contradictory meanings of the category "Asian Americans," which Kandice Chuh (Chuh 2001, 2003a) and Laura Hyun Yi Kang (Kang 2002, 2003) have conceived as both Western subjects and a racial minority within "the West." In a slightly different context, Candice Fujikane and Jonathan Okamura have explored the contradictory positionalities of Asian Americans as "settlers of color" in the context of Hawaiʻi (Fujikane and Okamura 2000).[3] As such, an increasing number of Asian North Americans have begun to explore their complex and contradictory positionalities as "Westerners of color" in the global terrain.

On the other side of the Pacific, Asian American studies as a *minority* discourse de-essentializes the meanings of race when the discipline is transplanted in a place where Asians constitute a racial, if not ethnic, majority. It can invite ethnoracial majority Asians to reflect upon the racial, ethnic, and (neo)colonial relations in and across Asia and the positions of power we occupy, albeit unevenly. The act of reorientation thus underscores the discontinuities within Asia, drawing attention to the histories of inter-Asian colonialism and imperialism. I contend that this reoriented trans-Pacific Asian American studies will equip Asians in Asia and Asian Americans with new self-perceptions at home and abroad while expanding the horizon on *both* sides of the Pacific.

Here I would like to add that the binaristic discussion of "Asia" and "Asian America" does not intend to negate the arbitrariness of those categorizations or erase the ambiguity of positions inhabited by in-between figures such as overseas students, "Asians in America" (rather than Asian Americans), returnees, Kibei, 1.5 generations, temporary migrants, and first-generation immigrants or refugees both across Asia and across the Pacific. On the one hand, a U.S.-trained returnee who works at an academic institution in Asia may be seen as occupying a position closer to an "Asian American," at least from the perspective of her/his fellow Asia-trained Asians. On the other hand, the returnees may feel more akin to minoritized Asian/Americans than the Asians who have stayed "safely" in Asia; they can be more acutely aware of the exclusionary practices within the discursive sphere of U.S. Asian American studies. The power dynamics between "Asians" and "Asian/Americans" shift and become complicated through gender, class, ethnic, regional, and other differences. Being an Asian North American in Asia is a complex position, which also depends on what Asian country one resides in, for how long, and with what Asian ancestries and linguistic fluency, and so on. Positionalities are relative and relational and are never essential.

What I want to emphasize is the usefulness of those positions (however arbitrary) to look at ourselves from the perspectives of others, so that we can question easy identifications among "Asians" while de-essentializing the meanings of race. The chapter also puts in question the tendency in minority studies whereby the practitioners view themselves primarily in alignment with the oppressed rather than examining our complicity with the dominant group. It is my hope that this study will help us raise new questions and engage in Asian American studies differently at the time when the "trans-Pacific" becomes a new paradigm of the discipline.

I begin with texts by two prominent U.S.-based Asian American literary scholars, King-kok Cheung and Sau-ling Wong, who delineate their pedagogical journeys to Asia and explore the differing significances of engaging in Asian American studies there. Their essays are collected in the anthology *Crossing the Oceans: Reconfiguring American Literary Studies in the Pacific Rim*, published in 2004 by Hong Kong University Press. I will also make an occasional reference to Wong's "Maxine Hong Kingston in a Global Frame" (Wong 2005), which appeared in the Japan-based *AALA Journal*. I reference those texts because they are full-length article treatments of the issue by practicing Asian American studies scholars who *literally* transported the discipline to various Asian locations and examined the significance of engaging in Asian American studies there. Their articles offer important insights into some of the differences between "Asians" and "Asian Americans" in terms of racialized subjectivities, perceptions, and experiences, in a place where Asians do not constitute a racial (even though they can be an ethnic) minority. While Cheung and Wong invite ethnoracial-majority Asians to perceive themselves as such, both critics warn against an easy identification through which the former empathizes with the experiences of minoritized Asian Americans.

Although Cheung and Wong's articles make an important critical intervention, their texts betray the kind of U.S.-centrism embedded in their projects. In particular, I point out how their trips take on the mode of an (unacknowledged) imperial mission in which renowned U.S. scholars travel to Asia to correct the misperceptions of Asian readers and to enlighten them. This is not to deny the importance of their intervention. Yet, the one-way internationalism that characterizes their pedagogical journeys risks relegating Asian readers to passive recipients of Western, albeit minority Western, knowledge production. It can prevent the encounter between Asia and Asian America from becoming a site of and opportunity for mutual learning. In stating this, I want to keep in mind that my critiques of these two scholars also apply to Asia-based Asian practitioners, especially those of us who have received training in the United States or Canada and engage in research and teaching in Asia, where we bring back that training.

To this extent and also to dehomogenize the Asian American scholars' representational practices, I read the two critics' journeys to Asia along with the discursive and literal journeys undertaken by other sets of U.S.-based Asian Americanists. In the latter part of the chapter, I look at critics whose encounters with Asia have triggered their critical self-reflections on their own discursive positions as minoritized U.S. subjects. In particular, I examine Laura Kang's article from the 2003 special issue of the *Journal of Asian American Studies (JAAS)*, "On Korean 'Comfort Women,'" and Lon Kurashige's short autobiographical piece, "Asian American History across the Pacific," included in this volume. The chapter ends with an examination of the possibility of Asian American studies as an inter-Asia as well as trans-Pacific project. My analysis of Asia in this chapter is limited to East Asia and does not explore more complex instances of Asian North Americans of South/east Asian ancestries, for instance, problematizing their relationships with East Asia.

While I question the way Cheung and Wong's trips to Asia fail to prompt a reexamination of their own U.S.-based minority positions, this is precisely what other critics, Kang and Kurashige along with Kandice Chuh and Lisa Yoneyama in the special issue, explore in their writings. At the same time, Cheung and Wong's pieces supplement, in an important way, the others' writings by offering critiques of the discursive practices of some ethnoracial majority Asians. Rather than denounce Cheung and Wong's works and praise Kang and Kurashige's, I suggest that those scholars' divergent engagements with Asia must be read in *supplement* with one another. In this way, I hope to show that Asian American studies' encounter with Asia, with internal power asymmetries in both groups, can create a place where we can learn from our differences as well as our commonalities.

Relocating Asian American Studies in Asia

In her article "Pedagogies of Resonance: Teaching African American and Asian American Literature and Culture in Asia," King-kok Cheung relates her experience of having taught U.S. ethnic literatures in various Asian locations: Taiwan, Japan, South Korea, Hong Kong, and Burma/Myanmar. Cheung claims that U.S. minority literature helps Asians in Asia self-reflect upon their own racial practices, which often remain invisible due to their majority status. Cheung writes of that pedagogical experience in Asia,

> Asian audiences easily understand or sympathize with the plight of racial minorities in the United States, but what is most intellectually satisfying is noting these audiences begin to identify social inequalities in their own countries and shift from empathizing with oppressed minorities elsewhere to seeing themselves as the dominant majority within their own homelands. (2004, 13)

Like Cheung, I believe this shift in perspective is a crucial part of studying minority experience *elsewhere*. After all, it is so much easier and safer to work on the "violence in another country."

Sau-ling Wong draws on the work of Mita Banerjee, who engages in Asian American studies in Germany. Wong makes a point similar to

Cheung's and critiques the displacement of U.S.-based Asian American studies abroad, which Banerjee calls "voyeurism of race," or how U.S. race issues are perceived in Germany "as a spectacle far from home," while occluding the ethnoracial differences "already existing in its midst" (Wong 2005, 31).

Indeed, focusing *solely* on foreign race issues without making a domestic linkage can risk the appropriation by dominant nationalist discourses to displace domestic oppressions onto the other. Cheung expresses that anxiety over the U.S. ethnic literary scholar's critique of "the dominant white culture," which "can play into chauvinistic or anti-American and anti-democratic sentiments in some Asian countries, leading to complacency rather than self-scrutiny" (Cheung 2004, 27). I cannot overemphasize this point, recalling what Lisa Yoneyama in a different context has aptly called "transnational warping" (Yoneyama 2001).

As witnessed in an increasing number of Japan-based Asian American scholarly works that engage in comparative racialization and/or empire studies (Takezawa 2005, 2009, 2011; Ikeuchi and Nishi 2006; Nakano 2007, 2012; Ishihara, Kina, and Yamashiro 2010; Yaguchi 2011), those works assist ethnoracial majority Japanese scholars to engage in Asian American studies differently. They help us view North American minority experiences not only through the sense of identifications but also through discontinuities and critical self-reflections as members of a dominant group.

To cite a few such endeavors within a Japanese context, Naoko Fujikura draws an interesting comparison between Japanese migrant laborers in the Americas in the early to middle twentieth century and the current Nikkei Brazilian and South/east Asian migrant workers in Japan (Fujikura 2009). As Fujikura explores their commonalities in terms of the ethnoracialized experience of displacement and labor exploitation in their similar and disparate economic and historical situations, the linkage disrupts, as it tears us away from the comfort of uncritical identification with the oppressed. Her analysis forces Japanese readers into a disquieting realization that many of us, with our differences, inhabit a position that is, in fact, much closer to the white majority's than to that of the exploited and racialized Asian migrant laborers of our familiar literary texts, despite our much desired identification with the latter. Studying racial minority literature elsewhere in this sense encourages Asians who have grown up as the majority to reflect upon their familiar reality and recapture it through the eyes of the other(s), often with a haunting sense of anxiety.

A similar perceptual shift occurred for me when I saw the 2005 documentary film *Dear Pyongyang,* directed by the Nisei Zainichi Korean filmmaker Young-Hee Yang. The film compelled me to look at the needs of ethnoracial minorities and their painful, coerced desire to distance themselves from their ancestral land, perhaps not unlike the anguish portrayed in John Okada's *No-No Boy*. Only this time, I saw it from the perspective of the dominant majority, who are ultimately responsible for creating such hostile social environments that force Zainichi Koreans, Japanese Americans, or any other minoritized population to take the stance of disinheriting their ancestral culture. My prior feeling of discomfort toward *No-No Boy*'s representations of Japan, however, also helped me interrogate Yang's Orientalist portrayal of North Korea, which is often overlooked in the mainstream Japanese appraisals of the film.

Elsewhere I have discussed the usefulness of what I call "the majority-minority twist," by which I refer to instances in which the ethnoracial *majority* of color (in this case, in Japan) study the histories and experiences of ethnoracial *minorities* in Western imperial nations, such as the United States, instead of studying race within the Japanese domestic/imperial contexts or in the formerly colonized nations. What this twisted perspective enables us to perform, I argue, is a simultaneous act of empathy and critique, or identification and disidentification, which *can* be put to productive use (Nakamura 2012b).

Working on war memories in Asian American contexts, I question what Eiichiro Azuma aptly called in the U.S. context "the cult of the internment," which I believe also applies to the dominant Japanese propensity to connect the Nikkei internment to the U.S. atomic bombings of two Japanese cities. Such a tendency aims to link Japanese and Japanese American experiences of the Asia-Pacific wars through the "same"—that is, anti-"Asian"—racism. While this anti-Asian, really anti-Japanese, racism presumably has its origin in white supremacy, "race" in its singularized form becomes the primary, if not the sole, factor that constitutes Asian/American experiences. Perceiving Asian American studies as *minority* discourse, however, compels us to situate Japanese American internment (*kyosei shuyo*) also in the context of, and in juxtaposition with, the Japanese state's mobilization of "Asians" for forced labor (*kyosei renko*), military sexual slavery, and other forms of ethnoracial and colonial violence. My work attempts to draw this linkage as it examines four literary works together: Joy Kogawa's *Obasan* and Mitsuye Yamada's *Camp Notes* and *Desert Run,* which deal with North American internment experiences, and Nora Okja Keller's *Comfort Woman* and Chang-rae Lee's *A Gesture Life*, which offer some Korean/American experiences of the same war.

In this sense, Asian American studies, particularly the literary studies, provides an important institutional site where those experiences can be discussed together in a single disciplinary terrain. The institutional division of labor has often prevented scholars from engaging in comparative studies, where the internment is addressed in (Asian) American studies and the forced labor and military sexual slavery constituting the topic for Asian and Japanese studies. Asian American studies can bridge this gap, as it allows us to engage with those histories across disciplinary boundaries as far as they are represented in its literature. Referencing Korean American perspectives is also important because, unlike South Korean or Zainichi Korean accounts, Korean *American* stories are scarce in Japan.

In this way, I agree with the critiques by Cheung and Wong. What I find missing in them is the awareness of a reverse gaze upon their own normalized Asian *American* perceptions, and subsequent need for them to learn from Asia. The double perspective they advance must also apply to them. Thus, while Cheung rightly encourages Asians to reflect upon their dominant positionalities within their societies, she never shifts her gaze to see herself as "the dominant majority" in the global order: namely, an American, *albeit minority*, scholar in Asia. Her work does not consider the possibility that her pedagogical journey constitutes a new imperial mission.

In a depiction of her visit to Taiwan, for instance, Cheung narrates an episode that delineates the impact that U.S. minority literature, in this case Maxine Hong Kingston's novel, has made in Taiwan. Citing "a Taiwanese scholar" who commented that the Taiwanese "should learn from Kingston's example and challenge the official history of the Republic of China, which has muffled the voices of its minorities," Cheung concludes, "In Taipei, I was thus made aware for the first time that American literature can hold a mirror to ethnic relations in Asia and can prompt an Asian audience to uncover repressed history concealed in its own soil" (Cheung 2004, 16). Although in agreement with that mirror effect, which Asian American literature can produce in Asia, I nonetheless find it surprising that Cheung never questions whether such efforts of resistance had (presumably) existed in Taiwan long before her introduction of Kingston and the importation of the Asian American model. Significantly, however, Cheung expresses no interest in learning about, let alone *from* those local Taiwanese endeavors; she is simply concerned with transmitting the Asian American "example" to them. That same attitude characterizes her visits to Japan, South Korea, and Hong Kong.[4] Sau-ling Wong's articles similarly display this lack of interest, paying little attention to the histories of racial resistance outside North America, whether in Asia or Germany.

Here I would like to emphasize that my critique of those scholars is not intended to negate the importance of Asians in Asia learning from Asian American struggles. I simply point to the extent that the Asian American critics and their texts remain the unmoving center that alone perform the pedagogical work, and how their cross-cultural journeys end up in one-way teaching rather than constituting a place and process of mutual learning. As many Asian American scholars have pointed out, Asian American studies as a Western discipline can risk participating in a (new) enlightenment mission.[5]

To this extent, I highlight the need for Asian American studies to learn from the struggles and scholarship produced in Asia. With regard to Japanese imperialism and colonialism, for instance, Asian studies and Japanese studies both in Japan and Asia have much longer histories of investments in the field than Asian American studies. Takashi Fujitani's recent book *Race for Empire: Koreans as Japanese and Japanese as Americans during World War II* (Fujitani 2011) provides an excellent example of a trans-Pacific comparative study of minority experiences. With its extensive references to the scholarship produced in Japan and South Korea, Fujitani's book elucidates the histories of Japanese American and Korean Japanese soldiers during the Asia-Pacific wars while engaging in a trans-Pacific dialogue across national and institutional boundaries.

Following Fujitani, I believe it is important that Asian American scholars in Asia/Japan connect their scholarship to Asian studies. For instance, reading Joy Kogawa's *Obasan,* which triangulates the Canadian internment, colonialism against Canada's indigenous peoples, and the United States's atomic bombing of Nagasaki, as minoritized discourse *in Japan* must evoke the histories of atomic bomb victims from the colonized and occupied territories of the Japanese empire: Korea, Taiwan, and China, among others. Although Kogawa herself does not make this linkage in her 1981 novel, it is crucial that Asian American studies fill in the gap by connecting her novel to the research findings of Asian and Japanese studies. The outcome not only disrupts the official claim of the Japanese government that the atomic attack constitutes the Japanese national tragedy but can also invite Asian

Americanists outside Asia to consider what they can learn from the scholarship and activism in Asia, whereby Asians themselves, including the survivors of Hiroshima and Nagasaki, have engaged with their own histories of aggressions and racism, as they condemn Japan's wartime aggressions and the discriminatory measures taken by the Japanese government against non-Japanese bomb victims.[6]

Writing/Reading "Asia" in Asian American Literature

Like Cheung, however, Sau-ling Wong, in "When Asian American Literature Leaves 'Home': On Internationalizing Asian American Literary Studies" (2004), does not question her U.S. vantage point; Wong criticizes Asians in Asia for being unaware of the discrepancies between Asia and Asian America. They thus fail to understand "properly" Asian American literary texts, she asserts. She goes on to diagnose the problem as one of "decontextualization" whereby Asian readers suffer from "a knowledge deficit" of Asian American culture and experience, which they mistakenly identify with their native Asian cultural experience. In other words, while Asian readers are "too remote" (Wong 2004, 32) from the original cultural context to fully understand Asian American literary works, their "superficial familiarity obscures the social, cultural and political matrix out of which the [Asian American] author operates and which profoundly alters their meaning" (33). Undoubtedly, this is a valid and important critique of misconceptions held by some Japanese who assume an unproblematized continuity between Japanese and Japanese Americans in terms of cultural and ethnic experiences.

However, by rendering Asians as "foreign" readers, Wong seems to assume the "native" reader to be the ultimate, if not sole, subject who performs *the* correct reading of Asian American texts. In this regard, nonnative readers are reduced to, when they are perceived only in terms of their deficiencies, cultural incompetents whose deficiencies require remediation if they aspire to produce a "proper" reading. It appears that Wong equates a "proper" reading with the U.S. Asian American way, and she does not allow the possibility of a cultural outsider perceiving what might be a blind spot to a native reader. As such, Wong dismisses and corrects those "misreadings" rather than explores their multiple meanings and potentials.

Perhaps this critique is especially pertinent to Asian American representations of Asia in which Asian readers become the objects of representations. Hyungji Park invites an exploration of "what Asia is to make of its own image as represented" in Asian American literature (Park 2010, 1). Park poses an important question, which is missing in Wong's article. Rather than dismiss or correct Asian readers' "misperceptions" of Asian American representations of Asia, Asian American scholars might address and take seriously the implications of those "misreadings." For instance, such misreadings, often accompanied by puzzlement and resentment, might stem from a sense of violation, an objection to what Asian readers might perceive as some Asian American writers' liberal, if not Orientalist, "(mis)use" of Asian culture and literature.

As I have mentioned earlier regarding Young-Hee Yang's representation of North Korea in *Dear Pyongyang,* such seemingly Orientalist construction of the ancestral land is not an unfamiliar practice by minority writers in Japan, as those writers negotiate with their need to devise representational strategies that can both satisfy and interrupt mainstream Japanese readers' desire for an exoticized other. Indeed, with what she termed "racial shadowing," Wong herself had given an elaborate analysis of such psychological mechanisms, illuminating some Asian American writers' desire for racial disowning before the advent of multiculturalism (Wong 1993). However, in "When Asian American Literature Leaves 'Home,'" which is characterized by its peculiar absence of the concept of Orientalism and imperialism, except toward Canada, Wong critiques "misperceptions" of Asian readers without considering the possibility that Asian American writers might *also* be responsible for those "misrepresentations."

The same can be said about Wong's charge of the erasure of racial issues by Chinese scholarly readings of *The Woman Warrior.* In "Maxine Hong Kingston in a Global Frame" (Wong 2005), Wong points out that despite China being a multiracial/ethnic nation, the racial minority discourse in Kingston's original text is translated into deracialized and heavily culturalized, hence less threatening, "East-West" relations in Chinese scholars' readings of the novel (28). Indeed, in many ways, Wong's critique is valid in Japan. For example, in a 1989 staging of *M. Butterfly* by the Japanese theatrical company Gekidan Shiki, *both* Song and Gallimard are performed by *Japanese* actors. Reviewers in popular magazines commonly interpreted the filmic adaptation of Marguerite Duras's novel *L'Amant* as a deracialized "love story," and more recently, Clint Eastwood's film *Flags of Our Fathers* was widely viewed as a deracialized, humanistic antiwar movie. Such erasures of race are a common practice in Japanese popular media. Another prominent example is the 1992 murder of Yoshihiro Hattori, an exchange student who was shot in Louisiana. In Japan, many viewed the shooting not so much as an instance of anti-Asian racism—in the way many Asian American scholars and activists interpreted the incident—but as an instance of a dysfunctional, gun-happy U.S. society, affirming the superiority of Japanese culture.

In this way, I fully empathize with Wong in her frustration with and critique of some Chinese scholars in their omission of race in their readings of Kingston as overseas Chinese literature rather than as U.S. minority literature (Wong 2005). Yet, Wong is equally culpable for her erasure of Orientalism and imperialism in her reading of Chinese receptions of Kingston. When the domestic racial minority issue becomes the only power asymmetry that the critic finds worthy of attention, it may not be surprising that Wong acknowledges Asian American dominance vis-à-vis Asian *Canadians* but not toward Asians in Asia who constitute an ethnoracial majority (Wong 2004). In that sense, Wong's article is like a reversal of some Asian scholars who point fingers to Western imperialism but not toward domestic racism.

Triggering "Self-Critical Reflection"

The need for Asian Americans to reflect upon their dominant American positionality is what Laura Kang and Lon Kurashige emphasize in their writings on the Asian American encounters with "Asia." Those encounters, they believe, disrupt the assumed positionalities of Asian Americans as solely minoritized subjects. In discussing Asian American women's engagements with the issue of Japanese military sexual slavery, for instance, Kang argues how this brutal act of sexual subjugation of (here) Korean women by the Japanese colonial regime needs to be viewed as constituting a site of "disidentification" (Kang 2003, 46) for them, as it instantiates "not their sameness but their distance and difference" (27) from the Korean victims.

In this way, Kang, like King-kok Cheung and Sau-ling Wong, perceives the encounter between Asia and Asian America as the site of differentiation rather than homogenization; Kang problematizes the process by which the Asian American artists and scholars' identification with the victims can eclipse the *American* part of their subject position vis-à-vis "Asia"/Korea. This is an important critique that also applies to some Japanese women's unproblematized, gender-based identification with the victims-survivors of Japanese military sexual slavery. Such identification can occlude the ethnoimperialist dimensions of that sexual violence. Although Japanese women were also mobilized for the military sexual slavery, the majority of those coerced were Asian women from the colonized and occupied territories of Japan. Furthermore, the primary means by which many Japanese women obtained their imperial citizenships was by assuming the position of "imperial mothers," thereby giving birth to soldiers who could act as potential rapists to those enslaved women (Nakamura 2005).

Significantly, then, Kang's argument confirms *and* supplements Cheung and Wong's insistence that ethnoracial majority Asians need to reflect upon their positionalities in engaging with Asian American literature. All three critics underscore the danger of appropriating the stories of others as one's own even though they comment on populations residing on different sides of the Pacific. Cheung and Wong invite Asians in Asia to recognize their majority position through their encounter with the minoritized Asian American population; Kang similarly prompts Asian Americans to identify their dominant American perceptions vis-à-vis Asia. Their respective articles point to the need of being read together to supplement one another.

As Kang elucidates the multiple, complex, and contradictory positionalities that "Korean/Americans" specifically inhabit, her article calls attention to the layered configurations of their affiliations rather than sustaining a simple binarization of homogenized Asia and Asian America. Drawing from Korean feminist scholar Cho Hae-joang, Kang suggests that Japanese military sexual slavery may provoke a stronger interest among Korean *American* women precisely because it embodies the combination of racial/colonial *and* sexual violence that Korean American women experience as double minorities in North America. At the same time, Kang calls for a critical examination of their identifications and investments "as distinctly American subjects of representation and knowledge production" (2003, 27). Citing Lisa Yoneyama's critique, Kang questions how those women might risk participating in the U.S. "imperialist myth of liberation and rehabilitation" (Yoneyama 2003, 74).

In the concluding chapter of her award-winning book *Compositional Subjects,* Kang looks at two documentary films by Korean American women that deal with U.S. military prostitution in South Korea. Kang sees the films as the place of an encounter between Korean and Korean American women, and her book problematizes the hierarchical division of labor that one of the films, *Camp Arirang,* assumes between those two groups of women. While the latter is assigned a position of power and authority in providing social commentaries, the former is deployed to offer personal experiences and testimonies that simply "support the broad observations and analyses articulated by the GIs and the Korean American women scholars" (Kang 2002, 265). Reminiscent of the Asians in King-kok Cheung's article, Korean women in that documentary are employed only to affirm and authorize, rather than challenge and intervene in, the normatized U.S. perceptions that the Asian American filmmakers already held in their travel to Asia, and in their assumed position of authority.

Kang warns against how those Korean American filmmakers unwittingly inhabit and inherit the discursive terrain constructed by U.S. imperialism, reproducing its narrative forms. As she maintains, "Instead of a refusal to represent, the challenge is to bring these issues to a transnational public discourse [. . .] without effacing our own specific positionalities as 'American' investigating subjects" (Kang 2002, 269). I would like to restate the importance of reading Kang, Cheung, and Wong together *in supplement* with one another. In that way, Kang's self-critique speaks to, as it resonates with the self-critiques of, ethnoracial majority Asians. The encounters between Asia and Asian America can thereby become a productive site of mutual learning and knowledge production.

Engaging in Dialogue with Other

Lon Kurashige's short autobiographical piece "Asian American History across the Pacific" points to the possibility of such dialogic encounters between "Asia" and "Asian America." In this essay, Kurashige documents his interactions with Japanese scholars and the subsequent self-interrogations they have generated: "how my encounters with Japan-based scholars have caused me to reflect upon the gospel of decolonization that I sought to spread throughout Japan" (Kurashige 2013, 17).

Kurashige's piece is particularly useful in that it traces the trajectories of his own deconstructed thoughts, norms, and assumptions as well as the learning processes involved. The essay provides a self-critique rather than a critique of his distant others. While I do not deny the importance of critiques directed at others, such criticisms can sometimes obscure our implications in the problems we project onto those others. This certainly applies to my critique of King-kok Cheung and Sau-ling Wong, and to a certain extent to Laura Kang's of her fellow Asian Americanists. Kurashige's piece not only invites us to consider what it means to engage in trans-Pacific Asian American studies; it makes us reflect upon the implications of our own enunciations.

What I find significant about Kurashige's conception of the trans-Pacific encounter is that it questions one-way pedagogical relationships and strives to engage in a conversation. Reflecting on his earlier, though well-intentioned, efforts to decolonize the Japanese academy—to enlighten it "with American counter-hegemonic empowerment" (Kurashige 2013, 15)—Kurashige questions the inherent premise of superiority, which one can assume even in advocating causes as valid and important as decolonization and antiracism.

Hence, in discussing the operation of (Asian) American studies in Japan, Kurashige stresses the need for U.S. scholars "to give up the missionary spirit of decolonization and instead to understand the relationships that Japanese scholars have to American studies on their own terms. This means appreciating the vast diversity of motivations that Japan-based scholars have for studying the US—motivations that often differ very much from my own" (Kurashige 2013, 16). Rather than presume and prescribe the singular truth and method that originates in the U.S. academy or else stipulate a separate and essentialist truth for its Japanese counterpart, Kurashige underscores the importance of understanding the operation of (Asian) American studies in its specific, localized academic context and thereby acknowledging the desires and motivations that are engendered therein.

It is important, I think, that Kurashige's call for a situated (Asian) American studies signifies the need to attend to the voices of others rather than simply endorse pluralism or relativism. As Joy Kogawa put it beautifully, "What draws us together is not sermon but story. Who are you? Who am I? What is your cause? What is mine?" (Kogawa 1984, 21). Similarly, Viet Nguyen emphasizes the need to "engage in dialogue with foreign others" rather than "theorize the international from a US vantage point" (Nguyen 2012, 160). All three authors underscore the value of engaging in conversation rather than preaching, whereby the former demonstrates an exchange that, unlike the latter, does not assume a single correct answer but searches for answers through that exchange.

Kurashige's writing also resonates with some Asian American and Canadian writers' efforts that I discussed elsewhere, as they attend to what to them sounds like "noise" rather than a "proper" (i.e., Western) language (Nakamura 2009). This act of attending exhibits a process by which the authors reflect upon their own assumed normativities, their preconceptions that have for them transformed certain sounds into "noise" or else into a "language." Certainly, this is much easier said than done. Instead of viewing Kurashige's piece as an accomplished ideal, I want to read it as an effort toward the difficult but important task of deimperializing (Asian) American studies, as we strive toward that end albeit in our imperfect ways.

Trans-Pacific War Memories and Asian American Studies across Asia

To close, I return to the "Asian American Studies in Asia" workshop in Taipei with which I began this chapter, as I intend to reexamine the meanings of Asian American studies from that location and perspective. In particular, I would like to discuss the special session entitled "Transpacific War Memories," in which a Chinese American poet from Hawaiʻi, Wing Tek Lum, read his poems on the Nanjing Massacre and a Japanese American critic, Gayle Sato, offered a commentary. What especially struck me was a question posed by one of the participants, the very lively discussion that followed, and the heterogeneity of voices that constituted responses from both U.S.-based and Asia-based scholars from Taiwan, South Korea, China, the Philippines, India, and Japan.[7]

At the outset of the question and answer period, Hsinya Huang, a scholar from Taiwan, posed a question in the form of an anecdote from her family history. With their parents having fled from mainland China after 1949, Huang and her husband were both born in Taiwan with "no direct geographical connections" (10/16) with the mainland. Her husband, however, "formed a kind of sentiment against Japan because of this Nanjing Massacre" (10/16), triggered by narratives of atrocities that "we read about the stories again and again in all historical books, again and again read the representations in the stories, in the poems" (10/16). As a consequence, her husband forbade Huang and her son to travel to Japan. Although Huang left the interpretation of her story/question to the audience, I understood it to address the responsibilities of artists, scholars, and readers to negotiate the need to remember and record atrocities with the importance of preventing such acts of memorialization from becoming an occasion to reproduce animosities toward a homogenized enemy/nation/other. I felt her story invited an important question for us to consider: how to pass on war memories without turning them into a new source of conflict.

Responses from the audience were various. One critic articulated the need to be conscious of "institutional mediation of narratives" (10/16) or, as another put it, the relationship between "locutions and locations: who gets to speak" (13/16) because of the physical, historical, and discursive spaces one occupies. Some insisted on the importance "to bear witness" (12/16) and to remember the atrocities as "important legacies of war" (14/16); others were more critical of such "ethical distance that a witness, testimonials" have to the extent that they can obscure the power one obtains "by becoming a subject of, speaking in proxy for the dead" (16/16). Some praised and endorsed the efforts; others were more skeptical. While one critic believed the poems were "perpetuating hate" (12/16), another felt what was on the table "is neither hate nor history" but "art and beauty: how words challenge the possibility of human extremities, what people are capable of in moments of great stress" (15/16). The two critics, despite their differing interpretations of the poems, however, questioned the one-sidedness of the picture: the "silence" of voices from Japan, as one South Korean scholar put it, in what she thought should be "a two-way conversation" (15/16).

The complex issues of one's positionality, "the locations and locutions," also induced responses from U.S.-based scholars. A Chinese American participant whose mother's family, like the mother of the poet Wing Tek Lum, had escaped from war-torn Nanjing, which was being occupied by Japan, interpreted the "refusal or inability to go to Japan" in terms of "justice," as what provokes the "question of aggressor and victim" (11/16). Another U.S.-based scholar, though of Japanese descent, stressed the need for Asian Americans to speak *also* as "Americans," especially at a time when the United States, which had "committed atrocities and were never charged for war crimes," is fighting its wars and "killing all these people." Citing "younger generation" (Asian) Americans who question the U.S. military aggressions at "global justice conferences" that seek reparations from Japan, she articulated the need for Asian Americanists to also respond to their questioning (16/16). Another Japanese American critic from Hawai'i, known for her pioneering critique of Japanese American settler colonialism, underscored the significance of "Honolulu" as the poems' "locution/location." Unlike Taiwan, where the massacre constituted a dominant national historical narrative, especially during the Guomindang era, the Japanese American ascendancy in Hawai'i, she explained, has eclipsed the histories of Japanese colonialism and military aggressions. She emphasized the contribution Lum's poems make in "that critical context" (14/16).

Significantly, a Taiwanese scholar whose parents had also moved from the mainland problematized the nationalist orientation by referring to "the 2.28 massacre," which he said "happened right here" (15/16). His statement caused me to reflect on the remark a Japanese participant made when she spoke of the atomic bombings without alluding to the Taiwanese, Korean, and Chinese *hibakusha* and the Japanese government's failure to compensate them for over half a century (15/16).[8] Such referencing, I thought, was crucial to prevent the enunciation of war memories from falling into competing claims of victimization.

I mention those exchanges for several reasons. What struck me immediately was the heterogeneity of voices that could not simply be explained by national affiliations. Equally important, the session challenged my preconception about the relationship between Japanese war crimes and Asian American studies, and the assumed commonalities in "our" perceptions toward the U.S.-based Asian American studies. Hence, prior to the session, I was much more critical of the tendency in Asian American studies to invest their energy in, to borrow one participant's words, "interethnic conflicts in Asian countries" (14/16) rather than the role that Asian Americans have played in various U.S. wars. I had thought that they were like some Japanese who condemn the Chinese government's suppression of human rights in Tibet or Xinjiang without denouncing atrocities committed by Japan, such as the Nanjing Massacre. In addition, it was my unconscious belief that matters relating to Japanese war crimes should be an *Asian* rather than an Asian American studies issue.

The session, however, gave me an important realization that Asian American studies constitutes a significant medium for U.S.-based and Asia-based scholars to engage in the histories of atrocities in Asia. Not only are practitioners such as Hsinya Huang direct descendants of those affected by Japanese war crimes; others, like Wing Tek Lum and many Chinese, Korean, Filipino/a, and other Asians, became "Asian American" as a direct consequence of Japan's invasion of their homeland as well. Hence, as Kandace Chuh and Lisa Yoneyama have pointed out, Japanese colonialism, military aggression, and their consequences constitute a significant segment of Asian American history (Chuh 2003b; Yoneyama 2003).

To that extent, the special session, in which Asian American studies in Asia engaged with literary representations of Japanese war crimes by a Chinese American poet, can serve as an important counterpart, if not a response, to the aforementioned *JAAS* 2003 special issue, which took up the theme of Japanese imperialism and military violence. However, unlike the special issue, which primarily addressed the challenges for U.S.-based scholars, the session in Taipei expanded the horizon to include the voices of Asia-based Asian Americanists, many of whom are descendants of people directly affected by Japanese colonial and military aggressions. The session invites a question of how the U.S.-based Asian Americanists' critique of the two empires may incite different responses in "Asia," even though I do not mean to homogenize those responses. In my limited experience of teaching the *JAAS* special issue in Japan, I noted Kang's article has drawn appreciation from Japanese students and mixed responses from South Korean students. While this imparts uniqueness to Asian American studies in Asia regarding its relationship with Japanese war crimes, the Taipei session can construct an important dialogue with the U.S.-based *JAAS* special issue and other like endeavors in examining the histories of violence within Asia.

The Taipei session also invites a question about the nature of intervention, which Asian American studies can make, especially in relation to Asian studies. As Daqing Yang points out, numerous works have been produced by Chinese *and* Japanese historians on the Nanjing Massacre, wherein scholars have formed cross-national dialogue. And in that dialogue, according to Yang, some Chinese historians' works have even come to reflect the interpretations of their Japanese counterparts (Yang 2006, 208). What, then, would it mean to address Japanese imperialism and war atrocities in Asian *American* studies rather than *Asian* studies? What new perspectives are enabled by the triangulation of war memories in Asia via Asian American studies in and across Asia and the Pacific? What is the role of literary studies?

These questions seem important when most of the practitioners of Asian American studies, unlike those of Asian studies, do not understand Asian languages, and when the practitioners are Asia-based Asian scholars, they often do not have linguistic skills in Asian languages that are not their own. (This is especially true in literary studies.) That linguistic shortcoming often prevents Asian Americanists from engaging in primary research in Asian languages in question or from learning about the resistant work undertaken in Asia, such as the critiques of Japanese imperialism in Japan, Korean nationalism in South Korea, or even settler colonialism in Taiwan, though such self-critiques are prevalent in Asian studies in Asia. While I include myself in this problem insofar as I work on Korean American literary representations without knowledge of the Korean language, Asian American (literary) critics certainly must find ways to compensate for our shortcomings by overcoming our monolingualism and by collaborating with scholars trained in different disciplines, languages, and national frameworks. We can thereby put our scholarships in perspective.

At the same time, as Chih-ming Wang stated, the special session was intended to create dialogue, to rearticulate "war memories in inter-Asian contexts" (13/16), and I thought it was important that the dialogue took place in English. Certainly, this is not to deny the possibility of using other languages. Yet, the use of English, despite its obvious problem of linguistic imperialism, helps open up the conversation to variously located Asian *Americanists,* where we can learn from one another's regionally based and informed researches. Kun Jong Lee, for instance, tells us that Korean American narratives on military "camptowns and sex workers" in South Korea are "not so 'unique' as many non-Korean scholars seem to presume," since such narratives have been widely published in South Korea since the 1940s. Lee also discusses some South Korea–based Asian Americanists' works that compare Korean and Korean American narratives on "military camptowns" (Lee 2012, 282).

Lee's argument makes me venture further to suggest that part of the responsibility of Asian Americanists in Asia is to introduce in English, and possibly in some other "common languages," the kind of "resistant researches" done in Asian languages. Yujin Yaguchi's critique of Japanese state and tourist imperialism in Hawai'i, available in Japanese, for instance, provides a useful counterpart to the previously mentioned critique of Japanese American settler colonialism by Fujikane and Okamura (Yaguchi 2011).

In my engagement with Korean/American literary representations of Japanese military sexual slavery *within* the context of Japan, I find authors like Chang-rae Lee and Nora Okja Keller help complicate the dominant Japanese perceptions of Korean/American responses to the issue, which are often conveyed in the homogenized, ethnonationalized discourses. Some Japanese claim that Korean/Americans exploit U.S. privileges and power to seek reparations (rightfully, in my opinion) from Japan, but in so doing they rarely criticize U.S. or Korean military violence. Reminiscent of the ways in which the U.S. conservative media depicted Japanese perceptions of the Asia-Pacific wars during the 1995 Smithsonian Enola Gay controversy, Korean/Americans in the right-wing Japanese discourses at present are largely portrayed as either being self-indulgent in their victimization, disregardful of their own aggressions, *or else* their self-critiques are appropriated to prove the Korean guilt and in turn the Japanese innocence. We recall that it is this twisted logic that Lisa Yoneyama addressed with her monumental term "the transnational warps" (Yoneyama 2001).

Lee and Keller draw the linkage between Japanese and U.S. imperialisms and military violence, thereby interrogating the Orientalized premise of Japanese exceptionalism and war crimes. Equally important, their works challenge the Japanese right-wingers' efforts to mutually exonerate the crimes by universalizing them, as Lee and Keller expose the brutality of sexual slavery instituted by the Japanese military empire. It becomes imperative then that Asian American studies transform the "transnational warps" into a proper circuit of transnational dialogue by bringing together the various critiques, so that the juxtaposition of disparate military violence will help us work toward achieving reparational justice rather than mutual exoneration. Worth recalling is that the exhibit originally planned by the Smithsonian National Air and Space Museum intended to juxtapose the brutality of Japanese military aggressions with the carnage caused by the bombings. As Lisa Yoneyama has eloquently argued, the 1995 documentary *In the Name of the Emperor,* directed by Christine Choy and Nancy Tong, condemns the atrocity of the Nanjing Massacre committed by the Japanese military; it also underscores the activism and critical voices in Japan that interrogate the Japanese government's suppression of this violent history and the complicity of the U.S. state (Yoneyama 2001).

Important then is that the writings of Lee and Keller resonate with the voices of critique in Asia, where intellectuals, activists, and the general public denounce the atrocities committed by their own governments as well as their adversaries. This includes the efforts in South Korea to problematize the exclusively nationalist framework in which Japanese military sexual slavery has been made into an issue. (By this, I do not mean to deny the important contributions Korean nationalism played in resisting Japanese colonial domination.) A particularly notable example occurred recently when a survivor of the Japanese military sexual slavery, Bok-dong Kim, called for an apology by the South Korean government for its sexual aggressions in Viet Nam.[9] It is crucial, I believe, that Asian Americanists link up Kim's activism to the activism of others in order to prevent possible appropriations: the women's peace group in Okinawa, for instance, who connect the U.S. military rapes to the rapes of women drafted for Japanese military sexual slavery. In this way, practicing Asian American studies across Asia and the Pacific can disrupt the "transnational warps" and create an alternative space where we can work toward reparational justice.

Notes

1 Asian American Studies in Asia workshop, Academia Sinica, Taipei, June 4–5, 2010; Nikkei Studies and Beyond conference, Kyoto University Tokyo office, July 27, 2012. See Wang (2012) for selected articles from the workshop.

2 More recent efforts of trans-Pacific and inter-Asia Asian American studies include the four-day Summer Institute in Asian American Studies, Asian American Studies through Asia: Fields, Formations, Futures, in Taipei in August 2013; the Gwangju Conference on Current Asian American Studies in East Asia, in South Korea in September 2013; and a roundtable at the

Association of Asian American Studies annual conference in San Francisco, The State(s) of Asian American Studies: Prospects in East Asia, April 2014.
3 Mitsuye Yamada's poems situate the mainland Japanese Americans in the desert, thereby constructing them as both "internees" and "settlers." See Nakamura (2009).
4 While Burma appears to be the exception where Cheung learns from the local struggles, the Burmese example confirms rather than challenges Cheung's idea of how "struggles" should take place, an idea she brought from the United States.
5 As I have discussed elsewhere, the anthology *Perilous Memories: The Asia-Pacific War(s)*, edited by T. Fujitani, Geoffrey White, and Lisa Yoneyama, elucidates a form of interactions that decenters U.S. minority norms. The anthology's narratives juxtapose the histories of U.S. racial minorities with the very heterogeneous racial and anticolonial struggles elsewhere, while mirroring and "kaleidoscoping" those experiences back to the decentralized U.S. perceptions and norms. See Nakamura (2012a).
6 See *Atom Bombs and Korean People,* vols. 1–7 (1986–2014); Park (1986); Ichiba (2000); Hirano (2009); for the English-language accounts, Yoneyama (1999), Toyonaga (2001), among others. See Nakamura (2014) for the analysis of *Obasan* in relation to non-Japanese bomb victims.
7 The session was moderated by Te-hsing Shan on June 4, 2010. The entire session ("Special Session Part 1/16–16/16") can be viewed online: http://www.youtube.com/user/ieasgovcc#p/u/30/lqtXHC26K8g. All citations are taken from this source and will be parenthetically indicated by the number of the video sequence. See also Lum (2013) for the poems.
8 The revised Hibakusha Assistance Law of 2008 allows survivors to apply for certificates from overseas, yet discrepancies still remain between Japanese survivors residing in Japan and those overseas. See Hirano (2009).
9 *Asahi Shimbun Digital,* March 8, 2014. Accessed July 30, 2014. http://www.asahi.com/english/articles/TKY201403080005.html. Kim Dae-jun apologized for South Korean military aggressions in Viet Nam in 2001 and Yohei Koho for the Japanese military sexual slavery in 1993.

References

Brada-Williams, Noelle, and Karen Chow. 2004. *Crossing the Oceans: Reconfiguring American Literary Studies in the Pacific Rim.* Hong Kong: Hong Kong University Press.

Cheung, King-kok. 2004. "Pedagogies of Resonance: Teaching African American and Asian American Literature and Culture in Asia." In *Crossing the Oceans: Reconfiguring American Literary Studies in the Pacific Rim,* edited by Noelle Brada-Williams and Karen Chow, 13–28. Hong Kong: Hong Kong University Press.

Choy, Christine, and Nancy Tong, dir. 1995. *In the Name of the Emperor.* 50 min. https://www.youtube.com/watch?v=OFGu7K_9cuU.

Chuh, Kandice. 2001. "Imaginary Borders." In *Orientations: Mapping Studies in the Asian Diaspora,* edited by Kandice Chuh and Karen Shimakawa, 275–295. Durham, NC: Duke University Press.

———. 2003a. *Imagine Otherwise: On Asian Americanist Critique.* Durham, NC: Duke University Press.

———, ed. 2003b. "On Korean Comfort Women." Special issue, *Journal of Asian American Studies* 6 (1).

Fujikane, Candace, and Jonathan Y. Okamura, eds. 2000. "Whose Vision? Asian Settler Colonialism in Hawai'i." Special issue, *Amerasia Journal* 26 (2).

Fujikura, Naoko 藤倉なおこ. 2009. バンクーバー高齢者施設に暮らす日系カナダ人一世 (Canadian Isseis Living in "Nikkei Home" in Vancouver). Unpublished paper presented at AALA meeting, Kyoto, January 10.

Fujitani, Takashi. 2011. *Race for Empire: Koreans as Japanese and Japanese as Americans during World War II.* Berkeley: University of California Press.

Fujitani, T., Geoffrey M. White, and Lisa Yoneyama, eds. 2001. *Perilous Memories: The Asia-Pacific War(s).* Durham, NC: Duke University Press.

Hirano, Nobuto, ed. 平野伸人. 2009. 海の向こうの被爆者たち――在外被爆者問題の理解のために (Understanding the Overseas Hibakusha). Tokyo: Hachigatsu Shokan.

Ichiba Junko 市場淳子. 2000. ヒロシマを持ちかえった人々――「韓国の広島」はなぜ生ま れたか (People Who Brought Back Hiroshima). Tokyo: Gaifusha.

Ikeuchi, Yasuko, and Shigehiko Nishi, eds. 池内靖子・西 成彦. 2006. 異郷の身体 (The Body in a Strange Land). Kyoto: Jimbun Shoin.

Ishihara, Masahide, Ikue Kina, and Shin Yamashiro, eds. 石原昌英・喜納育江・山城新編. 2010. 沖縄・ハワイーコンタクトゾーンとしての島嶼 (Okinawa, Hawai'i: Islands as a Contact Zone). Tokyo: Sairyusha.

Kang, Laura Hyun Yi. 2002. *Compositional Subjects: Enfiguring Asian/American Women.* Durham, NC: Duke University Press.

———. 2003. "Conjuring 'Comfort Women': Mediated Affiliations and Disciplined Subjects in Korean/American Transnationality." *Journal of Asian American Studies* 6 (1): 25–55.

Kido, Yoshiyuki 貴堂嘉之. 2002. アメリカ移民史研究の現在 (Historiography of American Immigration History). *Rekishi Hyoron* 625: 17–30.

Kogawa, Joy. 1984. "Is There a Just Cause?" *Canadian Forum* (1984): 20–24.

Kurashige, Lon. 2013. "Asian American History across the Pacific." In *Nikkei Studies and Beyond: Dialogue Between Scholars in Japan and the U.S.,* edited by Yasuko Takezawa, 12–19. Kyoto: Institute for Research in Humanities, Kyoto University.

Lee, Kun Jong. 2012. "An Overview of Korean/Asian American Literary Studies in Korea, 1964–2009." *Inter-Asia Cultural Studies* 13 (2): 275–285.

Lum, Wing Tek. 2013. *The Nanjing Massacre: Poems.* Honolulu: Banboo Ridge Press.

Nagasaki Zainichi Chosenjin no Jinkenwo Mamoru Kai, ed. 長崎在日朝鮮人の人権を守る会. 1986–2014. 原爆と朝鮮人 第1集〜7集 (Atom Bombs and Korean People, vols. 1–7). Nagasaki: Zainichi Chosenjin no Jinkenwo Mamoru Kai.

Nakamura, Rika 中村理香. 2005. 女・家族・国家／ディアスポラ——ノーラ・オッジャ・ケラーの『従軍慰安婦』にみる「二つの帝国」と脱出記の攪乱 (Narrating Two Empires, Re-narrating Escape/Rescue Narratives in Nora Okja Keller's *Comfort Woman*). In *Border-crossings, Marginalities, Diasporas in Three American Literatures,* edited by Noboru Matsumoto et al., 316–331. Tokyo: Nan'undo.

———. 2009. "Attending the Languages of the Other: Recuperating Asia, Abject, Other in Asian North American Literature." PhD diss., Rutgers University.

———. 2012a. "What Asian American Studies Can Learn from Asia?: Towards a Project of Comparative Minority Studies." *Inter-Asia Cultural Studies* 13 (2): 251–266.

———. 2012b. "Working on 'Race' as an Ethnoracial *Majority* of Color." Unpublished paper presented at the international symposium Dismantling the Race Myth, Kyoto, December 15.

———. 2014. "Addressing Japanese Imperialism via Asian American/Canadian Literature in Japan." Unpublished paper presented at the annual meeting of the Association of Asian American Studies, San Francisco, April 19.

Nakano, Satoshi 中野聡. 2007. 歴史経験としてのアメリカ帝国——米比関係史の群像 (The American Empire as Lived Experience: Scenes from the History of Philippine-U.S. Relations). Tokyo: Iwanami Shoten.

———. 2012. 東南アジア占領と日本人——帝国・日本の解体 (Southeast Asia and the Japanese Occupiers during World War II: The Dismantlement of an Empire). Tokyo: Iwanami Shoten.

Nguyen, Viet Thanh. 2012. "Refugee Memories and Asian American Critique." *Positions: Asia Critique* 20 (3): 911–942.

Park, Hyungji. 2010. "Imagined Asias, Imagined Americas: Reading Asian American Literature across the Pacific." Unpublished paper presented at the Asian American Studies in Asia workshop, Taiwan, June 6.

Park, Soon-nam 朴壽南, dir. 1986. もうひとつのヒロシマ (Another Hiroshima). Chigasaki: Airang no Uta Seisakuiinkai. DVD.

Son, Young-Ok, and Yong Kim, eds. 宋連玉・金栄. 2010. 軍隊と性暴力——朝鮮半島の20世紀 (Military and Sexual Violence: Korean Peninsula in the Twentieth Century). Tokyo: Gendaishi Shuppankai.

Takezawa, Yasuko, ed. 竹沢泰子. 2005. 人種概念の普遍性を問う―西洋的パラダイムを超えて (Is Race a Universal Idea?: Transcending the Western Paradigm). Kyoto: Jimbun Shoin.

———. 2009. 人種の表象と社会的リアリティ (Racial Representation and Social Reality of Race). Tokyo: Iwanami Shoten.

———. 2011. *Racial Representations in Asia*. Kyoto: Kyoto University Press.

Toyonaga, Keisaburo 豊永恵三郎. 2001. "Colonialism and Atom Bombs: About Survivors of Hiroshima Living in Korea." Translated by Eric Cazdyn and Lisa Yoneyama. In *Perilous Memories: The Asia-Pacific War(s)*, edited by T. Fujitani, Geoffrey M. White, and Lisa Yoneyama, 378–394. Durham, NC: Duke University Press.

Wang, Chih-ming, ed. 王智明. 2012. "Asian American Studies in Asia." Special issue, *Inter-Asia Cultural Studies* 13 (2).

Wong, Sau-ling C. 1993. *Reading Asian American Literature: From Necessity to Extravagance*. Princeton, NJ: Princeton University Press.

———. 2004. "When Asian American Literature Leaves 'Home': On Internationalizing Asian American Literary Studies." In *Crossing the Oceans: Reconfiguring American Literary Studies in the Pacific Rim*, edited by Noelle Brada-Williams and Karen Chow, 29–40. Hong Kong: Hong Kong University Press.

———. 2005. "Maxine Hong Kingston in a Global Frame: Reception, Institutional Mediation, and 'World Literature.'" *AALA Journal* 11: 7–41.

Yaguchi, Yujin 矢口祐人. 2011. 憧れのハワイ―日本人のハワイ観 (Longings for Hawai'i: Japanese Views of Hawai'i). Tokyo: Chuo Koron Shinsha.

Yang, Daqing 楊大慶. 2006. 南京残虐事件―原因論の考察 (Atrocities in Nanjing: Searching for Explanations), translated by Yoko Ihara. In *Iwanami Lectures on Asia Pacific Wars*, vol. 5, edited by Aiko Kurasawa et al., 181–214. Tokyo: Iwanami Shoten.

Yoneyama, Lisa 米山リサ. 1999. *Hiroshima Traces: Time, Space, and the Dialectics of Memory*. Berkeley: University of California Press.

———. 2001. "For Transformative Knowledge and Postnationalist Public Spheres: The Smithsonian Enola Gay Controversy." In *Perilous Memories: The Asia-Pacific War(s)*, edited by T. Fujitani, Geoffrey M. White, and Lisa Yoneyama, 323–346. Durham, NC: Duke University Press.

———. 2003. "Traveling Memories, Contagious Justice: Americanization of Japanese War Crimes at the End of the Post-Cold War." *Journal of Asian American Studies* 6 (1): 57–93.

———. 2014. "Enabling Aporia of Transnational Critique." Unpublished talk at the annual meeting of the Association of Asian American Studies, San Francisco, April 19.

PART VII

PEDAGOGIES

CHAPTER 13

Teaching Asian American Studies in Japan
Challenges and Possibilities

Masumi Izumi

Introduction

In one of my American studies classes in spring 2012, a student surprised me by declaring that she did not care if a policy was just or unjust, fair or unfair, "because that's the way things are in Japan." We were comparing immigration policies in Japan and the United States. The students learned that anyone born in a U.S. territory acquires U.S. citizenship, whereas Japanese citizenship is only granted to people who have at least one parent with Japanese citizenship, except in the case of a special permanent resident alien.[1] This means that if a person is born to Japanese parents in the United States, she can obtain U.S. citizenship, but if a person is born to American parents in Japan, she will not. After teaching students this information, I asked them, "Do you think this is fair?" and I received the above answer. The student did not try to justify Japan's immigration policy by arguing, for example, that immigrants would take jobs away from the Japanese, or that the crime rate would go up in our supposedly safe country. She just said, "Fair or unfair, just or unjust, that's the way things are." Other students appeared to be less sure, but since that student could speak English more fluently than any of her classmates, no one disagreed.

My student's flat dismissal of such notions as "fairness" and "justice" took me by surprise. Trained in the disciplines of American studies and Asian American studies, I have studied in detail how contested issues such as immigration, affirmative action, racial profiling, and even wartime or emergency detention based on race are debated in the United States vis-à-vis the notion of American "justice" or "fairness." In my PhD dissertation, I analyzed how the Supreme Court justified the removal and exclusion of Japanese Americans from the West Coast as a wartime measure, and how both liberal and conservative members of Congress justified the Emergency Detention Act (Title II of the Internal Security Act of 1950) by arguing that the act was less repressive and more just compared to the mass incarceration of Japanese Americans during World War II (Izumi 2004, 2009). In my classes, I teach about the *Dred Scott* and the *Plessy v. Ferguson* cases, explaining how the U.S. Supreme Court upheld slavery through the notion of property rights and sanctioned Jim Crow laws by adopting the infamous logic of "separate but equal." Also, in November 2012, I asked my students to watch the U.S. presidential debates to see how the two candidates, although advocating completely opposite policies, would assert that their policies were more in accordance with the American principles of democracy and the American way of life. In short, I have spent my academic career focusing on and teaching how American political debates over fiercely contested issues have been conducted based on the American principles of democracy and sense of justice and fairness. Minorities, including Asian Americans, also have made their demands throughout U.S. history claiming those discourses.

Listening to my student's dismissal of the notion of "fairness," I started to question my assumptions and wondered whether I had been naïvely importing into Japan an "American sense of justice" that I had internalized through my years of academic training in American and Asian American studies. Are American notions of justice and fairness applicable to the Japanese society in which my students live? Is fairness and justice universal, or does it vary from one society to another? Would scrutinizing in Japan the American sense of fairness and other issues relating to social justice illuminate some of the premises that American and Asian American studies take for granted? How does the teaching of Asian American studies in a different location complicate the notions and issues that the discipline has held to be relevant and important?

In this chapter, I focus on the Japanese university classrooms in which I teach as sites of intervention and explore some ways in which Asian American studies and related topics can be used not only to deconstruct some hegemonic social discourses on race, culture, ethnicity, and justice in Japan that my students might share but, at the same time, complicate some ideas held in Asian American studies by shifting the gaze from inside the United States to the outside. The majority of my students are Japanese who may or may not have experience living abroad; I also have a very small number of international and ethnic minority students. While I am not claiming that they are a typical sample of students in Japan as a whole, I have no reason to believe that their living environment and ideas are any different from most other university students in Japan. I will try not to overgeneralize with regard to the ideas expressed by my students; nonetheless, I would like to share some observations of my students from both inside and outside the classroom and offer, from a vantage point in Japan, some pedagogical ideas for teaching Asian American and Japanese migration studies. I think that exchanging ideas like these can be a productive part of a dialogue between Japanese and American scholars and teachers of Asian American studies. In an attempt to make the learning process reciprocal, I discuss both how Asian American studies can help Japanese students and how studies in Japan on related topics can benefit American students and scholars.

Complicating the Notions of Race in Japan and the United States

In the aforementioned American studies class, we studied the general history of immigration in the United States. In that class and in other classes, I noticed the students were not necessarily conservative in their opinions concerning diversity.[2] For example, when I asked a class of approximately forty-five students to analyze recent American debates on "illegal" (undocumented) immigration, the overwhelming majority supported the Dream Act, arguing that those who had entered the United States as young children had fulfilled the conditions required for permanent residency despite their "illegal" immigrant status.[3] Many also opposed the militarization of the U.S.-Mexican border from a humanitarian viewpoint, although about 20 percent saw tough measures against "illegal" immigration as being necessary.

Students seemed reluctant, however, to support open immigration policies in Japan that would increase the ethnic and racial diversity of the population. They did not think Japan and the United States should have similar immigration policies because, as the same student quoted at the beginning of this chapter said, "America is a country of immigrants while Japan is a homogeneous country." Talking with my students, I noticed that despite their opposition to an open immigration policy for Japan, they did not support discriminatory or exclusionary policies against foreigners or ethnic minorities already living in Japan, nor were they ignorant of the existence of ethnic communities in Japan. After thinking carefully about their double standard regarding diversity and immigration policies for Japan and the United States, as well as their apparently contradictory statements that although Japan was a "homogeneous" country, ethnic minorities in Japan should enjoy equal rights as Japanese, I realized that they did not connect the issues of immigration, diversity, and race in the same way they are conventionally connected in the United States.

Listening to my students, I started to see that in their minds the idea of "America" presupposed open access to its land and economic opportunities to people of diverse races and backgrounds, but the idea of "Japan" did not bear such a burden. Regardless of whether they considered America or Japan as an anomaly, they all thought of the two countries as polar opposites, with "America" being a multicultural society and "Japan" being a culturally homogeneous island nation. In a Skype discussion we had with students from the University of Southern California, one of our students referred to the Japanese as having a *"shima guni konjō"* (island nation mentality) and stated that their limited interactions with foreigners accounted for their lack of English proficiency.[4]

Although I did not have enough time for additional discussions on diversity and immigration in that particular class, I was reminded of the need to de-essentialize the contrasting images of Japan and the United States regarding the issues of immigration, diversity, and race. To contextualize the popular image of Japan as an island nation and to illuminate the historical contingency of this image, I now open my lecture course on diversity and immigration history by showing the maps included in this chapter.

Showing these maps, I explain that between 1868 and 1945, a substantial number of people migrated from Japan to all around the Pacific region. While the experiences of emigrants varied and the different waves of migration occurred for different reasons (military, colonial, labor, commercial, and so forth) and took place under different circumstances (free, forced, and so forth), one constant is that the Japanese had plenty of interaction with people outside the four main islands of Japan from the late-nineteenth century until 1945 (H. Yoneyama and Kawahara 2007, 10). The third map indicates that the overwhelming majority of Japanese in Asia and the western half of the Pacific region returned to Japan within several years after the end of World War II. The total amounted to about 6.6 million, if one combines military and civilian returnees (Sakaguchi 2007, 253–254). This means that as many as 10 percent of ethnic Japanese who lived in postwar Japan had been abroad

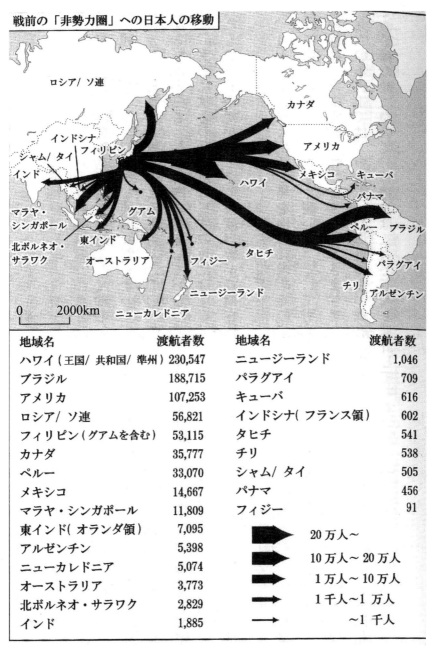

Map 13.1　Pre–WWII Emigration of Japanese to Areas outside Japan's Sphere of Influence
(H. Yoneyama and Kawahara, 9)

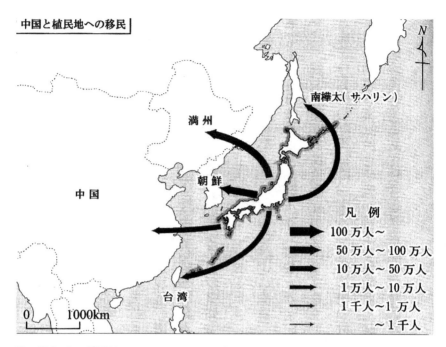

Map 13.2 Pre–WWII Emigration of Japanese to Areas within Japan's Sphere of Influence
(H. Yoneyama and Kawahara, 239)

for some time before or during World War II (Oguma 1995, 4).[5] By visually depicting Japanese overseas and return migration, I remind my students of their nation's colonial past and at the same time help them see that many Japanese had a pioneering spirit and courageously left their island nation to seek economic opportunities and better lives abroad.

Eiji Oguma has analyzed the historical shifts during the twentieth century of the hegemonic concepts in Japan regarding the "Japanese race." Between 1895 and 1945, Japan was an empire with overseas colonies, and as such needed racial discourses that somehow incorporated colonial subjects into the idea of the Japanese nation. After Japan's annexation of Korea, major scholars such as Kunitake Kume, Soho Tokutomi, and Shigenobu Okuma argued that the Korean and Japanese people shared a common ancestry (Oguma 1995, 92–103). Furthermore, the colonization of Manchuria was justified under the slogan of "*gozoku kyōwa*" (the harmony of the five races: Japanese, Korean, Chinese, Manchurians, and Mongolians) (Oguma 1995, 325–338).[6] After World War II, scholars dismissed the prewar impe-

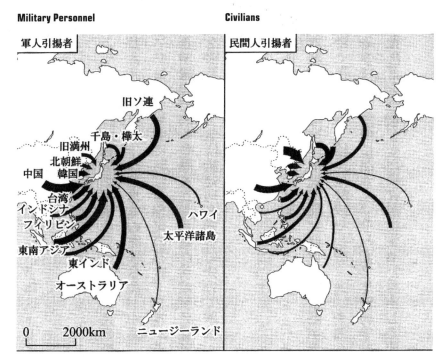

Map 13.3   Post–WWII Return Migration of Japanese to the Japanese Archipelago
(H. Yoneyama and Kawahara, 239)

rialist discourse surrounding the mixed-race origin of the Japanese nation and insisted that the Japanese were a distinct ethnic group that had occupied the Japanese archipelago since the Stone Age (Oguma 1995, 346–348). With the new constitution that defined the emperor as the "symbol of national unity," philosophers such as Tetsuro Watsuji claimed that the Japanese nation had always been "a cultural community that had one language, common customs, and shared history and value system" (quoted in Oguma 1995, 343). Scholars constructed the emperor as a national symbol of "cultural" integrity rather than an imperial figure with military and authoritarian power. In contrast to the prewar multiethnic empire, postwar Japan was imagined to be a democratic and peaceful nation consisting of only one ethnic group, the Japanese (Oguma 1995, 345). The large-scale return migration between 1945 and 1953 provided a useful discursive tool to Japanese opinion leaders who were trying to represent postwar Japan as a homogeneous nation. This representation was convenient in that it distanced ordinary

Japanese people from the militaristic imperialists and allowed them to dismiss the nation's expansionist period between 1895 and 1945 as a historical aberration. In the decades after World War II, the myth of Japanese homogeneity and denial of the nation's colonial past became deeply rooted among the Japanese.

Large-scale postwar return migration to Japan supported that historical amnesia not only in Japan but also in the Western world. The General Headquarters of the Allied Forces, headed by General Douglas MacArthur, ordered all Japanese in the Pacific region to return to the Japanese archipelago without considering the variety of circumstances surrounding people's migration and living situations.[7] In turn, about 56 percent of the 2.2 million Koreans who had lived in Japan as of August 1945 returned to Korea after the end of the war (Sakaguchi 2007, 254). The postwar reconstruction scheme for Asia, designed and enforced predominantly by the United States but also supported by Occupied Japan, was not designed to create a multiethnic postcolonial region in the western Pacific, but was based on the idea of restoring the "imagined communities" of Asian nation-states that had never existed in reality (Anderson 1991). Historically speaking, East and Southeast Asia had formed a large cultural sphere under imperial Chinese rule with a long and complex history of human migration. From the eighteenth century until World War II, when most of Asia was colonized by Western nations, human migration on an even larger scale occurred as a result of colonial transplantations of the labor force. The erasure of the memories of emigration by the Japanese to the Pacific region between the 1880s and 1945 was beneficial for both the Japanese nation and the West. By forgetting about Japanese aggression in Asia, the West could ignore its own colonial aggression and exploitation in the region (Fujitani 2011). Although anti-colonial wars continued for many decades in Asia after 1945, the Japanese who had returned to the Japanese archipelago were secluded from the disastrous battles that rampaged throughout the rest of Asia.[8]

Contextualizing Japanese racial discourses, on the one hand, can help students see the complexity of the notions of race in Japan and their contingent nature as sociohistorical constructs. Examining the Japanese concept of race, on the other hand, can complicate the notion of race in Asian American studies. In the United States, race has been discursively associated with people's skin color, even though the actual shade or pigmentation of a person's skin often had little to do with the category in which he or she was placed. Despite there being a considerable amount of scholarship on racial passing, the framing of race as an issue of "color" continues to lead people to primarily conceptualize it as something that can be seen from the outside. However, when one analyzes how Asian ethnic minorities or people of certain vocational lineages have been differentiated from the majority population in Japan, one can see that race as a human category does not necessarily require visible physical differences among the groups to create different social statuses or hierarchies based on racial discourses. For example, the anthropologist Yasuko Takezawa's anthology *Racial Representations in Asia* (2011) analyzes how race works in Asia, where biological or visible racial diversity does not seem to exist (Takezawa 2011). The volume includes papers that focus on how *zainichi* (ethnic/resident Koreans in Japan) and *buraku* (undercast) people have been racialized in Japan and elucidate the ways in which racial discourses differentiate between and exclude "invisible races" (Kurokawa 2011; S. Y. Lee 2011). Works by Japanese and Asian scholars like these can offer more complicated views of the interracial as well as intraracial dynamics from which structural inequalities emerge in different societies.

Furthermore, another one of Takezawa's provocative anthologies shows how racial or pseudo-racial discourses were constructed in Japan, India, China, and Africa in the modern era and questions the universality of the notion of race. In this anthology, Takezawa argues that the concept of race has three aspects: "race," "Race," and "RR" (Takezawa 2005, 28). The first refers to a social group's inherited political, economic, and social differences, which are created and maintained by institutions through hierarchies and exclusion; "Race" refers to the mapping and constructed categorizations of humans that are circulated as scientific notions; and "RR" stands for "race as resistance," an active notion utilized by socially disadvantaged groups in their activism and solidarity building. In this way, Takezawa differentiates the concept of race by its functions in a given society and expands its definition to include meanings beyond people's physical features such as skin color. By presenting different ways that race or race-like categories function in various regions in the world, her anthology challenges the conventional Western concept of race.

An expansion of the largely domestic focus of ethnic studies in the United States to include international perspectives is needed to illuminate the complex racial identities of non-white populations in a global context. Some works by Japanese scholars are helpful in widening perspectives on race. For example, Fumiko Sakashita has analyzed representations of African Americans in various newspapers and books in Japan before World War

II. The Japanese media imported prejudiced Western views of Africans and African Americans as being primitive and barbaric, while some liberal or leftist media outlets expressed sympathy toward the struggles of African Americans around civil rights issues. Their empathy toward racial minorities in the United States was connected to their own identities as members of a non-white country trying to be recognized as a first-class nation in a world that was still controlled by the hegemonic principle of white supremacy (Sakashita 2013, 207). Also, Hiromi and Tetsushi Furukawa have documented the emergence of coalitions between Okinawans and African American GIs living on American military bases in Okinawa in the context of the anti–Vietnam War and civil rights movements, despite the fact that the positions of local Okinawans and African American soldiers vis-à-vis the American military presence were completely opposite (Furukawa and Furukawa 2004). Furthermore, Yukari Takai has looked at the historically ambivalent relationships between Japanese and African Americans, finding that the former sometimes argued that they were better suited for American civilization than African Americans and the latter claimed that as U.S. citizens they were more entitled to jobs and privileges than immigrants from Asia (Takai 2006). Scott Kurashige, a Japanese American historian, has explored examples of everyday interactions and political alliances between Asian and African Americans (Kurashige 2008). Bringing together works by Japanese scholars and U.S. scholars like these can elucidate the complex positions developed and negotiated by Japanese in Japan and Japanese immigrants in the United States within the racial hierarchies both in their respective countries and across the globe.

Placing "Migration" at the Center of Analysis

Considering Japanese migration alongside colonialism and other issues can also provide us with ways of understanding the global context of human migration that do not get caught up in Japan's "national history debate" concerning Japanese colonialism while avoiding the simplistic views of Japanese migrants as either "victimizers" of other Asian peoples or "victims" of racial discrimination by whites. Because history education is highly politicized in Japan, students might refuse to listen to certain kinds of historical voices while privileging others if they are forced to take on certain positions when learning about the past. Some Japanese students are tired of so-called *jigyaku shikan* (self-deprecating national history), which allegedly overemphasizes Japan's colonial aggression and atrocities that were inflicted on Asia.[9] As victimizers' descendants, Japanese students carry historical burdens similar to those of white students in the United States and German students in Europe.

Although "*jigyaku shikan*" is right-wing political propaganda, given the growing conservatism expressed particularly through the Internet presumably by young people in today's Japan and the claim's educational and pedagogical effects, the idea cannot be taken lightly. At the same time, as Rika Nakamura has pointed out, Japanese scholars studying prewar Japanese migration to regions outside the country's sphere of influence tend to focus "*solely*" on foreign race issues without making a domestic linkage," and this could lead to its "appropriation by the dominant nationalist discourse, which can displace its domestic oppressions on to the other" (Nakamura 2012, 254). Through conversation and collaborations with Asian American studies in the United States, Japanese migration studies in Japan and Japan-based Asian and Japanese studies might be able to develop what Nakamura calls "comparative minority studies," which can "create channels through which we can link our disparate injuries and damages while turning them into possibilities for resistance" (264).

In postwar Japanese academia, Japanese who migrated to Japan's colonies overseas have been studied by scholars of Asian history in the field of colonial studies; the cultural and social adaptation of Japanese migrants to areas outside the Japanese colonies and the ethnicization of their descendants have been studied in the field of ethnic studies imported from the United States; and the factors for emigration have been studied by Japanese geographers. Those three academic fields had little contact with one another until the 1990s (H. Yoneyama 2007, 12–13). Integrating them requires the creation of a theoretical framework centered around "migration," which can help Japanese students deconstruct the myth of Japanese homogeneity and exceptionalism.

Through Asian American studies, students in Japan can see that the challenges Japanese migrants faced in North and South America such as cultural repudiation, structural racism, and even violence were common experiences among Asian immigrants. They can also learn that multiracial immigrant nations such as the United States are not necessarily tolerant of diversity; rather, that racial formation has been shaped by histories of struggles for equality as well as resistance to such changes. At the same time, they can learn that Japan had to cope with the reality of multiethnic empire building, and that the myth of Japan's homogeneity itself was a postwar construction that erased the nation's colonial past.

When we put migration at the center of our theoretical framework, we can begin to ask different sets of questions from those asked in colonial history or ethnic studies. What economic, political, and social factors induced migration from a particular location? Who brokered migration? Why did one village send immigrants to Hawai'i and a neighboring village send immigrants to New Caledonia, or Korea, for example? How did the emigrants to different regions affect their home village? How did migrants work and interact with people in their new homes? How did World War II affect migrants' lives? What happened to their property during and after the war? How did people live after returning to Japan?

Juxtaposing a variety of migratory patterns such as commercial, colonial, and labor migration, we can compare at macro, mezzo, and micro levels the experiences of Japanese migrants in the Asia-Pacific region who worked in many different locations—as plantation workers in Hawai'i, fishermen and cannery workers in Canada, nickel miners in New Caledonia, merchants in the Philippines, coffee planters in Brazil, company and store owners in Korea, and farmers in Manchuria and California. The positions these migrants took in their new communities varied, depending on the macro-scale relationships between Japan and the place to which they migrated as well as the social interactions they had with people of other ethnic backgrounds. Gender and class diversity among the people who migrated to the same area resulted in their different experiences as well. Seeing those different patterns of migration among the Japanese emigrants and theorizing the diverse interactions they had with the people of other ethnic backgrounds can give the students a better understanding of today's human migration in a globalized world, the complicated relationships between Japan and other Asian countries, and human diversity within Japan.

Additionally, the new perspectives emerging in Japanese migration studies resulting from the integration of scholarship on different emigration and return migration patterns can help those involved in Asian American studies in America to see the history of Asian Americans from a transnational point of view. By contrast, U.S.-centered Asian American studies has tended to see Asian migration as a one-way trip from Asia to the United States. In this view, once a "migrant" community discursively transforms into an "ethnic" community, "migration" becomes only a legacy from the past (Izumi 2010a). However, recent studies employing transnational perspectives, such as those by Brian Hayashi and Eiichiro Azuma, have found that substantial return migration occurred in Japanese American communities. If we include Kibei-Nisei, we can even say that Japanese Americans were made of three major groups: those who lived in America for some length of time and returned to Japan permanently, those who migrated in multiple directions (e.g., Kibei), and those who stayed in America permanently (B. Hayashi 1995; Azuma 2005). The first group was reintegrated into the Japanese nation-state, and like returnees from other areas in the Asia-Pacific region, they disappeared from the historiography of Japanese overseas migration. The second group was divided and reintegrated into two different nations depending on which side of the Pacific they ended up at the end of World War II. This group has probably been the most marginalized in both countries; their experiences have only recently become objects of academic research. The third group is composed of the mainstream Japanese American community. Their typical experiences became the hegemonic representation of Japanese Americans. By putting the stories of those who did not stay in the United States into the narrative of Asian American studies, we can avoid privileging the experiences of Nikkei and getting caught up in the "tyranny of the nation," and instead look at the experiences of the overseas Japanese from a Pacific-wide perspective.[10] Such a collaboration between Japanese and Asian American scholars will help both Japanese and American students overcome their respective national exceptionalisms.

Race in Cultural Discourses versus Race in Structural Discourses

Despite the existence of social critiques in Japan that insist young people generally have little interest in global issues, particularly in recent years, the experiences of Japanese Americans have gathered popular attention thanks to a number of non-scholarly works.[11] Almost without exception, those works explain the behavior of Japanese Americans in cultural terms, with notions such as *"Yamato damashii"* (spirit of the Yamato people) or *"Nihonjin-rashisa"* (Japaneseness), which implies *"gaman"* (endurance), *"nintai"* (patience), *"kinben"* (diligence), *"shōjiki"* (honesty), *"kenson"* (modesty), and *"sokuin"* (sympathy), traits they claim are unique to Japanese culture (Yanagida 2012, 18; Suzuki 2012). Also recently, visual images of Japanese Americans have been popularized through both documentary and fictional TV series and films, such as *99 Years of Love: Japanese Americans* (2011), *Time through the Lens of Toyo Miyatake* (2009), and *442nd Regimental Combat*

Team: Toughest Army in American History (Suzuki 2011). Those uncritically assume that Japanese and Japanese Americans share the same cultural traits and describe Japanese Americans' survival despite tragedies and/or their postwar success in terms of the "Japanese spirit." Students' knowledge about Japanese Americans, if any, is shaped by such popular images distributed through the Japanese media.

The problem with these images is that they essentialize the cultural traits of the "Japanese race" and affirm Japanese racial superiority with regard to other minority races in America. The belief that a particular race possesses some shared cultural traits is still very strong, and the general assumption expressed in the media that Japanese Americans have the same kinds of cultural virtues as Japanese in Japan reveals the fact that those virtues are believed to be "racial" qualities inherited by blood.

The attribution of certain personalities to a certain racial group seems to be less common in the United States, at least in public discourse today. Historically speaking, however, similar assumptions have been common in America. For example, Henry Yu has shown that sociologists of the Chicago school developed their theories on race relations using the writings and stories of Asian American sociologists. The problem in the Chicago school's explanation of Asian American marginality, Yu has pointed out, is that their survey, conducted in the 1920s and 1930s, started "with the assumption that the Orient was different from America," and it placed Asian Americans "in between two opposites." Robert E. Park and other Chicago school sociologists were fascinated with the stories of second-generation Asian Americans because they were thought to be unique in the sense that "unlike second-generation European immigrants who were merely divided from their parents by an attitude of cultural repudiation of the Old World, second-generation Orientals were also repudiated by white Americans," and thus "they were unable to find employment or social acceptance outside" their immigrant communities (Yu 2001, 100). Focusing on the cultural repudiation minorities faced, they paid less attention to the structural aspect of discrimination, namely, that Asian Americans were unable to find employment in mainstream society. The Chicago school failed to explore the relationship between cultural and structural inequalities—the sociocultural structure in which cultural repudiation resulted in discriminatory employment practices—because they focused on the cultural explanations of marginality experienced and expressed by their informants of color.

The development of ethnic studies and the proliferation of poststructuralism in academia have changed American views of race, shifting the focus to social structures rather than cultural or psychological issues. Michael Omi and Howard Winant's "racial formation" theory represented an important step forward in theorizing racialization. After critically reviewing contemporary theories related to race, they proposed an alternative theory for the United States that they called racial formation. The theory sees race as being shaped by the "process of historically situated *projects* in which human bodies and social structures are represented and organized" (Omi and Winant 1994, 55–56). In other words, they see race as something that arises and develops at the historically and culturally contingent intersection of social structure and cultural representation.

Even though it is often difficult for Japanese students to grasp the concept of racial formation since they do not share the experiences common among American racial minorities or have direct knowledge of what race means in America, teaching Asian American history through the structural view of racial formation can free them from cultural essentialism. When they believe in the unique virtues of the Japanese race, students can resent the historical prejudice and structural discrimination against Japanese Americans, but they tend not to see problems in the exclusion or persecution of other minorities, such as Chinese and Mexican Americans. In such a situation, comparing the experiences of different minorities can actually reinforce students' racial prejudice.

In her chapter in this book, Yuko Matsumoto analyzes how categories such as race and gender construct the discursive borders of the United States that include some people and exclude others. Similarly, the historian Gary Okihiro has argued that American history and its idea of citizenship have been shaped by various sets of binaries such as East and West, black and white, man and woman, and heterosexual and homosexual (Okihiro 2001). When I teach in the classroom, I also try to discuss race in relationship to other categories such as gender, nationality, class, and sexuality, applying the concept of "social formation" that he has recently proposed (Okihiro 2011).[12] For example, when I explain that Chinese Americans in the prewar period tended to form homosocial, ethnically concentrated communities while Japanese Americans were dispersed in large cities and various agricultural communities, I compare the Chinese Exclusion Act of 1882 with the Gentlemen's Agreement between Japan and the United States in 1907 and 1908 and emphasize that structural factors such as different immigration laws or diplomatic relationships between the home country and the host country generate differences in the social formation of different racial minorities.

While only a few Japanese scholars have examined the processes of the racialization of Asian Americans in their work, some are particularly useful for deconstructing the notion of race, thereby helping students see the connections between cultural discourses and structural relationships among the multiple racial groups that formed the United States and Asian America. For example, Fuminori Minamikawa (2007) has analyzed how Japanese Americans attempted to place themselves between whites and Chinese Americans in the U.S. racial-ethnic hierarchy by discursively replacing the hierarchy based on race with one based on culture or civilization. And Yoshiyuki Kido (2012) has examined how representations of the Chinese in a United States that was shifting its economic and social foundations from slavery to immigrant labor shaped its racialized discourses surrounding labor, gender, and imperialism.

While academic books and articles in English are often too difficult for Japanese undergraduate students, with the help of Japanese translations and Japanese scholars' interpretations of U.S. Asian American studies scholarship, they can learn about the theory of racial formation and the politics of racial representation.[13] By learning how economic and political interests and power relationships among diverse racial and ethnic groups have constructed race and generated racialized social and cultural hierarchies, Japanese students, who have not experienced race in the same way as American students of color, can understand how power works in a racialized society and race's relationship to other categories such as gender, class, and sexuality.

Asian American Studies and Academic Activism

In her chapter in this book, law professor Mari Matsuda touches on Okinawan and U.S. students' apathy toward political activism. The helplessness expressed by U.S. students seems to be shared by the Japanese students I teach. For example, the voting rate in the general election for the House of Representatives in December 2012 turned out to be the lowest out of all the post–World War II general elections. Voters between twenty and twenty-nine years old had the lowest turnout (37.89 percent), which was only half of the voting rate for people in their sixties (74.93 percent).[14] Young people's disappointment in politics derives from the fact that the government and politicians do not pay as much attention to younger people's needs as they do to those who are older. In the meantime, global competition and economic recession has hit the younger generation most severely, with private corporations and even the public sector decreasing the number of permanent full-time employees and relying more on contract laborers and part-time workers. Lifetime employment, which university graduates of older generations took for granted, is available only to a limited segment of the labor population in today's Japan.[15] The disastrous earthquake on March 11, 2011, might have added to the feeling among young people that life is unfair.

Thus, it appears that teachers of Asian American studies in Japan and the United States share a common challenge of restoring students' interest in political and social issues as well as showing that people in Japan, the United States, and the world have in the past struggled to obtain justice and correct wrongs in society. Learning about those struggles can promote more positive views toward politics and social activism among students. Naturally, the issues that need to be discussed in the two countries are different, so when teaching in Japan, we need to make the subject of Asian American studies relevant to what is at stake in the lives of our students.

Teaching Asian American studies in Japan, one has to deal with the question of how to relate to the identity politics of Asian American studies in the United States. Asian American studies developed as a part of the ethnic studies movement that took place on American university campuses in the 1960s and 1970s, beginning with the Third World Liberation Front student strikes on the West Coast in the late 1960s.[16] Although the relationship between the movement on campus and in the ethnic community might have been more complicated than portrayed in the self-reflective works on Asian American movements, there is no doubt that Asian American studies, even after it established itself as an academic discipline in American universities, has kept its commitment to the well-being of Asian American communities (Izumi 2010b).[17] By contrast, Asian American studies in Japan was imported from the United States purely as an academic discipline, and few scholars are directly committed or related to the Asian American community. In other words, at both the faculty and student levels, Asian American studies has been developed predominantly by community insiders in the United States, while in Japan, scholars and students of Asian American studies are studying "others."

Being an insider both helps and hampers one's study. Insiders share similar experiences with the people in the studied community, and thus are more likely to have a better understanding of unspoken sentiments, rules, and the epistemological significance of certain symbols within the community. Also, insiders often have better access to private information. However, they bear more responsibilities to the communities they research than outsiders. Being an outsider does not mean one is exempt from any ethical or political commitment to the studied community, but the relationship is more distant. In academic fields such as history, information that historians find about a community is not necessarily something that the community wishes to publicize. In that sense, insider scholars are more subject to the community's censorship as well as preferences for frameworks with which they can interpret information.

Asian American studies (particularly Japanese American studies) has had a strong inclination to represent Japanese Americans as either a "model minority" or a racial minority that resisted racialization (Minamikawa 2007). Such an emphasis on inclusion probably derives from Asian Americans' disadvantaged social status, which has been historically constructed by their exclusion from discourses of U.S. citizenship (R. Lee 1999; Ngai 2004; Izumi 2006). Their struggle for inclusion, however, has led the discipline to exclude "foreign" elements in the community from Japanese American history. Issei migrants, Kibei Nisei, those who left the United States, and those who sided with Japan in the World War II concentration camps have not been given due attention in Japanese American history until recently. Studies about those people were left to Japanese scholars with access to Japanese-language materials and less at stake in U.S. identity politics.

Moreover, since its foundation, the Asian American studies field has made use of scholarship in other groups such as African Americans, Latinas/Latinos, and Native Americans. Together, that has contributed to the uncovering of the cultural and social processes of racialization and discriminatory social formations in U.S. history. These works, including those coming from critical American studies, have had not only academic but also political consequences in U.S. society in that they repudiate "color-blind conservatism" and push society toward more egalitarian principles. In critical American studies, there is no separation between academic and political aims, and a scholar's academic pursuit is directly connected to the betterment of society. In ethnic and Asian American studies, students are encouraged to go out in the community and take part in local welfare projects or national politics to embody what they study.

For students in Japan, where the relationship between academia and social activism is more distant, the academic activism of Asian American studies could be inspiring, especially given the apathetic and apolitical atmosphere shared among the younger generation, which increasingly feels disadvantaged in today's globalized world. Japanese students need not necessarily relate to social issues pertinent to Asian American communities, but they can learn about the grassroots strategies and campaigns that American minorities have adopted and apply them to their own struggles against unfair conditions they find in Japan. If they understand how power works discursively, they can find inequalities contained in certain seemingly reasonable nationalistic or cultural discourses. Just as the theory of "racial formation" counters "color-blind conservatism" and Asian American history reveals the way discourses of inclusion and exclusion work to keep domestic racial hierarchies intact, Japanese students can learn how nationalist and cultural discourses can conceal racist and exclusionist policies in Japan and other places of the world. This can help them see in a new light not only issues of discrimination in Japan but also their own disadvantaged economic positions vis-à-vis older generations, which might encourage them to become involved in activism to change the status quo.

Moreover, if students get involved in Japanese social problems politically, they might start questioning U.S. hegemony over Japan and other countries. Rika Nakamura has pointed out that even though Asian American studies is sensitive to and critical about the power disparity between mainstream and racialized groups within the United States, some Asian American studies scholars lack sensitivity toward the hegemonic power they have outside their country as U.S. citizens (Nakamura 2012, 254). Nakamura has noticed such instances when Asian American scholars teach in Asia, and I have noticed a similar lack of sensitivity in historiography surrounding Nisei military service during World War II, the most celebrated aspect of Japanese American contributions to the U.S. nation-state. While their tremendous sacrifice and courage deserve praise, the way in which American and Japanese American history places Nisei soldiers and even Nisei draft resisters in the nationalistic, masculine discourse of military service without critically reflecting on militarism itself is problematic (Fujitani 2011).[18]

In Japan, U.S. militarism, particularly the military base problem in Okinawa, is one of the most serious social and diplomatic human rights issues. Seventy-five percent of U.S. military bases are located within Okinawa even though they occupy only 0.6 percent of Japanese territory. The residents around the bases are deprived of safe and quiet lives because of noise from military aircraft and risk the possibility of accidents. Rape and assault cases of local women and even young girls by U.S. servicemen enrage not only local Okinawan residents but also Japanese people as a whole, and despite efforts by the military administration to enforce discipline on servicemen, incidents continue to occur (Miyagi 2011). The disproportionate burden that Okinawa bears within Japan is the result of structural inequality between mainland Japanese people and Okinawans, and thus is a domestic problem. However, the base issue also reflects the unequal power relationship between the United States and Japan, as well as the geopolitical interest the former has in Asia. It is ironic that although Okinawa has been one of the major emigration prefectures within Japan, when military service of Japanese Americans is glorified, little connection is made between it and the suffering of Okinawans in Japan because of U.S. military bases.

Asian American studies, with its origins in the anti–Vietnam War movement, could recover its critical edge on a global scale if it expanded its framework beyond the Asian American community's inclusion into the discursive of the U.S. nation-state. Such a revision can connect critical voices and struggles for social justice in both Asia and America, and such a "transnational turn" would truly inspire both Asian American and Asian students.

Conclusion

Increasing collaborations between Asian- and American-based Asian American studies scholars have led to productive conversations in the form of exchanging not only research results but also constructive criticisms.[19] Asian American studies can benefit Japanese university students and scholars, and the different positions and perspectives of Japanese students and scholars can critically intervene in Asian American studies in the United States. For Japanese students, Asian American studies, more than other fields, is an example of the scholarship of "others" while seeing the connections between the history of their country and those of other nations. As such, the field can help both Japanese and American students build transnational coalitions of critical voices and acquire reflective and inspiring views on social issues close to their own lives and in the larger world.

Notes

1 "Special permanent resident aliens" (*tokubetsu eijū sha*) refers mostly to Koreans and Chinese people who came to Japan before the end of World War II and their descendants who chose not to obtain Japanese citizenship.

2 This class in spring 2012 was composed of ten students. One was an international student from Korea, and out of the nine Japanese students, four had either lived or studied abroad for varied lengths of time.

3 This was an ESL class, and I asked the students to write their opinions in English after reading a chapter on illegal immigration issues in America. All of the students were Japanese.

4 In May 2012, a group of fifteen students from the University of Southern California, led by Program Director George Sanchez, came to visit Japan. Our class had a Skype discussion in April in preparation for their visit. In May, we had a class discussion while the USC students stayed in Kyoto.

5 The population of the Japanese in the Japanese archipelago was approximately seventy million. The other thirty million were composed of Koreans, Taiwanese, and other people under the rule of the Japanese Empire.

6 Oguma argues that between 1932 (when Manchukuo was founded) and 1945 the majority of Japanese scholars supported the mixed-origin theory. They proffered arguments full of contradictions that tried to simultaneously emphasize the integration of East Asian nations based on paternalistic hierarchy under the Japanese imperial blood lineage and justify Japan's colonial rule over other Asian peoples.

7 For example, consider the case of Japanese people who had resided in New Caledonia before the war. During World War II, Japanese residents were rounded up and held in incarceration camps in Australia. Japanese men who were married to Japanese women were allowed to bring their families along, but those married to local women had to leave their wives and children. After the war, all the Japanese captives were sent to Japan, even though some wished to return to their families in New Caledonia. Many of these families were never reunited after the war (Nagata 1996).

8 Eiichi Hayashi has gathered cases of Japanese soldiers who did not return to Japan and stayed in Asia after the war. He speculates that the number of those ex-soldiers could be close to ten thousand. Many of them became involved in anticolonial battles in various Asian nations. Some children of prewar Japanese migrants were left behind in Asia when their parent or parents returned to Japan.

9 Just as neo-Nazi groups publish holocaust denial literature in Germany, right-wing media in Japan publish books and journal articles denying the occurrence of "the Rape of Nanking" and the large-scale abduction of Asian women as "comfort women" by the Japanese military.

10 I have taken the term "tyranny of the nation" from Donna Gabaccia's famous article in which she criticized the America-centered view of Italian immigrants (Gabaccia 1999, 3).

11　The Council on Promotion of Human Resource [*sic*] for Globalization Development, a policy council established under the Prime Minister's Office of Japan, has referred to the "inward looking attitudes" commonly found among Japanese youth. They state that this has resulted in a drop in the number of students who study abroad as well as fewer new company employees who wish to work outside the country (Grobaru Jinzai Ikusei Suishin Kaigi 2011).

12　Gary Okihiro has proposed expanding the concept of "racial formation" to "social formation" so that it includes other kinds of structural categories such as gender, class, and sexuality (Okihiro 2011).

13　Although many books on Asian American historical experiences have been translated into Japanese, only a few analytical works on Asian American racial formation and representations have been translated into Japanese. One example that is useful for students is the Japanese translation of Robert G. Lee's *Orientals* by Yoshiyuki Kido (R. Lee 1999).

14　Voting rates in the 2012 general election were 37.89 percent for voters in their twenties (49.45 percent in 2009), 50.1 percent for those in their thirties (63.87 percent), 59.38 percent for those in their forties (72.63 percent), 68.02 percent for those in their fifties (79.69 percent), 74.93 percent for those in their sixties (84.15 percent), and 63.3 percent for those seventy years of age or higher (71.06 percent). The overall voting rate in the 2012 general election was 59.32 percent, which was substantially lower than the 69.28 percent turnout in the 2009 election (Zaidan Hojin Akarui Senkyo Suishin Kyokai 2013).

15　The disadvantaged status of younger generations in the Japanese workforce can be most clearly seen by looking at the percentage of male workers irregularly employed in different age categories. In 2011, the percentage of irregular workers among male workers under twenty-four years old (excluding students) was 27.5 percent; between the ages of twenty-five and thirty-four, 15.3 percent; between the ages of thirty-five and forty-four, 8.5 percent, and between the ages of forty-five and fifty-four, 8.4 percent (Statistics Japan 2013).

16　Asian American studies' development out of the Asian American movement (also called the yellow power movement) is described in a number of contemporary anthologies (Tachiki et al. 1971; Gee 1976) and reflective works (Ho et al. 2000; Louie and Omatsu 2001). Karen Tei Yamashita wrote a novel on the movement in 2010 (Yamashita 2010).

17　I have found through my research on vernacular Asian American community movements in Los Angeles that Asian American studies literature has not covered off-campus movements as much as on-campus movements.

18 Eric Muller has produced scholarship on the Nisei draft resisters (Muller 2001). Unfortunately in my view, Muller's work uncritically places Nisei resisters within the nationalistic discourse of "American" masculinity in a similarly problematic way that the Japanese media praise Nisei soldiers for their samurai-like spirit, which is often constructed to shape the core of the "Japanese" psyche. T. Fujitani has criticized the ways the mainstream representations of Nisei soldiers have shifted in America during and after World War II (Fujitani 2011).
19 The journal *Inter-Asia Cultural Studies* published a special issue on Asian American studies in Asia in volume 13, issue 2 (2012).

References

Anderson, Benedict. 1991. *Imagined Communities: Reflections on the Origin and Spread of Nationalism*. London: Verso.

Azuma, Eiichiro. 2005. *Between Two Empires: Race, History, and Transnationalism in Japanese America*. Oxford: Oxford University Press.

Fujitani, T. 2011. *Race for Empire: Koreans as Japanese and Japanese as Americans during World War II*. Berkeley: University of California Press.

Furukawa, Hiromi, and Tetsushi Furukawa 古川博巳、古川哲史. 2004. 日本人とアフリカ系アメリカ人：日米関係史におけるその諸相 (Japanese and African Americans: Aspects in the History of Japan-US Relationship). Tokyo: Akashi Shoten.

Gabaccia, Donna R. 1999. "Is Everywhere Nowhere?: Nomads, Nations, and the Immigrant Paradigm of United States History." *Journal of American History* 86 (3): 1115–1134.

Gee, Emma, ed. 1976. *Counterpoint: Perspectives on Asian America*. Los Angeles: University of California Asian American Studies Center.

Grobaru Jinzai Ikusei Suishin Kaigi (Council on Promotion of Human Resource for Globalization Development). 2011. *An Interim Report of the Council on Promotion of Human Resource for Globalization Development*. Prime Minister of Japan and His Office, June 22. http://www.kantei.go.jp/jp/singi/global/120601interim_report.pdf.

Hayashi, Brian Masaru. 1995. *For the Sake of our Japanese Brethren: Assimilation, Nationalism, and Protestantism among the Japanese of Los Angeles, 1895–1942*. Stanford, CA: Stanford University Press.

Hayashi, Eiichi 林英一. 2012. 残留日本兵：アジアに生きた一万人の戦後 (Japanese Soldiers Who Remained Abroad: 10,000 Japanese Who Lived in Postwar Asia). Tokyo: Chuo Koron Shin Sha.

Ho, Fred, Carolyn Antonio, Diane Fujino, and Steve Yip, eds. 2000. *Legacy to Liberation: Politics and Culture of Revolutionary Asian Pacific America*. San Francisco: AK Press.

Izumi, Masumi 和泉真澄. 2004. "Japanese American Internment and the Emergency Detention Act (Title II of the Internal Security Act of 1950), 1941–1971: Balancing Internal Security and Civil Liberties in the United States." PhD diss., Doshisha University.
———. 2006. "Alienable Citizenship: Race, Loyalty and the Law in the Age of 'American Concentration Camps,' 1941–1971." *Asian American Law Journal* 13: 1–30.
———. 2009. 日系アメリカ人強制収容と緊急拘禁法：人種・治安・自由をめぐる記憶と葛藤 (Japanese American Internment and the Emergency Detention Act: Memories and Dilemma over Race, Security, and Liberty). Tokyo: Akashi Shoten.
———. 2010a. "Re-Interpreting Japanese Canadian Community Movement from Transcontinental and Transpacific Perspectives." In *Trans/American, Trans/oceanic, Trans/lation: Issues in International American Studies,* edited by Susana Araujo, Joao Ferreira Duarte, and Marta Pacheco Pinto, 209–218. Newcastle upon Tyne, UK: Cambridge Scholars Publishing.
———. 2010b. "Seeking the Truth, Spiritual and Political: Japanese American Community Building through Engaged Ethnic Buddhism." *Peace and Change 35* (1): 39–67.
Kido, Yoshiyuki 貴堂嘉之. 2012. アメリカ合衆国と中国人移民：歴史のなかの「移民国家」アメリカ (Chinese Immigrants in the United States: The Making of a "Nation of Immigrants"). Nagoya: Nagoya University Press.
Kurashige, Scott. 2008. *The Shifting Grounds of Race: Black and Japanese Americans in the Making of Multiethnic Los Angeles.* Princeton, NJ: Princeton University Press.
Kurokawa, Midori. 2011. "Markers of the 'Invisible Race': On the Film *Hashi No Nai Kawa.*" In *Racial Representations in Asia,* edited by Yasuko Takezawa, 32–52. Kyoto: Kyoto University Press.
Lee, Robert G. 1999. *Orientals: Asian Americans in Popular Culture.* Philadelphia: Temple University Press. Japanese translation by Yoshiyuki Kido オリエンタルズ：大衆文化のなかのアジア系アメリカ人. Tokyo: Iwanami Shoten, 2007.
Lee, Sung Yup. 2011. "Changing Faces: Colonial Rule in Korea and Ethnic Characterizations." In *Racial Representations in Asia,* edited by Yasuko Takezawa, 53–74. Kyoto: Kyoto University Press.
Louie, Steve, and Glenn Omatsu, eds. 2001. *Asian Americans: The Movement and the Moment.* Los Angeles: UCLA Asian American Studies Center Press.
Matsumoto, Yuko. 2015. "Americanization and Beika: Gender and Racialization of the Issei Community in California Before World War II." In *Trans-Pacific Japanese American Studies: Conversations on Race and Racializations,* edited by Yasuko Takezawa and Gary Y. Okihiro. Honolulu: University of Hawai'i Press, 161–182.

Minamikawa, Fuminori 南川文里. 2007.「日系アメリカ人」の歴史社会学：エスニシティ、人種、ナショナリズム (Historical Sociology of "Japanese Americans": Ethnicity, Race, Nationalism). Tokyo: Sairyusha.

Miyagi, Harumi 宮城晴美. 2011. 沖縄からの報告：米軍基地の現状と米兵によるレイプ事件 (A Report from Okinawa: The Current Condition of US Military Bases and Sexual Crimes by US Soldiers). *Ritsumeikan Gengo Bunka Kenkyu* 23 (2): 179–182.

Muller, Eric L. 2001. *Free to Die for Their Country: The Story of the Japanese American Draft Resisters in World War II.* Chicago: University of Chicago Press.

Nagata, Yuriko. 1996. *Unwanted Aliens: Japanese Internment in Australia.* St. Lucia: University of Queensland Press.

Nakamura, Rika. 2012. "What Asian American Studies Can Learn from Asia?: Towards a Project of Comparative Minority Studies." *Inter-Asia Cultural Studies* 13 (2): 251–266.

Ngai, Mae G. 2004. *Impossible Subjects: Illegal Aliens and the Making of Modern America.* Princeton, NJ: Princeton University Press.

99年の愛：ジャパニーズ・アメリカンズ (99 Years of Love: Japanese Americans). Directed by Sugako Hashida 橋田寿賀子. 2011. Tokyo: Tokyo Broadcasting System (TBS). DVD.

Oguma, Eiji 小熊英二. 1995. 単一民族神話の起源：「日本人」の自画像の系譜 (The Myth of the Homogeneous Nation). Tokyo: Shinyosha.

Okihiro, Gary Y. 2001. *Common Ground: Reimagining American History.* Princeton, NJ: Princeton University Press.

———. 2011. "Theorizing Social Formation." *In Proceedings of a Japan-based Global Study of Racial Representations 2010–2011: Racial Representations of Japanese/Asian Americans, January 8–10,* edited by Yasuko Takezawa, 1–21. Grant-in-Aid by Japan Society for the Promotion of Science, Institute for Research in Humanities, Kyoto University, March 31.

Omi, Michael, and Howard Winant. 1994. *Racial Formation in the United States: From the 1960s to the 1990s,* 2nd ed. New York: Routledge.

Sakaguchi, Mitsuhiro 坂口満宏. 2007. 新しい移民史研究に向けて(Towards New Studies of Migration History). In 日系人の経験と国際移動—在外日本人移民の近現代史 (Experiences and International Migration of the Japanese: Modern History of Japanese Overseas Migration), edited by Hiroshi Yoneyama and Norifumi Kawahara, 239–261. Kyoto: Jinbun Shoin.

Sakashita, Fumiko. 2013. "Lynching across the Pacific: Japanese Views and African American Responses in the Wartime Antilynching Campaign." In *Swift to Wrath: Lynching in Global Historical Perspective,* edited by Christopher Waldrep and William Carrigan, 181–214. Charlottesville: University of Virginia Press.

Statistics Japan 総務省統計局. 2013. 労働力調査 詳細集計 平成24年平均 速報結果。第二表「雇用形態、年齢階級別役員を除く雇用者数 (Labor Force Survey. Table 2: Number of Employees Categorized by the Type of Employment and Age). http://www.stat.go.jp/ data/roudou/sokuhou/nen/dt/index.htm.

Suzuki, Junichi. すずきじゅんいち (producer/director). 2009. 東洋宮武が覗いた時代 (Time through the Lens of Toyo Miyatake). Wakku. DVD.

———. 2011. 442日系部隊：アメリカ史上最強の陸軍 (442nd Regimental Combat Team: Toughest Army in American History). Tokyo: Film Voice. DVD.

———. 2012. 1941：日系アメリカ人と大和魂 (1941: Japanese Americans and the Yamato Spirit). Tokyo: Bungei Shunju.

Tachiki, Amy, Eddie Wong, Franklin Odo, and Buck Wong. 1971. *Roots: An Asian American Reader*. Los Angeles: UCLA Asian American Studies Center Press.

Takai, Yukari. 2006. "Blacks and Asians on the Move: A Comparative Study of the Great Black Migration and Asian Immigration from a Social History Perspective." *Journal of the Faculty of Foreign Studies, Aichi Prefectural University* 38: 29–51.

Takezawa, Yasuko, ed. 竹沢泰子. 2005. 人種概念の普遍性を問う：西洋的パラダイムを超えて (Is Race a Universal Idea?: Transcending the Western Paradigm). Kyoto: Jinbun Shoin.

———. 2011. *Racial Representations in Asia*. Kyoto: Kyoto University Press.

Yamashita, Karen Tei. 2010. *I-Hotel*. Minneapolis, MN: Coffee House Press.

Yanagida, Yukiko 柳田由紀子. 2012. 二世兵士激戦の記録：日系アメリカ人の第二次大戦 (Records of Battles Nisei Soldiers Fought: Japanese Americans in World War II). Tokyo: Shincho Shinsho.

Yoneyama, Hiroshi 米山裕. 2007. 環太平洋地域における日本人の移動性を再発見する (Rediscovering Migration of Japanese in the Pacific Rim Region). In 日系人の経験と国際移動：在外日本人移民の近現代史 (Experiences and International Migration of the Japanese: Modern History of Japanese Overseas Migration), edited by Hiroshi Yoneyama and Norifumi Kawahara, 9–23. Kyoto: Jinbun Shoin.

Yoneyama, Hiroshi, and Norifumi Kawahara, eds. 米山裕・河原典史. 2007. 日系人の経験と国際移動：在外日本人移民の近現代史 (Experiences and International Migration of the Japanese: Modern History of Japanese Overseas Migration). Kyoto: Jimbun Shoin.

Yu, Henry. 2001. *Thinking Orientals: Migration, Contact, and Exoticism in Modern America*. Oxford: Oxford University Press.

Zaidan Hojin Akarui Senkyo Suishin Kyokai 財団法人明るい選挙推進協会. (Association for Promoting Fair Elections). 2013. 衆議院選挙 (House of Representatives Election). http://www.akaruisenkyo.or.jp/070various/071syugi/693/.

CHAPTER 14

Japanese American Progressives
A Case Study in Identity Formation

Mari Matsuda

Over ozoni on New Year's Day of 2011, I told my 86-year-old father I was going to a conference to discuss racial identity of Japanese Americans. "How do you think people saw themselves?" I asked about the Issei Uchinanchu. "Did they think of themselves as Okinawan or just Japanese?"

He replied, "It depends, it depends who, where. Hawai'i? California? Southern California? It depends when. When did they come?"

"It depends" is probably the answer to the question proposed in many chapters in this book, as questions about racial formation always intersect with particular circumstances in complicated ways. The particularity explored in this chapter is Japanese American progressive political identity, including its race and ethnicity aspects.

"You know what they said about Okinawans in the old days . . . ," a Nisei community leader said to me conspiratorially at a luncheon at the Okinawan Center. "Buta kau kau. Aka. That's what they said about us."

The first phrase is an amalgam of Hawaiian and Nihongo, meaning, roughly, "they eat pig slop." The second phrase is political. Even in Hawai'i, which in my father's taxonomy was less progressive than Los Angeles, where he grew up, the taint of aka, red, Communist, is part of Okinawan identity. People whisper when they say it.

As a Sansei progressive, I have always traced my political lineage to the great Issei working-class scholar activists I was privileged to know as a child. Aka, by choice, at a time when this risked deportation, persecution, and execution. Some of the Issei, deported from the United States for their organizing, ended up in the Soviet Union, where they were reportedly killed in Stalin's purges (Ben Kobashigawa, conversation with author, 2000). Aka, vanished in a land they once considered a worker's paradise.

What drives my quest to understand the identity formation of those who came from nothing and risked everything for their vision of a better world is the question we must answer in this century, if we care about the survival of the human race. As the number of unstable nation-states that possess nuclear weapons increases, as we zoom past the atmospheric carbon dioxide load under which human life can flourish, as global capitalism gasps for breath, like a dying fish in a basket on a boat, we must answer this question: Under what conditions do ordinary people decide to act collectively to demand democratic control over the conditions that affect the quality of their lives?

I lectured recently to a group of visiting Okinawan law students. "Do you think it is right that the U.S. is dictating to your government the conditions under which military bases are built on your island, regardless of what the people of Okinawa want?" I asked. No, they said with great earnestness, it is wrong, it is not democratic, and it is not respectful. You could protest, I said, like the students in Japan who aggressively opposed the war in Vietnam and were an integral part of a worldwide peace movement that eventually ended that war. At pains to answer me honestly, they said, through their professor who was translating, that they are not protesters. They feel strongly that the bases should not be imposed on Okinawa, but they do not think of themselves as people who could stop bases. They do not think it would work. They would not know how to do it. They are not the ones who can act.

"Doshite?" I asked.

"Wakaranai," they answered, eyes full of regret.

In striking ways, they looked—with their pained, apologetic faces and their willingness to confess and explain their own absence of agency—exactly like my American students. It was not an absence of concern or an ignorance of the issues that paralyzed them. It was their identity. We are not the protesters; we are not the change-makers, that is someone else. I have heard this over and over from American students in many locations, and it breaks my heart, because it sounds like the death of democracy.

How is it that Issei, who could barely speak English, who had no legal status protecting them, who had no money or influence, risked the red-baiting and chose to participate in mass movements for worker rights? How is it that Nisei, faced with the assimilationist pressure of the war years, could form progressive organizations and remain steadfast, lifelong warriors for peace and justice? And what of the Sansei radicals who raised their fists in revolutionary defiance, alongside black and Latino nationalists; did they not raise their children to stand with the same militant pride? If the Issei and Nisei could do it in the middle of McCarthyism, why can my students, with all their privilege, not do it today? The withering of the belief that ordinary people can band together to make meaningful changes marked the opening years of the 2000s.

We faced the greatest economic crisis of our lifetimes, and yet there was no mass movement pushing back to demand jobs, housing, education, and an end to a system that benefits only corporations and warmongers. It is so obvious in this historic moment that the old order has failed us. Thus, in conversation, we explore the anatomy of silence.

"I have been thinking about the corrosive effect of cynicism," a film studies scholar said.

"It's possessive individualism," a sociologist said.

"Everyone is still at the mall, or on Facebook," a student said.

"My generation doesn't know how, we grew up after Reagan, there was no critique of capitalism," a Yonsei said.

While I wait for the answer, I look back at the experience of Japanese Americans who always had a critique and always knew where to go with it and how to convert it to action. Their experience may tell us something about where we need to go now.

These elements emerge as significant in shaping Nikkei activism: specific political study (i.e., reading Marx), connection to multiracial social justice movements, the presence of trained organizers, ethnic/social ties such that Nikkei identity was retained within political activism, cultural production, widely circulated left-leaning Nikkei publications, structural conditions—including race and class—that made injustice obvious, and finally, the presence of a global movement that people made part of their identity. These elements also emerge from the story of my family's political education, which I discuss below along with a brief history of Nikkei progressives.

Issei Progressives

At the end of the nineteenth century, Japan suffered from the same conflict between landed gentry and peasant farmers, alongside a growing urban poor, as did much of the world. Exploitation of workers in factory, mine, and field, burdensome taxes, and growing imperial ambitions imposed both a harsh material reality on large numbers of Japanese workers and farmers as well as a political awakening for progressives who studied Marx and watched intently as world events pushed class conflict toward revolutionary change (Kublin 1950, 322–328). The international involvement of Japanese leftists in the early 1900s is striking. They traveled to Europe and the Americas, participating in political action and organizing along the way. In the United States, they faced Palmer Raids and deportation, but they established a foothold, publishing radical/Marxist newsletters with wide circulations and working closely with the American left (Ichioka 1998, 380).[1] Lenin himself thanked Japanese leftists for their opposition to war against Russia (Yoneda 1975, 7).

Yuji Ichioka (1976) and others have documented the organizing and political education of Issei radicals. Prominent features include an international outlook and political action across racial lines. Issei participated in the Industrial Workers of the World (IWW) (Dubofsky 1969).[2] IWW activist Joe Hill traveled to Hawai'i, meeting workers in the early—largely unsuccessful—days of organizing on the plantations (Chinen 2010, 77). And Issei like Jack Kimoto—later arrested and tried under the Smith Act in Hawai'i—marched with the "army of the unemployed" in California demanding jobs during the Great Depression (Jack Kimoto, conversation with author, 1977).

Sen Katayama co-founded the American Communist Party and helped organize Japanese Workers Association branches in New York, Seattle, San Francisco, and Los Angeles.[3] His writing, translated into many languages and distributed globally, was part of his pledge to speak out on behalf of the oppressed: "I will be the bleeding mouth from which the gag has been snatched, I will say everything" (Katayama 1918, 39).

Katayama's comrades participated in the Oxnard sugar beet workers' strike of 1903, a landmark in the history of Japanese American and Chicano solidarity in the face of hostility from the reactionary arm of American labor, personified in Samuel Gompers (Street 1998, 193–199; Almaguer 1994). Katayama regularly published in Japanese American Communist publications, exhorting solidarity with workers in Korea and China, as Imperial Japan tightened its grip on those nations.

My father identifies a Meiji education as one of the ways in which Japan's "beat the West" mentality inadvertently nurtured a leftist consciousness. The Issei were from poor, peasant stock, but they could read. The newspapers and pamphlets promoted by Katayama and other radical intellectuals/organizers found a ready audience among the thousands of working-class Issei who were refugees from the exploitive economic practices of Imperial Japan. My grandfather, Jinkichi Matsuda, and his Okinawan comrades in Los Angeles were among them, active supporters of the International Labor Defense (ILD), a group that raised funds to support worldwide worker organizing and resistance to persecution of worker-radicals (Ginger 1983, 256–258).

The Issei arrived as young workers, learned political economy, and continued their political work after the bombing of Pearl Harbor, joining the United Front Against Fascism.[4] Abandoned by many on the U.S. left, the West Coast Issei were herded into internment centers. The Marxists among them supported the U.S. war effort, even as they were snubbed by the Communist Party. In its first issue published following suspension due to the internment, *Dōhō*, published by Seiji Fujii, proclaimed, "Today, it is the fundamental task of all pro-democratic Japanese Americans, both Issei and Nisei, to rally the people around the war policies laid down by the President" (Fujii 1943).

The Communist-affiliated *Dōhō* urged those eligible to volunteer for military service and those able to relocate under War Relocation Authority programs designed to settle loyal Japanese Americans in the Midwest and other inland locations.

After the war, Issei progressives continued their organizing efforts. They were persecuted during the McCarthy era, and they fought back, joining the Committee for the Protection of the Foreign Born to fight politically motivated deportations (Smith 1959, 46). In that group, they worked closely with Korean, Chinese, Mexican, and European immigrants (Garcilazo 2001). Although labeled a "Communist front group" (House Committee on Un-American Activities 1957, 7) by red-baiters, the committee included many liberals and civil libertarians who were not Marxists.

My childhood community, the Okinawans in Los Angeles, was active in all of this history.[5] Don Matsuda was born in Los Angeles in 1924. His father, Jinkichi Matsuda, was an Issei Okinawan forced off the land by taxes. Jinkichi Matsuda wrote of his experience.

> A letter came asking for money
> Traces of an unsteady brush
> Younger brother, just turned fourteen,
> Takes care of mother nearly sixty and two grandmothers, eighty and seventy-five
> So early for a full man's load of suffering on your back
> Taxes, taxes, emergency taxes
> Though a tiller of the land, your belly is half-empty
> And I went overseas! Three old women . . . living day by day
> Four lives and one horse?
> Younger brother! I will squeeze blood to raise the fifteen dollars.
>
> The struggle of the oppressed
> Promises victory in the end
> We will be victorious!
> Think that the future will be bright,
> Younger brother! To work is good
> But take care of yourself too.
> (J. Matsuda 1989, 171)

Seventeen-year-old Jinkichi Matsuda arrived literate, thanks to a Meiji-era education in Okinawa, and was able to teach himself English. The community pooled funds to lend him enough to go to college and graduate with a degree in dentistry from the University of Southern California.

Opening a dental practice in the middle of the Depression, serving poor Nikkei and Mexicans, he made little money, but as an educated man he was respected and called Sensei. Like his peers, working-class Okinawans with an interest in world affairs, he read Marx and Engels and struggled with other working-class immigrants for worker rights.

When I asked my father what his first memory of political activism was, he recalled being about five years old and watching his father and friends rehearsing a cultural performance of some kind that involved dancing and spears.[6] Drinking, studying, performing, and eating were all done communally, with social life and political life intertwined.

An unusual aspect was the inclusion of women. According to Don Matsuda, this was a direct response to the theoretical analysis of the position of women by Marx and Engels. Women participated in cultural production in this community of politicized working-class intellectuals. The progressive Okinawan Issei produced a journal, *LooChoo* (an alternative spelling of Ryukyu), which included essays and poems by women, including my grandmother, Tsuyuko Matsuda. When the Nisei were old enough, they became English-language contributors to this journal.

The rehearsals of song and dance were not just for performance within the Okinawan community. Performances in multicultural fund-raisers for the International Labor Defense brought together large numbers of left-wing immigrants of many races. Immigrant activists were under constant threat of deportation, and they joined together with other immigrant groups, including Jews, Slavs, and Mexicans, for mutual protection. I can remember from my own childhood sitting in the kitchen of Paul Kochi and Kiyo Oshiro, Issei leftists who barely spoke English, as they received visitors—black and white—who shared jokes and food over broken English conversation. In this period, Kochi-san was engaged in a legal battle fighting deportation, and allies of many races were supporting him. This is striking in contrast to the usual immigrant experience, which continues to this day, of the first generation isolated in a narrow silo of one ethnic community.

Food was another part of this cross-race organizing. The Los Angeles Committee for the Protection of the Foreign Born held large festivals at which each ethnic group prepared food from their country, often dressed in ethnic costume as they served from their national booth. Marathon chess games, folk dances, food, drink, horseshoes, and costume: this was political work, but it was also play, entertainment, culture, and friendship. These were considered "Communist front" activities and were subject to government surveillance. It took courage just to attend, particularly for vulnerable immigrants. The courage was bolstered by the wafting scent of teriyaki grilling, the sound of accordions playing polka, and guitarists singing mariachi style (Garcilazo 2001, 284).

These mass gatherings did not happen spontaneously. Organizers visited farmers, laborers, gardeners, and vegetable sellers, talking about the need to band together to pursue common ends. According to Don Matsuda, the hardcore organizers and propagandists were Naichi. They immigrated slightly later than the first group, many of whom went to Hawai'i at the turn of the century. They were more educated and more progressive, exposed to aka thought in Japan.

Organizers came to an audience ready for their message. Conditions in the United States were obviously stacked against immigrant workers, from racist immigration laws to exploitive labor systems. Tenant farmers were subject to crooked lease practices. Farm laborers toiled under starvation conditions. My father describes his father reading a letter secretly sent by the young daughter of a central valley farm family from the same furusato. She was begging for money in a ragged child's hiragana, because they were out of food and her own parents were too proud to ask for help—please, Uncle, send us what you can because the food ran out several days ago.

The idea of worker solidarity, class consciousness, and "internationalism" made sense given what the Issei could see around them. Paul Kochi (1937) wrote in his memoir of crossing over the desert through Mexico, helped by kind families who shared their meager provisions:

> What surprised me in having a good look at the mother was how much her type and her actions were exactly like my own mother's. And the daughter bore a close resemblance to a farmer's daughter back home. . . . The mother pulled out several thorns from the bottoms of my feet and gave me a pair of home-made zapatos—leather sandals. (Kochi 1978, 33–34)

They understood that this Japanese stranger was a poor peasant like them:

> It seemed for them we were all immigrants traveling the same road and they understood our situation from their hearts. This class consciousness cuts across race and nationality and promotes a mutual understanding which, if preserved and extended, would make the deserts bloom. (Kochi 1978, 39)

Indeed, given the obvious conditions of oppression that had forced the Issei out of Japan and that rendered their way so hard in the United States, the question is not so much "why did some Issei become socialists," but rather "why didn't they all?"

What seems unique to the radical Issei I knew was that they formed a community of like-minded people and actively read and studied political theory. This was a lifelong project. They were doing it as young men in the 1920s, and as old men in the 1970s, when Paul Kochi and Shingi Nakamura, whom I was privileged to know, would hold political texts under magnifying glasses to continue their study as their eyesight failed. Kochi-san and Shingi-san never ended their activism and served as leaders in the Los Angeles welfare rights movement in the 1970s.[7]

Active political study, professional organizers, mass circulation of Japanese-language progressive newspapers, and participation in multiracial leftist formations made it possible for these Issei to turn their natural understanding of the unfairness of life on the bottom into political activism. Growing up in this period, some Nisei started life well positioned to become radicals.

Nisei Progressives

Many in the Nisei generation, born in the United States, were naturally drawn to the leftist politics they were exposed to from two directions. The many left-wing formations and publications started by the Issei complemented political and cultural developments of the day. The New Deal, with the accompanying legitimization of unions; the romantic left of the intelligentsia, from John Reed to Picasso; the active organizing among college students and young workers that was part of a nationwide network of committed strategists, all reached the Nisei along with other members of their generation. A working-class Okinawan plantation worker from Hawai'i could attend "labor college" in California and gain firsthand experience in the details of running a successful strike, from soup kitchen to morale committee (Chinen 2010, 81). As Jere Takahashi (1982) has described, a Nisei college student could join a range of organizations—anarchist, socialist, Trotskyist, CPUSA, or some version of "democratic"—right on campus.[8]

For readers today, this organizational participation may seem like a naïve adherence to doctrinaire thinking, but this reading misses the reality that the left held commonsense appeal for young people who had seen their parents' labor exploited and who grew up amidst the vilest anti-Japanese race-baiting imaginable. The Communist Party, for example, called for equality and fairness for workers and immigrants. The Communist Party of Hawai'i, led by Nisei Charles Fujimoto, had the following platform in 1948:

> [We support a] program of government condemnation of large estates and resale of the land to the people for home sites and small farms at cost. We support the revision of present immigration laws, such as the Oriental Exclusion Act, to provide naturalization rights to all immigrants regardless of race or color. We urge the public ownership of all

public utilities. On taxation, we believe in the principle of taxation according to ability to pay, with personal exemptions. We support the granting of immediate Statehood for Hawai'i. (Butler 1949)

This platform was similar to the goals ultimately obtained by the Democratic Party in Hawai'i, run by Nisei who were liberals, not Marxists.

The dark days of McCarthyism meant that the most radical Nisei were persecuted. In Hawai'i, several were put on trial for treason under the Smith Act, and many more—the "reluctant 39"—were stigmatized and blacklisted because of their refusal to testify in witch-hunt hearings run by the House Un-American Affairs Committee (HUAC) (Chinen 2010, 86).[9] At that time, my family was living in Los Angeles. Under the blacklist system, my father was fired from thirteen jobs and finally opened his own television repair business in order for the family to survive.

For Nisei, like my father, who grew up with Issei Marxists and followed them to their meetings, it was natural to continue political work. My mother, Kimi Matsuda, was exposed to leftist politics as a university student active in the labor movement in Hawai'i. Study groups at the labor canteen[10]—a gathering place for visiting progressive GIs who would not patronize the segregated USO—were her introduction to Marx, and a labor canteen seminar taught by Ewart Guinier (father of critical race theorist Lani Guinier, and founder of black studies at Harvard University) was her introduction to African American history.

While Nisei progressives were a small subset of the Nisei population, they were not an insignificant presence. "Was it just a handful when you were in school?" I pushed my mother in a recent conversation. "Oh no," she insisted, rattling off names of members of Hawai'i Youth for Democracy (HYD), one of the many similar organizations with "Democracy" in their names, which stood for a version of democracy that included progressive analysis of political economy.

HYD, a University of Hawai'i student organization, was "an interracial, inter-faith youth organization dedicated to character building and education in the spirit of democracy and freedom." Begun in 1945 and officially recognized as a student organization in 1946, within the school, the group stood for "academic freedom, the right of students and professors to express themselves freely, and a campaign for more scholarships and dormitories." Beyond the university, HYD "strongly support[ed] the campaign for statehood" and supported "an America progressively freer of prejudice and poverty, and a nation working with the United Nations to preserve peace" (*Ka Palapala Yearbook* 1946, 93, 176). The group planned such events as International Student's Day, How Today's Youth Shapes the World of Tomorrow, Wages and Prices, Why You Should Vote, Post-War Japan, Russia's Foreign Policy, and Is the American Press Free, with a particular interest in labor issues. Noted feminist/progressive leaders Patsy Mink, later elected to Congress, and Jean King, who later served as lieutenant governor of Hawai'i, were members. The organized appeal to youth that generated the HYD is evident in this excerpt from a 1945 American Youth for Democracy recruiting pamphlet:

> You've got to see such things as AYD's first anniversary dinners held in New York, Chicago and Los Angeles, where such prominent youth and adults as Lieutenant-Colonel Evens Carlson, Frederic March, Sgt. Al Schmid, Norman Corwin, Howard Fast, Charlotte Hawkins Brown, Barney Ross, Orson Welles and others paid tribute to the youth of America and to their organization, AYD.
>
> There were big cultural events like AYD's Salute to "Fats" Waller, shortly after his death. Four thousand young people jammed Carnegie Hall to see the greatest names in the entertainment world perform in honor of the great Negro jazz artist. Among the sponsors and performers were such people as Duke Ellington, Leopold Stokowski, Count Basie, Deems Taylor, Bill Robinson, Jimmy Durante, Paul Whiteman and a list that made this AYD program an outstanding cultural event of the season. (American Youth for Democracy 1945, 22–23)

Don and Kimi Matsuda met in Chicago, where they traveled for a national Nisei for Wallace meeting.[11] Henry Wallace was the Progressive Party's candidate for president in 1948 (Hatfield 1997). The Nisei contingent of his campaign joined with other ethnic groups to encourage inclusion of racial justice and immigrant rights positions in the Wallace platform (Bahr 2007). This was well before the civil rights movement. The inclusion of antiracist positions showed the Wallace campaign's willingness to depart from the mainstream. Most significantly, the campaign refused to exclude Communists and succumb to red-baiting. It is difficult through today's lens to imagine an American political candidate so unafraid of leftist politics, and even more difficult to imagine Nisei, stereotyped as quiet assimilationists, as active participants.

The story of Nisei participation in the Wallace campaign and other militant, pro-labor, pro-peace, antiracist organized movements is undertold because it does not fit with the "good minority" story of the compliant Nisei. It was not a majority, but as my mother insists, it was more than a handful. In every city with a Nihonmachi, there were Nisei who were active at the union hall, who went to study groups on leftist theory, who walked picket lines. Some of their stories are recorded—including those of Kazu and Tak Iijima,[12] Yuri and Bill Kochiyama,[13] Ernest and Chizu Iiyama,[14] Lewis Suzuki,[15] and Karl Yoneda'[16] Kibei—but many more are unknown to recorded history.

A key feature of this cohort is their lifelong commitment. The Nisei for Wallace veterans went on to support the black civil rights movement, the anti–Vietnam War movement, and numerous labor and antipoverty struggles. They provided an elder presence when the Asian American movement blossomed in the 1970s, and they influenced Sansei activists by providing a solid counterexample to the valorized and obsequious "model minority."

Today, my father can barely walk, but he will show up at a peace demonstration in front of the Japanese consulate, calling for removal of U.S. bases in Okinawa. He is an active member of Veterans for Peace, walking with a cane but still carrying a peace placard, just as he did as a young man caught on camera by the FBI, protesting the U.S. invasion of the Bay of Pigs. This picture is a preserved souvenir of his political activism, courtesy of HUAC. Don Matsuda was called before HUAC and blacklisted during the McCarthy era. He was a decorated war veteran who had volunteered while at Heart Mountain Internment Camp, but they called him "un-American."

The patronizing tone of his interrogation by HUAC comes through the dry transcript. When Matsuda refused to identify himself in the photo from the Fair Play for Cuba Rally, the following exchange occurred:[17]

> *Rep. Scherer.* It is obvious to me that the picture in this photograph is that of the witness . . .
> *Mr. Doyle.* I agree that he is a good-looking native of California . . .
> *Mr. Scherer.* Well, let's not compliment him too much, taking the fifth amendment on his Communist Party activities.
> *Mr. Doyle.* Well I can compliment him on being born in the great State.
> [Later, the representatives discuss Matsuda's four battle stars.]

> *Mr. Doyle* . . . I don't understand how a man who has displayed the valor you displayed, to get four battle stars, in defense of our freedoms in the world, can do that and then be identified with an international conspiracy that openly says that, if necessary in its judgment, it will use force and violence to overthrow this Government. . . . And this man has had an education, attended the University of Chicago for a while. I want you to think pretty seriously, Matsuda. Aren't you in the wrong outfit? Do you belong there?

History shows that the red-baiters were actually the ones in the "wrong outfit," shamefully violating their oath of office by participating in harassment of law-abiding American citizens who were doing as the Constitution demands: speaking up as citizens, peacefully petitioning their government, perpetuating a government of the people and for the people. As the African American singer, actor, and activist Paul Robeson told HUAC:

> I am being tried for fighting for the rights of my people, who are still second-class citizens in this United States of America. . . . I stand here struggling for the rights of my people to be full citizens in this country. And they are not. They are not in Mississippi. And they are not in Montgomery, Alabama. And they are not in Washington. They are nowhere, and that is why I am here today. You want to shut up every Negro who has the courage to stand up and fight for the rights of his people, for the rights of workers, and I have been on many a picket line for the steelworkers too. And that is why I am here today. (Bentley 1971, 778–786)

Nikkei progressives from Hawai'i to New York stood in solidarity with Robeson, refusing to cooperate with HUAC, as they were wrongly accused of plotting the violent overthrow of the United States. My father and the Issei before him were judicious, gentle men whose weapons were pens and picket signs. Their commitment to the study of history and political theory, their constant debates, and their knowledge of world affairs teach a major lesson about the prerequisites of strong social change movements. It is a serious enterprise that requires courage, intellectual muscle, and intellectual work.

Sansei Progressives

The baby boom generation came of age in the ideological vacuum left by McCarthyism. Openly Marxist Japanese American publications no longer existed. Many active Issei and Nisei departed from visible political life after the scars and recrimination of the McCarthy period, and leftist Japanese American organizations disappeared. People who decide from a young age to side with the underdog and take risks for justice, however, never completely disappear.

The civil rights movement and the anti–Vietnam War movement were the call to action for the next generation. The predominant mainstream Nikkei political formation of the 1960s, the Japanese American Citizens League, was part of a coalition that sought passage of the civil rights acts and the end of Jim Crow in America. Marxists and radicals were allies in this struggle. My family participated in the No on Prop. 14 campaign, in a fight against the racially restricted housing covenants that kept Japanese Americans out of "good" neighborhoods in California. The campaign symbol in the Nikkei community was the character 家, the word for house, pronounced like the word for "no," reminding people to vote "no" so they could buy the house of their choice.

The Vietnam War, with its horrific imagery of massacred civilians—elders and babies alike—was viscerally offensive to Sansei, who had experienced domestic racism and believed the U.S. public tolerated the slaughter of civilians in Vietnam only because the victims were Asian. A new militancy emerged, as black power and Chicano and Puerto Rican nationalism altered the tone of political discourse. The idea that a group once despised and belittled in racist culture could change that culture by aggressive confrontation appealed to young Sansei who took to the streets in direct action. They revived Japanese cultural practices, such as Taiko drumming, as part of their anti-assimilationist worldview. Sansei also revived the tradition of serious political study, and once again long arguments about the correct interpretation of Lenin's "What Is to Be Done," echoed in Los Angeles Nikkei living rooms (Nakamura 2009).

Sansei were leaders in the ethnic studies movement supporting "our history our way" and the inclusion of Asian Americans as part of American history. In this sense, Sansei activism is directly responsible for the book you hold in your hands, because the serious study of the Japanese American experience would not have institutional support at major universities if not for an ethnic studies movement that occupied buildings, organized student strikes, and literally brought military tanks out into the streets of San Francisco, all over the question of whether books like this one should be written and studied.

Some Sansei radicals had direct ties to past generations of Japanese American progressives.[18] Chris Iijima, troubadour of the Asian American movement, was the son of Nisei Marxists who had dared to challenge the CPUSA on its support of the internment of Japanese Americans during World War II. Sansei deliberately sought out old-timers like Paul Kochi and Karl Yoneda, who were still studying, marching, and organizing as they had since before the war, and learned from them.

In Honolulu, former Smith Act defendants Charles and Eileen Fujimoto, Nisei, and Jack Kimoto, Issei, became active once again, in the Hawaiʻi Alliance, a branch of the National Alliance Against Racist and Political Oppression, an outgrowth of the Free Angela Davis movement. They brought in Sansei participants, myself included, to support initiatives like the National Coalition to Overturn the Bakke Decision—a California Supreme Court decision that had ended affirmative action in that state. Aiko Reinecke, former Smith Act defendant, served as patron to many Sansei activists and ultimately received an apology and reparations from the Hawaiʻi legislature (Matsuda 1998). Koji Ariyoshi, another Nisei radical who had fought alongside Mao Tse-tung in China, served as an adviser to Sansei activists in Honolulu (Joy Chong-Stannard, Director, Center for Biographical Research, University of Hawaiʻi, personal communication).

The Sansei story of activism echoes that of the two previous generations: it was part of a multiracial coalition, included cultural production, was international in outlook, and included critical political study at its core. McCarthyism left no mass political organizing in place when the Sansei came of age. There was much reinventing of the wheel. In contrast to the Issei and Nisei experience, there was a noted absence of experienced professional organizers and an absence of mass working-class participation. The Sansei movement, though powerful and significant, could not attain the reach of what the Issei had established in their radical beachhead in the Americas. This may be why the Yonsei generation feels it is on its own, and why the Yonsei return to culture, Okinawan spear dances and all, is devoid of politics.

Conclusions

At a recent union-sponsored organizing effort I participated in, a young student told me she was excited to talk to "real workers," a novelty in her political experience. After a screening of the film *Song for Ourselves*, chronicling the Sansei movement, a young viewer turned to me and said, "I am so jealous." Perhaps greater exposure to the long and gallant history of Japanese American progressives will serve as a useful tool to this generation that holds in its hands the biggest change-making contradiction ever given to an American Nikkei generation, the most obvious disparity of wealth and power, alongside the sweetest promise of democracy.

The students who tell me they "aren't protesters" have the wrong idea about what political work is. The protest is the last day. On the first day, you read history. On the second day, you meet with friends over food and drink, and argue about what history teaches. On the third day, you find other people who are doing the same thing and you meet with them, and so on, leading up to a mass demonstration of tens of thousands, making specific demands and extracting specific concessions, all strategically planned for and organized around.

Another key lesson is about the role of race and antiracism in all of this. The Issei radicals were internationalists; they never believed any story about the inevitability of race dictating x, y, or z. Common humanity and class unity were abiding themes for them, which meant an aggressive and explicit antiracist stance. Even as a child I knew how to tell the difference between progressive and nonprogressive Issei. Progressive Issei would never use words like "Kuro-chan," a diminutive and insulting term for black people. The most progressive allies in the broader left pantheon, like the IWW, the ILWU, and the Wallace campaign, were early adopters of anti-racism.

Racism was attacked. Race was not, however, denied. Issei LIKED being Japanese/Okinawan and had a great deal of chauvinistic pride about that. Ben Kobashigawa (2000) explained that Issei radicals like Shingi Nakamura embraced Okinawan performing arts in a deliberate effort to reject, "retokkan," the "haji," inferiority, imposed by the colonization of Okinawa. Elevating Okinawan culture brought self-respect, the groundwork for political strength. The focus on traditional ethnic forms of cultural production, particularly poetry, music, and dance, was a source of self-worth, and a gift to share with comrades of other nationalities. This was part of a political belief that folk culture belongs to workers and is therefore admirable and inalienable. It was also a part of organizing. Everyone came to the table with their differences intact and valued. The predominant impression I received from stories of culture night at the ILD was . . . it was great fun.

When my mother met Paul Robeson for the first time, she reports he gave her a warm hug and said that he loved singing in Hawai'i, where he was so warmly received. Nisei were among the organizers of Robeson's debut concert in Honolulu (Robeson 2010), and he spoke often of his solidarity with Asian peoples. Robeson, quite capable of opera, focused on folk songs of many races. The music of ordinary people, sharing international solidarity, was the old left soundtrack the Nisei progressives sang along to. My lullabies included the Irish freedom anthem "Kevin Barry" and the German "Die Gedanken Sind Frei" (Blood-Patterson 1988, 214–215). Like the SNCC army that took courage in the darkest hour from singing freedom songs, the inclusion of ethnically specific culture as a prominent part of political action is a strand in the Japanese American political experience.[19] This is seen most significantly with the Issei but continued with the role of culture in the Sansei/Asian American movement (see, e.g., the work of Chris Iijima and Joanne Nobuko Miyamoto and Janice Mirikitani)[20] and in politically aware Yonsei artists like the filmmaker Tad Nakamura,[21] who specifically reference that period.

The material conditions of deprivation and the overt racism my ancestors encountered resulted in both suffering and resistance. People suffer now, as well, but the cause is masked. Yonsei suffer from joblessness, poor housing options, absence of health insurance, heavy educational debt, and demoralization, but it is harder to see who or what is depriving them of the opportunity to thrive. With just a bit of political consciousness raising, the causes and potential solutions could become obvious, but there is no cadre of idealistic young organizers going door to door to start this conversation. Multiracial alliances with workers, serious political study, and professional organizing are the elements missing for the current generation. They tell me, and I hope they are right, that social media organizing can jump-start all of this. Nonetheless, the significant absence of mass-circulation, progressive news and analysis, whether in print or online, in the Asian American community stands in stark contrast to the record of thousands of regular readers reached by the progressive Nikkei press in the early twentieth century.[22] On the island of Kaua'i alone, the Marxist *Yoen Jiho* (Hawai'i

Star), with a primarily Okinawan readership on the island of Kaua'i, had a circulation of one thousand (Chinen 2010, 78).

The Issei and Nisei radicals whom I have loved and admired did not, as they dreamed, bring about a worker's paradise in their lifetimes. They thought it was possible, given advances in technology, to feed and shelter and educate everyone, if we simply shared, and that we could have a lot of time left over for cultural production. They talked long into the night about what this would look like and how it would come about. The word "democracy" was prominent in these discussions. It did not quite happen, but I am their child, and I believe it could, still.

Notes

1 One such newsletter published by Japanese immigrant Communists was *Kaikyūsen* (Class Struggle), published in San Francisco. Renamed *Zaibei Rōdō Shimbun* (Labor News) and then *Rōdō Shimbun* (The Japanese Worker), the newsletter then relocated to Los Angeles, where it remained, and was retitled *Dōhō* (Brotherhood).
2 The Industrial Workers of the World was a radically democratic, internationalist, antiracist union that sought to join all workers in "one big union." Unlike the reactionary and virulently anti-Asian traditional labor movement, the IWW actively recruited Issei members. For specific events demonstrating the IWW's role in Japanese American activism, see *Japanese American Activist Timeline: Legacy of Japanese American Activism*. Accessed June 1, 2012. http://jalegacy2011.wordpress.com/about/japanese-american-activist-timeline-five-generations-of-community-activism/.
3 Sen Katayama was one of the founders of the socialist and labor movements in Japan. When he moved to the United States in 1914, he began publishing a monthly journal called *Heimin* (The Commoner). "Under his influence, Japanese immigrant Communists, including Okinawans and women, appeared in the 1920s, and by the middle of the decade they organized Japanese Workers Association branches in New York City, Seattle, San Francisco, and Los Angeles." (Ichioka 1998, 380)
4 The United Front Against Fascism was a popular concept on the left during World War II. It required adherents to set aside ideological differences and the long list of left causes in order to focus all effort on winning the war. An editorial by the Japanese American Committee for Democracy explained the mission:

> First: To contribute to the smashing of fascism by aiding the war effort, and

> Second: To fight against all forms of racial discrimination, particularly those directed against Japanese Americans.
>
> . . . .
>
> In a previous editorial we pointed out that the Nisei problem is but a part of the entire minority problem in America. As such, it cannot be solved apart from the Jewish, Negro, or other minority problems, afflicting not only this country, <u>but many others</u>. When we recognize this, we are forced to cross boundary lines and to confront a ferocious form of racism, which only fascism can thrust upon us.
>
> If only because German and Japanese fascism constitute such an overwhelming menace compared to our native fascist fringe, a good case can be built for pushing the first plank of our program harder than the second. But if our thesis is correct—that our two basic aims are merely two arms of a pincer attempting to close in on fascism—then, it would be just as futile to push the first and ignore the second. For one arm of the pincer can do very little without the other, toward the defeat of fascism. (Japanese American Committee for Democracy 1945)

5 Ben Kobashigawa writes of the conflict between older Okinawan Issei and younger radical Issei who formed the "Seinenkai" in Los Angeles. "The Okinawan Seinenkai drew its political direction from the American Communist Party" (Kobashigawa 2000, 7).

6 Coincidentally, as this chapter was prepared for submission, the author witnessed a cultural performance with spears at the 2012 Eisa Festival in Honolulu on May 12, 2012. According to festival organizer Shari Y. Tamashiro (2012), the Young Okinawans of Hawai'i performed a Meekata (e-mail to Sara Lee, May 30, 2012).

7 In the 1970s "in Los Angeles, activists form[ed] Japanese Welfare Rights Organization in Little Tokyo with activist Shinsei Paul Kochi serving as its first president." *Japanese American Activist Timeline: Legacy of Japanese American Activism*. Accessed June 1, 2012. http://jalegacy2011.wordpress.com/about/japanese-american- activist-timeline-five-generations-of-community-activism/.

8 Discussion groups focusing on labor issues prompted many Nisei on college campuses to become politically active.

9 "The Hawai'i Seven" were individuals connected with the ILWU who were charged with plotting to overthrow the U.S. government.

10 The Honolulu Labor Canteen was established in mid-1945 on the initiative of the local labor movement. Jack Hall, regional director of the ILWU in Hawaiʻi, and Norval Welch, the NMU port agent, along with others developed the idea to establish a nonracist service canteen, because the USO and the Red Cross would not allow Asians or African Americans into their canteens. The canteen would emphasize the theme of labor-management harmony and offer labor education programs to people both in and out of the service. The canteen opened its doors on August 19, 1945. With the war ending, the canteen planned to transition to a peacetime community project with the following goal:

> Recognizing the need to promote harmonious relations and better understanding among all racial, religious, economic and political groups and wishing to supplement the facilities now provided by existing organizations, we, members of Labor, Business, the Armed Forces and the Community in Hawaii, acting upon the initiative of Labor and friends of Labor, have formed the Labor Canteen.

The Honolulu Labor Canteen became a center of labor education and a congregating place for leftists in and out of the service (Marquit 2002, 10).

11 Henry Wallace ran for president in 1948 on the Progressive Party ticket. His campaign was supported by many multicultural and progressive groups, including the Communist Party. Another such support group was the Nisei for Wallace (or Nisei Progressives) started by Japanese American activists who had been affected by the U.S. government's forced evacuation of Japanese Americans to internment camps.

12 See Ishizuka (2009) and Omatsu (1986–87).

13 See Fujino (2005).

14 See Taylor (1993); Kochiyama (2004); *San Francisco Chronicle* (2011); and *Rafu Shimpo* (2012).

15 See Bryant (2005).

16 See Yoneda (1983); Yoneda (1975); Streamas (1998); and Friday (2003).

17 United Front Technique of the Southern California District of the Communist Party: Hearings before the House Committee on Un-American Activities, 87th Cong. 2 (1962), statement of Don Matsuda.

18 Writer/professor Phil Tajitsu Nash, Sansei, says, "Yes, I am a progressive, working for what Adrienne Rich summarized as the creation of a society without domination" (Phil Tajitsu Nash, e-mail message to the author, May 30, 2012, quoting Rich). See "Adrienne Rich, Influential Feminist Poet, Dies at 82," *New York Times*, March 28, 2012, http://www.nytimes.com/2012/03/29/books/adrienne-rich-feminist-poet-and-author-dies-at-82

.html. Nash's ancestors included Issei pacifists and feminists and Nisei progressives involved in the Japanese American Committee for Democracy and other labor and civil rights movements. Nash was also influenced by Nisei Yuri Kochiyama, William Horhi, Minoru Yasui, Gordon Hirabayashi, and Fred Korematsu. "Issei–Nisei progressives were a vital component of my development," he says.

19 The Student Non-Violent Coordinating Committee was initially created in 1960 to coordinate the many sit-ins that began happening across the South after black college students in Greensboro, North Carolina, refused to leave a lunch counter after being denied service. As the civil rights movement grew, the SNCC was influential in organizing sit-ins, marches, demonstrations, and other actions such as the freedom rides and voter registration initiatives (Zinn 1964). Music and "freedom songs" were an integral part of the SNCC direct action method (Guttentag 2009). The SNCC eventually dissolved in the 1970s (Zinn 1964).

20 See Asian Women United of California (1989).

21 Tadashi Nakamura is a filmmaker whose critically acclaimed documentaries look back at the roots, key figures, and forward momentum of the Asian American movement. Nakamura's film *A Song for Ourselves* (2009), documenting the life of Chris Iijima, has won many awards at film festivals across the nation. Tadashi Nakamura, "Bio" (blog). Accessed May 30, 2012. http://tadashinakamura.com/Tadashi_Nakamura/Bio_-_Tadashi _Nakamura.html.

22 Similar radical Nikkei newspapers were published in several cities throughout the first half of the twentieth century. (See note 1.)

References

Almaguer, Tomas. 1994. *Racial Fault Lines: The Historical Origins of White Supremacy in California*. Berkeley: University of California Press.

American Youth for Democracy. 1945. *Dust off Your Dreams: The Story of American Youth for Democracy*. New York: American Youth for Democracy.

Asian Women United of California. 1989. *Making Waves: An Anthology of Writings by and about Asian American Women*. Boston: Beacon Press.

Bahr, Diana Meyers. 2007. *The Unquiet Nisei: An Oral History of the Life of Sue Kunitomi Embrey*. New York: Palgrave Macmillan.

Bentley, Eric. 1971. *Thirty Years of Treason: Excerpts from Hearings before the House Committee on Un-American Activities, 1938–1968*. New York: Viking Press.

Blood-Patterson, Peter, ed. 1988. *Rise up Singing*. Bethlehem, PA: Sing Out Corp.

Bryant, Dorothy. 2005. "The Suzuki Odyssey." *Berkeley Daily Planet*, January 28. http://www.berkeleydailyplanet.com/issue/2005-01-28/article/20625

?headline=The-Suzuki-Odyssey-By-DOROTHY-BRYANT—Special-to-the-Planet.
Butler, Hugh, with the Senate Committee on Interior and Insular Affairs. 1949. *Statehood for Hawaiʻi: Communist Penetration of the Hawaiian Islands.* Washington, DC: U.S. Government Printing Office.
Chinen, Joyce N. 2010. "Okinawan Labor and Political Activists in Hawaiʻi: Race, Ethnicity, Class and Social Movements in the Mid–20th Century." *IJOS: International Journal of Okinawan Studies* 1 (1): 69–94.
Dubofsky, Melvin. 1969. *We Shall Be All: A History of the Industrial Workers of the World.* Chicago: Quandrangle.
Friday, Chris. 2003. "Karl Yoneda: Radical Organizing and Asian American Labor." In *The Human Tradition in American Labor History,* edited by Eric Arnesen. Wilmington, DE: Scholarly Resources.
Fujii, Seij. 1943. *Dōhō* 2 (1) August 15.
Fujino, Diane C. 2005. *Heartbeat of a Struggle: The Revolutionary Life of Yuri Kochiyama.* Minneapolis: University of Minnesota Press.
Garcilazo, Jeffrey M. 2001. "McCarthyism, Mexican Americans, and the Los Angeles Committee for Protection of the Foreign Born, 1950–1954." *Western History Quarterly* 32 (3): 273–295.
Ginger, Ann Fagan. 1983. "Workers' Self-Defense in the Courts." *Science and Society* 47 (3): 257–284.
Hatfield, Mark O., with the Senate Historical Office. 1997. "Henry Agard Wallace (1941–1945)." In *Vice Presidents of the United States (1789–1993).* Washington, DC: U.S. Government Printing Office. http://www.senate.gov/arta ndhistory/history/resources/pdf/henry_wallace.pdf.
House Committee on Un-American Activities. 1957. *Communist Political Subversion: The Campaign to Destroy the Security Programs of the United States.* Washington, DC: U.S. Government Printing Office.
Ichioka, Yuji. 1976. "Early Issei Socialists and the Japanese Community." In *Counterpoint: Perspectives on Asian America,* edited by Emma Gee. Los Angeles: UCLA Asian American Studies Center.
———. 1998. "Japanese Americans." In *Encyclopedia of the American Left,* edited by Mari Jo Buhle et al. New York: Oxford University Press.
Ishizuka, Karen L. 2009. "Flying in the Face of Race, Gender, Class and Age: A Story about Kazu Iijima, One of the Mothers of the Asian American Movement on the First Year Anniversary of Her Death." *Amerasia* 35 (2): 24–48.
Japanese American Committee for Democracy. 1945. "Two Arms of a Pincer." Editorial. *Japanese American Committee for Democracy News Letter.*
Ka Palapala Yearbook. 1946. Honolulu: University of Hawaiʻi.

Katayama, Sen. 1918. *The Labor Movement in Japan*. Chicago: Charles H. Kerr & Co.

Kobashigawa, Ben. 2000. "Antinomies of Okinawan Immigrant Identity: Ethnic Pride and Shame within a Double Minority." Paper presented at the Uchinanchu Diaspora International Scholars Forum at the University of Hawai'i, Honolulu, July 2–5.

Kochi, Paul. [1937] 1978. *Imin No Aiwa: An Immigrant's Sorrowful Tale*. Translated by Ben Kobashigawa. Los Angeles: Author.

Kochiyama, Yuri. 2004. *Passing It On: A Memoir*. Los Angeles: UCLA Asian American Studies Center Press.

Kublin, Hyman. 1950. "The Japanese Socialists and the Russo-Japanese War." *Journal of Modern History* 22 (4): 322–339.

Marquit, Erwin. 2002. "The Demobilization Movement of January 1946." *Nature, Society and Thought* 5 (1): 5–39.

Martin, Charles H. 1985. "The International Labor Defense and Black America." *Labor History* 26 (2): 165–194.

Matsuda, Jinkichi. 1989. [Remittance]. *Amerasia Journal* 15 (2): 171–172.

Matsuda, Mari J. 1998. "Foreword: McCarthyism, the Interment and the Contradictions of Power." *Boston College Third World Law Journal* 19 (1): 9–36.

Morgan, Dwight C. 1936. *The Foreign Born in the United States*. New York: ACPFB.

New York Times. 1925. "Arrest 15 Picketing a Consulate Here." October 18.

Occidental College, Urban and Environmental Policy Institute. Timeline of the Progressive Movement in L.A.: 1940s. Accessed May 30, 2012. http://departments.oxy.edu/uepi/ plan/1940.htm.

Okinawa Club of America. 1988. *The History of the Okinawans in North America*, translated by Ben Kobashigawa. Los Angeles: Author.

Omatsu, Glenn, 1986–1987. "Always a Rebel: An Interview with Kazu Iijima." *Amerasia* 13 (2): 83–98.

Paul Robeson and Japanese Americans, 1942–1949. Accessed May 30, 2012. http://www.blackpast.org/ . . . /paul-robeson-and-japanese-americans-1942-1949.

Rafu Shimpo. 2012. "El Cerrito City Council Recognizes Ernest Iiyama." February 23. http://rafu.com/news/2012/02/el-cerrito-city-council-recognizes-ernest-iiyama/.

Robeson, Paul. 1978. "Robeson in Honolulu Backs Wallace, Denies Communist Peril." *Honolulu Star-Bulletin*, March 22, 1948. Reprinted in *Paul Robeson Speaks: Writings, Speeches, Interviews, 1918–1974*, 182–183. New York: Kensington.

Robeson, Paul, Jr. 2010. *The Undiscovered Paul Robeson: Quest for Freedom, 1939–1976*. Hoboken, NJ: John Wiley & Sons.

San Francisco Chronicle. 2011. "Iiyama, Ernest S." June 26.

Sherman, John W. 1989. "For Party and Proletariat: The American Committee for Protection of Foreign Born, A Communist Front, 1933–1959." Master's thesis, University of Toledo.

Smith, Louise Pettibone. 1959. *Torch of Liberty: Twenty-Five Years in the Life of the Foreign Born in the USA.* New York: Dwight-King.

A Song for Ourselves. Directed by Tadashi Nakamura. 2009. Los Angeles: Downtown Community Media Center. Film.

Soundtrack for a Revolution. Written and directed by Bill Guttentag and Dan Sturman. 2009. New York: Louverture Films.

Streamas, John. 1998. "Karl Yoneda and Japanese American Resistance." *Nature, Society and Thought* 11 (4): 489–499.

Street, Richard. 1998. "The 1903 Oxnard Sugar Beet Strike: A New Ending." *Labor History* 39 (2): 193–199.

Takahashi, Jere. 1982. "Japanese American Responses to Race Relations: The Formation of Nisei Perspectives." *Amerasia* 9 (1): 29–57.

Taylor, Sandra C. 1993. *Jewel of the Desert: Japanese American Interment at Topaz.* Berkeley: University of California Press.

Tsai, Michael. 2005. "Portrait of an Era." *Honolulu Advertiser,* May 5. http://the.honoluluadvertiser.com/article/2005/May/05/il/il01a.html.

Yoneda, Karl G. 1975. *The Heritage of Sen Katayama.* New York: Political Affairs Reprints.

———. 1983. *Ganbatte: Sixty-Year Struggle of a Kibei Worker.* Los Angeles: UCLA Asian American Studies Center.

Zinn, Howard. 1964. *SNCC: The New Abolitionists.* Boston: Beacon.

PART VIII

DIALOGUING SUBJECT POSITIONS

Notes from Shinagawa, July 28–29, 2012

Gary Y. Okihiro

Listening to my Japanese colleagues and reading their analyses and comparing them with what I understand to be Japanese American studies in the United States suggests to me several implications.

First, Japan-based scholars seem attentive to the notion of men and women as historical agents, an internal as opposed to external perspective. Whether as migrants, men or women, linguistic communities, commercial actors, Japanese scholars can understand the contexts of racism and sexism, but they appear more keenly attentive to the internal and individual voices and workings of Japanese America. Perhaps this arises from frames; scholars in Japan see Japanese America as extensions of self and Japan, while those in the United States are more focused, at present, on the (wider) contexts of Japanese America, perhaps beginning with the anti-Japanese movement to anchor that experience within U.S. history and society.

Second, Japan-based scholars speak more to intersectionality than racial formation. Perhaps that choice reflects gender (the scholar and subject matter), but it might also point to a difference of approach and relevance. In Japan, the matter of race has scant meaning; more important are gender, ethnicity, and class, whereas in the United States racial meanings, per racial formation theory, are deep and pervasive. Teachers are hard pressed to explain to Japanese students racial formation, or the ideas of majority/minority, notions that appear distant from the students' worldviews of themselves and Japanese society. Japanese students more readily grasp social constructs of gender and patriarchy, class and class struggle, and a normative heterosexuality and homophobia. They might thus form homologues, pedagogically, to race and racial meanings.

Third, language deserves far more attention than was given in this engagement. For instance, if language interpellates the subject, both author and topic, then writing in English must influence and constrain all of our authors whether they are Japan based or U.S. based. Writing in English forces unique methodologies, literatures, and presumed audiences. Some in Japan translate their writing, conceiving in Japanese and then translating that into English. How might that affect the work's readings, especially to native English speakers? Also, what are our assumptions here in using English words and concepts such as "race"? What about the translations that happen in fieldwork between Japanese scholars and Japanese American subjects?

Fourth, what are the implications of a possible identity and identification between Japanese and Japanese Americans? Is there an "imagined community" involved here among those involved in Japanese American studies, including on the part of Japanese students and their evolving and changing views of Japanese Americans? The rise of racism, nativism, and religious bigotry in the United States, for instance, following 9/11 intrigued and puzzled many Japanese students. Japanese American studies has provided a bridge linking anti-Asian, anti-Muslim sentiments and deeds following 9/11 to similar fears and hostilities following Pearl Harbor, including the Japanese American concentration camps. How might that imagined community in Japanese American studies constrain and restrict our imagination, narrowing rather than widening our consciousness, identifications, and solidarities? For instance, engaged histories of Japanese Americans and African Americans might have deeper and more consequential meanings than the histories of the solitary category "Japanese" (even if binational).

Fifth, even as Japanese American studies helps to comprehend the United States and the idea of an "American," Japanese American studies helps to understand Japan and Japanese history and subjectivities. For example, recordings and analyses of the Meiji-era language spoken by Issei and Nisei offer a rare opportunity to trace the evolution of Japan's Japanese language. There are oral history recordings of Issei, which are now being studied by linguists. The Latina/o dekasegi (migrant workers in Japan) destabilized the subjectivities of "Japanese." The question they pose is what or who is "Japanese"? Is it a "race" or biological category and/or a social construction?

Sixth, what is at stake here in Japanese American studies? For some, it is a matter of liberation, mind and body. In that sense, the field is directed at social activism. For others, it is mere intellectual curiosity or exemplars of other social phenomena that draws their attention. For them, the field is an academic, not political, concern. Even on the academic front, the division of fields into disciplines and then of nations and geographical regions leaves Japanese American scholars outside and between, as interdisciplinary, transnational, or translocal scholars. Is the field Japanese or Asian studies? Is it American studies? Is it emigration studies (from Japan) or immigration studies (within the United States)? Scholars in both Japan and the United States, because of the existing hierarchies within and among fields, often find themselves not merely perplexed in locating their work but more tangibly isolated and hence separated from power by dominant narratives of nation and outside disciplinary communities and conventions.

The challenge, then, is simultaneously to construct a field called "Japanese American studies" and to deconstruct its essentialism (the subject position termed "Japanese American"). It can also serve a conservative national agenda of both Japan (nationalism) and the United States (model minority). Both in the United States and the world, Japan/Japanese has undergone a "whitening" as the sole nonwhite member of the European/U.S. capitalist bloc, much like the transformation occurring with the onset of the "browning" of America. Insofar as Japanese America posits a racialization and a national category, it works to advance a conservative agenda. But Japanese America can also retard, if not reverse, that object. This is the opportunity and burden of this and future articulations of Japanese American studies.

Thoughts on Positionality

Noriko K. Ishii

The question of positionality is a crucial one in academic pursuits. As a Japan-based historian of U.S. social and women's history with a PhD from a U.S. university, I was struck by Professor Gary Okihiro's question on our subject-positions and our stakes in Japanese American studies. His query reminded me of a life-changing incident during my first year of graduate school. Although this experience first turned me away from the field of Japanese American studies, it was an important learning experience and a critical turning point in my academic career. In short, it made me think about the meaning of my positionality as a Japanese person in relation to my academic research in U.S. history and American studies.

In 1988, when I began my first semester as a graduate student in Washington, DC, I casually selected Japanese American internment during World War II as my first research topic. I must confess that at that point I had neither a fixed agenda for my graduate program nor a clear awareness of my positionality. I thought Japanese American studies was an obvious choice for a Japanese graduate student. In addition, by choosing to work on internment, I was able to fulfill a requirement for a course I was taking to use non-written materials as a primary source because my location provided me with easy access to the National Archives, where I could work with films and photographs held in the War Relocation Authority records.

However, an interview I conducted with the head of the Washington chapter of the Japanese American Citizens League discouraged me from choosing Japanese American studies as a dissertation subject. After our main interview session was over, the Japanese American woman, reflecting on the

African American agitation against Japanese racism at the time, said something along the following lines: "If you are Japanese, please pass on our Japanese American message to Japanese politicians and business people. Tell them to be responsible in the statements they make about race and the American people, even when addressing a Japanese audience in Japan. Every time a Japanese political leader makes a remark with racial prejudice against African Americans, all the Japan-bashing from African Americans and other ethnic groups in the United States ends up being targeted toward us Japanese Americans. We are the ones who suffer from those racist comments. Please be more responsible." I was totally appalled. I will consider in detail why this was the case later in this discussion, but first I would like to consider the political and economic context of the time and then the meaning of her statement.

This was in the late 1980s, when the trade friction between the United States and Japan was at its peak. Japan was the world's second-largest economic power, and the United States was suffering from a growing trade deficit with Japan. It can now be seen in retrospect that Japan was at the height of its "bubble economy," or financial boom, which would collapse three years later in 1991, plunging Japan into two decades of economic stagnation that some have called "the Lost Decades." By 2011, Japan's position had dropped to the world's third-largest economic power, with China taking its place. In this social and economic context, Japanese political leaders making racist remarks and Japanese "Little Black Sambo" products angered African Americans.

In August 1988, only two weeks before I started graduate school, the *Washington Post* ran a story that groups led by the Congressional Black Caucus were threatening to boycott Japanese products to protest Japanese companies' use of black racial stereotypes, which could be seen in toys, children's books, and black mannequins in Japanese department stores (Shapiro 1988a; Bloomquist 1988). Prior to this, Japanese political leaders had made racially derogatory statements about African Americans, presumably unaware of their own racial prejudices and how much their statements could hurt African Americans and U.S.-Japan relations at large. In 1986, Prime Minister Yasuhiro Nakasone commented publicly that African Americans and Hispanics lowered the overall U.S. intelligence level. In July 1988, two weeks before the boycott threats by black groups in the United States, Michio Watanabe, a leading politician under Nakasone's wing of the ruling Liberal Democratic Party, publicly remarked, "American blacks don't mind filing for bankruptcy."

Alarmed by the threat of a boycott, Japanese manufacturers and publishing houses moved quickly to abandon all controversial products and stop printing and selling *Little Black Sambo,* one of the most popular children's books and which had been on the market for ninety years (Shapiro 1988b, 1989). Despite those actions, protests by African Americans in front of the Japanese embassy in Washington continued, and public sentiment against Japanese racism and cultural insensitivity lingered. African American protests against racism were justified, but U.S. public sentiment might have arisen from anti-Japanese sentiment rather than solidarity with African Americans. It might have also been true that Japanese politicians and businessmen harbored feelings of self-conceit that Japan was superior to the United States in terms of its economic power and diligent, thrifty labor force.

Why, to return to my story, did the Japanese American woman head of the DC chapter of the Japanese American Citizens League ask a Japanese graduate student to pass on a message from Japanese Americans to Japan, expecting me to change Japanese public sentiment, that of a public ignorant of the multiracial culture of the United States? What were her motivations? I have come to understand her admonition to me in several ways.

First, she might have felt uncomfortable with the chasm that lay between her and me, a Japanese graduate student. This relates closely to the question of positionality. Since I was a student interested in the history of Japanese Americans purely from an "outsider's" academic perspective, the Japanese American woman probably wanted to make me realize that for her and others the history of Japanese Americans is not something of the past, but rather something that is continually being made as part of the search for social justice. As a civil rights activist, she was probably aware of the history of collaborations and contestations between Japanese Americans and African Americans during the civil rights movement that had been uncovered by scholars since the 1990s. Fearing the danger of losing solidarity between African and Japanese Americans, she probably thought it crucial to "enlighten" the Japanese so they would become aware of how their actions connect across national borders to affect race relations in the United States. Accordingly, she welcomed me as a Japanese graduate student new to the field of Japanese American studies, and she tried to create good "bridges" between Japan and the United States by turning me and other Japanese graduate students into "mediators."

Second, the social position of Japanese Americans was closely and directly related to their country of ancestry and its power relative to the United

States. In other words, Japan's post–World War II economic recovery and advance as a strong U.S. ally in East Asia during the Cold War era might have affected the position of Japanese Americans in the multiracial hierarchy of the United States. At the same time, however, my interviewee, the Japanese American woman, was likely aware of how the racial formation of Japanese and Japanese Americans operates in the United States and knew that whites and non-whites would not distinguish between Japanese and Japanese Americans.

But why was I appalled at the Japanese American woman's comment? As a naïve, first-year graduate student, I immediately felt overburdened by her suggestion that I take on the responsibility of a mediator. Why did I feel overburdened? It was because I wanted to have a distance between me and my object of study. As a student of history, I believed that distancing was indispensable for objectivity, a desired end of history and academic work generally. Her comments disrupted that distance and threw me unexpectedly into the middle of the conflict between African and Japanese Americans. I felt threatened, and was uneasy, filled with discomfort and fear. This was the beginning of the process by which I came to realize my positionality as a Japanese national.

Her comments illuminated the fact that Japanese Americans live in the contested terrain of a multiracial society and that their position and welfare are partially directed by their relations with other groups, including African Americans. Thus, their quest for social justice as a racial minority in a white-dominated society is enormously complex. In addition, underlying their social activism is the traumatic memory of the World War II internment that Japanese Americans, the Nisei and Sansei, and the first-generation Japanese immigrants (Issei) shared.

Through her comments, I realized how different the political stakes are between Japanese Americans and Japanese who were temporarily residing in the United States. I felt I could never have an equal stake in or properly treat the Japanese American quest for social justice without having a collective memory of the World War II internment that was shared by family members and friends. Being an "outsider," I could always return to Japan, where I was a member of the dominant group in society, a significantly different position from Japanese Americans who remained a racialized minority group in the United States. In this way, I became aware that I could never claim a Japanese American positionality in Japanese American studies.

Despite that fact, I was stunned to discover that white Americans on the East Coast generally perceived Japanese Americans and Japanese nationals as being no different. Those in my department, both faculty and students, who were predominantly white (there were no Asian Americans), failed to understand the differences between Japanese and Japanese Americans or even between Japanese and Chinese. Therefore, when I discussed my uneasiness and fear with my professors, no one could understand why I could not identify with Japanese Americans. It was quite a revelation to me that the racialized perception in American culture that lumps together Japanese nationals and Japanese Americans supersedes notions of nationality and even national borders.

A discussion with one of my professors also helped me realize the importance of positionality. Having a long-standing interest in racial discourse in U.S. history, I found myself discussing with a professor of African American history the possibility of pursuing a career in that field. He advised me against that if I was seriously considering a future of presenting my work in U.S. academia because, the professor advised, nobody would accept a Japanese woman as a serious African American studies scholar. Without having shared the experience and historical memory of African Americans, my audience would think that I could never understand my subjects' political stakes and feelings. This was another revelatory, learning experience because I had naïvely believed that I could specialize in whatever field I had an academic interest in.

From those experiences, my identity as a Japanese woman, as well as my understanding of the differences between Japanese nationals and Japanese Americans, came into focus. In other words, I came to realize that nationality was a central constituting factor of my positionality. Furthermore, I learned how important it is to identify one's positionality and political commitments when engaging in academic research. Ever since, I have pursued academic research that is rooted in what I see as a positive set of political commitments that are guided by my positionality as a Japanese woman. The question of positionality, as a Japanese historian based in Japan, has become my first and foremost point of reference when I choose to undertake academic research in the fields of U.S. history and American studies.

More than two decades have passed since academic organizations such as the Organization of American Historians called for the internationalization of American history and American studies. The July 2012 Shinagawa conference organized by Professors Yasuko Takezawa and Gary Okihiro provided a rare opportunity for both U.S.-based and Japan-based scholars to engage in provocative dialogues involving fundamental epistemological questions. Such an exciting forum, I believe, reflects the fact that the internationalization of American studies has entered a new phase in which substantial transnational exchanges can produce new knowledge.

References

Bloomquist, Randall. 1988. "Blacks Protest Japanese Bias; Boycott Hinted." *Adweek,* August 15, Midwest edition, LexisNexis Academic.

Shapiro, Margaret. 1988a. "Old Black Stereotypes Find New Lives in Japan; Marketers Defend Sambo Toys, Black Mannequins, Insist Racism Was Not Intended." *Washington Post,* July 22, A18.

———. 1988b. "Japanese Companies Recall 'Little Black Sambo' Products." *Washington Post,* July 29, A15.

———. 1989. "Japanese Publishers Ban Sambo." *Washington Post,* January 25, C1, C2.

Asian American History across the Pacific

Lon Kurashige

I have never had the opportunity to reflect on my developing interest in Japan, so I welcome the invitation by Professors Takezawa and Okihiro to consider my positionality as a researcher of Asian American history. I do this in light of the exchange between U.S.-based and Japan-based scholars of Nikkei studies held in Shinagawa (Tokyo) in July 2012. This reflection is rooted in personal views, memories, and experiences, because these have been the most powerful influences on my thinking. Yet in focusing on the personal I will not ignore structures of colonialism and racism that have shaped my personal identity within the United States and Japan.

As a historian, I cannot help but work chronologically in constructing the narrative of how I, an American and a U.S.-based scholar, came to my current positionality vis-à-vis Japan-based scholars. Before I begin, let me state that my relationship to Japan today is based in a deep respect and appreciation for the contributions that Japan-based scholars and scholarship have made to my understanding of Asian American history. My feelings, however, did not start out this way.

As an undergraduate, I cut my scholarly teeth researching California's Alien Land Law, nourished by the work and perspective of Roger Daniels's *Politics of Prejudice: The Anti-Japanese Movement in California and the Struggle for Japanese Exclusion*. Upon entering graduate school I again followed Daniels to embrace social history by shifting my attention from the white "victimizers" to the Asian American "victims." This shift stemmed from my involvement with the movement for Asian American social justice, which taught me firsthand that oppressed peoples had historical agency; they were not inert blocks of wood but active agents able to influence their own histories. As a young scholar, I embraced the project of empowering present-day racial minorities by reclaiming the historical agency of Asian Americans. In so doing, I embraced racial nationalism, an ideology that cast racialized communities as "internal colonies" whose subjects often have internalized white racism. The goal, as I saw it, was for racial minorities to "decolonize" their minds, control their own communities, and forge alliances with other oppressed groups (blacks, Latinos, women, the poor and working classes, etc.) in order to unite for progressive change. In some ways it was not hard for me to become a racial nationalist. Having grown up in a self-segregated Nikkei community with a preponderance of former internees, I had never really trusted white America—even though some of my friends were white. Yet it was hard to totally resolve the internalized racism that told me that as a Japanese American I was lesser than the dreaded, feared, and idealized "*hakujin*."

As a racial nationalist, I turned increasingly toward scholars who were Asian American and who in their own way also were struggling to decolonize their minds. When I started graduate school in the late 1980s, the two historians who stood out were Professors Yuji Ichioka and Ronald Takaki. Ichioka's pioneering studies of the Issei proved the most useful for my research on Japanese Americans; but his emphasis on using Japanese-language sources and recovering one's buried language ability proved too much for my limited undergraduate study of Japanese. So it was that Takaki exerted the stronger influence. Yet the important point is that I began to distinguish between two types of Asian American history—one rooted in the social history of Asian immigrants and their vernacular sources, and the other in second and later generations—and their English-language sources. I identified with the latter and wrote a dissertation and subsequent book focusing on Nisei identity formation. As a result, I saw Ichioka, and other scholars of the Issei, as secondary relations—connected to my research interests but outside my immediate kin.

The border between my primary and secondary kin relations started breaking down through deepening personal and professional ties with Professor Brian Masaru Hayashi. Beyond our common scholarly interests, Hayashi was familiar to me because we both grew up in Los Angeles and, as Sansei, played in the same Japanese American basketball leagues. But he was unlike any of my Nikkei friends because he was fluent in Japanese, worked in Japan, and traveled back and forth across the Pacific. When I shared with him my views about Japan, he would shake his head saying, "You need to go to there and see for yourself!" This was his polite way of saying how naïve and uninformed were my views.

As mentioned, I had studied Japanese in college and, in addition, had been around Japanese-speaking people my whole life, but I still managed to see Japan, as historian John Dower might say, through "Western eyes." I remember reading David Mura's memoir *Turning Japanese* and imagining myself vicariously living his Tokyo adventures—although his internalized racism, I thought, was more extreme than mine, since he grew up bereft of an ethnic community. Yet, for me, growing up in Los Angeles in the 1970s and 1980s gave me added incentive to misrecognize Japan because I was in frequent contact with busloads of camera-toting Japanese businessmen and tourists. My Sansei friends and I derogatorily called them "FOBs" (Fresh off the Boat), trying as hard as we could to distance ourselves from their embarrassing Asian accents, style of dress, and mannerisms. Another kind of FOB in my social orbit were recent Asian immigrants and refugees (some of whom were Japanese but most Korean, Chinese, and Vietnamese) who started showing up in my public junior high. My identity as an American required that I distance myself physically and psychologically from FOBs. But no distance was great enough to prevent white classmates from calling me racist names and lumping me, in their minds, with Asian immigrants and foreigners.

Brian Hayashi was a revelation to me because he was not an FOB and yet he was at home with Japanese language and culture, and was living in Japan. His biculturalism exposed the constructedness of the ethnic binary that I had used to distinguish Japanese Americans from FOBs. In this way, Hayashi restimulated the interest in Japan I developed while taking Japanese-language classes in college. Consequently, I applied for and received a Fulbright lectureship and with Hayashi's help taught for the 2003–2004 academic year at Kyoto University. While I do not have enough time and space to describe what a transformative experience it was for me and my family to live in Japan, I will share one example that reveals my evolving positionality vis-à-vis Japan-based scholars.

Hayashi and fellow Kyoto University professor Yasuko Takezawa asked me to speak at a symposium on Nikkei history that was attended by a good number of Japan-based scholars. Out of the many papers given, I believe mine was the only one from a scholar currently working in the United States. This became painfully apparent in the wrap-up session when I asked why all of the scholars there were using conceptual frameworks based on U.S.

historiographies or Western thinkers such as Edward Said. I voiced my disappointment that none had relied on Japan-based historiographies or conceptual frameworks—that is, on what I consider more authentic Japanese perspectives. I gave an example saying that the scholars might have relied on Zen Buddhism for their inspiration.

I forget the general response that my comment provoked, but I do remember one person pointedly asking whether I had the right to presume that only Westerners could use the work of someone like Edward Said. Why was it all right for U.S.-based scholars to appropriate his theories and not for scholars based in Japan? When he raised this question, I realized that I had hit a nerve in the audience, and thus quickly shut up.

The enormity of my ignorance, however, had yet to fully reveal itself to me. After all, I had come to Japan not just to deconstruct my own identity but to undermine the colonialized mentality that I imagined had caused Japan-based scholars of American studies to idolize the United States—and the scholarship created there. This colonial relationship with respect to American studies in Japan has been carefully analyzed in Takeshi Matsuda's *Soft Power and Its Perils: US Cultural Policy in Early Post-War Japan and Permanent Dependency*. Like the white do-gooders in Matsuda's book who sought to bring American democracy to Japan, I too sought to enlighten Japanese scholars, but with American counter-hegemonic empowerment rather than liberal democracy. I wanted to expose and eliminate the effects of America's deeply rooted cultural colonization. To do this meant stretching my old racial nationalism to include the people of Japan, thus creating a transnational racial identity in opposition to white colonial mentality imposed and internalized in Japan as well as Asian American communities. The FOB syndrome that once distanced me from Japan was a thing of the past.

After my Fulbright year, I returned to Japan a number of times to teach graduate students, conduct research, and visit with friends. During this time, I worked closely with a number of students and young scholars from Japan. I am not sure when, but some time amidst my frequent contact with Japanese scholars and students, I realized that being a missionary for the gospel of decolonization was no different from preaching the kind of democratic modernization that Matsuda exposes as a form of white colonialism. My attempt to decolonize Japan gave little thought to the historical and contemporary agency of its people; it assumed that Western knowledge and experience could help "save" them from their unenlightened state, which created a huge psychological chasm between U.S.-based and Japan-based scholars. I had begun to cross this chasm before the Shinagawa conference, but that meeting (and subsequent discussions I have had about it), for the first time, left me with five thoughts about how I can, and why I should, bridge this divide.

First is to stop trying to help Japan. This means relinquishing the goal of decolonization and, instead, trying to understand the relationships that Japanese scholars have to American studies on their own terms. Doing so requires appreciating the vast diversity of motivations that Japan-based scholars have for studying the United States—many of which differ very much from my own. Jettisoning the missionary spirit, I have come to realize, also means appreciating the diversity of graduate training in, and institutional situations for, American studies at Japanese universities.

A second factor is to understand the historical milieu in which Japanese scholars were raised and currently operate. This means crossing the often difficult border between American studies and Japanese area studies. I have found that such border crossing is better facilitated by identifying as a scholar of trans-Pacific studies, rather than Japanese American studies. One indication that I had progressed as a trans-Pacific scholar occurred during the workshop session of the Shinagawa conference when we discussed Professor Sachiko Kawakami's paper (see in this book) about Korean immigrants in San Francisco's Nihonmachi. Kawakami used the concept of "post-coloniality" to explain the Koreans' motivations for forging interpersonal bonds with Japanese Americans. One Japan-based scholar noted that her paper revealed a "Japanese sensibility," which I inferred to mean that she had an acute awareness of the legacy of Japanese colonialism on the Korean peninsula. I could understand that from Kawakami's perspective it was not so strange to see older Korean immigrants, who had been schooled in the Japanese language, seeking out friendly gatherings with Japanese Americans. After all, Zainichi Koreans in Japan often have no problem forging interpersonal relations with mainstream Japanese.

My point here has less to do with Kawakami's use of postcolonialism than with the fact that I could understand what she meant by it. A few years earlier I do not think I could have done so, because I would have read the good relations between Korean immigrants and Japanese Americans as a sign of "pan-ethnicity," the notion, central to Asian American studies, that Asians in the United States have shared a racial identity as outsiders in white America. Until I could see beyond the pan-ethnicity concept and cross the border into Japanese-area studies, I would not be able to appreciate Kawakami's Japanese sensibility. Consequently, I would have missed a chance to see experiences in San Francisco's Nihonmachi from a totally different, and equally valid, perspective.

The third bridge across the chasm separating Japan-based and U.S.-based scholars originates from the second one. In appreciating a "Japanese sensibility," I need to pay special attention to the fact that Japan has its own important history of ethnic minorities. This history can serve as a crucial point of comparison with U.S.-based studies of Asian Americans. Too often, seemingly homogeneous countries like Japan are dismissed as irrelevant for the study of immigration and ethnicity. This is unfortunate and flies in the face of a rich vein of studies conducted on Japan's ethnic minorities, especially but not limited to Zainichi Koreans. A brilliant example of comparative possibilities is Takashi Fujitani's *Race for Empire: Koreans as Japanese and Japanese as Americans during World War II*. Fujitani's book bridges the chasm across the Pacific by highlighting Japan's very real multiethnic ideology during World War II. This ideology, he argues, mirrored America's simultaneous switch from "vulgar racism" to a new multiethnic ethos that he calls "polite racism."

Fujitani's criticism of national histories raises a fourth point about bridging scholarship across the Pacific that highlights what Japan-based scholars can contribute to the study of Asian Americans. In her own reflection on the Shinagawa conference, Rika Nakamura poses a crucial question to U.S.-based scholars: "How does Japan/Asia help you question your normative perception and truths as the Westerner of color in the global terrains?" I've already answered this question by showing how my encounters with Japan-based scholars have caused me to reflect on the gospel of decolonization that I sought to spread throughout Japan. But there is another answer with which I would like to end this reflection. This centers on the ability of Japan-based scholars to better deconstruct nationalism than their U.S.-based counterparts.

In wrestling with Japan-based scholarship I have learned how American I am. Specifically, I have realized that my racial nationalism is not so much anti-American as it is anti-white. In this way I can appreciate Asians, blacks, Latinos, or native peoples as true Americans who have a more inclusive sense of national identity than do most whites. I celebrate the possibility of creating an American identity that is inclusive of all aggrieved groups. In this way, I am for making nationalism better (more inclusive and aware of power relations and their effects). I am not for getting rid of nationalism altogether or portraying it as always inherently wrong. For many Japan-based scholars, the litmus test of nationalism is the horrendous death and destruction committed in its name during World War II. Yet for me, and perhaps other U.S.-based scholars, the test comes with the civil rights movement and the tremendously positive changes (including social movement organizing) that have occurred in the United States since racial minorities have become recognized as legitimate Americans. In the final analysis, such a difference in appreciating nationalism promises to enliven discussions of Asian American history and should be encouraged.

Such discussions are not entirely new to Asian American studies. One thread about nationalism and denationalization has circulated within U.S.-based scholarship since the 1990s, but for some reason it is only now that I have come to connect this subject to the study of Asian American history. Why the delay? It can be explained in part by the stubbornness of my own racial nationalism and monolingualism, which has limited my research interests to the U.S. side of the Pacific. Yet another reason for the delay is that the existing discussion of nationalism and denationalization has been rooted in questions of diaspora and transnational migration—see, for example, the extended dialogue with Sau Ling Wong's critique of denationalization in Rhacel Parrenas and Lok Siu's *Asian Diasporas: New Formations, New Conceptions.* Because my research has focused less on migrants and more on later generations and questions of their mainstream belonging and loyalty, I have treated books like the one by Parrenas and Siu as secondary kin relations. This brings me to my fifth and final point about why and how I can cross the Pacific in my research.

In reflecting on the Shinagawa conference, I have realized that Japan-based scholars and scholarship have made it possible to globalize my work not just by researching diaspora and transnational migration. Rather, I also can cross the Pacific by learning about the history of Zainichi Koreans and other minorities in Japan, and comparing them, like Fujitani does, to second-generation and later Japanese Americans. Consequently, I look forward to a trans-Pacific discussion regarding minority studies that will include not just issues of diaspora and trans-Pacific migration but also questions of identity formation, political and cultural citizenship, community formation, and social movements, as well as mainstream ethnoracial politics, ideology, and discourse. Thus, it is through comparative minority studies that racial nationalist and monolingual U.S.-based scholars like me can perhaps best benefit from the tremendous opportunities that Japan-based scholars present.

Japanese Americans in Academia and Political Discourse in Japan

Okiyoshi Takeda

I am a political scientist specializing in Asian American politics. Although I earned my PhD in the United States, my initial interest was in the U.S. Congress and not in Japanese American studies or Asian American studies.

What shifted my interest toward Asian American studies was that I had witnessed firsthand a campus sit-in at the Princeton University president's office, where students were fighting for the establishment of an Asian American studies program. Witnessing such an incident, I realized that Asian Americans were an understudied topic in the field of political science. There is also a tendency for scholars from Japan to focus exclusively on Japanese Americans and to disregard other Asian American ethnic groups. Since I did not start out my study on Asian Americans in a graduate school in Japan with an interest in Japanese Americans, I have been able to avoid taking that kind of path.

It becomes problematic when scholars choose their research group based on a nationalistic attitude—for example, Japanese scholars choosing to study Japanese Americans based solely on Japanese linkage. I share a certain level of discomfort when Japanese authors publish books and state in an afterword that we should understand Japanese American history because "after all, we are Japanese."

For example, it is extremely rare for Korean residents in Japan to be included in the concept of "we, the Japanese" and in the mind of Japanese scholars who study Japanese Americans. I have come across a book on

Japanese American history published during the 1990s by a Japanese scholar who implied that because Japanese Brazilians and other Latin Americans of Japanese descent were coming to Japan in great numbers, we should pay greater attention to Japanese Americans as a close comparable minority group. The problem with this argument is that we have had Korean and Chinese people who had been long-time residents and lived among us long before Japanese Latin Americans came to Japan.

On the other hand, it is true that Japanese American history is not well understood among the Japanese public (and Asian American history is even lesser known). Japanese high school textbooks seldom discuss Japanese American history (or for that matter, the Japanese occupation of Korea, Taiwan, Manchuria, and Oceanian islands and flow of peoples between these areas and Japan). The only aspect about Japanese Americans that is briefly taught in high schools is the history of internment. It is therefore not surprising that the main actress in the twelve-hour television drama *99 Years of Love* commented in a news conference that she "didn't know there were such Japanese people who immigrated to the United States until I played this role." Needless to say, some questioned whether she was qualified to play the lead role in the drama.

Furthermore, it is worthy to note that the Japanese internment case is sometimes "used" and "abused" in the Japanese political discourse.

Specifically, the left-wing media and critics in Japan often point to the U.S. government's apology to people of Japanese ancestry as a result of the redress movement as an example of how the Japanese government should act by offering a similar apology to the war victims in Asia (including, but not limited to, "comfort women," or sex slaves). *Asahi Shimbun*, the leading left-wing newspaper, often runs articles and op-ed pieces that argue for a similar step to be taken by the Japanese government.

An article published on December 20, 2007, for example, reported a public lecture given in Matsuyama, Ehime, whose main message was to push for the Japanese government to apologize to "comfort women." The lecturer, who was the president of the *Onna Tachi no Sensō to Heiwa Shiryōkan* (Women's Active Museum on War and Peace) in Tokyo, was reported to state that righting a wrong and overturning injustice were the basics of solving the "comfort women's" issue, citing President Ronald Reagan's apology to people of Japanese descent in 1988 as an example. Another article on June 30, 2006, entitled "From the Window of an Editorial Writer," described the Bataan Death March's survivors' activities. The survivors' association held an essay contest, and a Japanese college student who was one of the winners joined the survivors' annual meeting. The student pointed out that the U.S. government has apologized for the internment of people of Japanese descent during World War II, and then stated, "As an aggressor country, it is a natural thing to apologize [to the victims of the Bataan Death March], and I cannot understand why Japan does not."

The right-wing media and critics in Japan also tend to use the internment case to their own advantage. *Sankei Shimbun,* the leading right-wing newspaper, often interprets Japanese American history in a way that promotes their nationalistic cause. For example, Yoshihisa Komori, the newspaper's Washington-based senior editor who has written extensively against Korean and Korean American residents' demands for an apology for the sexual enslavement of "comfort women," published an editorial entitled "A Government Would Never Easily Apologize" on August 21, 2010. In this editorial, Komori pointed out:

> Presidents Reagan and Bush [Sr.] apologized to Japanese Americans for their internment during World War II, and President Clinton apologized for the occupation of Hawai'i by armed forces. But there are very few examples in which the United States apologized to other countries. It is clear that the United States colonialized the Philippines by force, but it has not apologized to them. The same is true with the atomic bombs dropped in Japan.

In Komori's logic, the U.S. government's redress is used as a reason that Japan does *not* have to apologize to Korea, because the redress is an apology to the country's own people and does not transcend national borders.

Sankei Shimbun is also known for arguing for strengthening U.S.-Japan military ties. Interestingly, in the newspaper, wartime experiences of Japanese American soldiers are often positively connected to the current U.S.-Japan security alliance. One editorial writer, Yoshirō Toriumi, praised Jun'ichi Suzuki's documentary film *MIS: Human Secret Weapon* and the members of the Military Intelligence Service who joined the mission in an editorial on October 6, 2012. In his conclusion, Toriumi wrote, "From listening to one testimony after another in the film, I was able to appreciate the foundation of the U.S.-Japan alliance that the second-generation Japanese Americans worked hard to build." Here, the link between the Military Intelligence Service and the U.S.-Japan alliance is not made explicit. Second-generation

Japanese Americans, however, are "used" to support the interpretation that they have contributed to the current U.S.-Japan alliance.

Toriumi wrote another editorial on November 27, 2010, this time on awarding a Congressional Medal of Honor to the 442nd regimental combat team, a unit composed almost entirely of soldiers of Japanese ancestry. After writing about the harsh experiences of several former soldiers in the European Theater of Operations, he noted that these soldiers were taught *bushidō* (the code of the samurai) by their parents. Toriumi then concluded that the Japanese "ought to pay more attention to the footsteps made on current Japan's most important ally by second-generation Japanese Americans who followed Japanese spiritual beauty." Again, Japanese Americans are evaluated on whether they are useful to the current Japan's military status.

A more extreme case of praising Japanese American soldiers for demonstrating Japanese cultural virtues can be found in the right-wing historical bimonthly magazine *Rekishitsu* (The Knowledgeable of History). In its November 2010 issue, which featured the 442nd regimental combat team and a related documentary film by Jun'ichi Suzuki, the magazine carried an article entitled "442 Was the Imperial Army among the U.S. Forces." It likened the soldiers of the 442nd team to the Imperial Army of Japan because "they fought according to the teachings of their Japanese parents[:] 'Haji' (shame), 'meiyo' (honor), 'gaman' (perseverance), 'shinbō' (patience), 'doryoku' (efforts). . . . They were an 'imperial army' in America" (p. 11). Here, the fact that the 442nd team fought against the Axis powers, which included Japan, is conveniently ignored. Emphasis is placed on the spirit of the 442nd team and its similarities in virtues of Japanese culture.

As the foregoing analysis suggests, the study and treatment of Japanese Americans in Japan and their history are shaped by the politics and ideologies held by opposing constituencies in Japan. The way in which Japanese Americans are studied, analyzed, and discussed is different in Japan from how the subject is treated in the United States. Whether or not such treatment is healthy is another matter for discussion; however, it is probably true that most Japanese Americans would not know how they and their history are discussed in their country of ancestry.

Location, Positionality, and Community
Studying and Teaching Japanese America in the United States and Japan

Yoko Tsukuda

Issues surrounding the differences between U.S.-based and Japan-based Japanese American studies have been important to me as a person who has pursued degrees at graduate schools in both countries. I first became interested in the history of Japanese Americans in my junior year of college when a visiting white professor from Seattle told me the story of how her father helped his Japanese American friends during World War II. Because I was unaware of what the "camps" meant, I was shocked to learn about the internment experience of Japanese Americans. After writing my senior thesis based on a month of fieldwork in Los Angeles's Japanese American community, I enrolled in an ethnic studies master's course at San Francisco State University. Later, I returned to Japan and completed an American studies PhD in the Area Studies Department at the University of Tokyo. Presently, I teach at a Japanese university. My experiences in both the United States and Japan have often led me to questions surrounding my positionality as a Japan-based scholar who engages in Japanese American studies.

To the United States and Back to Japan

While a graduate student at San Francisco State from 2000 to 2004, I actively participated in the Japanese American community by volunteering and interning. Inspired by my American classmates in the ethnic studies program, who often spoke from their own ethnic or racial community's standpoint, I was seeking to find "my own community" through research and community service. That involvement in the Japanese American community soon made me realize the boundaries and connections between Japanese Americans and Japanese nationals.[1] At the time, the meanings and roles of the community were being questioned, with San Francisco's Japantown losing Japanese American residents and businesses and a Japantown preservation movement growing among Japanese American community leaders. I wondered how Japanese Americans and Japanese nationals could maintain a unified ethnic community. Japantown had become a mere symbol of ethnicity for younger Japanese Americans (many of whom had dispersed into suburban areas), although it continued to provide Japanese nationals with Japan-related everyday commodities such as food and various kinds of Japanese-language services. I occasionally heard criticisms from the two groups directed at each other: some Japanese American community leaders criticized Japanese nationals for their lack of respect of Japanese Americans' past struggles against racism, while some Japanese business owners insisted that Japanese Americans should understand how much the economy of Japantown is dependent on Japanese businesses, such as those catering to tourists. In my master's thesis, I examined the relationship between those two groups based on interviews in and participant observation at several community organizations. Although I had no intention of staying in the United States after completing my graduate studies, I regarded my study as a contribution to the development of San Francisco's Japanese American community and positioned myself as one of its members.

When I returned to Japan and resumed my studies at a Japanese university, it seemed natural for me to continue to pursue my interest in the relationship between Japanese nationals and Japanese Americans. However, moving my base back to Japan and Japanese academia gave me an opportunity to reconsider Japanese American studies not only from a perspective outside the Japanese American community but also in the wider framework of American studies and U.S. history. Thinking back to when I was in San Francisco, I found it strange to place the Japanese nationals I met there in U.S. immigration history in the same way as the prewar Issei generation. Just as I spent four years in the United States as a student and then moved back to Japan, many Japanese today have high levels of mobility among Japan, the United States, and beyond. I wondered, given that situation, could those mobile Japanese really be called "immigrants" and be understood as being part of U.S. immigration or Japanese American history? How and when do they become "immigrants"? How and when do they stop being "immigrants" (if such a thing is possible)? These questions led me to write a doctoral dissertation that considered the (dis)similarities between immigrants and non-immigrants in the United States through case studies of contemporary Japanese/Japanese American communities. In that way, my research interests have always been linked to my positionality and location.

Beyond Nation-Based Frameworks

Dialogues between U.S.-based and Japan-based Japanese Americanists have offered a very important opportunity for both groups to make clear and share their own "investments" (to borrow a word from Professor Gary Okihiro) in the field, as well as reflect on the different paths shaped by domestic contexts the field has taken in the two countries. In the United States, Japanese American studies was born out of the civil rights movement at the same time as studies of other racial minorities arose. Japanese American studies contributed greatly to the success of the redress and reparations movement and succeeded in giving Japanese Americans a historical place similar to immigrants from Europe in the larger U.S. story of the inclusively multiculturalistic "nation of immigrants." Japanese American studies in the United States takes for granted the fact that its mission is social justice and works from a nation-based framework that has rarely been challenged. In Japan, however, interest in Japanese Americans or *Nikkei Amerika jin* grew in academia beginning in the late 1970s and 1980s, though a few studies about Japanese emigration had existed before those decades. This interest then spread into popular culture, as can be seen by the appearance of television drama series such as the adaptation of the novel *Futatsu no sokoku* (Two Homelands, 1983) entitled *Sanga moyu* (Burning Mountain and River, 1984) as well as *99 nen no ai: Japanese Americans* (99 Years of Love, 2011). Those representations draw sympathy for early Japanese immigrants and their descendants from Japanese audiences by depicting them as victims of U.S. racial discrimination, and they end up incorporating Japanese Americans' postwar socioeconomic success as a "model minority" into a nationalistic narrative in order to prove the superiority of the Japanese "race."

In this context, dialogues between Japan-based and U.S.-based Japanese Americanists can play a rather important role if they explore the transnational perspective of "Japanese America" without being trapped by nation-based frameworks. However, I do not mean that we should be free from ideas of location such as the United States or Japan. While the various technological developments in today's globalized world tend to give us an illusion that we can conduct any kind of research wherever we are, the location, audience, and language of our studies as well as our own positionalities continue to matter, and we should always be keenly aware of those contexts and factors. Without a doubt, our positionalities limit our audiences and resources as well as mirror our different epistemological foundations. I am often reminded of this when I teach Japanese American studies in Japanese universities. Some Japanese college students have never been abroad and have no doubts about the idea that Japanese society is homogeneous. However, many other Japanese college students have a wide variety of overseas experiences; some have mixed heritage or dual nationalities, and others were born or spent their childhood overseas, or have recently studied or traveled abroad. They have often asked me questions like, "Am I Japanese American?" or "How can I become an immigrant?" These questions have made me realize how the Japanese in Japan can relate to the Japanese in the United States individually and "transnationally" in a way that goes beyond the nation-based frameworks of each country. I hope our dialogues will continue and generate productive outcomes amid a growing interest in transnational Japanese America.

Note

1 Here, I am not using the phrase "Japanese nationals" to refer only to people with Japanese citizenship. I am also including in the category Japanese business expatriates and their families as well as postwar Japanese immigrants who may have become naturalized Americans and not retained their Japanese citizenship.

Positions In-Between
Hapa, Buddhist, and Japanese American Studies

Duncan Ryûken Williams

In reflecting on my positionality vis-à-vis Japanese American studies, one of the first things that come to mind is the multiplicity of positions that make up my identity. I am neither fully Japanese nor American nor Japanese American. Given that my father is British and my mother Japanese, my heritage is at least dual. Given that I was born and brought up in Japan initially as a British citizen with an alien registration card and then as a dual citizen from fifteen to twenty years old, and since twenty, as solely a Japanese citizen, it is sometimes hard to know how to define my position to Japanese America. Yes, I have lived and worked in the United States on various visas, and more recently, with a green card for the past twenty-five years. So I suppose that as a person with a Japanese passport who has permanent residency in the United States, I am technically an Issei, a first-generation Japanese immigrant to the United States.

But identities are complex—both given and chosen. In addition to being a slightly nontraditional Issei, I would also closely identify as a person of mixed roots and mixed-race heritage (I grew up using the Japanese term *hafu*, and in recent years the U.S. term *hapa*, and now both interchangeably) that resists simplistic national or racial categorizations.

Perhaps the person I most identify with in Japanese American history is Fred Kinzaburō Makino, the British-Japanese community leader in Hawai'i and founder of the influential *Hawai'i Hochi* newspaper, who had emigrated and settled in Honolulu after growing up in Yokohama. He took his Japanese mother's maiden name after his father died when he was four, but before his transformation into a Japanese American community member, he was primarily identified as a son of the Higgenbotham family in Yokohama's international community. His brother, Jō, who had immigrated to the Big Island earlier and was awarded U.S. citizenship there, found that when he moved to New York City, his citizenship was revoked by the state because of his part-Japanese heritage. In a curious way, there is a long history of those of part-Japanese heritage ending up identifying more closely with the Japanese aspect of their identity while in America's racial landscape.

Identities are also multiple. In addition to my studies of Japanese American religious history and mixed-race histories, my primary field of research is the study of Japanese Buddhism, and I was ordained as a Zen Buddhist priest in Nagano, Japan, some twenty years ago. This has oriented me to focus on Japanese-language texts, both primary material from and secondary scholarship about Japanese America, especially as I realized that so much of Japanese American history and religion as produced in the United States has been so biased by an exclusive focus on English-language sources by Christians, who for most of the first half of the community's history have been a small minority.

My training in religious studies and Buddhist studies has alerted me to a number of other challenges in Japanese American studies. First, because of the emergence of Japanese American (and Asian American) studies in the United States from within the framework of ethnic studies and leftist and activist politics, the field has been weak in the study of the religious life of the communities. The legacy of the political left's myopic views on religion has meant that the field has long missed the centrality of religion to community formation. This has only been partially corrected in recent years with the publication of a handful of works on Japanese Buddhism and Christianity. I am sure the fact that my positionality as a priest in Japanese American Buddhist communities informs this view.

Second, despite the imminent shift of the roughly 1.3 million-person Japanese American community into the first Asian American group that is majority multiracial, the study of persons of mixed roots and race in Japanese America has been woefully inadequate. The first Japanese Americans to settle in Hawaiʻi, Oregon, and California in the 1860s–1870s were all multiracial. The first Nisei, born in 1870, was Mary Schnell, born at the Wakamatsu Tea and Silk Farm Colony in California to the German John Henry Schnell and his Japanese wife, Oyo. In addition to the first major wave of Japanese migration to the United States, the second wave after the near-complete ban in 1924 was the post–World War II migration of Japanese war brides and mixed-race orphans. While some scholars have rightly noted the need for further research on the so-called Shin Issei community, it should be highlighted that much of that migration also involves multiracial families. So, it is not just that we need to attend to the changing Japanese American community, which will only become increasingly majority multiracial in the future, but we need to attend to families and persons of the multiracial and mixed-roots heritage (e.g., Japanese-Korean, Japanese-Filipino, Japanese-Chinese). I am sure the fact that my positionality of mixed roots and an Issei migrant informs this view as well.

Finally, we might consider some of the questions raised at the Shinagawa gathering about insiders and outsiders or U.S.-based and Japan-based scholarship in light of other fields of academic discourse. Again, given my position as a religious studies scholar, I am keenly aware of debates around emic and etic views of religion and the comparative advantages of insider/outsider frames to deepen our understanding of any religion. At this juncture in the field of religious studies, a field that admittedly has had more time to digest and think through these issues, the consensus is that a Christian scholar of Christianity, for example, while having certain advantages (access to archives, a phenomenologically sensitive view from the practitioner's perspective, and a longer familiarity with the tradition), certainly does not hold any special status. Excellent research on Christianity has emerged from Christian scholars, but equally excellent research has emerged from Jews, atheists, and Muslims. Subpar and poor research has also come from both Christians and non-Christians alike. While certain divinity schools may still hang onto an antiquated notion that only Christians can study Christianity properly, this is really not a serious nor sustainable position given the actual results of the broad spectrum of scholarship on the subject.

It seems to me that it is also high time that we recognize that Japanese American scholars of Japanese America have produced excellent research as well as subpar dribble. And the same can be said for non-Japanese American scholars (whether Euro-Americans or Japanese nationals). It is time we recognized the value of scholarship across the Pacific by scholars with multiple positionalities who are all contributing to a fuller understanding and picture of Japanese America.

Toward More Equal Dialogue

Yasuko Takezawa

For the benefit of young scholars in both countries, I would like to present one more story following Professor Noriko Ishii, about the experience of a Japanese student studying Japanese Americans in the United States during the 1980s.

First, I have to confess that when I embarked on my path as a scholar in the United States, I was rather naïve, with my approach to Japanese American studies being shaped by the cultural baggage I had carried from Japan. After spending my undergraduate years there majoring in comparative culture and cultural anthropology, I had hoped to continue and deepen my studies by focusing on Japanese American acculturation and ethnic identity in an American graduate program. Through the fieldwork, however, I came to realize that such an approach positioned Japanese Americans on a continuum linking the two poles of "American" and "Japanese" culture—precisely the framework critiqued in the introduction to this volume.

After several years of living in Seattle, I grew steadily uneasy with being labeled simply as a "Japanese" person; culturally and psychologically, I felt a strong sense of affinity with my Sansei friends. However, I came to realize that one decisive factor would forever separate me from them regardless of how many years I stayed in the United States: I did not have parents, aunts, uncles, and grandparents who were sent to the concentration camps.

A theatrical performance I watched one day with my Japanese American friends at the Asian American Theatre in Seattle in 1985 marked a turning point in my approach to the lives and experiences of Japanese Americans, and consequently in my understanding of their culture. The performance, which was followed by a talk by the late Gordon Hirabayashi, was a fund-raising event to support his lawsuit against the U.S. government. The play, entitled *Breaking the Silence,* was by the Seattle playwright Nikki Nojima Louis and focused on the voices of the Issei, Nisei, and Sansei, depicting how they came to break the silence surrounding the camps. Like the moment when a clear picture emerges from a jigsaw puzzle, everything I had encountered in my academic and social life in Japanese America suddenly made sense. I decided then and there to change my dissertation topic.

Living in Seattle in the 1980s, I was fortunate to be in the right place at the right time to study issues surrounding redress. While it was clear to me from my conversations in the Japanese American community that wartime incarceration and the redress movement were immensely significant in terms of Japanese American ethnic identity, there was a dearth of serious studies on such issues at the time. As I pressed forward in my fieldwork and personal interviews, people shared stories with me that they had hardly discussed with even their own family members. Although I might have felt uncomfortable about being labeled as a "Japanese from Japan," their perception of me as such gave me privileged access to such stories. Like many other anthropologists, as years passed, I deepened my relationship with the people who were the topic of my research, and when I finally had to leave Seattle for Japan, members of the community said to me, "You really became one of us."

However, whereas I felt the people in the Japanese American community accepted me, my experience with the Asian American studies academic community was rather mixed. At a session on employment during one of the annual meetings of the Association for Asian American Studies (AAAS) around 1990, I raised a question regarding the credentials necessary to hold a teaching position in Asian American studies. The professor who was moderating replied, "First, you have to be Asian American, not an Asian from Asia. You need to grow up in the community—otherwise, you may sympathize, but you cannot empathize with the people." I was appalled and embarrassed, as it was obvious from my name and accent that I was Japanese from Japan.

This U.S.-centric framework also reared its head at another annual meeting in the mid-1990s, at which I served as a commentator for a panel and touched upon the importance of adopting a transnational framework. During the question and answer period, a renowned professor replied that Asian American studies and Asian studies should be clearly distinguished, with the former focusing on issues only within American society. I experienced a number of similar episodes in those days.

Furthermore, at a certain point I also discovered that at research universities, though such bias was understandable when placed against the social and political context of the time, student representatives on hiring committees (who often had one vote among several) sought role models from their own community in new hires, thus limiting the opportunities for those who did not fit this mold to participate in and help develop the field.

These cases illustrate one aspect of Asian American studies in the late 1980s and the early 1990s, a time when the field had yet to witness the rise of first-generation immigrant researchers and the "transnational" approach. Many senior scholars who developed Asian American studies out of the civil rights movement were extremely sensitive to the general public's conflation of Asians and Asian Americans.

The pressure to maintain a clear distinction between the two was stronger for Japanese scholars from Japan for a number of reasons. First, unlike their Chinese or Korean counterparts, very few Japanese scholars from Japan engaged in Asian American studies. Second, there were various incidents that created a heightened sense of urgency surrounding Japanese American issues in the field, including the 1980s U.S.-Japan "trade war," the murder of Vincent Chin in 1982, and some Japanese politicians' racist remarks about other minority groups in the United States. And third, one can also point to the then-increasing presence in the field of scholars who had recently emigrated from Asia, a trend that was beginning to call into question the relevance of the common ground and history upon which Asian American studies originally based itself.

After teaching Asian American studies at UC Santa Barbara for a short period, in 1990 I returned to Japan and began teaching in the academic world there. I came to commit myself to two projects, decisions that stemmed from my previous involvement in the Japanese American community. First, following the 1995 Great Hanshin earthquake in my hometown of Kobe, I became involved in *tabunka kyōsei* (literally, "multicultural coexistence") policy making in Hyogo Prefecture. Second, for four consecutive years starting in 2001, I served with Irene Hirano (then executive president of the Japanese American National Museum) as a co-organizer of a conference for the Japanese American Leadership Program, which was sponsored by the Japan

Foundation and the Japanese Ministry of Foreign Affairs. I learned a great deal from the Japanese American delegation and the discussion that took place there.

Finally, I would like to add a few words relating to my topic selection process for my first book and my chapter on the three artists in this anthology. In particular, I want to call attention to a choice I made to reject the research privileges and boundaries that have come to be applied to Japanese scholars in or from Japan. In my graduate years, a number of professors both inside and outside of my academic institution in the United States strongly encouraged or even pressed me to use my language skills through archival studies of Japanese-language materials in the Japanese American community or interviews with the Issei (the immigrant generation). Though there were exceptions, including my supervisor, with such a climate shaping people's academic development, at least in my generation, the overwhelming majority of Japanese anthropologists who earned PhD degrees from American universities wrote dissertations based on their fieldwork in Japan. This reflects the existence of an attitude—which some may say lingers on—that students from Japan and Asia are able to contribute to the field of Asian American studies as well as other fields in the United States only by making full use of their linguistic abilities.

Perhaps sharing some parallels observed in the expressions of resistance of Shizu Saldamando, one of the three artists featured in my earlier chapter, I have struggled with the assumptions, stereotypes, and pressures by American scholars that Japanese scholars in or from Japan are most suitable for, or must conduct, research using Japanese-language skills, although I was fully aware of the importance of research engaging in the Issei and the use of Japanese-language resources, as well as my substantial handicap in English capability and a skewed access to U.S. literature. Instead of feeling confined by these expectations, I chose to disrupt them by conducting my research for *Breaking the Silence* through interviewing people who identified themselves as Nisei and Sansei (second- and third-generation Japanese Americans, respectively) in English—except a few Kibei (second-generation Japanese Americans who were educated in Japan)—to see what new possibilities might arise in the spaces of my language insecurity and the positionality of being from Japan.

The extent to which the AAAS has changed over the years is interesting and deserves mention here. In 2012, after giving a talk at Kyoto University,

Mary Yu Danico, then president of the AAAS, who is a so-called 1.5 generation Korean American, suggested we start an exchange program for junior scholars between the AAAS and the grant project I lead. I felt that this reflected the emergence of what we discussed in Shinagawa about "more equal dialogue." Japanese and Asian American studies have without a doubt entered a new and exciting phase.

Contributors

Eiichiro AZUMA is Alan Charles Kors Term Chair Associate Professor of History and the director of the Asian American Studies program at the University of Pennsylvania. He is specialized in Asian American history with an emphasis on Japanese Americans and trans-Pacific migration, as well as Japanese colonialism and U.S.-Japan relations. Azuma is the author of *Between Two Empires: Race, History, and Transnationalism in Japanese America* (Oxford University Press, 2005) and a co-editor with Yuji Ichioka of *Before Internment: Essays in Prewar Japanese American History* (Stanford University Press, 2006), and the *Oxford Handbook of Asian American History* (Oxford University Press, forthcoming 2016).

Andrea GEIGER is an associate professor of history at Simon Fraser University in British Columbia, Canada. Her research interests include trans-Pacific and borderlands history, race, migration, and legal history. Her particular interest in Japanese immigrants stems from her experience living in Japan as a child. She is the author of *Subverting Exclusion: Transpacific Encounters with Race, Caste, and Borders, 1885–1928* (Yale University Press, 2011), awarded the 2013 Association for Asian American Studies History Book Award and the 2011 Theodore Saloutos Book Award (Immigration and Ethnic History Society).

Noriko K. ISHII is a professor of U.S. history, women's history, and American Studies at Sophia University in Tokyo, Japan. Her research interests include transnational women's history, race, gender, war memories, and U.S.-Japan relations. Her major works include *American Women Missionaries at Kobe College, 1873–1909: New Dimensions in Gender* (Routledge, 2004) and a chapter each of *Christianity in America: Continuities and Transformations* (Sophia University Press, 2011, in Japanese) and *Introduction to North American Studies* (Sophia University Press, 2015, in Japanese).

Masumi IZUMI is a professor of American Studies at the Department of Global and Regional Studies, Doshisha University, in Kyoto, Japan. Her research interest is cultural history of postwar Japanese American and Japanese Canadian communities. Her English publications include "Alienable Citizenship: Race, Loyalty and the Law in the Age of 'American Concentration Camps,' 1941–1971," *Asian American Law Journal* 13 (2006), "Seeking the Truth, Spiritual and Political: Japanese American Community Building through Engaged Ethnic Buddhism," *Peace and*

Change 35: 1 (2010), and "The Japanese Canadian Movement: Migration and Activism before & after World War II," *Amerasia Journal* 33: 2 (2007).

Sachiko KAWAKAMI is an assistant professor of anthropology and immigration studies at the Department of Global Affairs, Kyoto University of Foreign Studies. Her major works include *Korean Immigrants in San Francisco's Japantown: Affinity and Liminality* (Tokyo: Ochanomizu Shobo, 2014, in Japanese), "Contact Zone Expanding from 'Cool Japan': Cultural Creation and Manga/Anime Industry in San Francisco Japantown" in *Humanities in Contact Zone IV*, edited by Masakazu Tanaka and Naoji Okuyama (Kyoto: Koyoshobo, 2013, in Japanese), "Why Do Korean Immigrants Start Businesses?: Examining the Studies of Overseas Korean Immigrant Entrepreneurship in an Era of Globalization" in *Current Address of Overseas Koreans: The Voices of the People and Japanese Researchers*, edited by Toshio Asakura and Shinpei Ōta (Seoul: Hakyoun Press, 2012, in Korean).

Yuko KONNO is a lecturer at the Center for Language Education and Research at Sophia University. Her research interests include trans-Pacific migration, fishing history, and U.S.-Japan relations. She is the author of "Transnationalism in Education: The Backgrounds, Motives, and Experiences of Nisei Students in Japan before World War II," *Journal of American and Canadian Studies* 27 (2009), and a Lucie Cheng Prize–winning essay, "Localism and Japanese Emigration at the Turn of the Twentieth Century," *Amerasia Journal* 38: 3 (2012).

Lon KURASHIGE is an associate professor of history at the University of Southern California. He is the author of *Japanese American Celebration and Conflict: A History of Ethnic Identity and Festival, 1934–1990* (2002) and "Perfect Storm of Exclusion: Asian Americans, Political Debate, and the Making of a Pacific Nation," a book manuscript currently under contract. He has edited and authored U.S. history textbooks as well as "Conversations in Transpacific History," a special issue of *Pacific Historical Review* (June 2014).

Mari MATSUDA is a professor of law at the University of Hawai'i at Mānoa, specializing in the fields of torts, constitutional law, feminist theory, critical race theory, and civil rights law. She is the author of *Where Is Your Body?: Essays on Race, Gender and the Law* (Beacon Press, 1996) and co-author of *We Won't Go Back: Making the Case for Affirmative Action* (Houghton-Mifflin, 1997) and *Words That Wound: Critical Race Theory, Assaultive Speech, and the First Amendment* (Westview Press, 1993).

Valerie J. MATSUMOTO is a professor of history and Asian American studies at the University of California, Los Angeles. Her research interests include Japanese American history, women's history, and foodways. Her publications include *City Girls: The Nisei Social World in Los Angeles, 1920–1950* (Oxford University

Press, 2014), *Farming the Home Place: A Japanese American Community in California, 1919–1982* (Cornell University Press, 1993), and *Over the Edge: Remapping the American West* (co-edited with Blake Allmendinger, University of California Press, 1999).

Yuko MATSUMOTO is a professor in the Department of Literature at Chuo University. Her research interests include ethnicity, race, gender, and class in early twentieth-century America. Professor Matsumoto is the author of *Constructing the American Nation: Boundaries of Citizenship in the United States* (University of Tokyo Press, 2007, in Japanese) and "Race and World War I—The Comparison of Racism between France and the United States," *Journal of the Faculty of Letters, Chuo University* 60 (2015), and co-editor of *Migration and Crossing of Cultures* (with Toshie Awaya, Akashi-shoten, 2011, in Japanese).

Fuminori MINAMIKAWA is an associate professor of sociology at the College of International Relations, Ritsumeikan University. He specializes in historical sociology of ethnicity and race in the United States, focusing on the experience of the Japanese Americans. His publications include *E Pluribus Unum: A Sociology of Multicultural America* (Kyoto: Horitsu Bunka-Sha, forthcoming, in Japanese) and "Japanese American Success Story and the Intersection of Ethnicity, Race, and Class in the Post–Civil Rights Era," *The Japanese Journal of American Studies* 23 (2011).

Rika NAKAMURA is a professor at Seijo University. Her research area includes Asian North American literature and the representations of "war memories." Major works include "What Asian American Studies Can Learn from Asia?: Towards a Project of Comparative Minority Studies," *Inter-Asia Cultural Studies* (2012), and "'Allied Masculinities' and the Absent Presences of the Other: Rehabilitation of Japanese Soldiers in the Age of American Wars in Iraq and Afghanistan—An Analysis of *Flags of Our Fathers* and *Letters from Iwo Jima*," *PAJLS* (Rutgers University Press, 2010).

Gary Y. OKIHIRO is a professor of international and public affairs and the founding director of the Center for the Study of Ethnicity and Race at Columbia University. Professor Okihiro is one of the founders of the fields of Asian American and comparative ethnic studies. His expertise in comparative ethnic studies stresses the idea of power and its location and articulations in human society for the dismantling of those hierarchies of race, gender, sexuality, class, and nation. Among his books are *American History Unbound: Asians and Pacific Islanders* (California, 2015), *Pineapple Culture: A History of the Tropical and Temperate Zones* (California, 2009), and *Island World: A History of Hawai'i and the United States* (California, 2008).

Michael OMI is a professor of ethnic studies and the associate director of the Haas Institute for a Fair and Inclusive Society (HIFIS) at the University of California, Berkeley. He is the co-author with Howard Winant of *Racial Formation in the United States,* 3rd ed. (Routledge, 2015). Other publications include "'Slippin' into Darkness': The (Re)Biologization of Race," *Journal of Asian American Studies,* 13: 3 (October 2010), and "The Changing Meaning of Race," in *America Becoming: Racial Trends and Their Consequences,* edited by Neil Smelser, William Julius Wilson, and Faith Mitchell (National Academy Press, 2001).

Okiyoshi TAKEDA is an associate professor of political science at the School of International Politics, Economics, and Communication, Aoyama Gakuin University, Tokyo. Having earned a PhD from Princeton University, he has published *Asian American Politics* (with Andrew L. Aoki, Polity Press, 2009), "One Year after the Sit-In: Asian American Students' Identities and Their Support for Asian American Studies," *Journal of Asian American Studies* 4: 2 (2001), and "The Japanese American Leadership Delegation Program: The Emergence of a New Network of Japanese Americans Involved in U.S.-Japan Relations," *Imin Kenkyu Nenpo,* 18, 2012 (in Japanese).

Yasuko TAKEZAWA is a professor of anthropology at the Institute for Research in Humanities, Kyoto University. Her research interests include race, ethnicity, migration, and human diversity. Her English publications include "Human genetic research, race, ethnicity, and the labeling of populations," *BMC Medical Ethics* 15: 33 (2014), *Racial Representations in Asia* (ed., Kyoto University Press /Trans Pacific Press, 2011), and *Breaking the Silence: Redress and Japanese American Ethnicity* (Cornell University Press, 1995). She is also the series editor of three volume anthologies, *Dismantling the Race Myth* (University of Tokyo Press, 2016, in Japanese).

Yoko TSUKUDA is an assistant professor of American Studies at the Faculty of Law (General Education), Seijo University. Her research interests include postwar Japanese immigration to the United States and contemporary Japanese American communities. Her PhD dissertation is "The Making of 'Immigrants' in the United States: Case Studies in Contemporary Japanese/Japanese American Communities" (University of Tokyo, 2011). Her publications include "Place, Community, and Identity: The Preservation Movement of San Francisco's Japantown," *Pacific and American Studies* 9 (2009).

Wesley UEUNTEN teaches in the Asian American Studies Department at San Francisco State University. He has published articles on Okinawan identity and is the cofounder of Genyukai Berkeley, a group that performs Okinawan music. His major publications include "Okinawan Diasporic Identities: Between Being a Buffer and a Bridge," in *Transcultural Japan: At the Borderlands of Race, Gender, and Identity,* edited by David Blake Willis and Stephen Murphy-Shigematsu (Routledge, 2007), and "Japanese Latin American Internment from an Okinawan Perspective," in *Okinawan Diaspora,* edited by Ronald Y. Nakasone (University of Hawai'i Press, 2002).

Duncan Ryûken WILLIAMS is the chair of the University of Southern California's School of Religion and the director of the USC Center for Japanese Religions and Culture. He is the author of a monograph entitled *The Other Side of Zen: A Social History of Sôtô Zen Buddhism in Tokugawa Japan* (Princeton University Press, 2005) and co-editor of a number of volumes, including *Issei Buddhism in the Americas* (University of Illinois Press, 2010), *American Buddhism* (Routledge/Curzon Press, 1998), and *Buddhism and Ecology* (Harvard University Press, 1997). He is currently completing a monograph titled *Camp Dharma: Buddhism and the Japanese American Incarceration during World War II* (University of California Press) and writing a manifesto for Japan in the twenty-first century titled *Hybrid Japan.* He is also the founder of a database on mixed-race Japanese people, the Hapa Japan Database Project.

Index

Figures and tables are indicated by page numbers in italics.

AAAS (Association for Asian American Studies), 397–398, 399–400
Abiko, Kyūtaro, 175
absent presence, 277, 281n14
The Accidental Asian (Liu), 56
"Achievement, Culture and Personality" (Caudill and De Vos), 43–44
activism: and Asian American studies, 332–333, 334, 336nn16–17; encouraging students toward, 331, 332–333; lack of identity for, 343; and racial categories and identity politics, 77; student apathy for, 330. *See also* Asian American movement; black power movement; civil rights movement; identity politics; Japanese American progressive politics; Sansei (third generation) Japanese American women activists
affirmative action, 53–54, 54–55
African Americans: black exceptionalism, 41; black power movement, 186, 189, 197; contemporary Japanese politicians' racist comments on, 372–374; depictions of by Japanese immigrants, 115–116; Japanese scholarship on Japan and, 323–324; and racism, 46, 51; and U.S. membership, 161
agriculture: and gender, 165–166; and Issei experience, 265, 266, 267

Alba, Richard, 46
Alien Contract Labor Law (1885), 89
Alien Land Laws, 128n14, 260, 266, 267, 295
An American Diary series (Shimomura), 65
American Hello Kitty (Shimomura), plate 5
American Indians, 161
American Infamy #2 (Shimomura), 65–66, plate 2
Americanization movement, 161–162, 163, 169, 174, 178n2, 188–189. *See also* Beika (Americanization); Beika (Americanization), and gender
American studies, 14
Americans Who Became Japanese Soldiers (documentary), 32n4
American vs. Japs 2 (Shimomura), plate 4
American Youth for Democracy (AYD), 352
Ancheta, Angelo N., 42–43
Annual Review of Migration Studies (journal), 14
Arab Americans, 66
Ariyoshi, Kōji, 356
Art of Gaman (exhibition), 9n1
arts: and Asian Americans, 74; and multiracialism, 60, 63; pressure on artists of color, 71–72; and social and political issues, 62. *See also* Asian American artists

Asian Americans: and art, 74; invisibility of, 15–16; population growth of, 40; and racism, 43, 51, 75; socioeconomic indicators for, 47. *See also* Asian American artists; Asian American movement; Asian American studies; Japanese Americans; racializations, of Asian Americans; women, Asian American

Asian American artists: approach to, 4, 61, 63–64, 78n5; and Asian American label, 67; and multiracialism, 62; and portraits, 63; and social and political issues, 62. *See also* arts; Kina, Laura; Saldamando, Shizu; Shimomura, Roger

Asian American Hardcore, 207n12

"Asian American History across the Pacific" (Kurashige), 291, 292, 301

Asian American literature, 295, 297–298, 300

Asian American movement, 186–187, 188–189, 190–192, 193, 353. *See also* Japanese American progressive politics; Sansei (third generation) Japanese American women activists

Asian American Political Alliance, 206n3. *See also* Sansei Concern

Asian American Portraits of Encounter (exhibition), 63, 72

Asian American studies: and activism, 332–333, 334, 336nn16–17; borrowing from related disciplines, 332; and comparative studies, 295; exclusion of scholars from, 16, 17; impetus for, 15–16, 16–17, 331; insiders and outsiders in, 331–332; and institutional production of knowledge, 18–19; and Japanese migration studies, 326–327; and linguistic skills, 306, 399; and nationalism, 384; U.S.-centrism of, 397–398. *See also* Asian American studies, in Asia; Asian American studies, teaching in Japan; Japanese American studies; Japanese American studies, and trans-Pacific dialogue; Japanese American studies, in Japan

Asian American studies, in Asia: approach to, 7–8, 288, 289–291, 290–291; Asian conferences on, 288–289, 308n2; and Asian erasure of racial issues, 298–299; and Asian studies, 296–297; and inter-Asian colonialism, 289–290, 294–295, 299, 305–306, 307–308; and language considerations, 306–307; and majority-minority twist, 294; and minority complicity with U.S. imperialism, 289, 290, 299, 300–301; and misreadings of Asian American texts, 297–298; as outsiders, 332; and positionality, 290, 300; and studying foreign race issues, 292–294; and transnational warping, 307–308; and trans-Pacific dialogue, 301–302; and U.S.-centrism, 291, 295–296, 297, 302, 333, 381. *See also* Asian American studies; Asian American studies, teaching in Japan; Japanese American studies; Japanese American studies, and trans-Pacific dialogue; Japanese American studies, in Japan

Asian American studies, teaching in Japan: approach to, 316–317, 334; and activism, 331, 332–333; citizenship laws example, 315–316; classes in study on, 335nn2–4; and identity politics in U.S. Asian

American studies, 331; immigration policies example, 317–318; and Japanese migration, 325–326; and race in Japan, 322, 323; and racial formation theory, 329, 330; students' racial perceptions from popular culture, 328; translation of English texts for, 330, 336n13. *See also* Asian American studies; Asian American studies, in Asia; Japanese American studies; Japanese American studies, and trans-Pacific dialogue; Japanese American studies, in Japan

Asian American Studies in Asia workshop, 288, 303–306, 306–307

Asian Diasporas (Parrenas and Siu), 384

Asian Sisters, 194, 205

Asian studies, 296–297, 306, 397–398

Asian Women's Center (AWC), 194, 205, 207n14

assimilation: and Americanization, 174; arguments for, 129n20; contemporary scholarship on, 46; and interracial marriage, 48; and Japanese immigrant leaders, 118–119; Sansei on, 184; sociological research on, 118, 128n18, 279n5. *See also* Americanization movement; Beika (Americanization); Beika (Americanization), and gender

Association for Asian American Studies (AAAS), 397–398, 399–400

atomic bombings, 294, 296, 304, 309n8, 387

Australia, 89, 92, 335n7

AWC (Asian Women's Center), 194, 205, 207n14

AYD (American Youth for Democracy), 352

Azuma, Eiichiro, 4, 16, 128n10, 175, 294, 327

bar hostess (*shakufu*), 123–124

Bataan Death March, 386–387

beauty pageants, Japanese American, 49–50

"The Beige and the Black" (Lind), 46

Beika (Americanization), 171–172, 174, 175–176, 177, 178n3, 184. *See also* Beika (Americanization), and gender

Beika (Americanization), and gender: approach to, 6, 163, 177; and family life, 171; importance of, 170; and Japanese womanliness (*Yamatonadeshiko*), 172–174; and living standards, 171–172; and picture marriages, 164–165; and self-racializations, 168–169; and women's labor, 165–167, 175–176; and youth culture, 174. *See also* Beika (Americanization); Sansei (third generation) Japanese American women activists

Bhagat Singh Thind, United States v. (1923), 43, 117

Biographical Dictionary of Japanese in the United States, 168

black exceptionalism, 41

black power movement, 186, 189, 197. *See also* Student Non-Violence Coordinating Committee

blacks. *See* African Americans

Blue Hawai'i series (Kina), 70

Bonilla-Silva, Eduardo, 42

Boot and Shoe Repairers Association, 146

Breaking the Silence, 9n1, 397

British Columbia, 138–139, 140, 141–142, 144, 153n32
Brodkin, Karen: *How Jews Became White Folks and What That Says about Race in America*, 45
Burakumin. *See* outcaste status/classes
Burnight, Ralph, 172

California: anti-Japanese fishing bills in, 100; discourses on Japanese in, 260–264, 269–270; integration of Mexicans in, 162
California Japantown Preservation Pilot Project, 245
Camp Arirang (documentary), 300–301
Camp Notes (Yamada), 294–295
Canada: exclusionary legislation in, 139–140; Royal Commission on Chinese and Japanese Immigration (1902), 138, 153n32. *See also* British Columbia
capitalism, 27, 32n7, 162, 343
Caudill, William: "Achievement, Culture and Personality," 43–44
Central Japanese Association, 167, 168
Certeau, Michel de, 217
Cheung, King-kok: approach to, 291, 292, 301; *Crossing the Oceans*, 290–291; on ethnoracial majority Asians reading U.S. ethnic literature, 292, 293, 300; "Pedagogies of Resonance," 292, 293; U.S.-centrism of, 295–296, 309n4
Chicago school, of sociology, 118, 279n5, 328
Chicana. *See* Mexican American women
Chicana Action Service Center, 193
Chicano. *See* Latinos; Mexican Americans
China, 22, 24, 139, 141, 298

Chinda, Sutemi, 25–26, 30, 32n8
Chinese, in Japan, 334n1
Chinese Americans: negative attitudes toward, 42, 50; in prewar period, 329; in racial hierarchy, 330; token acceptance of, 188. *See also* Chinese immigrants
Chinese Exclusion Act (1882), 30, 137, 150n9, 329
Chinese immigrants: Japanese rhetoric against, 140; women, 163–164. *See also* Chinese Americans
Chou, Rosalind: *The Myth of the Model Minority*, 52–53
Christianity, conversion to, 140, 152n21
Chronicle of Higher Education (journal), 54
Chuh, Kandice, 289, 292, 305
civic nationalism, American, 127n7
civil rights movement, 73, 186, 355, 374, 384, 391. *See also* Asian American movement; black power movement; Japanese American progressive politics
class, 27, 149n6. *See also katō shakai*
coal mining, 143–144, 153nn32–33, 154n34
colonial studies, 325
colorism, 53
Comfort Woman (Keller), 295
comfort women, 299–300, 309n9, 335n9, 386
Committee for the Protection of the Foreign Born, 346, 348
communication studies, 127n5
Communist Party, 345, 346, 350, 360n5, 361n11
Communist Party of Hawai'i, 350–351
comparative minority studies, 325, 384
comparative studies, 295

Index   411

Compositional Subjects (Kang), 300–301
Conference of Pacific Relations (1925), 117
Council on Promotion of Human Resource for Globalization Development (Japan), 336n11
counter public sphere, 127n5
The Courtship of Eddie's Father (TV series), 196
"Crafting Ethnic Studies" (Okihiro), 228
credit associations, rotating (*tanomoshi-kō*), 124
critical American studies, 332
Critical Mixed Raced Studies conference and journal, 62
Crossing the Oceans (Cheung and Wong), 290–291. See also Cheung, King-kok; Wong, Sau-ling
cultural imposters, 49
Cumberland (BC), 138–139, 144, 153n32

Daily Bruin (newspaper), 53
dance, Okinawan, 229–231, 235n12
Daniels, Roger, 378
Dear Pyongyang (documentary), 294, 298
decolonization, 302, 381, 382, 383
Democratic Party of Hawai'i, 351
denationalization, 384
Desert Run (Yamada), 294–295
Devon Ave. Sampler series (Kina), 68–69, 76, plate 9
De Vos, George, 43–44, 149n6
Dialogue. *See* Japanese American studies, and trans-Pacific dialogue
diasporic imagination, 127n5
difference, 238–239, 251
Dōho (newspaper), 175, 346, 359n1

Double Cross (Harden), 44
Dower, John, 380
draft resisters, Nisei, 333, 337n18
Dream Act, 317
drug abuse, 194–195, 207n12
Duras, Marguerite: *L'Amant*, 298

East San Pedro. *See* Terminal Island Japanese community
East to America (Wilson and Hosokawa), 26
Eastwood, Clint: *Flags of Our Fathers*, 298
economic activities: and racial difference, 238–239, 248, 250, 251
education: affirmative action and Asian Americans, 53–54, 54–55; history education in Japan, 324–325; Japanese-language schools, 175; race depictions in textbooks, 21–22, 23–24; surveillance and silencing in academia, 228. *See also* Asian American studies, teaching in Japan
eggs (hapa), 49
Eisa Festival, 360n6
"The Emergence of Yellow Power in America" (Uyematsu), 188–189
emigration. *See* Taiji, Japan, immigrants from
emigration agencies, 14
English language, 306–307, 370
ethnic identity, 50
ethnicity, concept of, 127n6
ethnic minorities. *See* minorities, ethnic and migrant
ethnic studies: on antiracist activism, 239; approach of, 228–229, 332; international perspectives needed for, 323; and Japanese Americans, 1; on Japanese migrants, 325; and San Francisco State strike, 187, 331; and

ethnic studies (cont.)
  Sansei, 355; and scope of research, 17; and views on race, 329
ethnic way of seeing, 108, 126n1
ethnographic present, 126n3
ethnoracial formation, 110

fairness, 316
family models, 171
Farewell to Rohwer (Saldamando), 72, plate 14
Farming. *See* agriculture
Fawn Killer: "In the Movement Office," 190–191
Feagin, Joe: *The Myth of the Model Minority*, 52–53
Flags of Our Fathers (Eastwood), 298
442nd regimental combat team, 388
442nd Regimental Combat Team (film), 327–328
"from a lotus blossom cunt" (Tanaka), 191
"The *Fūchibā* Porridge Song," 214–215, 215–216, 234n3, 235n6
Fujii, Sei, 170
Fujii, Shūji, 346
Fujimoto, Charles, 350, 356
Fujioka, Shirō: *Pioneers of Japanese Development* (*Minzoku hatten no senkusha*), 265
Fujitani, Takashi: *Perilous Memories*, 309n5; *Race for Empire*, 296, 337n18, 383
Fukuzawa, Yukichi: *Sekai kunizukushi* (All the Countries of the World), 21–22, 22–23, 32n6
Fulbeck, Kip, 60, 62

Gabaccia, Donna, 335n10
gambling, 122–123

gender: and Japanese American studies in Japan, 19–20; and race, 168. *See also* Beika (Americanization), and gender; women
Gentlemen's Agreement (1907–1908), 89, 90–91, 133, 164, 329–330
geography, 325
Gerstle, Gary, 127n7, 129n20
A Gesture Life (Lee), 295
Gidra (magazine): introduction to, 6, 186, 187–188; Asian Women's Center's statement in, 194; financial issues, 206n5; gun imagery in, 207n22; on sexism, 190, 207n18; on third world liberation movement women, 199, 201; and women, 189, 198–199, *200*, 207n19
Glenn, Evelyn Nakano, 169, 278, 281n15
Gobineau, Joseph-Arthur, 119
Gompers, Samuel, 346
Goodyear, Anne Collins, 67
Gordon, Milton, 48
Gosei (Kina), 70, plate 12
Gramsci, Antonio, 4
Great Hanshin-Awaji Earthquake (1995), 2, 398
Guinier, Ewart, 351
Guinier, Lani: *The Miner's Canary*, 55

Hacker, Andrew: *Two Nations*, 45–46
Hall, Jack, 361n10
Hamano, Merilynne. *See* Quon, Merilynne Hamano
Hane, Mikiso, 153n33
hapa (mixed-race), 49, 61, 62, 78n2. *See also* multiracial identity
Hapa Soap Opera series (Kina), 67–68, plate 7
Hapa studies, 31
Harden, Jacalyn: *Double Cross*, 44

Hata, Donald Teruo, Jr.: *"Undesirables,"* 25–26
Hattori, Yoshihiro, 298–299
Hawai'i: Americanization in, 169; discourses on Japanese in, 261–263, 264, 267, 273, 278, 279nn6–7; positionalities of Asian Americans in, 289; progressive politics in, 350–351, 351–352
Hawai'i Alliance, 356
Hawai'i Seven, 360n9
Hawai'i Youth for Democracy (HYD), 351–352
Hayashi, Brian Masaru, 18, 280n9, 327, 379–380
Highland Park Luau (Saldamando), 71, plate 13
Hill, Joe, 345
Hinman, George Warren, 169
Hirabayashi, Gordon, 361n18, 397
Hirano, Irene, 9n1, 398
Hmong Americans, 47
Hollinger, David, 68
Honolulu Labor Canteen, 351, 361n10
Horhi, William, 361n18
Hosokawa, Bill: *East to America*, 26
House Un-American Activities Committee (HUAC), 353–354
How Jews Became White Folks and What That Says about Race in America (Brodkin), 45
How the Irish Became White (Ignatiev), 45
HUAC (House Un-American Activities Committee), 353–354
HYD (Hawai'i Youth for Democracy), 351–352

Ichihashi, Yamato: *Japanese in the United States*, 148n5, 263–264
Ichioka, Yuji, 15, 16, 30, 174, 345, 379

identity: and activism, 343; complexity of, 393, 394; ethnic, 50. *See also* hapa (mixed-race); multiracial identity
identity politics, 71, 76, 77, 248, 331. *See also* activism
Ignatiev, Noel: *How the Irish Became White*, 45
Iijima, Chris, 356, 362n21
ILD (International Labor Defense), 346, 348
imagined community, in Japanese American studies, 370
Immigration Act (1924), 92, 117, 129n20, 260
immigration history, 127nn5–6
immigration policies, Japanese students on, 315, 317–318
incarceration. *See* Japanese American internment.
Indochinese Women's Conference, 199, 207n21
Industrial Workers of the World (IWW), 345, 359n2
Inter-Asia Cultural Studies (journal), 337n19
intermarriage, 46, 48–49, 50, 61
International Labor Defense (ILD), 346, 348
Internment. *See* Japanese American internment
internment studies, 267–269, 270, 280n9
interracial marriage, 46, 48–49, 50, 61
intersectionality, 369–370
"In the Movement Office" (Fawn Killer), 190–191
Irish, 45
Iriye, Akira, 152n23
Iseri, K., 171
Ishii, Kikujirō, 133–134

Ishii, Noriko K., 372–373, 374–376
Ishimoto, Shidzue, 153n33
Issei (first generation) Japanese Americans: coded meanings in term, 272; pioneer thesis, 265–266, 267, 280n10; and progressive politics, 345–346, 348–350, 354, 357–358, 358–359; and translation, 107; and U.S. membership, 15. *See also* Beika (Americanization); Japanese immigrants; Japanese immigrant vernacular representations
Issei Oral History Project, 176
Issei pioneer thesis, 265–266, 267, 280n10
Ito, Kazuo, 144
IWW (Industrial Workers of the World), 345, 359n2

JAAS (*Journal of Asian American Studies*), 291, 305–306
JACL (Japanese American Citizens League), 49, 270, 271, 277, 280n10, 355. *See also* Japanese American Research Project
"Jap," 111, 120, 143
Japan: capitalism in, 27, 32n7; colonial rule by, 128n17; concerns about European colonialism, 22–23; erasure of race in popular media, 298–299; history education in, 324–325; Japanese American tourists to, 202–203; minorities in pre-WWII, 6, 335n5; political apathy of youth, 327, 330–331, 336n11; postwar return migration to, 318, *321*, 322, 327, 335n7; pre-WWII migration from, 318, *319–320*, 320, 325; racial discourses in, 20–22, 23–25, 320–322, 335n6; racist comments against African Americans, 372–374; Sansei on, 202–204; stereotype of as insensitive to minority issues, 16; U.S. military in, 333–334, 343; views on Japanese Americans, 327–328, 386–388, 391; voting rates in 2012 general election, 330, 336n14; WWII atrocities denial in, 335n9; WWII soldiers who did not return to, 335n8; youth in workforce, 336n15. *See also* Meiji government
"A Japan-based Global Study of Racial Representations" project, 2
Japan Emigration Service, 14, 18, 31n2
Japanese Americans: and African Americans, 372–373; citizenship status of, 15, 20, 25; comparative income of (1965), 206n6; complexity of quest for social justice, 375; grand narrative of, 19, 220–221; and intermarriage, 48–49; Japanese awareness and use of, 386–388; as overseas Japanese, 15; popular attention to, 1, 9n1, 18–19; popular attention to in Japan, 19, 327–328, 391; and return migration to Japan, 327; scholarship on, 1; social position based on perception of Japan, 185, 250, 374–375; as tourists to Japan, 202–203; and translation, 107. *See also* Asian Americans; Beika (Americanization); Issei (first generation) Japanese Americans; Japanese American internment; Japanese American progressive politics; Japanese American racial formation; Japanese immigrants; Japanese immigrant vernacular representations; Japantown (Nihonmachi), San Francisco; Nisei (second generation) Japanese

Americans; racializations, of Asian Americans; Sansei (third generation) Japanese Americans; *Takao Ozawa v. United States* (1922); women, Japanese American; Yonsei (fourth generation) Japanese Americans

Japanese American Association, 170

Japanese American beauty pageants, 49–50

Japanese American Children's Home of Los Angeles, 78n4

Japanese American Citizens League (JACL), 49, 270, 271, 277, 280n10, 355. *See also* Japanese American Research Project

Japanese American Committee for Democracy, 359n4

Japanese American internment: cult of, 294; and Japanese American identity, 19, 396–397; and Japanese American National Museum, 18; Japanese awareness and use of, 386–387; justification for, 316; as lesson on racism, 1–2; and mixed children, 78n4; progressives in, 346; and racial formation, 259; scholarship on, 267–269, 270, 280n9; translation of books on, 14

Japanese American Leadership Delegation program, 9n1, 398–399

Japanese American National Museum, 18, 60, 62, 278

Japanese American progressive politics: approach to, 8, 342, 343, 344–345; and Asian American movement, 353; and author's family, 346, 347, 348, 351, 353–354, 355; deportation of from U.S., 342–343; development of, 344, 348–349, 350, 357; and Issei, 345–346, 348–350, 354, 357–358, 358–359; lack of contemporary progressive identity, 343, 344, 357, 358; multicultural nature of, 348, 349, 356, 358; and Nisei, 350–351, 352–353, 354, 358–359, 360n8; publications by, 345, 358–359, 359n1, 359n3, 362n22; and race and antiracism, 357–358; and Sansei, 355–356; and Wallace campaign, 352–353, 361n11; women in, 348; and Yonsei, 344, 356, 358. *See also* Sansei (third generation) Japanese American women activists

Japanese American racial formation: approach to, 258–260, 278; complexity of, 342; exclusion based on, 276–278, 279n2; future work on, 278; generational compartmentalization in, 264, 272–273; and internment studies, 259, 267–269; and Japanese American Research Project, 259, 270–275; and Japanese American scholarship, 259; justification of Nisei experience, 270–272; legal national membership focus, 270–271; and myths about Issei pioneers, 265–267, 280n10; and postwar Japanese immigrants, 257–258, 277, 279n2; and racism, 259, 260, 276, 279n1; regional biases in, 258, 260–264, 269–270, 273–275, 279n4; terminology for discussing, 279n1; translation of texts on, 336n13

Japanese American Research Project (JARP): and Beardsley, 273–274; and Chinda memorandum, 26; generational definitions of, 272–273; history of, 270, 280n10; and Japanese-language documents,

Japanese American Research Project (JARP) (cont.) 126n2; lack of postwar research, 275; official publications of, 271, 280n11; and racial formation, 259; regional bias in, 273–275; and Yasui, 274–275

Japanese American studies: approach to, 2–3, 9; and civil rights movement, 391; contributors to book, 3; differences between U.S.- and Japan-based scholars, 17, 19; excluded groups from, 2, 332; future of, 31; imagined community in, 370; impetus for, 15–16, 371; and institutional production of knowledge, 18–19; intellectual and subjective interactions for, 233–234; Japanese diaspora approach to, 8; and Japanese-language primary sources, 108–109; and Japanese-language skills, 17, 399; metaphors in, 218–219; and positionality, 1, 2–3, 9, 371; and redress and reparations movement, 391; representations of Japanese Americans in, 332; research framework of, 7; scope of topics by American-based scholars, 17–18; and study of multiracials, 394–395; and study of religion, 394; translation issues in, 20, 108; widening scope of, 31, 217. *See also* Asian American studies; Asian American studies, in Asia; Asian American studies, teaching in Japan; Japanese American studies, and trans-Pacific dialogue; Japanese American studies, in Japan

Japanese American studies, in Japan: approach to, 4, 13; Asian American views of, 16, 17; and assumptions of commonality, 385–386; development of, 13–15, 32n3; and emigration studies, 14; and English language, 370; gender imbalance in, 19–20; internal perspective of, 369; and intersectionality *vs.* racial formation, 369–370; and local history, 13–14, 31n1; and Nihonjin-ron (theories on Japanese uniqueness), 14–15; popular awareness and interest in, 14, 386, 391; for understanding Japan, 370. *See also* Asian American studies, in Asia; Asian American studies, teaching in Japan; Japanese American studies; Japanese American studies, and trans-Pacific dialogue

Japanese American studies, and trans-Pacific dialogue: appreciating diversity of Japan-based scholars, 382; and ethnic minorities in Japan, 383; Kurashige on, 301–302; and minority studies, 384; and nationalism, 383–384; and nation-based frameworks, 391–392; topics emerging from, 2; and understanding Japanese milieu, 382–383; and value of scholarship, 395. *See also* Asian American studies; Asian American studies, in Asia; Asian American studies, teaching in Japan; Japanese American studies; Japanese American studies, in Japan

Japanese American women. *See* women, Japanese American

Japanese American youth clubs, 186, 205n2

Japanese Association of America, 165

Japanese Association of Los Angeles, 123, 124, 129n22

Japanese Association of Southern California, 165
Japanese Association of the Pacific Coast, 25
Japanese Chamber of Commerce, 124
Japanese diaspora, 8, 18
Japanese family, 171
Japanese Fishermen's Association, 100, 101
Japanese immigrants: businessmen and racial attitudes, 116; contemporary high mobility of, 390–391; and conversion to Christianity, 152n21; and culture, 218–219; laborers, 150n9; and *mibunsei* (status system), 142–146, 147, 152nn29–30; origins of, 29–30; and outcaste classes, 30, 149n7; proposed scholarship directions for, 325–326; in rural areas, 175–176. See also Beika (Americanization); Japanese immigrant vernacular representations; Taiji, Japan, immigrants from
Japanese immigrant vernacular representations: approach to, 5, 109, 125–126, 126n3; on assimilation, 118–119, 128n18; conflation of local with international issues, 116–117; domination of by immigrant leaders, 122, 124; and economic survival, 111; ethnocentric focus of, 117–118; failure of against racism, 126; false assumption about, 108; *jinshu* (race), 115, 118, 119–120; *minzoku* (race/nation/ethnicity), 112–114, 119–120, 121; as moral reform and disciplinary tool, 122–124, 129n24, 129nn21–22; of other racial minorities, 115–116, 128n16; and racial equality, 117; and racial formation, 259; as resistance against racism, 111–112, 120–121, 265–266; for seeking place in racial stratification, 121–122; for self-identification, 109–111, 120–121; sources for, 108, 127n8; translation of, 108–109, 127n9. See also *jinshu* (race); *minzoku* (nation/race/ethnicity)
Japanese in the United States (Ichihashi), 148n5, 263–264
Japanese-language education, in U.S., 175
Japanese-language primary sources, 17, 108, 126n2, 379
Japanese Latin Americans, 236n15, 385–386
The Japanese Problem in the United States (Millis), 260–261
Japanese Produce Dealer's Association, 129n24
Japanese Shoe Repairers Association (*Nihonjin Kakō Dōmeikai*), 145–146, 154n35, 155n40
Japanese war brides, 274, 275, 277–278, 281nn14–15
Japanese Welfare Rights Organization, 360n7
Japanese Workers Association, 345, 359n3
Japan International Cooperation Agency (JICA), 18
Japan's kasō shakai (*Nihon no kasō shakai*) (Yokoyama), 27
Japantown (Nihonmachi), San Francisco: changing nature of, 390; commercialization of, 243; cultural preservation of, 244–245; demographics in, 245; elderly in, 245; history of, 242–243; Japanese

Japantown (Nihonmachi) (cont.)
American identification with, 241; other ethnic minorities in, 251. *See also* Korean immigrants, in Japantown; Little Tokyo, Los Angeles

JARP. *See* Japanese American Research Project

JICA (Japan International Cooperation Agency), 18

jigyaku shikan (self-deprecating national history), 324–325

Jim Crow laws, 316

jinshu (race): approach to, 5, 127n9; basis for, 118; in China, 29; and conflation of local with international issues, 116; as "race problem," 115; and reductionist view of race relations, 119; use of in Japan, 119–120; vernacular use of by immigrants, 120. *See also* Japanese immigrant vernacular representations; *minzoku* (nation/race/ethnicity); race

jinshu byōdō (racial equality), 116, 120, 122

Journal of Asian American Studies (*JAAS*), 291, 305–306

justice, 316

Kaigai ijū (*Emigration Overseas*) (journal), 31n2

Kang, Laura, 289, 291, 292, 299–301, 306

Kanzaki, Kiichi, 169, 172

kasō shakai (low strata society), 27–28, 29. See also *katō shakai*

Kasuri (Kina), 69–70, plate 10

Katayama, Sen, 345–346, 359n3

katō shakai: approach to, 4; as anachronistic projection, 30–31; context for use of, 29–30; first use of, 25–26, 32n8; and outcaste classes, 30; translation of *katō*, 27–29; use of in American newspapers, 26–27

Kawakami, Kiyoshi K., 262–263, 382

Kawasaki, Kanichi, 104n7

Keywords (Williams), 27

Kibei, 7, 257, 268, 269, 276, 290, 327, 332

Kikumura, Akemi: *Through Harsh Winters*, 143, 152n28, 175

Kim, Bok-dong, 307, 308

Kimochi, 247

Kimoto, Jack, 345, 356

Kina, Laura: approach to, 4, 63–64; on ambiguity of marginalized positions, 71, 76; and Asian American/hapa label, 68, 76, 78n2; audience of, 70, 79n22; background of, 68; and Critical Mix Raced Studies conference and journal, 62; and diasporic issues, 70; and family history, 69–70; and intermingling of place, history, and identity, 68–69; and *Loving v. Virginia* (1967), 68; mixed-race focus of, 67–68; and racism, 75–76; self-description of, 68; and social categories, 77, 78. *See also* Asian American artists; Kina, Laura, works by

Kina, Laura, works by: *Blue Hawai'i* series, 70; *Devon Ave. Sampler* series, 68–69, 76, plate 9; *Gosei*, 70, plate 12; *Hapa Soap Opera* series, 67–68, plate 7; *Kasuri*, 69–70, plate 10; *Loving* series, 68, plate 8; *Soldier Boys*, 70, plate 11; *Sugar/Islands*, 70; *Sugar* series, 69. *See also* Kina, Laura

King-O'Riain, Rebecca Chiyoko, 49–50
knowledge, institutional production of, 18–19
Kobashigawa, Ben, 357, 360n5
Kobe Center for Overseas Migration and Cultural Interaction, 18
Kochi, Paul, 348, 349–350, 356, 360n7
Kochiyama, Yuri, 353, 361n18
Kogawa, Joy: on coming together, 302; *Obasan*, 294–295, 296
Korea, 299, 320, 322. *See also* Korean immigrants, in Japantown; Koreans, in Japan; South Korea
Korean American studies, 7, 295
Korean American women, 300
Korean immigrants, in Japantown: approach to, 7, 239–240; and commercial racializations, 248, 250; elderly, 245–247; and global status of Korea, 250; history of, 243–244; methodology for study of, 240; as peripheral, 248–249, 249–250; and post-coloniality, 382–383; representation of Japantown by, 241, 249; silent affinity of, 239, 241, 242, 249, 250–251; small business owners, 248. *See also* Japantown; Little Tokyo, Los Angeles
Koreans, in Japan, 323, 334n1, 382
Korematsu, Fred, 361n18
Kotsubo Incident, Taiji, 91
Kume, Kunitake, 320
Kurashige, Lon: approach of, 299, 378; American identity of, 383; "Asian American History across the Pacific," 291, 292, 301; development of positionality of, 378–379, 380–382; and Hayashi, 379–380; in Japan, 380–381; and racial nationalism, 379; on trans-Pacific dialogue, 301–302, 382–384; views of Japan and FOBs, 380

L'Amant (Duras), 298
language: English, 306–307, 370; Japanese, 370; Okinawan, 213–214, 223–224; skills in, and Asian American studies, 17, 399; vernacular, 109, 126n4, 127n5. *See also* Japanese immigrant vernacular representations
La Otra Gerry (Saldamando, Shizu), 77, plate 17
Latin Americanization, of race relations, 42
Latin Americans, Japanese, 236n15, 385–386
Latinos, 7, 41–42, 46, 55, 186. *See also* Mexican Americans
leatherwork, 154n35, 155n36
Lee, Chang-rae, 295, 307, 308
Lee, Robert G.: *Orientals*, 336n13
Liang Qichao, 29
Lippard, Lucy R., 65
Lipsitz, George, 54
Little Friends Playgroup, 194
Little Tokyo, Los Angeles, 111, 122–123, 125, 129n22, 252n1. *See also* Japantown (Nihonmachi), San Francisco
Liu, Eric, 43, 56
livelihood, 242
living standards, 171–172
local history, 13–14, 31n1. *See also* Taiji, Japan, immigrants from
localism. *See* Taiji, Japan, immigrants from; Terminal Island Japanese community
LooChoo (journal), 348
Looking at Art series (Saldamando), 74, 79n27, plate 16

Lopéz, Ian Haney: *White by Law*, 43
Los Angeles, 94, 111, 113, 128n11. *See also* Little Tokyo; Terminal Island Japanese community
Los Angeles Japanese Association, 165
Los Angeles Women's Group, 193
Loving series (Kina), 68, plate 8
Loving v. Virginia (1967), 60, 62, 68
Lowe, Lisa, 50, 168
Lum, Wing Tek, 303, 305

Machida, Margo, 70
Madame Butterfly (opera), 298
"A Major Ethnic Disaster" (*Pacific Citizen* article), 49
majority-minority twist, 7–8, 41, 294
Makino, Fred Kinzaburō, 393–394
"Male Perspective" (Yamamoto), 192
Manchuria, 320
marriage difficulties, 168–169
marriages, picture, 164–165
Matsuda, Don, 347, 348, 352, 353–354
Matsuda, Jinkichi, 346, 347
Matsuda, Kimi, 351, 352, 358
Matsuda, Takeshi: *Soft Power and Its Perils*, 381
Matsuda, Tsuyuko, 348
"Maxime Hong Kingston in a Global Frame" (Wong), 291, 292, 298, 299. *See also* Wong, Sau-ling
McClatchy, V. S., 172
Meiji government: arguments against racism, 137, 138–142, 146–147; history associated with progress in, 152n23; and Japanese racial and international standing, 136–137, 151n19; understanding of racism, 146, 150n9, 151n11, 168; and *Yamato minzoku* (Japanese race), 155n38. *See also* Japan
membership, in U.S. nation-state, 161–163, 270–271. *See also* Beika (Americanization), and gender
Mexican Americans, 115–116, 162, 163. *See also* Latinos; Mexican American women
Mexican American women, 190, 193, 201
mibunsei (status system): approach to, 5, 136; continued importance of, 135–136, 147; Haworth on, 134–135; and immigrant passport situation, 133–135, 148n5; and Japanese immigrants, 142–146, 147, 152nn29–30; and Meiji arguments against racism, 137, 138–141, 146–147, 150n9, 151n11; overview of, 148n5; and racism, 136, 143; terms used for, 149n6; U.S. and Canadian awareness of, 148n4. *See also* outcaste status/classes
migrant minorities. *See* minorities, ethnic and migrant
migration studies, Japanese, 325–327
Millis, Harry A.: *The Japanese Problem in the United States*, 260–261; on Japanese women, 166
The Miner's Canary (Guinier and Torres), 55
Mink, Patsy, 352
minorities, ethnic and migrant: alignment of, 290; as complicit with U.S. imperialism, 289; and foreign policy, 185; in Japan, 2, 6, 334n1, 335n5; Japanese immigrant treatment of, 115; new critical attention on in Japan, 18, 383; and *Perilous Memories* (Fujitani, White,

and Yoneyama), 309n5; and social status, 323
minority studies, 19, 289, 290, 384. *See also* comparative minority studies
minzoku (nation/race/ethnicity): approach to, 5, 127n9; basis for, 122; in China, 29; as educational tool, 122–123; ethnic minority sense of, 113–114; first uses of, 23; flexibility of term, 112; nationalistic sense of, 112–113; racial sense of, 114; and racial stratification, 121; as resistance against racism, 111–112, 120; translation of, 128n10; use of in Japan, 119–120; vernacular use of by immigrants, 120. *See also* Japanese immigrant vernacular representations; *jinshu* (race); race
Mio, Japan, 88, 89, 104n8
MIS: Human Secret Weapon (film), 387
Mitsugu, Matsuda, 232
mixed-race identity. *See* multiracial identity
Mixed Remixed Festival, 60
Mixed Roots Film and Literary Festival, 60
Miyakawa, T. Scott, 275, 281n13
Miyasaki, Peggy, 183–184, 204, 205n1, 207n28
Mochizuki, Carol, 193, 206n9, 206n11
model minority, 43–44, 45, 270–271, 332
moral reform campaigns, 122–123, 129nn21–22, 163–164, 165–167
"The Mountain Movers" (Ling), 206n8
multicultural coexistence, 2, 398
multiracial identity: and activism, 61; and art, 63; and Asian American artists, 60, 62; assertiveness of, 4; implications of growth of, 49; in Japanese American community, 394–395; optimistic views of, 61–62; ostracization of, 78n4; problems with, 61; and racial authenticity, 49–50; and racism, 62; and social stratification, 42. *See also* hapa (mixed-race)
Mura, David: *Turning Japanese*, 380
Murakami, Chris: "My Friend," 201
Murase, Mike, 187, 206n5
music: and Okinawan identity, 225–226, 229–231; Okinawan *sanshin*, 223, 231, 234n4, 235n8; as resistance, 214, 233. *See also* Nakayoshi Group; Okinawan music
"My Friend" (Murakami), 201
The Myth of the Model Minority (Chou and Feagin), 52–53

Nakamura, Tadashi "Tad," 358, 362n21
Nakasone, Yasuhiro, 373
Nakayoshi Group: approach to, 6, 219, 233; and Battle of Okinawa, 216, 221–222; Dolly's life story, 222; formation of, 224–225; and "The *Fūchibā* Porridge Song," 214–215, 215–216; humor by, 220; and identity, 234; introduction to, 215; and Japanese American grand narrative, 221; and marginalization, 224, 225; methodology for study on, 219; and music, 214, 222, 223, 226, 231–232, 233; and Okinawan language, 223–224; provocative ironies of, 216–217; and resilience of Okinawan culture and identity, 216
Nanjing Massacre, 303–304, 306, 335n9
Nash, Phil Tajitsu, 361n18

National Alliance Against Racist and Political Oppression, 356
National Coalition to Overturn the Bakke Decision, 356
nationalism, 383–384
Native Americans, 161
nativist movements, 162, 178n2
Naturalization Act (1790), 20
neighboring effect, 104n2
New Caledonia, 335n7
"The New White Flight" (*Wall Street Journal*), 51–52
New York Times, 53–54
Nguyen, Viet Thanh, 288, 289, 302
Nichibei Shimbun (newspaper), 108
Nihon (*Japan*) (newspaper), 23
Nihonjin (*Japanese People*) (magazine), 23
Nihonjin Kakō Dōmeikai (Japanese Shoe Repairers Association), 145–146, 154n35, 155n40
Nihonjin-ron (theories on Japanese uniqueness), 14–15
Nihonmachi. *See* Japantown; Korean immigrants, in Japantown
Nihon no kasō shakai (Japan's *kasō shakai*) (Yokoyama), 27
Niisato, Kannichi, 168–169, 174
Nikka Noho (newspaper), 175–176
Nikkei Studies and Beyond conference, 288
99 Years of Love: Japanese Americans (TV drama), 9n1, 327–328, 386, 391
Nisei (second generation) Japanese Americans: and American cultural influences, 174; and assimilation theory, 279n5; coded meanings in term, 272; draft resisters, 333, 337n18; in Hawai'i, 169; in internment studies, 268–269; as model minority, 43–44, 270–272; policing of group boundaries by, 277, 281n14; and progressive politics, 350–351, 352–353, 354, 358–359, 360n8; representations of WWII soldiers, 175, 337n18; and social organizations, 192–193, 205n2
Nishi, Setsuko Matsunaga, 44
Nojima Louis, Nikki: *Breaking the Silence*, 9n1, 397
No-No Boy (Okada), 14, 294
Nosse, Tatsugoro, 140, 151n16
Not Pearl Harbor (Shimomura), plate 3

Obasan (Kogawa), 294–295, 296
O'Brien, Eileen: *The Racial Middle*, 53
Oguma, Eiji, 128n13, 320, 335n6
Ohnuki-Tierney, Emiko, 153n33, 155n36
Oka, Seizo, 154n35
Okada, John: *No-No Boy*, 14, 294
Okamura, Jonathan, 289
Okihiro, Gary: on Asian racializations, 42, 52; on ethnic studies, 228; on impetus for Japanese/Asian American studies, 15, 16; questions posed by on Japanese American studies, 3, 288; on social formation, 329, 336n12; on U.S. membership, 329
Okinawa: and African Americans, 324; and *Blue Hawai'i* series (Kina), 70; dance, 229–231, 235n12; food, 236n14; genealogies in, 235n13; and Japanese colonialism, 235n9; language of, 213–214, 223–224; reputation of, 342; resilience of culture and identity, 216; U.S. military in, 333–334, 343; women in, 232–233. *See also* Nakayoshi

Group; Okinawan diaspora; Okinawan music
Okinawa, Battle of, 216, 221–222
Okinawan diaspora: and genealogies, 235n13; keys to understanding, 227; marginalization of, 224, 225; and Okinawan language, 214; postwar immigration, 234n5; and progressive politics, 347, 357–358, 360n5. *See also* Nakayoshi Group
Okinawan language, 213–214, 223–224
Okinawan music: in diplomacy, 230; "The *Fūchibā* Porridge Song," 214–215, 215–216, 234n3, 235n6; and identity, 225–226; under Japanese colonialism, 230–231, 233; *sanshin*, 223, 231, 234n4, 235n8; and social formation, 229–230; "Tinsagunu Hana" (song), 226–227, 235n11; transnational spread of, 231–232; "Unna Bushi" (song), 232–233
Ōkuma, Shigenobu, 320
Omatsu, Glenn, 187
One Way or Another: Asian American Art Now (exhibition), 63
"On Korean 'Comfort Women'" (Kang), 291, 306. *See also* Kang, Laura
Oriental Concern, 206n3. *See also* Sansei Concern
Orientalism, 16–17, 248, 298, 299
Oriental Masterprint series (Shimomura), 64, plate 1
Orientals (Lee), 336n13
Ōta, Masahide, 225
outcaste status/classes: abolishment of, 150n8; and arguments against exclusionary measures, 139; and coal mining, 153n33; emigration of, 30; and experience of racism, 143; and Japanese migration history, 149n7; and; scholarship on racializations of, 323; and shoemaking and leatherwork, 155n36; in status system, 134–135, 135–136, 148n5; *yotsu* term used for, 143, 152n28
outsiders, 332
Oxnard sugar beet strike, 345–346
Ozawa, Takao, 20, 24–25, 43, 114, 117, 128n12

Pacific Citizen (newspaper), 49, 273, 280n10
Park, Robert Ezra, 118, 328
Parrenas, Rhacel: *Asian Diasporas*, 384
"Part Asian, 100% Hapa" (Fulbeck), 60
passionate detachment, 227
passports, Japanese immigrant, 133–135, 148n5
"Pedagogies of Resonance" (Cheung), 292, 293. *See also* Cheung, King-kok
Perilous Memories (Fujitani, White, and Yoneyama), 309n5
Peru, 236n15
Petersen, William, 45
picture marriages, 164–165
Pioneers of Japanese Development (*Minzoku hatten no senkusha*) (Fujioka), 265
polite racism, 383
political activism. *See* activism
portraits, 63
positionality: as 2012 Kyoto conference focus, 2–3; effects of, 392; Ishii on, 371, 372, 374, 375, 376; reflections on from Taipei conference, 304;. *See also* Japanese American studies, and trans-Pacific dialogue

post-coloniality, 382
post-structuralism, 329
postwar Japanese immigrants (Shin Issei), 7, 257, 258, 272–273, 277–278, 279nn2–3, 395
primary sources, Japanese-language, 17, 108, 126n2, 379
Princeton University, 53–54, 385
progressive politics. *See* Japanese American progressive politics
prostitution, 163–164
Pulido, Laura, 206n8, 207n19, 207n22

race: approach to, 13, 20; and activism, 77; in Asia, 298–299, 323; and Chicago school, 328; depictions of in textbooks, 21–22, 23–24; flexibility of categorization, 162; and gender, 168; international perspectives needed on, 323–324; Japanese discourses on, 20–22, 23–25, 128nn12–13, 320–322, 335n6; Japanese immigrants' views on, 115–116; Japanese perceptions through popular culture, 328; scenarios for racial stratification in U.S., 41–42; and *Takao Ozawa v. United States* (1922), 24–25; Takezawa on, 323; in U.S., 41, 322–323. See also *jinshu* (race); *minzoku* (nation/race/ethnicity); racial formation theory; racializations; racializations, of Asian Americans; racism
Race for Empire (Fujitani), 296, 337n18, 383
racial alienation, 46
racial bribe, 55
Racial Equality Proposal, 25
racial formation, 325, 369–370. *See also* Japanese American racial formation

racial formation theory, 55–56, 109, 329, 333. *See also* social formation
racializations: approach to, 2; and activism, 77; of Asian women, 168–169, 191, 195–196, 197–198, 207n16; black/white paradigm in, 42–43; and changing demographics in U.S., 41; and economic activities, 238–239, 248, 250, 251; and immigrant history, 127n6. *See also* racializations, of Asian Americans
racializations, of Asian Americans: approach to, 4, 40, 42; and assimilation, 46; and black/white paradigm, 42–43; and colorism, 53; conferences on, 1; and intermarriage, 48–49, 50, 61; of Japanese and Japanese Americans as identical, 376; and marriage customs, 164–165; model minority, 43–44, 45; as on par with whites, 47; as perpetual foreigners, 50; and racial authenticity, 49–50; and racial bribe, 55; and racial positioning, 52–53; as racial project, 55–56; as racial threat, 51–52; and self-racializing, 168, 177; and *Survivor* (TV show), 39–40; and university affirmative action, 53–54; and whiteness, 45–46, 56. *See also* racializations
The Racial Middle (O'Brien), 53
racial minorities. *See* minorities, ethnic and migrant
racial nationalism, 379
racial project, 55–56
Racial Representations in Asia (Takezawa), 323

racial shadowing, 298
racial stratification, 41–42, 56, 121–122
racism: and African Americans, 46, 51; commercial forms of, 238–239, 248, 250, 251; De Vos on basis of, 149n6; as disguised, 238; Japanese immigrants encounters with, 111, 143; Meiji arguments against, 137, 138–142, 146–147; Meiji understanding of, 146, 150n9, 151n11, 168; and *mibunsei* (status system), 136, 143; *minzoku* (race/nation/ethnicity) used to counter, 112–114; and multiracialism, 62; nativist movements, 162, 178n2; and *Nihonjin Kakō Dōmeikai* (Japanese Shoe Repairers Association), 145–146; polite, 383; popular understanding of, 51; and racial formation, 276, 279n1; and scholarship, 217–218; and Shimomura, 75; and U.S. foreign relations, 51; vernacular resistance against, 111–112, 120–121, 126, 265–266; and whiteness claims, 43. *See also* Japanese immigrant vernacular representations; racializations; racializations, of Asian Americans
Rafu Shimpo (newspaper): on Alien Land Law (1920), 128n14; on black issues, 115, 128n15; on Japanese colonial rule, 128n17; on Los Angeles demographics, 128n11; on Ozawa case, 115; pluralistic understanding of U.S. in, 113; as source for vernacular representation, 108, 127n8. *See also* Japanese immigrant vernacular representations

The Real Japanese Question (Kawakami), 262–263
redress and reparations movement, 17, 386, 387, 391, 397
Reich, Wilhelm, 198
Rekishitsū (The Knowledge of History) (magazine), 388
religious studies, 394, 395
Rice, W.M., 137–138
Rich, Adrienne, 361n18
Robeson, Paul, 354, 358
Rosaldo, Renato, 126n3, 227–228
Rostow, Eugene, 268
Royal Commission on Chinese and Japanese Immigration (1902), 138, 153n32
Russell, John, 21

Saldamando, Shizu: approach to, 4, 63–64; ambiguity in work of, 71, 76, 77, 78; artistic vision of, 72–73; background of, 71; and ethnic art labels, 71–72, 73; focus of on Los Angeles youth culture, 71; parents of, 73; profile of, 74; and racism, 75–76; on social categories, 77; and tattooing, 74; work of as personal narrative, 73–74, 76. *See also* Asian American artists; Saldamando, Shizu, works by
Saldamando, Shizu, works by: *Farewell to Rohwer*, 72, plate 14; *Highland Park Luau*, 71, plate 13; *La Otra Gerry*, 77, plate 17; *Looking at Art* series, 74, 79n27, plate 16; *Stay Gold* series, 73; *Waiting for the Band in Between Sets*, plate 15. *See also* Saldamando, Shizu
San Francisco. *See* Japantown; Korean immigrants, in Japantown

San Francisco State strike, 187, 206n4, 228, 331
Sanga moyu (Burning Mountain and River) (TV drama), 391
San Pedro (CA), 94–95. *See also* Terminal Island Japanese community
Sansei Concern, 187, 206n3
Sansei (third generation) Japanese Americans: Okinawan, and genealogies, 235n13; and progressive politics, 355–356, 357. *See also* Sansei (third generation) Japanese American women activists
Sansei (third generation) Japanese American women activists: approach to, 6, 184–185, 205; activism by, 184; on Americanization, 188–189; and Asian American movement, 190–191, 190–192; and drug abuse, 194–195, 207n12; and *Gidra*, 198–199, *200*, 207n19; on Japan, 202–204; organizations by, 193–194, 204–205; and other minority women groups, 206n8; Peggy Miyasaki example, 183–184, 204, 205n1, 207n28; self-definition and aims of, 189; and sexism, 189–192, 193; and sexist stereotypes of Asian women, 195–197; and sexual stereotyping during Vietnam War, 197–198; social climate for, 185–188; and third world liberation movements, 199, 201, 207n21. *See also* Beika (Americanization), and gender; Japanese American progressive politics
sanshin Okinawan music, 223, 231, 234n4, 235n8
Satō, Shōsuke, 22

Sekai kunizukushi (All the Countries of the World) (Fukuzawa), 21–22, 22–23, 32n6
sexism, 189–192, 193, 195–197, 197–198
Shah, Nayan, 167
shakufu (bar hostess), 123–124
Shibusawa, Naoko, 185
Shimomura, Roger: approach to, 4, 63–64; and Americanism, 67, 75; on Asian American label, 67; on Asian Americans and art, 74; collection of "stereotype" items, 64, 78n8; inspiration for work, 64; issues of race and stereotypes in works of, 64–66, 66–67, 74, 75; and Japan, 75; and multiculturalism in art world, 66; and social categories, 75, 77, 78; Western misunderstandings of work, 65, 79n11. *See also* Asian American artists; Shimomura, Roger, works by
Shimomura, Roger, works by: *An American Diary* series, 65; *American Hello Kitty*, plate 5; *American Infamy #2*, 65–66, plate 2; *American vs. Japs 2*, plate 4; *Not Pearl Harbor*, plate 3; *Oriental Masterprint* series, 64, plate 1; *Shimomura Crossing the Delaware*, 66–67, 79n15, plate 6. *See also* Shimomura, Roger
Shimomura Crossing the Delaware (Shimomura), 66–67, 79n15, plate 6
Shin Issei (postwar Japanese immigrants), 7, 257, 258, 272–273, 277–278, 279nn2–3, 395
Shin Sekai (newspaper), 143, 175
silent affinity, 241–242, 249
Simpson, Caroline Chung, 278, 281n14
Siu, Lok: *Asian Diasporas*, 384
Smith, Anthony D., 126n4

SNCC (Student Non-Violence Coordinating Committee), 358, 362n19
social categories, 61, 71, 77, 78
social formation, 329, 336n12. *See also* racial formation theory
social movement theory, 77
social sciences: manly ethic in, 227–228
Soft Power and Its Perils (Matsuda), 381
Soldier Boys (Kina), 70, plate 11
Song for Ourselves (film), 357, 362n21
South African model, 41–42
Southern California Japanese Christian Churches Association, 172
Southern California Japanese Fishermen's Association, 100–101
South Korea, 307, 308, 309n9. *See also* Korea; Korean immigrants, in Japantown
special permanent resident aliens, 334n1
Spickard, Paul R., 281n15
status system. See *mibunsei*
Stay Gold series (Saldamando), 73
strategic essentialisms, 4
Student Non-Violence Coordinating Committee (SNCC), 358, 362n19
Subverting Exclusion (Geiger), 5
Sugar/Islands (Kina), 70
Sugar series (Kina), 69–70
Survivor (TV show), 39–40
Suzuki, Lewis, 353

Taiji, Japan, immigrants from: approach to, 4–5, 86–87, 87–88; and anti-immigration laws, 89, 90–91, 92, 104n5; conclusions from, 104; destinations for, 89, 92; emigrant education for, 93; financial support from, 98; illegal migration, 91–92; importance of local connections, 88–89, 91–92, 93; income remitted by, 92–93, 104n6; popularity of emigration, 89–91, 92; reasons for emigration, 88, 104n2; as research focus, 86; and Taijijin-kai (Taiji Village Association), 85, 98; and village culture, 93. *See also* Terminal Island Japanese community
Taijijin-kai (Taiji Village Association), 85, 98
Taiji-jinkei Club (Taiji People's Club), 85
Takahashi, K. T., 139, 142, 151n16
Takaki, Ronald, 379
Takao Ozawa v. United States (1922), 20, 24–25, 43, 114, 117, 128n12
Takezawa, Yasuko: and Japanese American Leadership Delegation program, 398–399; and Kurashige, 380; and linguistic abilities expectations, 399; and multicultural coexistence policy making, 398; on race, 323; *Racial Representations in Asia*, 323; on racism, 238; on representation as resistance, 127n5; as scholar in U.S., 16, 396–398; workshops organized by, 288–289
tanomoshi-kō (rotating credit associations), 124
teaching. See Asian American studies, teaching in Japan; education
Terminal Island Japanese community: and adaptation to America, 87, 94, 100, 101–102; and anti-Japanese fishing legislation, 100; conclusions from, 103; demographics of Terminal Island, 95–96; as East San

Terminal Island Japanese community (cont.)
Pedro, 95–96; establishment of, 95; history of Terminal Island, 94; involvement of in home communities, 98–99; occupations in, 96, *97*; origins of immigrants in, 97–98; precursor abalone fishermen to, 94–95; and Principal Walizer, 102–103; relations with whites over fishing concerns, 100–101; and *sonjin-kai* (village associations), 98. See also Taiji, Japan, immigrants from
Thind, Bhagat Singh, 43, 117
Third World Liberation Front strike, 187, 206n4, 228, 331
third world liberation movement women, 199, 207n21
Through Harsh Winters (Kikumura), 143, 152n28, 175
Times through the Lens of Toyo Miyatake (film), 327–328
"Tinsagunu Hana" (song), 226–227, 235n11
Tokutomi, Soho, 320
Torres, Gerald: *The Miner's Canary*, 55
Tosa Maru (ship), 133
translation, 20, 107, 108–109, 370. See also Japanese immigrant vernacular representations
transnational warping, 293, 307
trans-Pacific dialogue. See Japanese American studies, and trans-Pacific dialogue
trans-Pacific studies, 382
Tsurumi, Yūsuke, 117
Turning Japanese (Mura), 380
Two Nations (Hacker), 45–46
tyranny of the nation, 327, 335n10

UC (University of California), 54–55
Uchida, Masao: *Yochishiryaku* (Condensed geography), 21, 32n6
UCLA (University of California, Los Angeles), 194, 207n13, 270
"Undesirables" (Hata), 25–26
United Front Against Fascism, 346, 359n4
United States of America: Americanization movement, 161–162, 163, 169, 174, 178n2, 188–189; apologies to Japanese Americans, 386–387; membership in, 161–163; military in Japan, 333–334, 343; nativist movements, 162, 178n2; political apathy of U.S. students, 330; race in, 41, 322–323; and racial minorities, 185. See also California; Hawai'i
university admittance, 53–54, 54–55
University of California, Los Angeles (UCLA), 194, 207n13, 270
"Unna Bushi" (song), 232–233
Uno, Kiku, 199, 207n21
Uyematsu, Amy, 186, 188–189, 197, 206n6

vernacular language, 109, 126n4, 127n5. See also Japanese immigrant vernacular representations
Viet Nam, South Korea in, 308, 309n9
Vietnam War, 197–198, 355
"Visible & Invisible: A Hapa Japanese American History" (exhibition), 60, 78n1

Waiting for the Band in Between Sets (Saldamando), plate 15
Wakayama prefecture, Japan, 88. See also Taiji, Japan, immigrants from

Wallace campaign, 352–353, 361n11
Wall Street Journal: "The New White Flight," 51–52
war brides, Japanese, 274, 275, 277–278, 281nn14–15
Washington Crossing the Delaware (painting), 79n14
Watanabe, Kazan, 22
Watanabe, Michio, 373
Watsuji, Tetsuro, 321
Weber, Max, 227–228
"When Asian American Literature Leaves 'Home'" (Wong), 297, 298. *See also* Wong, Sau-ling
White, Geoffrey: *Perilous Memories*, 309n5
White by Law (Lopéz), 43
white exceptionalism, 41
whiteness, 45–46, 53, 56
whiteness studies, 127n6, 162
Who Is White? (Yancey), 46, 48
Williams, Raymond: *Keywords*, 27
Wilson, Pete, 54
Wilson, Robert A.: *East to America*, 26
women: and Americanization movement, 162, 163; Korean American, 300; Mexican American, 190, 193, 201; Okinawan, 232–233; in progressive politics, 348. *See also* Beika (Americanization), and gender; women, Asian American; women, Japanese American
women, Asian American: and Americanization, 188–189; and drug abuse, 194–195, 207n12; as immoral, 163–164; and intermarriage, 48; sexualization of, 191, 195–196, 197–198, 207n16. *See also* Sansei (third generation) Japanese American women activists; women, Japanese American
women, Japanese American: approach to, 5–6; and labor norms, 165–166; and marital difficulties, 168–169; organizations by, 168, 175, 192–193; and picture marriages, 164–165; racialization of, 168–169; roles of, 172–174, 176; as *shakufu* (bar hostess), 123–124; and youth culture, 174. *See also* Beika (Americanization), and gender; Nakayoshi Group; Sansei (third generation) Japanese American women activists; women, Asian American
Women's Association of the Los Angeles Japanese Methodist Church, 173
Wong, Sau-ling: approach to, 292; *Crossing the Oceans*, 290–291, 292; on denationalization, 384; on ethnoracial majority Asians reading U.S. ethnic literature, 292–293, 297, 298, 299, 300, 301; "Maxime Hong Kingston in a Global Frame," 291, 292, 298; on racial shadowing, 298; U.S.-centrism of, 295, 296; "When Asian American Literature Leaves 'Home,'" 297, 298
World War II: *Americans Who Became Japanese Soldiers* (documentary), 32n4; Japanese Latin Americans in, 236n15; Japanese soldiers who did not return to Japan, 335n8; Nisei soldiers and draft resisters, 337n18; postwar reconstruction in Asia, 322. *See also* Japanese American internment

Yamada, Mitsuye, 294–295, 309n3
Yamato minzoku (Japanese nation), 111–112, 155n38. *See also* Japanese immigrant vernacular representations; *minzoku* (nation/race/ethnicity)

Yamatonadeshiko (Japanese womanliness), 172–174
Yancey, George: *Who Is White?*, 46, 48
Yang, Young-Hee: *Dear Pyongyang* (documentary), 294, 298
Yasui, Minoru, 274–275, 281n12, 361n18
Yellow Brotherhood, 206n5, 207n12
yellow power. *See* Asian American movement
Yochishiryaku (Condensed geography) (Uchida), 21, 32n6
Yoen Jibo (Hawai'i Star) (newspaper), 358–359
Yokohama Japanese Overseas Migration Museum, 18
Yokoyama, Gennosuke: *Nihon no kasō shakai* (Japan's *kasō shakai*), 27

Yoneda, Karl, 353, 356
Yoneyama, Lisa, 292, 293, 300, 305, 307, 309n5
Yonsei (fourth generation) Japanese Americans: in Japanese American grand narrative, 221; Okinawan, and genealogies, 235n13; and progressive politics, 344, 356, 358
Yoshimura, Evelyn, 197–198, *200*, 202, 203, 207n17
youth clubs, 186, 205n2
youth culture, 174

Zaibei Fujinn no Tomo (journal), 167, 170, 173, 174, 178n4
Zaibei Nihonjinshi (*History of Japanese in America*), 266
zainichi (Koreans in Japan), 323, 334n1, 382